The Free People –
Li Gens Libres

PARKS AND HERITAGE SERIES
ISSN 1494-0426

The Parks and Heritage series focuses on topics related to national parks and historic sites in North America. Both historical and contemporary, these books raise our awareness about the many facets of national parks, including the warden service, religion, ethnohistory, and environmental studies.

No. 1 · **Where the Mountains Meet the Prairies: A History of Waterton Country** Graham A. MacDonald

No. 2 · **Guardians of the Wild: A History of the Warden Service of Canada's National Parks** Robert J. Burns with Mike Schintz

No. 3 · **The Road to the Rapids: Nineteenth-Century Church and Society at St. Andrew's Parish, Red River** Robert J. Coutts

No. 4 · **Chilkoot: An Adventure in Ecotourism** Allan Ingelson, Michael Mahony, and Robert Scace · Copublished with University of Alaska Press

No. 5 · **Muskox Land: Ellesmere Island in the Age of Contact** Lyle Dick

No. 6 · **Wolf Mountains: A History of Wolves along the Great Divide** Karen R. Jones

No. 7 · **Protected Areas and the Regional Planning Imperative in North America** Edited by Gordon Nelson, J.C. Day, Lucy M. Sportza, James Loucky, and Carlos Vasquez · Copublished with Michigan State University Press

No. 8 · **The Bar U and Canadian Ranching History** Simon Evans

No. 9 · **Heritage Covenants and Preservation: The Calgary Civic Trust** Edited by Michael McMordie, Frits Pannekoek, E. Anne English, Kimberly E. Haskell, Sally Jennings

No. 10 · **The Lens of Time: A Repeat Photography of Landscape Change in the Canadian Rockies** Cliff White and E.J. (Ted) Hart

No. 11 · **Farmers "Making Good": The Development of Abernethy District, Saskatchewan, 1880–1920, Second Edition** Lyle Dick

No. 12 · **The Free People – Li Gens Libres: A History of the Métis Community of Batoche, Saskatchewan** Diane Payment

The Free People – Li Gens Libres

A History of the
Métis Community of
Batoche, Saskatchewan

UNIVERSITY OF
CALGARY
PRESS

Diane P. Payment

© 2009 Diane P. Payment

University of Calgary Press
2500 University Drive NW
Calgary, Alberta
Canada T2N 1N4
www.uofcpress.com

No part of this publication may be reproduced, stored in a retrieval system or transmitted, in any form or by any means, without the prior written consent of the publisher or a license from The Canadian Copyright Licensing Agency (Access Copyright). For an Access Copyright license, visit www.accesscopyright.ca or call toll free 1-800-893-5777.

LIBRARY AND ARCHIVES CANADA CATALOGUING IN PUBLICATION

Payment, Diane
    The free people - Li gens libres : a history of the Métis community of Batoche, Saskatchewan / Diane P. Payment.

(Parks and heritage series, ISSN 1494-0426 ; 12)
Previously published under title: "The free people, Otipemisiwak," Batoche, Saskatchewan, 1870-1930.
Includes bibliographical references and index.
ISBN 978-1-55238-239-4

1. Métis–Saskatchewan–Batoche Region–History. 2. Métis–Saskatchewan–Batoche Region–Social life and customs. 3. Batoche Region (Sask.)–History. 4. Métis–Government relations. 5. Indians of North America–Saskatchewan–History. I. Payment, Diane. Free people, Otipemisiwak, Batoche, Saskatchewan, 1870-1930. II. Title. III. Title: Gens libres. IV. Series.

FC3545.B36P393 2008   971.24'2   C2008-906187-X

The University of Calgary Press acknowledges the support of the Alberta Foundation for the Arts for our publications. We acknowledge the financial support of the Government of Canada through the Book Publishing Industry Development Program (BPIDP) for our publishing activities. We acknowledge the financial support of the Canada Council for the Arts for our publishing program.

Cover design, page design, and typesetting by Melina Cusano

In memory of Métis elders
Alexandrine Fleury Nicolas (1887–1987)
and Médéric McDougall (1903–1989),
witnesses of a harsh and glorious past.

To all the men and women of Batoche who have
re-affirmed their identity and pride in their Métis heritage.

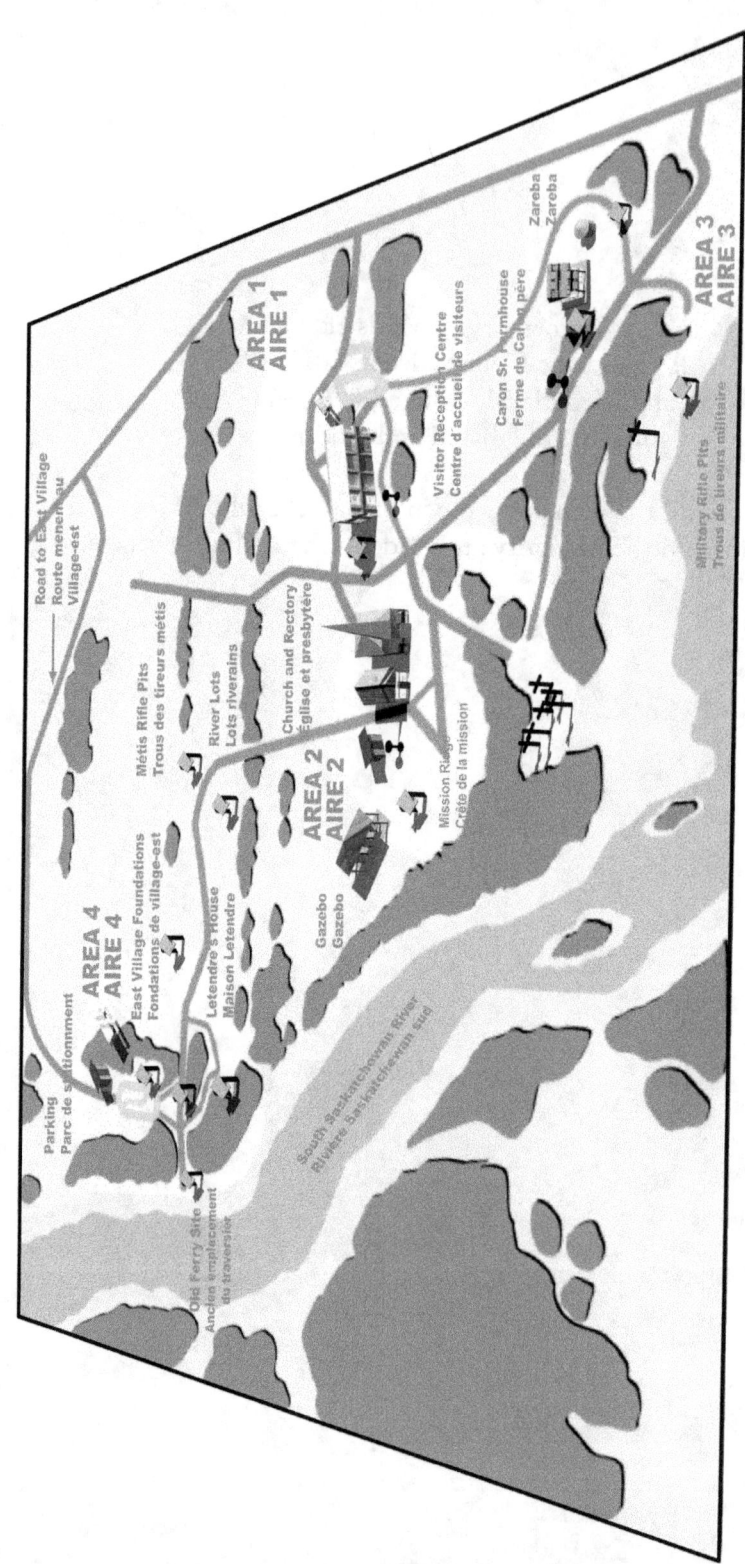

CONTENTS

Foreword — XI

Testimonials — XV

Author's Preface — XVII

Acknowledgments — XVIII

Abbreviations — XIX

List of Illustrations — XX

Introduction — 1
    Review of Major Literature and Interpretive Trends since 1985
    Methodology
    The Long Road to Batoche

1: Society and Culture — 33
    Social Organization and Family
    Customs and Traditions
    Social Issues
    Relations with First Nations
    Relations with Settlers

2: The Métis and the Roman Catholic Church   93

   Cultures in Conflict
   1885: The Riel Factor
   The General and the Priests
   Relations after 1885

3: Political Activism   123

   St. Laurent Council and Territorial Government Era
   A National Feast Day, A Flag, An Anthem
   The Last Stand: Armed Resistance
   Métis Rights after 1885

4: Economy   163

   The Early Commerce: Fur Trade, Buffalo Hunt, Freighting, and Other Enterprises
   Merchant Trading
   The Later Years

5: Land Claims on the South Saskatchewan River   203

   Customary Landholding and the Manitoba Precedent
   Aboriginal Land Claims through Scrip in 1886 and 1899–1900

6: Hard Times and Coming of Age: Batoche since the 1930s   249

   Women's Work and More
   Off to War
   Political Resurgence and Growth
   Cultural Revival and Renewal

Appendices   301

   1.1. Métis Wintering at St. Laurent de Grandin Mission 31 December 1871

   1.2. Families of St. Antoine de Padoue Parish, Batoche, 1924

   1.3. Métis Songs

   2.   Claims for Losses Suffered in 1885, Batoche and Vicinity

   3.   Notes on Quantitative Analysis of Homestead Declarations

   4.1. Beneficiaries of Land Scrip, Batoche and Vicinity, 1885–87

   4.2. Beneficiaries of Land Scrip, Batoche and Vicinity, 1900

Notes   323

Selected Bibliography   363

   Oral History Interviews
   Unpublished Manuscript Sources
   Published Sources

Index   379

FOREWORD

It is with great pleasure that I write this foreword to Diane Payment's *The Free People – Li gens libres: A History of the Métis Community of Batoche, Saskatchewan*. When asked by Diane to write the foreword, I was humbled, but was, at the same time, eager to complete this task. Ever since I first became employed with the Gabriel Dumont Institute in 1996, I have been interested in her work. One of the first books about the Métis that I read was her first fascinating monograph on Batoche, the community at the centre of the 1885 Resistance. Reading this book enabled me to better understand Batoche in both time and place, and outside of the strict confines of the 1885 Resistance. Steeped in the oral tradition and sympathetic to the Métis, Batoche: 1870–1930 is still the most accessible printed resource relating to the history of this community. I strongly recommended this book as the essential introduction to the Métis community of Batoche.

The Free People – Otipemisiwak: Batoche, Saskatchewan, 1870–1930 was a seminal work. It was one of the first books about a Métis community that was heavily reliant on oral history and sympathetic to a Métis perspective. Furthermore, while the tragic events of 1885 were important to the book's narrative, Diane amply demonstrated that community life continued for several decades after this cataclysm. The book was a social and cultural history, and as such it did not bog the reader down with battle details from the 1885 Resistance, nor did it contain reams of information about Louis Riel. Instead, the book rightly concentrated on Batoche's matriarchs and patriarchs, and the village's community life. Perhaps most importantly, the book gave agency to Métis women. Later in her career, Diane would write more exclusively about the women of Batoche.[1]

Diane was one of the first historians to write that the Métis were not static primitives doomed to the dustbin of history, a well-worn and racist trope advanced by G. F. G. Stanley, Donald Creighton, Marcel Giraud et al. Her monograph convincingly argued that the Métis adapted, and fit into the new socio-economic milieu as well as many of their Euro-Canadian and European neighbours, and in the case of some families, such as the Bouchers or Boyers, even better. Simply put, Batoche was a society in constant flux, and adapted to the new economic realities without abandoning its Aboriginal heritage. It was only when Prairie society became more stratified, with the majority population holding a dim view of miscegenation, that the Métis became socially, economically, and politically marginalized.

Diane outlines many important aspects of Batoche's history in this book, including the community's society and culture, its ambivalent relationship with the Catholic Church, its long tradition of political activism, which continued well after the 1885 Resistance, its entrepreneurial spirit, and its preference for practising mixed farming and wage labour rather than cereal agriculture, as well as its dispossession through the fraudulent Scrip System. Diane compellingly argues that the Scrip System, as it did elsewhere in the Canadian West, failed to adequately resolve the issue of the Batoche Métis' Aboriginal land tenure, and left them largely dispossessed.

In the book, Diane pays homage to the Michif (Michif-French)/Métis French language. Peppered throughout are several instances of Michif-French which was traditionally spoken by the Batoche-area Métis. As Diane asserts, it is very distinct from the neighbouring "Canayen," Walloon or Old World French. While derived from the "Canayen" French of the Métis' French-Canadian voyageur ancestors, Michif-French is a Métis language that evolved to meet Métis needs. Written phonetically, with many different word meanings, and employing Cree/Ojibway syntax, Michif-French was once the object of fierce ridicule by European-born and Euro-Canadian Francophones. As a result of this linguistic and cultural discrimination, it is on the verge of becoming extinct. Fortunately, Michif-French is still spoken in Manitoba, particularly in St. Laurent and St. Eustache.

Throughout her career, Diane has worked as a public historian. In her role as a Parks Canada historian, she got to know Batoche's Elders and storytellers, and was on intimate terms with many of them. Did this colour her perceptions as a historian? It likely did; however, the Elders and community people only shared with her because they trusted her. If she had taken on the role of the "objective," "scientific" historian she would not have been able to tell the history of Batoche from the perspectives of the Métis community. Within Métis Studies, building trust with community people is very important because there is a deep mistrust of non-Métis academics within the Métis community. In addition, as anybody involved in Métis Studies can attest, the Métis' historical record is fragmentary. Often, oral memories are selective or are non-existent, and sometimes archaeological research—in addition to a keen understanding of the local oral tradition and printed primary and secondary sources—is needed to better understand a particular Métis community's past. As a result, telling Métis stories and writing about Métis history involves reconstruction work. This multifaceted approach allowed Diane to write her narrative about Batoche. For instance, archaeological fieldwork conducted by Parks Canada at the village site and on the battlegrounds, along with oral history interviews and printed sources, enabled her to write her memorable narrative of Batoche's ante- and post-bellum community life.

Diane clearly did not toe the party line at Parks Canada. They wanted a sanitized narrative about Batoche that would run parallel to the dominant English-Canadian discourse about the incorporation of the Prairie West into the new Dominion of Canada. That Diane wrote sympathetically about the Métis, while also documenting where the federal government and, by extension, the larger non-Aboriginal population had marginalized the Métis, was out of sync with the then-official Parks Canada view. Unfortunately, we still see a similar mindset in our "national" institutions.[2]

Parks Canada is beginning to change its perspective about how it interprets the 1885 Resistance. Recently, Parks Canada, Batoche National Historic Site, the Gabriel Dumont Institute, and local Elders and community people (including Rose Fleury, who is mentioned in the second edition's conclusion) worked to have the Métis name Tourond's Coulee ("la couli des Tourond" and "li couli dii Tourond" in Michif-French and Michif-Cree) restored to the Parks Canada interpretation of the Battle of Fish Creek, which took place on April 24, 1885. Henceforth, the site will be known as "Battle of Tourond's Coulee/Fish Creek Historic Site of Canada."

There are some important changes in the second edition. For instance, the Métis' generally poor relations with the local "Canayen" (French-Canadian) population who discriminated against the Métis are better documented. As Diane indicates in the second edition, the local Métis were actually called "Batochiens"—the 'dogs from Batoche" by their French-Canadian cousins. Many old wounds still resurface between the Métis and the "Fransaskois" (the descendants of the Canayen, Walloon, and Old World French farmers and shopkeepers) living near Batoche. In July 2007, I was part of the organizing committee for a roundtable at Batoche which hoped to bring local Métis and Francophones together in a constructive and meaningful dialogue. It became apparent during the roundtable's discussions, however, that after more than one hundred years of living together and intermarrying[3], the Métis and the Fransaskois are still struggling to address past wounds, particularly those affecting group identity, racism, and cultural retention. The clichéd dictum of the French-Canadian nationalist historian Lionel Groulx, "Notre maître, le passé," ("Our Master: the Past") applies itself well to these two founding peoples who retain their long collective memories of injustices, and marginalization (albeit at differing scales) at the hands of the dominant Anglophone majority.

The second volume also includes a historiography of more recent developments in Métis Studies as well as a discussion of the creation of Batoche National Historical Site. It also includes the sometimes difficult decisions which a historian sympathetic to the Métis had to make when faced with a Parks Canada bureaucracy that wanted to maintain the historical status quo (read: the English-Canadian interpretation of the 1885 Resistance) at the expense of better explaining the Métis' rationale for taking up arms in 1885.

A summation of Batoche history after 1930 is also included in the second edition. As Diane correctly asserts, Batoche did not disappear. For the Métis, Batoche will always remain hallowed ground. For it was here that their ancestors briefly held off the Dominion of Canada and the British Empire so long ago. Batoche has become the heart of the Métis Nation, particularly during Back to Batoche Days, the annual gathering place of Métis from across the Métis Homeland. Many local Métis – direct descendents of the original settlers at Batoche – live in neighbouring communities, and many others have Batoche in their hearts despite living far away. Batoche and its environs have produced many talented leaders, thoughtful and compassionate Elders, artists, and academics who have contributed immensely not only to the Métis Nation, but to Canadian society as well. Today, the community is a ghost town; however, it lives on in story, in song, and in film, but perhaps most importantly, it lives on in the collective memory of the Métis. Presently, Friends of Batoche, the Batoche Métis Homeland Local 51 of the Métis Nation – Saskatchewan, as well as Parks Canada staff and local Elders, artists, and community people are working to revitalize Batoche.

Darren R. Préfontaine,
Gabriel Dumont Institute
November 2008

TESTIMONIALS

This history invoked many sad memories...Your study of Batoche has brought to light many things that I ignored. The early prosperity and persistence of the community is particularly revealing as I did not observe that in the 1930s...The book has made me aware of Batoche's survival and the fact that things have changed dramatically in Western Canada since I was there (translation).

> Marcel Giraud author of *Le Métis Canadien*, Nice (France), 1992

Diane has reported all of our history – even our differences with the Church. I am proud of her work and the fact it was done in our language, French... I also have to say that I got to know Diane pretty well when she was gathering oral histories. The Métis community has a debt of gratitude to Diane for researching our history at this time when more and more of us are rediscovering our culture and seeking recognition nationally.

> Médéric McDougall, special friend and mentor, 1985

Diane and I worked together for many years. It was a challenging and rewarding journey. We were a team – I knew the land and its people and she transcribed the ideas and histories into written words. Batoche will always be in our hearts. This book celebrates the people of Batoche and their important contribution to the history of the Métis Nation and Canada.

> Edward Bruce, Batoche Elder, 2008

Thank you for completing the 2nd English edition of *Li Gens Libres – The Free People* – especially for including our stories and celebrating our Michif French heritage. I offer you an Eagle Feather – compliments of «Celui qui nous surveille tous» (the One who watches over us).

> Rose Fleury, Batoche Elder, 2008

AUTHOR'S PREFACE

> We left Manitoba because we were not free, and we came here to what was still a wide open country in order to be free. And still they [outsiders] will not leave us alone. – Memoirs of Gabriel Dumont [ca. 1902] (Archives of Manitoba, MG10, F1, translation).

The history of Batoche, the community, and its people was largely forgotten or misrepresented until the 1980s. It was portrayed by outsiders as the seat of the North-West Rebellion, the site of the Métis' last stand and "defeat" to be followed shortly after by their social and economic disintegration and dispersal. However, a fresh look at the history of Métis communities along the South Saskatchewan River, in particular Fish Creek (originally la couli des Tourond), Batoche, St. Laurent (de Grandin), and St. Louis (de Langevin), disputes this view and suggests continuity of political, social, and economic activity. There was no mass exodus by the Métis after 1885. In fact, some of the families who sought refuge across the border and further north eventually returned to the homeland. At the turn of the twentieth century, family, culture, and lifestyle continued to shape and distinguish Métis society. The community resisted an unprofitable farming economy, pursuing a variety of traditional and new occupations. It also continued to assert its rights as the new nation of the Northwest. Poverty, fear, and discriminatory Canadian policies towards Aboriginal peoples were serious impediments to survival and growth, but a few families managed to prosper. By the 1920s, many youth relocated to other regions of Western and Northern Canada to find employment while families who remained on the small riverlot farms of their grandparents lived a life of subsistence and isolation from surrounding Eurocanadian communities. Oral history accounts by Batoche elders revealed an enduring hidden pride in their Métis heritage, and by the 1960s there began a quiet but determined action by people to assert their rights and resist discrimination. Following in the footsteps of their patriotic ancestors, many local Métis became active in local and Saskatchewan Métis organizations.

Batoche has changed dramatically from the prosperous trading community of the early 1880s and the small insular mixed farming community of the 1920s. But it remains the "Métis capital of Canada," an evocative and enduring cultural landscape of riverlots, wooded bluffs and winding trails. It is a spiritual place where people gather around July 24 each year to celebrate, and pray in the little cemetery up on the hill where the spirits of ancestors such as Gabriel Dumont, Xavier Letendre, Josephte (Paul) Tourond, and Marguerite (Dumas) Caron continue to lead and inspire them.

ACKNOWLEDGMENTS

I would like to thank the present and former staff at Batoche National Historic Site of Canada and colleagues in the Western and Northern Service Centre (Winnipeg) for their support and assistance, in particular Rose-Marie Carey, Mark Calette, Greg Thomas, and Dave Beeusaert. I would also like to thank Darren Préfontaine, Gabriel Dumont Institute, and Gilles Lesage, La Société historique de Saint-Boniface, and Diane Lamoureux, Missionary Oblates, Grandin Archives, for their assistance and access to their collections. I would like to acknowledge the encouragement and inspiration of individuals such as Frits Pannekoek, Athabasca University, Lloyd Rodwell (1927–1996), Saskatchewan Archives Board, and Lionel Dorge (1934–2001), La Société historique de Saint-Boniface, and Les Éditions du Blé.

A special heartfelt « mârci » to all the people of Batoche, St. Laurent de Grandin, St. Louis, Duck Lake, and Bellevue, who shared their memories of the past and present, in particular, Marguerite Perillat (1909–89), Edward Bruce, Art Fisher, Réal Boucher, and Brenda Boyer Percell. They provided ongoing information during visits, conversations and correspondence and their "stories" are part of "this story."

This study could have been completed without the total support and love of my husband, Roxroy West, and my furry companions, Minette (1983–2003), Okima, and Babette.

ABBREVIATIONS

AM	Archives of Manitoba.
DA	Deschâtelets Archives, Oblates of Mary Immaculate, Ottawa.
DCB	Dictionary of Canadian Biography.
EAA	Edmonton Archdiocese Archives.
GA	Glenbow Archives.
GNMA	Grey Nuns of Montreal Archives.
HBCA	Hudson's Bay Company Archives, Manitoba Archives.
LAC	Library and Archives Canada.
PAA	Provincial Archives of Alberta, Oblates of Mary Immaculate.
PADA	Prince Albert Diocesan Archives.
SAB	Saskatchewan Archives Board, Saskatoon.
SBHS	St. Boniface Historical Society.
SBAA	St. Boniface Archdiocesan Archives.
UAA	University of Alberta Archives.

LIST OF ILLUSTRATIONS

Front cover images:
1. 1885 Flag in custody of Nault family of Ste. Rose du Lac (Manitoba) - Diane Payment. (Illustration 3.4 in book).
2. Family gathering on occasion of 50th wedding anniversary of Jean-Baptiste Arcand and Nancy McKay at Maskeg Lake, 1914 - Provincial Archives of Alberta, OB 3804. (1.13 in book).

Back cover images:
1. Boyer, Breland, Dumont and Ouellette family gathering at St. Laurent de Grandin, ca. 1910 - Provincial Archives of Alberta, OB 3805.
2. Background image of couple with two children: Frédéric and Mélanie Parenteau (St. Germain) and children, Joseph and Caroline ca. 1915 - Parks Canada, donated by Marguerite (St. Germain) Caron.

Inside front cover images:
1. Antoine Ferguson of St. Laurent with daughters Emma (left) and Ernestine (right), ca. 1915 – Saskatchewan Archives Board, R-A5225.
2. Patrice Fleury (1840–1941) veteran of 1885 Resistance in front of Batoche monument, 1935 – donated by Marcel Giraud.
3. Standing left to right: Baptiste Primeau, John-Baptiste Letendre and seated: Azarie Letendre in 1914 before they left for overseas to serve in World War I – Parks Canada, donated by Stella Parenteau.
4. Mme Josephte (Paul) Tourond (1831–1928) on her farm at Batoche, ca. 1920 – Parks Canada, Brenda (Boyer) Percell Collection. (3.7 in book)
5. Joe Caron with horse team, ca. 1940s – Parks Canada, donated by Russell Porter.

Inside back cover images:
1. "Mme Veuve" (Widow) Tourond's claim to the North-West Rebellion Claims Commission – Library and Archives Canada, RG 15, Vol. 914, No. 21. (3.8 in book).
2. Map of Batoche National Historic Site of Canada, courtesy, Parks Canada.

Intro. 1. Métis Landscape, North West Territories, 1880–1905.
Intro. 2. Métis Communities on North and South Saskatchewan River, ca. 1920.
Intro. 3. Batoche and district today.
1.1. François-Xavier Letendre *dit* Batoche (1841–1901) – Parks Canada, Louis Venne Collection.
1.2. Marguerite (Parenteau) Letendre (1843–1937) – Parks Canada, Louis Venne Collection.
1.3. Panoramic view of Batoche Village, 1891 – Archives of Manitoba, N855.
1.4. Letendre house and family probably on wedding of Florestine Letendre and Bruno Venne, September 4, 1894 – Saskatchewan Archives Board, R-A5634.
1.5. Elders of Batoche and St. Laurent de Grandin, ca.1910. Seated, William Boyer and Julienne (Bousquet) Boyer; standing left to right: Clémence (Boyer) Gervais, Élisabeth (Dumont) Ouellette, Gilbert Breland, Moïse Ouellette, Jean-Baptiste Arcand, Baptisens Parenteau, Father François-Xavier Simonin, Nancy (McKay) Arcand, Félicité (Boyer) Breland, Hélène (Boyer) Racette, Jonas Moreau – Provincial Archives of Alberta, Parks Canada, Edmond and Berthe (Ladéroute) Boyer Collection.
1.6. Jean Caron (1833–1905) and Marguerite (Dumas) Caron (1843–1937) with granddaughters Emma and Marie and son Albert in front of their house at Batoche, ca. 1900 – Provincial Archives of Alberta, OB 3827.
1.7. Théophile Caron and third wife Lisa (Gervais) Caron with their children and Kokum Clémence (Boyer) Gervais, ca. 1915 – Parks Canada, donated by Walter and Marie Fidler.
1.8. Ludger Gareau (1855–1954) and Madeleine (Delorme) Gareau (1868–1958) and their family in Pincher Creek, Alberta, ca. 1905 – Parks Canada, donated by Gérard Chamberland.
1.9. Voyageur and ancestor Jean-Marie Boucher (1793–1870) and Boucher family of St. Louis, ca. 1915. On the wall are portraits of parents Jean-Baptiste Boucher and Caroline Lespérance. Standing left to right: Baptiste Jr., Rose-Délima, Charles-Eugène, Salomon, Frédéric, Élise and Joseph. Seated left to right: Sara, Caroline, Marguerite, Emma (Grey Nun), Marie-Rose, Alvina (« La Pie ») – Parks Canada, courtesy St. Louis Historical Committee.
1.10. Antoine Ferguson of St. Laurent with daughters Emma (left) and Ernestine (right), ca. 1915 – Saskatchewan Archives Board, R-A5225.
1.11. Christine (Dumas) Pilon and daughters Octavie Lépine (left) and Adélaïde Pilon (right), ca. 1920 – Parks Canada, Omer Ranger Collection.

List of Illustrations XXI

1.12. « Sur le cou de ma bouteille » (Good Cheer) at Batoche, ca. 1914. Seated Louis Letendre at left and Alexandre Parenteau; standing Joseph « Caton » Pilon Jr., a Dubois – Parks Canada, Omer Ranger Collection.

1.13. Family gathering on occasion of 50th wedding anniversary of Jean-Baptiste Arcand and Nancy McKay at Maskeg Lake, 1914 – Provincial Archives of Alberta, OB 3804.

1.14. L-R: A.M. Frigon, Indian Agent, Maxime Lépine Jr. and Marguerite (Boucher) Lépine, "Farmer-Instructors" at One Arrow First Nation, ca. 1915 – Parks Canada, Omer Ranger Collection.

2.1. St. Antoine de Padoue Parish, Batoche, ca. 1897 – Saskatchewan Archives Board, S-B6756.

2.2. Father Julien Moulin and parishioners, St. Antoine de Padoue, Batoche, ca. 1902 – Parks Canada, donated by Justine (Caron) St. Germain.

2.3. First schoolhouse at Batoche (1894–1917), ca. 1907; standing at far left is teacher Mlle Onésime Dorval and at right, Father Moulin with school children – Saskatchewan Archives Board, R-B1771.

2.4. Sisters Faithful Companions of Jesus and boarders at Duck Lake Industrial School, 1900 – Saskatchewan Archives Board, S-B6759.

2.5. Prophet and Politician Louis Riel (1844–1885), ca. 1880 – Library and Archives Canada, C-86500.

2.6. General Middleton, Father André, Indian Agent R.S. Mackenzie and Chief Beardy (seated with hat) at Duck Lake, 1885 – Library and Archives Canada, C-18951.

2.7. Monument in honour of Métis, Cree and Dakota who died in the 1885 Resistance erected in the Batoche cemetery in 1901 – Provincial Archives of Alberta, OB 60.

2.8. Father Georges Roussel with Adélaïde (Pilon) Ranger (left) and Marie (Caron) Parenteau (right) in front of rectory in 1977 – Diane Payment.

3.1. Louis Schmidt *dit* Laferté (1844–1935), politician and land agent in Prince Albert – Archives of Manitoba, N10414.

3.2. Louis Riel and Mistahimaskwa (Big Bear) at Duck Lake, 1884 – *La Liberté et le Patriote*, 21 septembre 1951, p. 13.

3.3. Remains of a picture of Our Lady of Lourdes which was pinned on a white flag flown by the Métis during the 1885 Resistance. Below is a prayer by Louis Riel and the names of his children, Jean and Marie-Angélique – Library and Archives Canada, C-15527.

3.4. 1885 flag in custody of Nault family of Ste. Rose du Lac (Manitoba) – Diane Payment.

3.5. Adjutant-General Gabriel Dumont (1837–1906) – Union St. Jean Baptiste, Woonsocket, Rhode Island, Mallet Collection.

3.6. "So much sadness, so much fear": Métis in chains in front of Regina prison,1885: L-R Ignace Poitras, Johnny Sansregret, Pierre Parenteau, Pierre Gariépy, Philippe Garnot, Albert Monkman, Pierre Vandal, Baptiste Vandal, Toussaint Lussier, Maxime Dubois, James « Timous » Short, Patrice Tourond and Emmanuel Champagne – Saskatchewan Archives Board, R-B714.

3.7. Mme Josephte (Paul) Tourond (1831–1928) on her farm at Batoche, ca. 1920 – Parks Canada, Brenda (Boyer) Percell Collection.

3.8. "Mme Veuve" (Widow) Tourond's claim to the North-West Rebellion Claims Commission – Library and Archives Canada, RG 15, Vol. 914, No. 21.

3.9. Charles Nolin (1837–1907) and Rosalie (Lépine) Nolin (ca. 1850–1927) of St. Laurent de Grandin and Onion Lake– Provincial Archives of Alberta, OB 3810.

3.10. Maxime Lépine (1837–1897) member of Manitoba legislature 1874–78 and councillor of Métis Provisional government of 1885 – Archives of Manitoba, N10909.

3.11. Charles-Eugène Boucher (1864–1926), member for Batoche, Legislative Assembly of the North West Territories, 1891–1898 – Parks Canada, donated by Boniface and Agnès Fidler.

3.12. Charles "Le Marquis" Fisher (1865–1907) member for Duck Lake, Territorial and Saskatchewan legislature, 1898–1905 – Parks Canada, donated by Justine (Laviolette) Pambrun.

4.1. George Fisher Sr. (1830–98) merchant of St. François-Xavier (Manitoba), Fort Qu'Appelle and Cypress Hills (Saskatchewan). Parks Canada, courtesy of Arthur Fisher.

4.2. Batoche merchants in Winnipeg, 1878: standing left to right, Baptiste Boyer, Xavier Letendre; seated, left to right, Alexandre Boyer, George Fisher Jr., William Letendre and François Gingras of St. Joe (now Walhalla), North Dakota – Parks Canada, donated by Beatrice (Boyer) Gervais.

4.3. Batoche and Duck Lake businessmen in front of Massey-Harris office in Duck Lake, 1894: seated, left to right, Charles-Eugène Boucher, Xavier Letendre and W.J. Pozer; standing, left to right, George Fisher Jr., Damase Racette, Gustave Fournier, W.S. Urton, L. St. Louis de Gladiou, Patrice

4.4. Parenteau and R.S. Mackenzie – University of Saskatchewan Library, C55/2/10.5M.
4.4. North West Mounted Police Barracks (former Boyer store and house), Batoche, 1891. Interpreter and scout Napoléon Venne is standing in the centre, arms crossed – Parks Canada, Fort Battleford National Historic Site Collection.
4.5. Road construction gang near Batoche, ca. 1925 – Parks Canada, courtesy of Marguerite (St. Germain) Caron.
4.6. Pile of buffalo bones and skulls waiting for shipment in Saskatoon, 1890 – University of Alberta Archives 74169/15/93.
4.7. Baptiste Larocque's steam threshing outfit at Duck Lake in 1908 – Saskatchewan Archives Board, R-A8248(1).
5.1. Land Claims at Batoche in the 1870s – Parks Canada, compiled from Saskatchewan Archives Board, Homestead and Lands Branch files and Surveyors' notebooks.
5.2. Riverlot settlements along the South Saskatchewan River – Saskatchewan Archives Board, Prince Albert District Map [ca. 1900].
5.3. Map and claims at St. Louis (de Langevin) after 1889–90 resurvey – Marilyn Croot.
5.4. Map and claims at St. Laurent (de Grandin) ca. 1884 to 1930 – Marilyn Croot.
5.5. Map and claims at Batoche, ca.1884 to 1930 – Marilyn Croot.
5.6. Map and claims at Vandal and Gabriel's Crossing, ca. 1884–1930 – Marilyn Croot.
5.7. "Halfbreed Scrip Commission" at Batoche village, 1900 – Saskatchewan Archives Board, S-B9737.
5.8. "Halfbreed Scrip Commission" headquarters in former Letendre house now North West Mounted Police Post, Batoche village, 1900 – Saskatchewan Archives Board, S-B9738.
5.9. People waiting for Scrip Commission at Duck Lake, 1900 – Saskatchewan Archives Board, S-B9722.
5.10. Scrip certificates valued at (a) $160 in 1885 and (b) 240 acres in 1905 issued by the Department of the Interior – Library and Archives Canada, RG15, Vol. 1391, 1406 (C-132171 and C-13272).
5.11. Scrip awarded to John Letendre *dit* Batoche in 1900 – Saskatchewan Archives Board, Homestead files 989 and 671 (S-B8302 and S-B8303).
6.1. Alexandrine (Fleury) Nicolas seated left with friends at Duck Lake picnic, 1983 – Diane Payment.

6.2. Kokum Mary-Jane (formerly Racette, née Ouellette) Charette besides Riel's grave in St. Boniface (Manitoba), 1935– donated by Marcel Giraud.

6.3. Joe Caron with horse team, ca. 1940s – Parks Canada, donated by Russell Porter.

6.4. Ferryman Napoléon Fayant at Batoche's Crossing, 1963 – Saskatchewan Archives Board, R-A22306-2.

6.5. Wedding of Eveline Caron and Joe Boyer, Batoche, October 16, 1944 – Parks Canada, Derek Bodington Collection, courtesy of Annette Boyer.

6.6. Children of Edmond Boyer and Berthe Ladéroute, 1930s – Parks Canada, Brenda (Boyer) Percell Collection.

6.7. Standing left to right: Baptiste Primeau, John-Baptiste Letendre and seated: Azarie Letendre in 1914 before they left for overseas to serve in World War I – Parks Canada, courtesy Stella Parenteau.

6.8. Edmond Boyer (1897–1966) veteran of two World Wars – Parks Canada, Brenda (Boyer) Percell Collection.

6.9. Elders of l'Union Nationale Métisse St. Joseph du Manitoba celebrating la fête nationale in Riel Park (St. Vital, Manitoba) in July, 1917: standing left to right: Alexandre and Joseph Riel (brothers of Louis), André Nault, Elzéar Lagimodière, William Lagimodière; seated: Paul Proulx – Parks Canada, donated by André Nault Jr. family of Meadow Lake, Saskatchewan.

6.10. Damase Carrière (1848–1885) who died at the battle of Batoche on May 12, 1885 and was reportedly "finished off" by the North West Field Force in retaliation for Captain French's death and Pélagie Parenteau (1854–1920), married (1) Damase Carrière and (2) Maxime Dubois – Parks Canada, courtesy of Mrs. Jean Groat.

6.11. Patrice Fleury (1840–1941) veteran of 1885 Resistance in front of Batoche monument, 1935 – donated by Marcel Giraud.

6.12. RCMP constable Archie Lépine (1938–1962) who died on duty – Parks Canada, courtesy of Octavie (Pilon) Lépine.

6.13. Marie-Anne (Lépine) McDougall and Médéric McDougall on their 50th wedding anniversary, 1983 – Courtesy of Doris McDougall.

6.14. "The man who would be bishop:" Monsignor Alfred Boucher (1901–1984) – Prince Albert Diocesan Archives.

6.15. Prime Minister J.G. Diefenbaker at official opening of Batoche Museum, June 28, 1961 – Saskatchewan Archives Board, S-MN-B3101.

6.16. Edward Bruce at work at Batoche National Historic Site of Canadam, ca. 1995 – Parks Canada.

6.17. Official Opening of Caron House, Batoche NHS, July 18,1992 – Diane Payment.

6.18. Rose (Gariépy) Fleury, Mark Calette and Edward Bruce at Batoche NHS, 2005 – Parks Canada.

6.19. Brenda (Boyer) Percell: "Proud to be Métis," ca. 1995 – Brenda Percell.

6.20. Wagon rides, Back to Batoche Days, July, 2005 – Diane Payment.

Introduction

REVIEW OF MAJOR LITERATURE AND INTERPRETIVE TRENDS SINCE 1985

The hundredth anniversary of the 1885 Resistance resulted in a proliferation of studies on the Métis and Louis Riel.[1] The Métis, a "forgotten people," outside mainstream First Nation and Eurocanadian society, were suddenly remembered or came to the forefront. More importantly, the Métis were starting to reclaim "their" history. The most important publications of that decade were *The New Peoples: Being and Becoming Métis in Western Canada* edited by Jacqueline Peterson and Jennifer S.H. Brown and *The Collected Writings of Louis Riel/Les écrits complets de Louis Riel*, under the general editorship of George F.G. Stanley. These studies brought new insights into Métis ethnogenesis, communities and lifestyles, and the complex personality and activities of their spiritual and political leader, Louis Riel. They were accompanied by heated debates on the armed conflict of 1885, Métis land rights, and Riel's character, beliefs, and leadership.[2]

The diversity and complexity of Métis experience also came to the forefront during this period as scholars from both within and outside the Métis community began looking beyond traditional themes such as origins, "the golden years" of the early nineteenth century, and resistance and dispersal. Studies of Métis communities such as Batoche (Saskatchewan),

St. Laurent (Manitoba), and Turtle Mountain and Pembina (North Dakota) revealed the complexity and diversity of the North American Métis experience and more importantly, their persistence into the twentieth century.[3] Biographies of individuals such as Xavier Letendre, Charles Nolin, Louis Schmidt *dit* Laferté, and Johnny Grant[4] were important additions to our knowledge of "ordinary" Métis men, but except for a few wives and mothers of prominent men, Métis women remained largely absent from the literature.

The last two decades have witnessed the broadening of the scope of Métis history and inquiries by Métis themselves. Among the most active in this undertaking were Antoine Lussier, who documented the tenuous relationships between the Métis and the clergy and French Canadians in Manitoba, Emma LaRocque, who addressed issues of identity, and Ron Bourgeault, who identified Western capitalism and colonialism as the main agents of Métis subjugation.[5]

Métis activist and professor Howard Adams was one of the main challengers of what he called "the politics of colonization" and an advocate of a Métis perspective(s) of history.[6] Critical of the government of Canada and its institutions, he became increasingly disillusioned with Métis associations whom he identified as the new oppressors. He argued that Aboriginal history should not be written by "white settlers" who cannot avoid their ingrained Eurocentric ideology or fully understand Métis culture and knowledge. His pessimism and personal intolerance of non-Métis were not very constructive, but his work inspired many Métis (and some non-Métis) writers and scholars towards new inquiries, methodologies, and a more "total" Métis history.

From Riel to the Métis[7]

The execution of Louis Riel in 1885 fostered a heated exchange between French and English-speaking Canada, but the Métis were largely forgotten or dismissed as a marginal and doomed people in English-Canadian literature. Although Riel and Dumont were not forgotten in Quebec nationalist literature,[8] the discourse was largely paternalistic and assimilationist. In the 1930s, French ethnologist Marcel Giraud came to Western Canada to inquire about the Métis, visiting Batoche and other communities in the throes of the Great Depression. His monumental survey history, *Le Métis*

Canadien, was ground-breaking in terms of scope, sources, and field work, but his view of the Métis as a weak, "primitive," and vanishing people unable to adapt to a superior Western civilization has since been disproved. The same held true for his English-speaking contemporary, George F.G. Stanley, who presented similar ethnocentric views in *The Birth of Western Canada*. These views were adamantly disputed by the Métis who were determined to vindicate their actions and those of their leader in Manitoba in 1869–70 and in Saskatchewan in 1885. In the 1920s, the Comité historique of the Union Nationale Métisse St. Joseph du Manitoba, founded in 1887, went to Saskatchewan to interview participants and witnesses of the 1885 Resistance. These accounts and government documents were the basis for their national history: *L'Histoire de la Nation Métisse*, published in 1936. Unfortunately, the book was largely dismissed in Western academic circles due to its lack of annotations and polemic tone and remained unknown to English-speaking audiences until it was translated and republished in 1982. But if one returns to the main sources for the book, the collection of the Société historique métisse, it is evident that a large body of largely untapped oral history material can be reconstructed to recover Métis voices and perspectives. The memoirs of Gabriel Dumont and other Métis witnesses of the armed conflict of 1885 were collected by the society in 1902–03. Dumont's memoirs were edited, translated, and published in 2006, but many Métis accounts are still unpublished.[9]

Although Riel continues to be the subject of many controversial analyses and there is a need to look beyond him or at other Métis men and women, he is still largely misunderstood. Riel remains a cult figure, at the forefront of Canadian history: a symbol of French language and political rights to francophones in Quebec and Canada and a social reformer by many Western Canadians. To the Métis, however, he is generally recognized as a legendary spiritual and political leader and "founding father," although not all agree on the scope and importance of his role in their struggle against colonialism. According to Ron Bourgeault, Riel was a nineteenth-century liberal democrat and theologist who challenged the agenda of the Canadian state and the rigidity of the Roman Catholic Church.[10] He was an intellectual in conflict within himself, a leader who became frustrated with his inability to negotiate the rights of his people. Howard Adams, a descendant of 1885 Provisional government councillor Maxime Lépine, is more critical of Riel, perhaps because he followed a moderate course of action or did not want to resort to an armed uprising, both in 1869–70 and in 1885. The Métis were divided in their objectives and the revolutionary agenda of leaders such as Maxime Lépine and guerrilla warfare tactics of Gabriel Dumont were superseded by Riel's moderate and conciliatory agenda. According to Adams, Riel had become a spiritual rather than a political reformer by 1885. He states that if Riel had not been at Batoche, the Métis (and First Nations) may have had a better chance of winning the war and maintaining control over their territory and that, today, many non-Métis and the government continue to exploit false images and myths about Riel to obscure real issues, assuage their guilt, and divide the Métis.[11]

The conflicting images of Riel as madman, mahdi, and villain persist in contemporary literature. Thomas Flanagan, who recently published a second edition of *Louis 'David' Riel: Prophet of the New World*,[12] maintains that Riel's religion was a form of millenarianism but that he was insane. He argues that Riel provoked rebellion against established authority, that he killed an innocent Ontarian, and that his actions provoked the downfall of the Métis. It is a harsh and overly simplistic view of Riel. Other factors must be addressed, such as his charismatic qualities, which made him a supernatural and superhuman power in the eyes of his people. He was an intermediary between the dominant Eurocanadian and Métis societies and entwined both cultural perspectives. The persecution, exile, and execution of Riel by the Canadian government created a martyr-hero, and he became a symbol of the Métis struggle and oppression. Riel's personal journey, in particular the syncretic nature of his spiritual and political beliefs, remains largely unknown. In *Riel: A Life of Revolution*, journalist Maggie Siggins draws an evocative if romanticized portrayal of the man and his cause. The material for the book is largely borrowed from other writers but is original in its interpretation of Riel's actions and behaviour in the context of other world struggles and oppression. The letter by Douglas Daniels (in Addendum 3) is a particularly insightful analysis of the persistence of Riel's critics to dismiss him as an unstable megalomaniac rather than an intelligent devoted man loyal unto death to his God and his people and a human being who will forever confound his critics.[13]

Riel's memory and spirit are very much alive today in communities such as St. Vital (Manitoba) and Batoche, where he is generally revered like a saint and a martyr who died for his people. His pivotal role in the struggle for the recognition of Métis rights is acknowledged by all Métis communities across Canada. According to Métis leader Yvon Dumont:

"Louis Riel means something to the Métis that is not shared by others.... He is very important because he is a significant part of our sense of nationalism."[14]

Riel was officially recognized as a founder of Manitoba by the province and the federal government in 1992. One of the most current controversial issues surrounding Riel is whether he should also be exonerated and recognized as a founding father for bringing Manitoba into Confederation. In the last decade, a number of Bills to honour him and set aside his conviction have been presented in the House of Commons and the Senate but none have made it beyond first reading. In a Statement of Reconciliation with Aboriginal Peoples of Canada in 1997, the Minister of Indian Affairs stated that the federal government wanted to acknowledge his contribution to Canadian history, but this remains largely rhetoric. The proposals to "rehabilitate" Riel were denounced as historical revisionism by some mainstream academics while the Métis themselves are not unanimous in their support of this initiative. The Riel family and members of the oldest Métis organization in Canada, l'Union Nationale Métisse Saint-Joseph du Manitoba, support his exoneration, while the Manitoba Métis Federation and others argue that it is a strategy to deflect the larger Métis land claims issue and could prejudice its outcome. Riel remains a liability and his memory continues to be manipulated by groups and individuals for various political ends.

Métis economy has been the subject of numerous inquiries in the last decades, particularly in conjunction with the land claims issue and the marginalization of a society. Historian Gerhard Ens used a Western European class model in *Homeland to Hinterland* and in an article on Métis trader Johnny Grant[15] to argue that the Métis hunters and farmers, a peasant class, were unable to adapt to the Western capitalist economy. According to Ens, the merchant class may have been innovative and adaptive, but its members lacked the business skills and connections to make the transition to the nascent industrial economy of the Western interior. There was also an inherent flaw in their Métisness, which made them move back and forth between both parent cultures. As a result, they were unable to succeed in capitalist society and were pushed aside.

Métis scholars such as Howard Adams and Ron Bourgeault disputed these arguments and argued that "White Settler" colonialism and associated institutions were the main reasons for the marginalization of the Métis. Adams stated that Aboriginal peoples were conquered by European colonizers who imposed Western ideologies of racism and capitalism and waged war. The colonization experience led to what he called the "ossification" of Aboriginal society after 1885.[16] Bourgeault also applied a Marxist framework to his study of Métis society whom he described as a segregated wage-labour class in a capitalist state and economy. He argued that hunting-gathering Aboriginal peoples of the Plains were egalitarian societies based on kinship and communal modes of production and exchange.[17] There was no dominant class who exercised power and appropriated surplus until merchant capitalists such as the Hudson's Bay Company transformed communal modes of production and created an Aboriginal class of wage labourers or a working class based on exploitation and not mutual and reciprocal trade relations as has been argued by conservative and liberal economists. He maintains that capitalism is at the core of the ethnogenesis of a mixed Euro-Indian labouring class rather than ethnic blending and culture.

Nicole St-Onge has also applied a non-Aboriginal Marxist model to her study of the Métis communities of Pointe-à-Grouette and St. Laurent (Manitoba), but she has incorporated oral history sources and traditional knowledge into her inquiries. She reconstructed family and kinship networks to illustrate the importance of identity and economic and social change in these complex and diverse communities.[18] Heather Devine's recent publication, *The People Who Own Themselves*, traces the origins and movements of her large extended Canadien and Métis family from the St. Laurent valley to the Northwest. The author used genealogical records and personal family histories to document the complex identities and cultural values of the Desjarlais family and its varied roles in Métis society.[19]

Land and political rights remain at the forefront of Métis history. The adversarial forum or historical debate of the 1980s and 1990s between academic experts such as D.N. Sprague (on behalf of the Manitoba Métis Federation) and Thomas Flanagan (on behalf of the federal Department of Justice) on Métis land and Aboriginal rights has produced heated exchanges but no consensus on the "real story" behind the reality of the Métis loss of their traditional land base, poverty, and marginalization by the 1930s. One of the weaknesses of the Flanagan argument of voluntary sale of Métis lands and exodus from Manitoba is that it is based almost exclusively on selected documents and perspectives created by the Canadian government and Eurocanadian agencies and that it does not validate or include Métis oral tradition and history. Flanagan is also associated with an anti-Métis agenda and subscribes to what Métis lawyer Paul Chartrand refers to as the "perverse effect thesis," which argues that the recognition of the inherent rights of the Métis will not benefit them and will "degrade the dignity of individual Métis human beings."[20]

The betrayal and dispossession arguments advanced by Sprague and Métis agencies did not have the benefit of a comprehensive Métis paper record or "hard evidence" and only limited oral evidence. But whether through circumstance or wilful intent, the terms of the Manitoba Act were never fulfilled and the Métis were ultimately deprived of a communal land base or territory. There is also the overriding factor of Métis moral and political rights, which were identified in the *Royal Commission on Aboriginal Peoples Report* in 1997.[21] Sophisticated computer technology may prove to be a great asset in untangling the web of evidence relating to scrip issued by the government in conjunction with Métis land rights.[22] However, the debate between defendant (Government of Canada) and plaintiff (Métis) is far from over and to date inconclusive.[23] Claims research has raised the complexities and challenges of "courtroom history" and its ultimate validity or credibility in both legal and academic circles.[24]

The Métis were identified as an Aboriginal people in section 35 of the Constitution Act of 1982, but their rights were not defined. As a result, the Métis have had to prove these rights before the courts, a situation which has resulted in a number of cases relating to Aboriginal title and resource rights. There are two landmark cases relating to Métis constitutional rights now before the courts. The Supreme Court of Canada acknowledged the validity of the Manitoba Métis land claims case and it finally went to trial in 2006.[25] Some critical issues raised in the Manitoba Métis Federation Statement of Claim – issues that the courts have to deal with – are whether the Métis are Indians under the Constitution Act of 1867 (section 91(24)) and whether the Manitoba Act was a treaty and the fiduciary obligations of the Crown were breached, depriving the Métis of their collective land rights. In 1994, the Métis of Northwest Saskatchewan filed a land claim on behalf of the Métis of that area, claiming Aboriginal title to the land they occupied and harvested, a right which was not extinguished through government scrip grants.[26]

The Métis obtained a historic victory in the Fall of 2003 when the Supreme Court affirmed for the first time that the Métis enjoy constitutionally guaranteed Aboriginal rights to natural resources. The court upheld the acquittals of Steve Powley and his son of Sault Ste. Marie

(Ontario), who were charged with unlawful hunting and possession of game in 1993. The court recognized the historic Great Lakes Métis community and its right to land and resources under the Constitution Act of 1982.[27] On the other hand, the hunting rights of Ernie Blais of Manitoba pursuant to the Natural Resource Transfer Agreement of 1930 were denied on the basis that, at the time, the Métis were not viewed or identified as "Indians" by both the Métis and the Crown.[28]

The courts have stated that the government is in a trust-like relationship with the Métis people and must consult and negotiate with them in good faith. The Métis likewise are committed towards the reconciliation of their historic rights pertaining to lands, resources, and governance.

Resistance-Rebellion Debate

Eurocanadian literature related to 1885 usually focuses on the military engagement between the Government of Canada and Aboriginal peoples of the Northwest and ignores or minimizes the broader, complex, and more significant social and political contexts of the confrontation. In response to a call for a more holistic presentation of the conflict at National Historic Sites of Canada such as Riel House and Batoche, terms such as "North West Rebellion" and "Métis Resistance" have been adopted to reflect dual or differing perspectives of the event.[29] There is a long tradition of confrontation and mistrust on both sides, however, and the presentation of differing views poses peculiar challenges and requires thorough and ongoing research and analysis. Terms such as armed conflict, uprising, and insurrection, which are perceived as more positive or less confrontational, are also used by Métis and non-Métis writers. In some contexts, such as in Upper and Lower Canada in 1837, the terms "rebel" and "rebellion" have a positive connotation, perhaps because these events are part of mainstream history or did not involve Aboriginal peoples. The term "resistance" has acquired legitimacy and acceptance in relation to events of 1869–70 in Manitoba due to its use by eminent Manitoba historian W.L. Morton, who argued that, since Canada had not assumed authority in Red River, the Métis had a legal right to resist. He and other historians of the same period, such as George F.G. Stanley, would claim, however, that the armed uprising of 1885 was a rebellion as Canada had assumed legal ownership of the North West Territories. This argument has been disproved in the last decades by the recognition of the inherent right of self-government of Aboriginal peoples and the fact that the Government of Canada did not confirm the land and political rights of the Métis of the North West Territories by 1885.[30]

From a Métis perspective, the 1885 Resistance and others that preceded it were reactions to western colonialism or the need to defend their rights as the "New Nation of the Northwest." The Métis tried to deal with the dominant society or protect their social organization and economy through negotiation, but when this failed they were "forced" to take up arms. According to Ron Bourgeault, the "second insurrection" of 1885 "was the manifestation of a resistance to the policies of internal colonialism propagated by the Canadian state."[31] It was fought with a clear understanding on the part of the Métis that there could be no military victory but that the upholding of the tradition of resistance was necessary for their survival and future. Howard Adams expands this view by arguing that initially the Métis were part of a broad-based coalition of Aboriginal and non-Aboriginal groups who protested against the policies and actions of the federal government who proceeded to isolate the Métis and force them into a second revolution.[32] Laura Caso Barrera, who has compared the nineteenth-century struggles of the Canadian Métis and the Mexican Mayas, argues that it is important to look at the resistance as a social movement or crisis in Métis history. In 1885, the Métis fought to maintain their autonomy, social organization, and customary land rights, which were threatened by invading colonial forces.[33]

Perhaps one of the most controversial recent publications dealing with 1885 is *Loyal till Death*.[34] The authors argued that the First Nations were loyal to the Queen, that they did not "rebel" or take up arms against the government alongside the Métis, and that it was the latter who were the disloyal or the real rebels and forced some First Nations to take up arms. The book provided a long-needed First Nations perspective on 1885 and argues convincingly against a concerted uprising by Aboriginal peoples. It states that the First Nations had their own strategies for dealing with the Canadian government and that it did not include rebellion. However, the First Nations position is presented as a single narrative or does not deal with the varied positions of Cree and Assiniboine bands and individuals.[35] For example, there is evidence that Métis Farmer-Instructor Michel Dumas pressured members of Kàpeyakwàskonam (One Arrow) Cree Nation close to Batoche to take up arms in 1885. But there was also much discontent and resentment against the government on the poor reserve and long-standing kinship ties with the Dumont, Cayen, and Gariépy [Gardipy] families were also instrumental in the decision of some warriors from Kàpeyakwàskonam and Kàmiyistowesit (Beardy) reserves to join the Métis.[36] The portrayal of the First Nations as innocent victims of both the Canadian government and the Métis is both far-fetched and potentially self-defeating to the First Nations' cause. The revival of the image of the "evil Halfbreed"[37] will not help heal old wounds and promote renewal between the two Aboriginal groups.

It is well documented in Métis literature that there were important cultural differences and long-standing disputes between the Métis and First Nations. By the mid-nineteenth century, territorial and hunting rivalries had alienated many Métis and First Nations, in particular the Assiniboine and Dakota. Dumont himself spoke of an old hunting feud between him and Mistahimaskwa (Big Bear), which had alienated the two chiefs[38] and might explain the latter's unwillingness to support him and the Métis at Batoche in 1885. As brokers between Eurocanadians and First Nations, the Métis were isolated and resented by both groups who did not appreciate their separate national aspirations. This role was particularly evident in the making of the treaties where the Métis acted as interpreters and were perceived by both Eurocanadians and First Nations as fostering their own positions and agendas. A complex and diversified community, the South Saskatchewan River Métis were not fully united in the resort to arms in 1885 and leaders such as Louis Riel, Gabriel Dumont, and Charles Nolin had different strategies and agendas. This is a story that remains to be told.

A comprehensive article entitled: "Parks Canada and the 1885 Rebellion/Uprising/Resistance" by former Parks Canada historian Alan McCullough raises important issues regarding differing views of the events of 1885. The author traces the evolving interpretation of the conflict identified by the Historic Sites and Monuments Board of Canada as a "rebellion" precipitated by the Métis (or Halfbreeds as they were then called) in the 1920s but now interpreted primarily as a Métis "resistance" at Batoche National Historic Site.[39] Acknowledging that every generation writes its own histories and that nation states strive to produce a single, unifying account of their past, the author deplores the fact that, at Batoche, the "subordinate competing"[Métis] version has supplanted the "dominant" [Eurocanadian] or official version. He argues for a return to what he perceives as the more balanced national view of the conflict. This interpretation suggests the persistence of an anti-Métis bias in Canada, where the Métis are still viewed as "the opposition" or obstructionists rather than as a minority group struggling to find its just place within the larger Canadian family or as a "nation within a nation." Parks Canada's Cultural Resource Management Policy acknowledged the requirement for the presentation of multiple, differing views and stated that it would not be an arbiter of history.[40] The interpretation of the complex historical experience may be idealistic or unattainable, but sites commemorating Métis persons or events, such as Batoche and Riel House, were subject to increased scrutiny by Parks officials in recent years. This action may be associated with the reassertion of Métis political consciousness and numerous Métis rights cases now before the courts. Even though Canada prides itself in being a multi-ethnic federation, a strong Western Canadian Métis voice is perceived as a threat to the national identity or "dominant story." Canada is still in the process of nation-building and its Aboriginal peoples and other ethnic groups want their versions of events to have priority at places specifically associated with their history. Only time will tell if, as a nation, we will have the strength and tolerance to achieve "unity within a diversity."

Women: "Centre and Symbol"[41]

Métis society past and present cannot be fully understood without the inclusion of women and children who have been largely ignored or are "missing from history." It is only recently and primarily by women, both Métis and non-Aboriginal, that Métis women have been incorporated into broader aspects of Métis history. Other family members, in particular children and elders, have also been the subject of more inquiries, especially in films and recordings. Maria Campbell's novels delved into Métis cultural experiences and lifestyles, inclusive of women and children, thus filling an important gap in the literature. *Halfbreed*[42] was the first to challenge existing stereotypes of Aboriginal women. Writing of her personal experiences with discrimination and poverty while growing up in the 1940s and 1950s, she brought women's experiences to the forefront. Both Campbell and Christine Welsh[43] have recorded the voices of their grandmothers in an attempt to understand and reclaim their heritage. Métis children's world has been primarily depicted through historical fiction such as Noëlie Palud-Pelletier's *Louis: Fils des Prairies* and Thelma Poirier's *The Bead Pot*.[44]

The primary role of women in the ethnogenesis of the Métis in association with the fur trade was documented in the 1980s by Sylvia Van Kirk and Jennifer S.H. Brown, who emphasized the role of family and kinship.[45] Recent inquiries by Nathalie Kermoal, Sherry Farrell-Racette, Diane Payment, and Nicole St-Onge have documented themes such as material culture and artwork, roles as cultural and economic brokers, involvement in political and armed resistance, and specific cultural and gender issues.[46] More information on individual women who were "strong like two people" is emerging through oral and family histories. The reconstruction of women's lives and roles in Métis society is particularly challenging and requires innovative research tools and techniques. In her recent work on Catherine Lacerte Mulaire, Diane Boyd applied the methodology of "controlled speculation" to fill in the gaps in this Métis teacher's life.[47] Some women elders, such as Madeline (Mercredi) Bird, recorded memoirs that were published as biographies.[48] Genealogy or family history is also an important tool in the piecing together of Métis women's lives. The work of Heather Devine and Margaret Clarke in reconstructing families through genealogical and other records has given a name and sometimes a small voice to forgotten or silent women.[49] In terms of more recent history or experience, more Métis women are telling their stories and addressing issues such as poverty, racism, sexism, and family breakdown in publications such as *In Our Own Words: Northern Saskatchewan Women Speak Out*.[50] There is evidence that Métis women in the past and present played a vital role in the cultural and economic expansion of their families and communities. However, much work remains to be done before the diverse experience of Métis women is fully understood and integrated into general Métis history.[51]

Culture, Language, and Spirituality

Métis culture has always been the subject of much misunderstanding and speculation by other groups as it does not fit into a specific category like its parent cultures and is often confused with both. Métis culture is syncretic or combines elements of European and Aboriginal cultures in a new distinct Métis culture. Métis ideological culture (*mentalité*) is not well documented and has not received the same attention as its more tangible material culture, although the latter is often misidentified or appropriated by others in museum collections. The Michif language has also been dismissed by outsiders as bad French or erroneously referred to as a dialect or jargon. Métis cosmology or religious beliefs, amalgams of indigenous and Christian spirituality and traditions, are also often misinterpreted as superstitions or *médecine sauvage* (primitive medicine) in Western literature. Oral history has facilitated the collection of historical narratives (*les histoires*) and stories (*les contes*) and confirmed that Métis culture has been passed on by elders from generation to generation and, like other cultures, is fluid and changing. But there is an urgency to pursue this collection with the present-day generation of elders.

There have been numerous initiatives by the Métis to document their heritage in the last decade. A recent publication, *Métis Legacy II*,[52] focuses on culture and folkways recorded by Michif elders and lay people as well as scholars. Oldtime and new Métis music is being recorded in videos such as *John Arcand and his Métis Fiddle*,[53] *Richard Lafferty: The Muskeg Fiddler*,[54] and Lynn Whidden and Ray St. Germain's *A Métis Suite*.[55] Maria Campbell has recorded traditional stories and legends,[56] and Auguste Vermette's reminiscences provide firsthand accounts of Métis lifestyle, customs, and important events of Métis history such as the Resistance of 1869–70, which his parents witnessed.[57] Leah Dorion has documented the enduring cultural traditions and lifestyles of the road-allowance community of Crescent Lake.[58] Métis material culture such as art work, clothing, and articles of trade and transportation are being re-interpreted and reproduced by both research specialists and individuals at large. A recent publication, *Expressing our Heritage: Métis Artistic Designs*,[59] provides annotated illustrations of historical and contemporary Métis clothing and art work. The Métis Infinity flag and the sash *(ceinture fléchée)*, perhaps the most distinctive symbols of Métis culture, are also examples of cultural adaptations and renewal. Another enduring symbol, the Red River cart was replicated using traditional and new construction techniques for a historic journey from Pembina to Red River (Winnipeg) during the 2002 North American Indigenous Games. Artist writer and historian Sherry Farrell-Racette has analyzed and compared the distinctive art forms of the Métis. She raised the complexity of this task and the need to merge Métis history (such as genealogy, family, and community studies) with the study of clothing and artistic expression. She noted that the understanding of the varied and complex Métis experience is crucial to the identification and contextualization of its material culture.[60]

The belief in a balanced reciprocal relationship between human life and natural life and the syncretism of indigenous and Christian beliefs in Métis cosmology is a theme that requires investigation and documentation. It is known through oral history and observer accounts such as those of Father Émile Petitot[61] that Métis beliefs and rituals incorporated elements of both Aboriginal and Canadien traditions, but it is not clear how and to what extent Métis people fused Aboriginal spiritualism with Roman Catholicism. Martha McCarthy and Raymond Huel have discussed the contributions of the Métis as auxiliaries of the Catholic missionaries and their instrumental roles as cultural brokers and interpreters in the propagation of the faith amongst Aboriginal peoples.[62] Huel documented aspects of the tenuous relationships between the Métis and Oblate missionaries and the need of the Church to re-define spirituality or incorporate Aboriginal values and traditions in an emerging indigenized "Third Church."[63] Métis anthropologist and priest Father Guy Lavallée has reflected on these themes in a personal journey of spiritual discovery and renewal. He has written prayers in Michif in an effort to indigenize Catholicism.[64] The visions of Métis prophet and leader Louis Riel need further comparative analysis in the context of contemporary Aboriginal spiritual movements. Questions such as how Christianity was accepted by the Métis or elements of indigenization, syncretism, and religious dualism remain largely unanswered.

Language and culture are inextricably linked, and the survival and revival of language is crucial to a people's identity and culture. The Michif language has been the subject of extensive academic inquiries and debates in recent years. According to Dutch linguist Peter Bakker, Michif (or Michif Cree) is a new language that combines Plains Cree and some Ojibwe verb forms and French Canadian noun forms.[65] This mixed language is based on Cree and French grammatical systems, but it is a new or unique language, which cannot be understood by unilingual French or Cree speakers. He argues that Michif-French is more specifically a unique dialect of Canadian French. Robert Papen, on the other hand, points out that Michif-French or French-Michif, which is spoken in Métis communities such as St. Laurent (Manitoba), predated Michif-Cree and that it is an integral part of the identity of the people of that community.[66] Métis linguists are also divided on this issue. Norman Fleury argues that there are really three Michif languages: Michif-French, Michif-Cree, and Michif-Saulteaux or Ojibwe, while Bruce Flamand says that there is only one Michif language (Michif-Cree). In communities such as St. Laurent (Manitoba) and Batoche (Saskatchewan), the Michif (or Mitchif) spoken is primarily French, although the syntax is Cree. In Ile à la Crosse, Cree is predominant, although the nouns are French or a variant form, and in Turtle Mountain (North Dakota) the verbs are a mixture of Cree and Ojibwe (Chippewa) and the noun forms, although French in origin, have been anglicized in pronunciation.[67]

Politics and power are also factors as to whether a language is given status. Métis lawyer Paul Chartrand, originally from St. Laurent, has aptly noted that a dialect is a language when there is an army behind it. There is a multilingual tradition among the Métis, which should be respected. In 2000, the Métis National Council declared the Michif language, more specifically the Michif-Cree mixed language, as the official historic language of the Métis Nation in 2000, opening the door to some divisions within the Métis community. There are other issues. The dissemination of Michif or Michif languages requires a spelling system, curriculum materials, and funding status under the Official Languages Act.

Recent History and New Interpretive Trends

It was argued in the mid-1990s that the Métis had been poorly served by historians and mainstream academics and that there was a need for Métis perspectives of history. Métis writers tended to adopt a more radical stance or look primarily at Métis history in terms of racism and class conflict. However the resurgence of nationalism and ethnic pride promoted the re-interpretation of events such as the Battle of Seven Oaks, the documentation of more recent community histories and the place of the Métis in a modern multicultural Canadian society.[68]

There were important milestones in the recovery of Métis history and its integration into mainstream Canadian history in the 1990s and early 2000s. *The Report of Royal Commission on Aboriginal Peoples*, included a chapter entitled "Métis Perspectives," which dealt extensively with Métis land rights and self-government and important themes such as identity and culture and included other Métis communities in Labrador, Quebec, the Maritimes, and the Northwest Territories. It also identified current issues such as racism, education, and employment.[69] In *The Myth of the Savage and the Beginning of French Colonialism in the Americas*, Olive Dickason dispelled some myths concerning miscegenation in New France (French Canada), while her overview of Aboriginal history, *Canada's First Nations: A History of Founding Peoples from Earliest Times*, focussed primarily on First Nations but included important discussions on the origins, movements, and contemporary issues of Métis history.[70] Her own personal journey as a Métis woman who discovered and affirmed her identity is a remarkable one and an inspiration to others.

Picking Up the Threads: Métis History in the Northwest Territories is a collaborative work between Métis and non-Métis.[71] It traces the history of the comparatively unknown Métis communities of the Athabasca-Mackenzie in Canada's north. Based extensively on oral history and visual sources, the publication was a follow-up to a popular illustrated history published in the 1970s.[72] *Picking Up the Threads* documented the unique history of northern Métis and linkages with southern communities and confirmed the diversity and complexity of the Canadian Métis experience. As a result, François Beaulieu, Métis patriarch and one of the eighteenth-century founding fathers, was designated as a person of national historic significance in 2000. Other important individuals such as Catherine Beaulieu Bouvier Lamoureux, an entrepreneur and community leader who established enduring kinship networks in the Deh Cho and North Slave regions, were also documented.

The most important recent survey history is undoubtedly *Metis Legacy*,[73] a Canada millennium project with the Louis Riel Institute and Gabriel Dumont Institute of Métis Studies and Applied Research. In Chapter One,[74] Leah Dorion and Darren R. Préfontaine "deconstructed" Metis historiography written largely by "outsiders" or "others" and brought fresh Métis perspectives to themes such as resistance, oral traditions, and spirituality. They identified important gaps in contemporary issues such as health, justice, and economic development and the ongoing absence of Métis history in Canadian and North American mainstream history. They argued that Métis history is often presented in the context of Western frameworks such as the fur trade and the Churches. It is a history which remains largely "hidden" or conserved in the memories of elders, due to a primarily oral tradition and the pervasive biases against Métis in Canada and Mestizo peoples in America generally.

Metis Legacy also addressed the multinational and multidimensional aspects of Métis heritage and culture in North America, including the Northwest Territories, Missouri, and Montana. "Many voices" of the northern Métis were heard in two articles on the Métis in the Northwest Territories, which provide the reader with different perspectives from the region. An essay on the Métis-Cree community of Cumberland House is an important contribution to the study of individual communities. A biography of Manitoba Métis activist Elzéar Goulet, and articles on the Dorion trading family from northern Saskatchewan and twentieth-century Alberta political activists who influenced resistance and renewal in the West are other important essays. Historical and contemporary Métis art works are highlighted in two chapters, while a special pictorial section illustrates their rich material and visual culture. One of the most useful sections of the book for researchers is the comprehensive annotated bibliography and references to the large collection of music, films, and other audio material produced on the Métis in the last decades.

Another important recent addition to the study of the Métis is *From Rupert's Land to Canada: Essays in Honour of John E. Foster*.[75] Although the articles in the book deal primarily with the fur trade, Frits Pannekoek provides an insightful and comprehensive review of Métis studies and suggestions for future research, in particular on the period 1900 to 1950, which had a strong influence on present-day politics, culture, and identity. An article on the Desjarlais family by Métis historian Heather Devine draws on genealogical sources as well as fur trade records to reconstruct this extended family whose activities and lifestyle were inspired by both Cree and Canadien culture and ultimately evolved into a new freeman Métis culture and identity. The reprinting of the late John Foster's article on the origins of the Métis of the Western Plains and a bibliography of his work acknowledge his important contribution to the field.[76]

In 2001, this writer published an article on the Métis of the western plains in the *Plains* volume of *The Handbook of North American Indians*.[77] The main themes discussed were language, origins and territories, identity and culture, external relations, political and economic traditions, and current issues. As Métis history is "in motion" and is undergoing a resurgence, there is little doubt that new themes and issues will be identified and research gaps on the Métis diaspora, women, mythology, and literature (oral history and stories) will require more frequent updating of survey articles. Other family and community histories are required to illustrate the varied

Métis experience across North America and provide comparative frameworks.

Recent technological developments have been a boon to Métis history. Databases and websites have been developed by universities, archives, resource centres, and associations, enabling Métis to trace their genealogy, family histories, and land claims.[78] The last decades have witnessed the production of many films and videos by and on the Métis.[79] Plays on controversial themes such as *La Trahison/The Betrayal*, a historical dramatization of the conflict between Gabriel Dumont and Father Julien Moulin at Batoche (1997),[80] and Crossings (*The Bell of Batoche*)[81] by Millbrook, Ontario, playwright Robert Winslow, whose ancestor fought against the Métis, in collaboration with Métis playwright Bruce Sinclair, illustrate the "coming of age" of the Métis. The Gabriel Dumont Institute produced *The Métis People: Our Story*, an interactive CD-ROM that traces Métis history from past to present.[82] Another excellent multimedia package is a Québécois production entitled *Riel: Plaidoyer musical pour la réhabilitation d'un juste*,[83] a musical portrait of Riel's life, career, and execution, using varied period accounts, traditional and modern compositions, and poetry to create an original and stimulating representation of the Métis leader. In 2003, Les Productions du Rapide-Blanc of Montreal produced *Sur les Traces de Riel*, a documentary, which, despite its title, focuses on the life of an inspring Métis elder, Rose (Gariépy) Fleury, of Duck Lake, Saskatchewan. Another historical documentary, focussing on the thriving community of St. Laurent, Manitoba, entitled: *Le Monde qui parlait aux arbres*, was produced by Productions Rivard of St. Boniface in 2003.

METHODOLOGY

Revisiting one's work is always a risky and daunting proposition. Although many of my interpretations, developed in the late 1970s and 1980s, remain valid or plausible, ongoing interaction with people at Batoche and surrounding communities have altered my original views. Additional oral history sources and memoirs have also provided new insights and perspectives. The sense of an ongoing evolving "cultural community" at Batoche or what has been described as psycho-cultural persistence[84] is more evident in my mind, notwithstanding increased exodus to urban areas and to other provinces and north since the 1920s and particularly since the 1950s. Some of the changes that I previously somewhat naively attributed to difficulties in adapting to a new Western social and economic order are better understood in the context of a marginalized society that was resilient and innovative. The cultural landscape of Batoche has changed dramatically in the last decades. Some of the changes parallel population shifts in Saskatchewan, which has experienced an exodus of its youth in search of employment opportunities and an increased elderly population. Many old families sold their farms and retired to neighbouring towns and cities. Many of these lands have been consolidated into larger farms without the traditional farmstead or have been acquired by the One Arrow Cree Nation under Treaty Land Entitlement.

Batoche has been a long journey of personal "re-discovery" with a commitment to help reclaim its painful and stirring history. In the past, the community was largely ignored by writers and the media or portrayed as a "primitive" buffalo-hunting Aboriginal society that had "rebelled" against government forces in 1885 and disappeared "into the bush." These perceptions have changed or have been disproved since the 1980s. There has been a resurgence of Métis pride in Canada and Mestizo pride throughout North and Central Americas. Cultural pluralism and Aboriginal self-determination are accepted principles, and Batoche is now very much at the forefront as "the heart of the Métis Nation." The agendas of both government and Métis organizations have also impacted on the community in recent decades, although local Métis themselves have not always been involved in political developments and historical debates. According to most people I have talked to, the most important cultural issue is reclaiming their identity and rehabilitating a history that was absent or misrepresented in mainstream history. I was pleased to hear that they found the first edition of this book an important source of information about their families and a contribution to the reinstatement of Métis history.

When I wrote the first edition of the book in the 1980s, I was more pre-occupied with scholarly requirements for interpretive frameworks and quantitative analysis, or what was identified as a "scientific" methodology. It was also important to justify the use of oral history and traditional knowledge, approaches that were not widely accepted or recognized in academic circles. My reconstruction of Batoche is not based on structural and quantitative methods (except to some extent, the chapter on land claims). I would argue that the understanding of Métis culture cannot be based on Eurocanadian theoretical models. There is a requirement to describe the society from within or according to culturally based open and flexible frameworks and, in the case of oral history, stories rich in meaning but sometimes ambivalent and rarely definitive. There is a system of checks and balances in a community to ensure that the appropriate people are interviewed. Elders or spokespersons at Batoche identified the people who should be interviewed or who were respected for their integrity and knowledge. These "keepers and transmitters of knowledge" expressed different views and varying interpretations of events such as the 1885 Resistance and issues such as land claims. No oral history account and tradition remains intact over time. Each teller brought his or her own perspective to the account or emphasized certain facts depending on the time, the audience, and the purpose. Métis oral histories tend to stress family and genealogy, resistance to external or outside authority, mobility, homeland, and cultural values. Family and kinship ties shaped Métis society. Interpersonal alliances guided the strategic behaviours that ensured cultural continuity, community development, and external relations. In this inquiry, I have strived to be unbound by my own categories and open to discovery and challenge, with the realization that an unbiased or objective history is impossible.

I will define my approach as a primarily intuitive inquiry based on written materials produced by non-Métis and records left by the Métis in the form of dictated and written accounts and more recent oral history narratives and personal observations since my association with Batoche in the 1970s. In the case of records by "others" such as explorers, fur traders, government officials, settlers, and missionaries, it is sometimes possible to re-contextualize their accounts and even reconstruct the oral voice embedded in the text. However fragmentary and partial, it is a record of direct association and experience. A rich repertoire of visual materials from archives and family collections was another invaluable source of information. In the case of absence or limited information, as in the case of women, it is possible to use comparative information and innovative methodologies such as "controlled speculation" to reconstruct the past.[85]

The story of Batoche is that of an evolving cultural reality, a complex and divergent community, which one can attempt to recreate with the awareness that the story that is presented is a reconstruction and not the "real" or "only" one. Without a doubt, however, it is a story of struggle, survival, and renewal.

THE LONG ROAD TO BATOCHE

In the eighteenth and nineteenth centuries, the term "Métis" (pronounced "Mitchifs" from the original "Métifs") identified a new people with its own identity, culture, and economy.[86] Today the term "Métis" includes all peoples of mixed (First Nation and European ancestry) in Canada and more recently the United States, many of whom, especially in Quebec, British Columbia, and Montana, have only formally identified as such or used the term in the last few decades. The use of the modern term "Aboriginal people" to identify Métis is also often misleading. Although the group includes Métis, the term is often mistakenly used in the context of First Nations. Identification as Métis usually implies affiliation with a representative cultural or political group. However, Métis identity is fluid and varied, and some people of mixed heritage do not identify themselves as Métis or are not recognized as Métis because they are not culturally associated with historic Métis communities of the Northwest. To many people today, Métis, the people and the term, remains ambiguous and unclear.

New France and « le pays d'en haut »

Métissage occurred during the period of first contact between First Nations and Europeans on the east coast in the sixteenth century or earlier. Since historical memory in Métis society is largely orally based, it is extremely difficult to trace the development of early Métis group identity. There is recorded evidence of an early mixed heritage population in the Atlantic provinces and in Labrador.[87] According to Olive Dickason, based on letters of French missionaries and New England newspapers, the Acadians were described as a mixed French, Micmac, and Maliseet people in the mid-eighteenth century.[88] The Canadiens of New France were also described as "swarthy brethren" of the Amerindians. French policy was that of one nation or integration of Aboriginal peoples into the French nation, and, although this did not materialize and there are few official records of mixed marriages, it does not mean that they did not occur. For example, Louise Dechêne recorded only seven mixed marriages in Montreal for the period 1642–1715 but cautions that these do not include the more prevalent customary marriages that were not recorded by missionaries or state officials.[89] Dickason noted that there were 120 official or civil marriages in New France[90] but the extent of intermarriage or *mariage à la façon du pays* (according to the custom of the country) will never be known. There is, however, an oral tradition and visual evidence of métissage in many French Canadian families. One of the enduring oral traditions is that of « les chavages ont passé » which refers either to the practice of unmarried French Canadian women of giving away children born out of wedlock or the custom of Aboriginal people of adopting non-Aboriginal children and raising them as their own. Parish records did not always state the ethnic origins of spouses or children who came from *les pays d'en haut*. Métissage was probably quite extensive for political and economic reasons in New France but not officially acknowledged and recognized by French officials. It did not give rise to a separate or new ethnic group as in the Northwest. French Canadian historians of the nineteenth and early twentieth century downplayed the Métis origins of French Canadians at a time when miscegenation was looked down upon and a racist ideology prevailed.

Seventeenth- and eighteenth-century European explorers and travellers in North American projected images of both the "noble" and "ignoble savage,"[91] but increased contact with First Nations gradually strengthened the view of the "ignoble" and "barbaric Indian."[92] These racial theories were also applied to mixed peoples. Nineteenth-century European imperialism fostered racial theories condemning mixing of the races, which was perceived as degenerative and dangerous.[93] Western literature described the Métis as an uncivilized people whose culture and values were an obstacle to economic and social progress or the civilized aspirations of Eurocanadians. Victorian travellers to the Northwest such as Captain Butler, the Earl of Southesk, and the Marquis of Lorne appreciated Métis hospitality and their abilities as hunters and interpreters, but they described them as lazy, improvident, and shifty.[94] Métis were perceived as inferior to "real Indians" or "nothings." These racial theories and prejudices predominated well into the twentieth century and explain why a mixed heritage was hidden or Métis were forced to "pass as white" or identify as "real Indians." In many cases, they were scorned or rejected by both groups. It is only in the last thirty years or so that a positive image of "métisness" has emerged and fostered pride in Métis identity and heritage in Canada and North America.

It was in the "middle ground"[95] or Great Lakes region that a Métis counter-ideology contesting the dominant doctrine of racial purity and cultural pluralism emerged. By the late seventeenth century, the French frontier had moved westward from the St. Lawrence valley to the *pays d'en haut* (Great Lakes and the Ohio valley) in what is now the American Midwest. Marriage *à la façon du pays* was a primary component of social and economic interactions between the Eurocanadian fur traders and First Nations women. Many of the *coureurs de bois* (unlicensed traders and freemen) established families in military posts such as Michilimakinac and villages such as Green Bay and Prairie du Chien.[96] Peterson estimates that by 1820, the population of the Great Lakes communities was between ten and fifteen thousand.[97] The mixed heritage people of these communities were intermarried with or related to over a dozen First Nations peoples. These individuals identified themselves as *Chicots* or *Bois-Brûlés*, a surname possibly acquired from the "burnt stump" agriculture that they carried out, along with the harvesting of game, fish, and wild rice. Métis communities in the Great Lakes preceded or developed alongside those of the Red River valley and some families from the Great Lakes migrated to that region in the early 1800s. For example, Jean-Baptiste Nolin told Alexander Ross in the 1850s that he came to Pembina and the Forks of the Red and Assiniboine rivers in the 1770s.[98]

Red River: Cradle of the Métis Nation

Métis origins in the Red River Valley can be traced to around the mid-eighteenth century and the western explorations of the La Vérendryes and others from New France. They established trading posts in present-day Manitoba and Saskatchewan and entered into relationships with local Aboriginal peoples. Accounts suggest that some and perhaps many *engagés* under contract in the western posts refused to return to Quebec after the cession of 1760 or remained out west *en dérouine* (trading on their own) and intermarried with Ojibwe, Cree, Dakota, and Assiniboine women.[99] This development is also corroborated by Antoine Champagne in his work on La Vérendrye.[100] Databases incorporating information from parish and census records, voyageurs' contracts, and other sources may eventually enable researchers to identify these individuals and their families.[101] Hudson's Bay Company "servants" from the British Isles and voyageurs of the North West Company and other concerns also came to the region to trade in the eighteenth century. The first generations of Métis born in the North-West integrated into their Aboriginal mother's culture. In the few recorded cases where children (mainly sons) were sent to Montreal or Scotland by their fathers, they adopted their paternal heritage.

By 1805 or earlier, some of the descendants of these mixed families had staked land in an area called « la pointe » near the junction of the Seine and Red rivers in present-day Saint-Boniface (Manitoba).[102] It is not known specifically when these "new people" began to identify as Métifs (Métis) but the term is noted in 1814–17 Red River missionary correspondence. The descendants of First Nations and Scottish and English employees of the Hudson's Bay Company were identified alternately as "Native English," "Mixed bloods," and "Halfbreeds" in nineteenth-century fur trade and government records, although it is doubtful they called themselves by those names.

Church affiliation, language, and culture, as well as occupation, generally distinguished various Métis groups in the Red River Settlement but the distinctions were also blurred.[103] Some, described as "Halfbreed Indians"[104] followed Aboriginal lifestyles, while others adopted French Canadian and British customs. Intermarriage between the two groups, guided by social and economic factors, integrated one partner, more often the "Native English," into the parent Métis society. This trend is documented in the censuses of the Red River Settlement. The Métis, who were largely (at least nominally) Catholic and Michif-speaking, established themselves in the riverlot communities of St. Boniface, St. Norbert, and St. François-Xavier. Their Protestant and English or Bungee speaking (a Cree-Ojibwe-Gaelic dialect) compatriots settled in the parishes of the "Lower Settlement" north of the Red and Assiniboine rivers. British kinship and fur trade connections enabled more "Native English" to rise to administrative positions (primarily postmasters) within the Hudson's Bay Company, while French Canadian voyageurs hired after the early 1800s occupied labouring positions. The traditional hierarchy and ethnic bias were reduced somewhat after the union of the North West Company and the Hudson's Bay Company in 1821. The Nor'Westers, who obtained commissions in the new company after 1821, fostered the promotion of a few of their promising French Canadian employees. The appointment of Georges Deschambault and Henry Fisher as Chief Traders and of Horace Bélanger as Chief Factor were important, if exceptional, occurrences.[105] A large number of Métis were engaged as labourers for the Hudson's Bay Company boat brigades on a seasonal basis or under contract at the trading posts in various districts. Those who took up residence in Red River also pursued activities such as fishing, trapping, and farming. But an increasing number of Métis from the "French parishes" were freemen or *gens libres* who organized buffalo hunts, produced pemmican, freighted (transported furs and merchandise), and traded independently. Marie Desmarais Delorme, François Gingras, Narcisse Marion, Cuthbert and Daniel McGillis, Louis Letendre, and Emmanuel Champagne were among a number of prosperous independent traders at Red River by the mid-nineteenth century.

During the first half of the nineteenth century, the Métis developed a strong national consciousness and affirmed their sovereignty as a "new nation." Under the leadership of Cuthbert Grant, they rose in armed protest against economic sanctions on the sale of pemmican imposed by the Hudson's Bay Company. Métis songwriter Pierre Falcon commemorated the Métis victory at "La Grenouillère" (Seven Oaks) in 1816 with a national anthem.[106] The trial of free trader Guillaume Sayer in 1849 provided another opportunity for the Métis to challenge the Company's authority.[107] The cry of « le commerce est libre » ("the trade is free") followed the news that the Company's trading monopoly had been broken. The increasingly inept and unrepresentative council of Assiniboia, the Company's local political authority (1835–70), became the focus of subsequent protests as well.

The New Nation of the Northwest formed the majority of the population at Red River. It had developed specific political and economic traditions while a strong kinship network and land base fostered national consciousness. There were a variety of occupational groups and political leaders in Red River by the 1850s, for example, the merchant and freighting entrepreneurs, composed of families such as the Lagimodières, Gingras, Marions, Kittsons, and their relations. Also, there was an influential political elite of men such as François Bruneau, Louis Riel Sr., and James McKay in the 1850s and 1860s who were succeeded by Riel Jr., Charles Nolin, and Pierre Delorme.[108]

Red River society was diverse and complex. Differences in political and economic traditions and specific kinship ties had fostered various alliances. The Breland, Dease, and Hamelin families of St. François-Xavier (White Horse Plain), for example, were politically conservative (favouring the status quo or the administration of the Hudson's Bay Company), while the Riels, Carrières, Lépines, and Naults of St. Vital were adherents of free trade and self-government.[109] Similarly, the Goulets, Vennes, and Charettes of St. Norbert were ambivalent in their support of Riel and the resistance to Canadian annexation in 1869–70, while the Carons, St. Germains, and Champagnes were strongly committed. Divergent political views were also in evidence at Pointe-à-Grouette (Ste. Agathe).[110] But the common bonds of culture and heritage also ensured a certain solidarity. The majority of Métis rallied around Riel and supported the Provisional Government in its demands for guarantees of land and political and cultural rights. Negotiations with the Canadian government for the creation of a Métis province were protracted and difficult, but the persistence of the Métis negotiators resulted in the confirmation of existing land holdings (section 32 of Manitoba Act) and an entitlement of 1.4 million acres (565,000 hectares) for Métis children (section 31 of the Manitoba Act), provincial status, and the guarantee of linguistic and religious rights. However, the Manitoba Act was subject to numerous amendments and orders in council in the 1870s, effectively alienating Métis rights. The Canadian government dispatched a military expedition to take control of Manitoba, Riel was forced into exile, and the Métis were persecuted and isolated from power. Delays in the confirmation of existing land holdings and in the distribution of the Métis grant meant that much of the land was allocated to newcomers. The distribution of Métis land entitlement as negotiable scrip created opportunities for unscrupulous land agents, and even government officials, to defraud Métis landholders. The land grants were widely dispersed rather than being concentrated in areas contiguous to existing Métis communities, thus frustrating Métis dreams of a cohesive homeland in Red River. While there is some scholarly debate on the extent of Métis dispossession and forced relocation, the Métis themselves maintained and continue to maintain that they were discriminated against and pushed out.[111]

"Families All Over the Country": The Far Northwest and the Saskatchewan

Métis communities were established at Ile à la Crosse (Saskatchewan), Lac Ste. Anne and Lac la Biche (Alberta), the Athabasca (*le Rabasca*), and on la grande rivière (Mackenzie River) in the late eighteenth and the mid-nineteenth century. Although the ethnic origins of the western Métis were similar to that of the Red River Métis, there were important distinctions. Many of these families had Dene rather than Cree origins and their voyageur ancestors were not from Red River but had made their way further west inland or via the English (Churchill) River route. Métis presence in the north may have predated or accompanied the establishment of southern communities. For example, François Beaulieu, who led Alexander Mackenzie on his voyages, was in the Athabasca-Mackenzie by the 1770s, where he established a large extended Dene-Métis family.[112] The Métis of the Northwest had family and work connections with Red River through the Portage La Loche brigades and travelled south to trade and socialize. Northern families such as the Normands, Frobishers, and Lespérances relocated to Red River in the 1840s–50s, while the Mercredi (originally Macardy) and Bouvier families moved north.[113] Northern and southern Métis shared many cultural traditions but the communities had distinct economies and lifestyles.

Métis presence in the South Saskatchewan River region dates back to the late eighteenth century when French-Canadian voyageurs such as Jean-Baptiste Letendre *dit* Batoche, and his Cree wife, Josephte, travelled from Montagne de Roche [Rocky Mountain House] to the Saskatchewan River to hunt and trade.[114] By 1810 Letendre was a freeman who operated a post to which he gave his alias "Batoche" at Muskootao Point, west of Fort à La Corne on the north bank of the Saskatchewan River. The family was at Red River by 1825 but continued to trade in the Saskatchewan district. Louis Letendre and Marie Hallet, the parents of Xavier Letendre, who later founded the community of Batoche along the South Saskatchewan River, were at La Montée, the North West Company post opposite Fort Carlton in the early 1820s.[115] Other Métis families such as the Dumonts and Montours had a *pied à terre* in the region during that period.

By the 1840s, Métis from Red River had established *hivernements* (wintering camps) in the Qu'Appelle Valley, at Touchwood Hills and in the vicinity of Wood Mountain and the Cypress Hills, a territory that is now part of Saskatchewan. One of the most important of these early gathering places was at couli Chapelle (near present-day Willow-Bunch).[116] By the 1860s, the Métis of St. François-Xavier and parishes along the Red River had also established seasonal encampments further north and west: at Prairie Ronde (near present-day Dundurn), Grosse-Butte (near present-day Humboldt) and Petite-Ville (vicinity of present-day Fish Creek) on the west bank of the South Saskatchewan River.[117] It was at the latter site that a hunting-trading party led by Gabriel Dumont established a community in 1868. Petite-Ville was the forerunner of the St. Laurent Settlement (which included la couli des Tourond, Batoche, St. Laurent, and St. Louis), where the Métis relocated from Manitoba between 1872 and 1882, and later.

The families who came to the banks of the South Saskatchewan River included traders, freighters, hunters, and mixed farmers who sought a new life in a region unencumbered by settlers. They were a politically conscious group, most of whom had witnessed infringements on their rights by newcomers in Manitoba. They relocated to traditional lands further west to avoid discrimination, maintain their identity and culture, and diversify their economic activities.

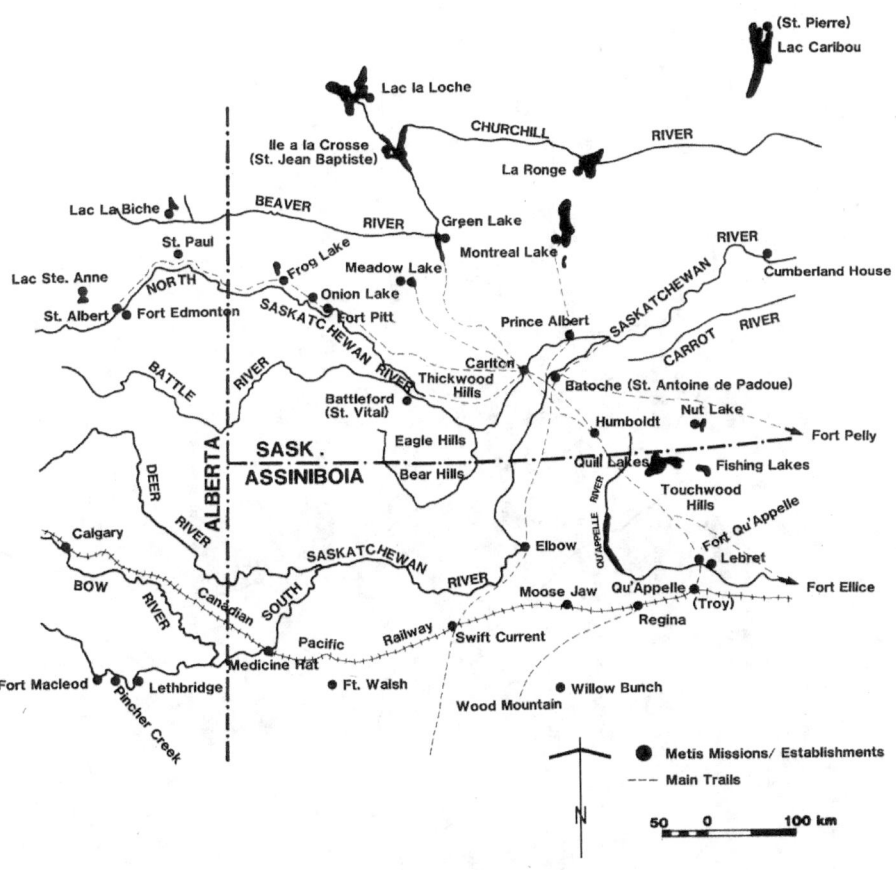

Intro. 1. Métis Landscape, North West Territories, 1880–1905.

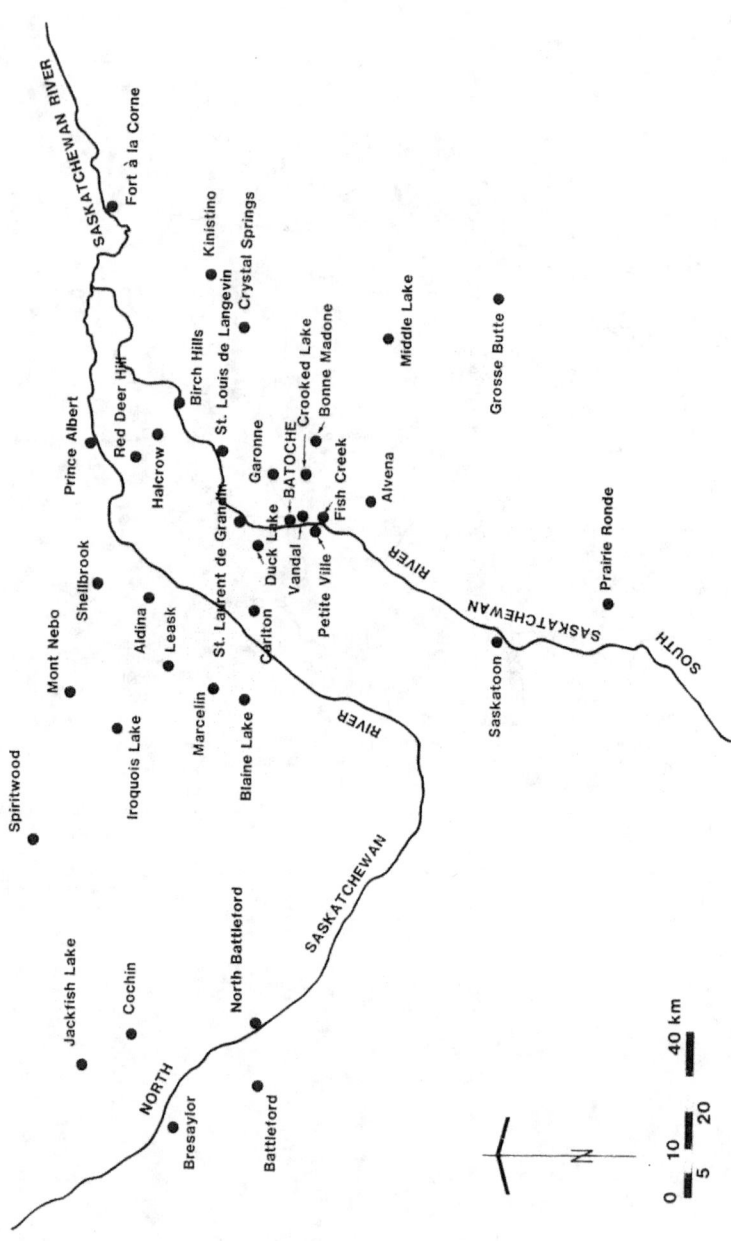

Intro. 2. Métis Communities on North and South Saskatchewan River, ca. 1920.

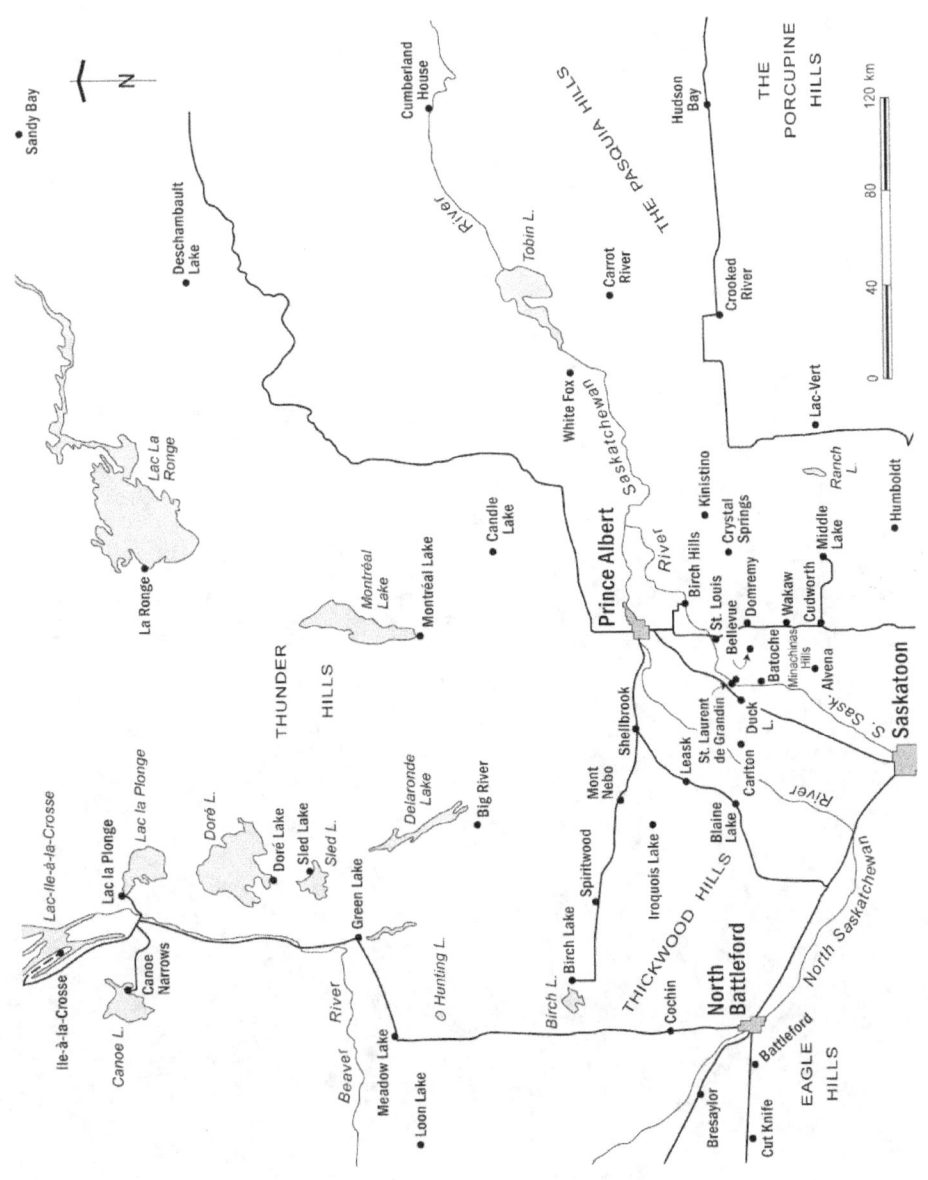

Intro. 3.   Batoche and district today.

Society and Culture

"Follow in the footsteps of your ancestors... preserve the customs... and above all, keep your language"
— *Louis Schmidt*

SOCIAL ORGANIZATION AND FAMILY

The first families of hunters and winterers who took up lands around Batoche in the 1870s came almost entirely from the winter camps of the North-West. As early as the 1840s, several French Canadian voyageurs had already settled around Fort Carlton with their Aboriginal families. During the 1850s, a large number of Métis families were reportedly wintering in the proximity of the Qu'Appelle River, File Hills and Gros Ventres Forks (South Saskatchewan River).[1] But around 1865, there was a rapid increase in the number of winter camps in the Fort Carlton area. The most important one was the Petite Ville encampment on the west bank of the South Saskatchewan River.

It was at this time and following the political and social turmoil of the Red River community in 1869–70 that the Métis of the district decided to establish themselves on the banks of the South Saskatchewan. Other circumstances conspired to hasten their decision. The area around Fort Carlton was not favourable for a permanent settlement. The soil was fairly swampy and unsuitable for farming, there was little wood, and it became increasingly difficult to obtain provisions. Finally, in 1870, a smallpox epidemic spread fear and consternation throughout the Métis wintering sites.

Although it took relatively few victims among the Saskatchewan Métis, the epidemic strengthened their desire to relocate.

On 31 December 1871, a meeting of the local Métis elders was held under the chairmanship of Lawrence Clarke of the Hudson's Bay Company at Fort Carlton, with the support of Father Alexis André, OMI.[2] Among the "patriarchs" were Isidore Dumont *dit* Aicawpow, Louison Letendre *dit* Batoche, and Jean Dumont *dit* Chakasta. The group's objective was to choose a site for a new community. After three years, they finally agreed on an area centred on the new St. Laurent de Grandin mission on the west bank of the South Saskatchewan. They set aside an area, "taking as the boundary of the colony the two sides of the river ten miles below the crossing and ten miles above the present winter camp [St. Laurent]."[3]

According to a Hudson's Bay Company (HBC) census in 1871, the population of the new "St. Laurent Settlement" numbered 322 persons.[4] It rose to 450 in 1877 and to more than five hundred people in the following year, after a wave of immigration from Manitoba.[5] This was less than the figure of fifteen hundred forecast by Chief Factor Lawrence Clarke for 1873, but it was a stable rate, which would be maintained during the following decade. All these figures must be regarded as approximate, for the population at the time was seasonal or mobile. During the 1870s, the settlements were more like base camps. Among the first families to settle along the South Saskatchewan were the following:[6] in the north, at Gardepuis' [or Gariépy's], Philippe Gariépy, James Short, and Mrs. Marguerite Ouellette (widow of Pierre), there since 1870; in the south, on the west bank, some families had taken up lands around the St. Laurent de Grandin mission since shortly after its founding in 1871. Among the first arrivals were Baptiste and Alexandre Hamelin, Antoine Fleury, Jonas Moreau, and Pierre Landry. The families of Isidore and Jean Dumont, Joseph Ouellette, Antoine Ferguson (Fercuson), Charles Racette, and Baptiste Boyer settled on the east bank. The Letendre *dit* Batoche family settled in the vicinity of the crossing set up by Xavier Letendre in 1873. They were joined by the families of Joseph "Dodet" and Baptisens Parenteau, Cuthbert "Corbet" Fayant (Failhant), and Pascal and Abraham Montour. Others took up lands in the vicinity of Gabriel Dumont's Crossing, while Ignace Poitras and Baptiste Vandal had settled earlier to the south along the trail from Humboldt. Other families included in the 1870 enumeration of the district settled in the vicinity of Fort Carlton, and in particular at Duck Lake.

In 1878, another group of about fifty families arrived from Manitoba and the North West Territories. Some of them had already spent time in the North-West, and in particular in the Qu'Appelle River, Wood Mountain, and Cypress Hills area, before joining their relatives or compatriots on the South Saskatchewan.

Another group, this one mainly from Manitoba, arrived in the spring and summer of 1882. This was the largest contingent, and it turned Batoche, St. Laurent, and the new parish of St. Louis into permanent settlements. According to a report by Father André in 1883, the population of the district was distributed as follows: St. Laurent (which included St. Louis at the time), 400; St. Antoine (which included la couli des Tourond, now Fish Creek), 500; and Duck Lake, 600,[7] for a total of 1,500 for the entire Métis population in the area. Excluding Duck Lake, which is not located on the South Saskatchewan River, the Métis population of the area numbered 1,000. However, these figures are not precise, for another diocesan report mentions eight hundred people at St. Antoine in 1883.[8] On the other hand, this figure takes into account the rural population of the parish. In the case of the 1884–85 census of the territory,[9] the Métis settlements are enumerated together with Prince Albert, thus making any valid reconstruction impossible. The limits of these communities were not clearly defined at the time. During the 1880s and 1890s, Batoche included not only a village but also a fairly extensive rural sector. The only clearly defined boundaries were those of the parish of St. Antoine de Padoue. In 1885, the parish extended to the north as far as lot 17; to the east it included the area of the present parish of St. Isidore de Bellevue, which was founded only in 1902; to the west it included the farms of the first subdivided lots of township 43 along the west bank of the South Saskatchewan River, and to the south it extended as far as the Tourond coulee (township 41-1-3), a distance of about twenty-five kilometres. The parish of the Immaculate Conception in Fish Creek was detached from Batoche in 1900. When the parish of St. Laurent de Grandin was closed in 1893, the residents on the east bank were divided almost equally between Batoche and St. Louis (according to distance).

Métis communities were largely self-governing before 1905. Saskatchewan municipalities were only established after 1909. The provincial and federal censuses taken before 1911 are very approximate as far as the Métis population on the South Saskatchewan is concerned.[10] Parishes are thus the best sources of information on population. In fact, parish registers allow us to establish birth, marriage, and death rates and, with less precision, to arrive at a figure for the population as a whole. According to a summary analysis of the St. Antoine de Padoue (Batoche) registers for the period 1885–1920,[11] the birth rate was 7.28 per cent and the death rate 3.5 per cent: the difference between the two was therefore positive. Moreover, an annual average of 3.4 weddings for the same years leads us to believe that a high proportion of young people left the parish. The registers also show that families were large: about ten to twelve children per couple living up to the age of forty-five or completing more than twenty years of marriage. On the other hand, infant mortality (less than five years) was high, at four deaths per family. The relatively high birth rate helped to compensate for the many deaths that occurred during the flu epidemics in 1890–91 and 1897 and the tuberculosis epidemics between 1899 and 1904. During the period 1894–1904, there were 191 deaths, an average of nineteen a year. The birth rate was barely able to make up for these losses. In sum, thanks to a high birth rate and large families, which filled the gaps left by deaths and departures, Batoche succeeded in maintaining a population figure of close to 450 inhabitants from 1885 to 1920.

Though somewhat homogeneous in origin, the Métis community on the South Saskatchewan River organized into several groups soon after its foundation, and there were signs of social stratification. More than 75 per cent of the population that settled in this area during the 1870s and 1880s came from Red River, the Pembina area, and the St. Joseph (St. Joe) area in Dakota.[12] These families were united by close ties. Apart from a few exceptions, they were also of First Nation (especially Cree and Ojibwe) and French Canadian descent. The families whose European ancestors were Scottish, Irish, or English had already been living for several generations in the Métis parishes in Manitoba, including St. Norbert and St. François-Xavier. They had become integrated in the Métis community by language, religion, mentality, and lifestyle. These families continued to intermarry almost without exception, as they had before coming to the Saskatchewan district. Life was simple, even for the well-to-do: people lived to satisfy their immediate needs and followed the rhythm of the seasons. Until the mid-1870s, Métis life revolved around the bison hunt, which was the Métis' main source of food. Residences were temporary and based upon seasonal bison movements. The timing of social activities and births was also influenced by the hunt. Weddings were held mainly in January and February, while births seemed to be more frequent in late fall or early winter, which were periods of rest. After 1885 and at the turn of the century, daily life was less subject to seasonal fluctuations and population movements. The Métis maintained a mobile lifestyle, but since the mixed farming they were increasingly engaging in required some continuity, they now travelled less for reasons of work than to "visit relatives." Some people went regularly to see their relatives who had moved north of Batoche and less frequently their "cousins in Manitoba."[13]

During the 1870s, the population was small and there were few class distinctions. In fact, most of the Métis were hunters, farmers, and labourers with few aspirations to commercial leadership. Nonetheless, certain individuals stood out[14] because of their economic status or social involvement, together with such factors as traditional knowledge, schooling, family origins, and even gender. Although status was largely influenced by economic activities, formal education and professional training were also prestigious.

The missionary who accompanied the hunters on the prairies or wintered with them enjoyed special esteem and influence. Father André assisted the leaders with the interpretation of "external" rules or laws laid down by the Canadian government. The same applied to the leader of a hunting expedition and the president of a local administrative council. Gabriel Dumont occupied these two positions during the 1870s. His large herd of cattle and horses were not only a sign of economic success but also a source of prestige among his compatriots. Similarly, Louis(on) Letendre Sr., Isidore Dumont *dit* Aicawpow, Jean Dumont *dit* Chakasta, Joseph Hamelin, and a few others who owned more than fifteen horses each were also regarded as well off and influential.[15] Their prestige also rested on the fact that they had resided in the area since the 1860s. The entrepreneurs Xavier Letendre, Salomon Venne, and Emmanuel Champagne also figured among the leaders of their community.[16] Persons who had specialized skills or knew how to read and write were also held in high regard, such as carpenters Ludger Gareau, teacher Ferdinand Ladret, and convent-educated Christine (Dumas) Pilon. During the 1880s, social classes were in evidence but there was a lot of mobility. The hunters and freighters saw their numbers and influence decrease. Batoche and vicinity were going through a transitional period. Politicians such as Louis Schmidt, Charles Nolin, and Maxime Lépine arrived from Manitoba to breathe new life and debate into the politics of the South Saskatchewan River Métis. These men were regarded as the new leaders of the community. A new class of

1.1. *François-Xavier Letendre dit Batoche (1841–1901) – Parks Canada, Louis Venne Collection.*

1.2. *Marguerite (Parenteau) Letendre (1843–1937) – Parks Canada, Louis Venne Collection.*

1.3. Panoramic view of Batoche Village, 1891 – Archives of Manitoba, N855.

diligent farmers was also being formed: Jean Caron Sr., Joseph Ouellette, Baptiste Boucher, and Joseph Pilon were known as hard-working, enterprising, and tenacious. Many of their adult sons followed in their footsteps. In the early 1880s, other people came to settle near the Métis. They were French, Québécois, and Acadians from eastern Canada who took up lands east of Batoche (in the area that would become Bellevue) to farm or set up businesses. The Gareau brothers, Ludger and Azarie, and Philippe Chamberland were among the first French Canadians to settle in the area. Some French immigrants settled nearby at Duck Lake. Among them were Louis St. Louis de Gladiou, Baron Huysmans de Neftal, and Louis Riguidel. Most of these individuals integrated into Métis society, filling certain gaps among the professionals and workers.

During the 1890s and at the turn of the century, the situation changed as several merchants left Batoche for more promising localities or to pursue other more lucrative ventures. New families assumed the leadership of the community. The majority of the people were farmers and skilled workers who had little leisure time to worry about the outside issues of the day. In the rural society of the time,[17] this role went traditionally to the parish priest, the parish council, the school trustees, and the postmaster. The lay elite was generally recruited from among the entrepreneurs-merchants, skilled workers, and some of the more prosperous farmers. Then came the tradesmen, farmers, skilled workers, seasonal workers, and unskilled labourers.[18] All these groups were represented at Batoche.

Several factors determined membership in a group or an individual's social standing. Family antecedents, occupation, and prestige were important criteria. Schooling seemed to be a way of reaching a "higher" class. In Batoche and St. Louis, there were examples of stratification within certain families.[19] On the other hand, it seems that the Métis attached less importance to material wealth and social conformism than did Eurocanadians. In most cases, an individual's personality, initiative and abilities were the source of his prestige and his ascendancy over his compatriots.

At the turn of the century, there were "cliques" or groupings by family, age, economic and social status, and political interest to be found in Batoche and vicinity. The socio-economic elite included the Boucher, Letendre, Venne, Champagne, and Fisher families. Some personalities stood out because of their specifically political interests or their community leadership: conservatives Charles Nolin, Maxime Lépine, and Philippe Gariépy were generally opposed to the comparatively left-wing group composed of

Alex Fisher, Philippe Garnot, and Abraham Montour.[20] There was also the "Caron clique"[21] (the brothers Pierre, Théophile, and Patrice), friends of Father Moulin who were very active on the parish council.

As in European society of the time, Métis women's status was closely tied to that of their fathers or husbands. Nuns and spinsters of a certain age enjoyed a privileged status, but always according to special norms. As a general rule, a woman's role was essentially family-oriented and domestic, but she was recognized as the boss within the home. A woman's limited field of action offered her few economic or social prospects outside the home and family. However, seniority and schooling seemed to be sources of prestige. Métis women generally had more formal education than their husbands and many could read and write. These women were valued in a society where the written word was gaining ascendancy. The Métis owed their Aboriginal heritage mainly to Cree and Ojibwe women and valued the cultural and linguistic training they had received from their mothers and grandmothers. In their writings, Métis leaders such as Louis Riel and Charles Nolin insisted on the need to respect and honour their maternal ancestors.[22]

The family was at the core of Métis society. Whole families, consisting sometimes of three generations, relocated along the South Saskatchewan River. We have as example, the case of Pierre (Pierriche) Parenteau, aged sixty-eight, and his son Moïse, who came to join their daughter and sister Marguerite, wife of Xavier Letendre, in 1882. Xavier's octogenarian parents also lived with him in the village. His elder brothers André and Louis and their large families also established themselves in the area. Their sisters Marie (wife of Emmanuel Champagne), Hélène (wife of Charles Thomas), and Sophie (wife of Édouard Dumont) also settled on farms very close to the village of Batoche.

This "chain migration" was practised by almost all families. Parents, children, brothers, and sisters settled on neighbouring or nearby lots, often close to their "in-laws." The Caron and Pilon families claimed several adjoining lands. The Vandal and Fidler families occupied lands south of Gabriel's (Dumont's) Crossing, while the Boyer, Ouellette, and Dumont families formed the largest contingent of colonists in St. Laurent de Grandin. The Lépine and Boucher families constituted by themselves almost the entire population of St. Louis. This network of relationships gave the whole area, including Duck Lake to the west, the character of a "big family." The community was homogeneous, united (in spite of typical internal

1.4. *Letendre house and family probably on wedding of Florestine Letendre and Bruno Venne, September 4, 1894 – Saskatchewan Archives Board, R-A5634.*

divisions), and, at least in the early years, self-sufficient. The social and moral support that came with what is called "family immigration" made it easier to adapt to a new environment. However, in everyday life, the family in each rural community functioned more according to the principles of a nuclear society. Aged parents often stayed with one of their children, generally one of the younger ones. A father who had settled on a piece of land tried to reserve the neighbouring lots for his sons. This practice facilitated mutual aid and social interaction. A young couple usually moved into a separate home, even if it was close to that of their parents. An unmarried son who reached the age of majority generally left home, unless he was to inherit it or paid for his room and board. The nineteenth-century Métis Canadien family was guided by the principle of unity, the need to maintain traditional values, and the primacy of the collectivity over the individual. It was a rural society which integrated the individual but imposed certain obligations on him for the sake of collective survival. The roles of each family member were clearly defined, even though precarious economic and social circumstances might cast doubt on these definitions and require family members to adapt and be flexible. The same conditions prevailed in several similar societies at that time. According to studies of the nineteenth-century rural North American family, "the model that emerges is one of diversity and flexibility, the kind of controlled disorder that varied in accordance with pressing social and economic needs."[23]

Within the family, tasks were clearly divided. The father and the sons were responsible for the heavy farm work and often took seasonal jobs that brought in "wages." They would also "winter" far away with the cattle. The mother and the daughters were responsible for "housekeeping." They also cultivated the vegetable garden, which together with the hunt provided the Métis with their basic diet. Métis women rarely worked in the fields, but milking the cows, taking care of the chickens, and collecting the eggs were included among their tasks.[24] Moreover, families often received help from an aged grandparent or unmarried aunt they had taken in, or from a cousin they were putting up temporarily.

The roles of family members, though precisely defined, were at the same time interdependent. Grandparents were involved in the life of the nuclear family, both socially and economically. Widows usually lived with one of their children, whether at home with the heir or with one of their married daughters. They took part in domestic work and child care and education. Aged parents usually lived alone in a separate home, generally close to that of one of their children. Grandparents unable to do the farm work alone or take care of the maintenance called on their children for help. Elders were treated with respect and tenderness. There were no "big pensions" (old-age security) and no welfare at the time, nor any retirement homes. The lives of aged parents remained intertwined with those of their children. During their active lives, people tried to put aside some savings to meet their needs in old age, but custom required children to take care of their aged and needy parents if they survived.

The family or "household" was composed of father, mother, and children. The father's role was to be "head of the family" and provider. He was the one in charge, at least in theory. Families were always enumerated under the father's name.[25] According to the teachings of the Church, the mother or wife had to submit to her husband. Such popular appellations such as "*la créature*" or "*la mère*" suggested a lower status, but in most families the mother was roughly equal to the father. She was responsible for the children's education and for running the household. Even though the structure was clearly patriarchal, in practice the mother exercised some authority in the home, and children gained their independence when they came of age or left home.

Few couples had a long family life cycle. Until the turn of the century, as a result of the high death rate of women due to too many or too closely spaced pregnancies, as well as of the generally lower life expectancy of men, few "lived out their lives" with the same spouse. According to a study done in the United States, before 1900 only 40 per cent of the female population had an ideal family life cycle (up to age 50 with the same spouse).[26] Given the more precarious situation of a people marked by more poverty and illness, this percentage was probably lower in the Métis communities. But there were exceptions. A woman who had safely passed "the critical period" or fertile years had a good chance of reaching old age and hence of surviving her husband. The average age at death in Batoche during the period 1885–1905 was 63 for women and 56 for men,[27] and only 15 per cent reached the age of 75.

Children were an important source of labour: boys outside the home and girls inside. However, since boys ensured the family's succession and provided more economic potential, they enjoyed more freedom. Young children were pampered, but as soon as they reached adolescence, they were called on to take part in domestic work. Orphans were never abandoned to strangers. They were taken in by their grandparents or an older

1.5. *Elders of Batoche and St. Laurent de Grandin, ca.1910. Seated, William Boyer and Julienne (Bousquet) Boyer; standing left to right: Clémence (Boyer) Gervais, Elisabeth (Dumont) Ouellette, Gilbert Breland, Moïse Ouellette, Jean-Baptiste Arcand, Baptisens Parenteau, Father François-Xavier Simonin, Nancy (McKay) Arcand, Félicité (Boyer) Breland, Hélène (Boyer) Racette, Jonas Moreau – Parks Canada, Edmond and Berthe (Ladéroute) Boyer Collection.*

sister or brother. In Batoche and vicinity, there were several examples of children "adopted" by relatives or even friends. It was not rare for a widower or widow to remarry twice[28] so that the children of two or three families found themselves living under the same roof. Young people married early, especially girls, who usually married before the age of 20 and often between 16 and 18. Boys married a little later, usually after the age of majority (21). For economic as much as social reasons, few people remained single. In fact, young women still unmarried at the age of 25 were called "old maids." Some single women were valued for their artistic abilities, business acumen, and generosity towards the family, but this status was only possible in cases of wealthy families or when fathers ensured the financial independence or security of their adult daughters.

In Batoche, St. Laurent, and St. Louis, people rarely married outsiders. Endogamy was practised for several generations, almost without exception, until 1940. This was common practice in societies having a distinct cultural identity and national consciousness. Social class and economic status or parents' occupations were of prime importance in the choice of a spouse. In Red River and especially St. François-Xavier, there were several examples of such "class marriages" between Métis of French Canadian descent and those with Scottish or English ancestry.[29] In the South Saskatchewan River communities, where the Métis were primarily of Cree and French Canadian descent, people married within their social class and among relatives. When they arrived, the families were tied by third- and fourth-degree blood relations, and some, like the Letendre-Champagne, Boyer-Fisher, and Dumont-Ouellette families, were first cousins by marriage. During the 1890s and 1900s, the marriages between the children of these families created a society that could be called a "family" in the wide sense. All relationships were present: one could be both the aunt and sister-in-law of the same person, or both the husband and cousin. Social intercourse was confined to a very narrow circle, and the ramifications of a first marriage created friendships leading to new unions. Family endogamy cured the insecurity and solitude that accompanied migration. The closeness of the dwellings along the river and the custom of sons' settling on lands adjacent to those of their parents helped to develop strong emotional ties.

There were several types of marriage in the communities on the South Saskatchewan River: (1) unions or marriages according to social class, (2) intermarriage, limited in the first and second generations but more frequent in the third (at the turn of the century), (3) marriages between cousins of various degrees, beginning with the second generation, and (4) a few cases of exogamy, or marriage with a person from the outside, and hence cases of a person leaving the community and becoming integrated into another group. The Boucher and Letendre families illustrate the first two categories. Jean-Baptiste Boucher Sr. and his wife Caroline Lespérance were unrelated as far as we know. Their family of fourteen living children had what is called an "ideal" life cycle (survival into adulthood, marriage, and death after 50), which was rare at the time.[30] Their daughter Emma became a Grey Nun, and their thirteen other children married and raised families of five children on the average. Counting two second marriages, ten of the spouses were Métis, and five were French Canadians from the same social class. The Bouchers married into the Letendre (Xavier), Lépine (Maxime), and Schmidt (Louis) families and had what are called "successful marriages," that is economically and socially advantageous ones. One Boucher daughter married a sergeant of the North West Mounted Police (NWMP) and another married a civil servant, which were considered "honourable positions" at the time. By the 1890s, the Boucher family and its descendants constituted the majority of the population of St. Louis.

In comparison, Xavier Letendre's family was better off economically but was more severely affected by infant mortality and illness, which decimated its members in 1901–02. This family, one of the richest in the area between 1870 and 1895, became tied by marriage to other merchants families, namely the Fisher, Venne, and Parenteau families. There were several marriages between the family of Louis(on) Letendre (Xavier's older brother) and his third wife Angélique Dumas and the Joseph Pilon family. Two of Joseph's sons married two of Louis's daughters, and another Pilon son married one of Xavier Letendre's daughters. One of Louis's daughters, Henriette, married a first cousin, Daniel Dumas.[31] In almost all these families, marriages between blood relations and in-laws still occurred in the third generation or after 1910. The result was a network of very close relationships throughout the area.

The Caron and Parenteau families illustrates the third type of marriage. Jean Caron Sr., the patriarch of this family, was married to Marguerite Dumas, sister of Angélique Dumas-Letendre. Several of their children married into the family of Moïse Parenteau and Véronique St. Germain, who was the first cousin of Jean Caron (on the maternal side). Moïse Parenteau was himself the son of Marie-Anne Caron, sister of Jean Caron, and

1.6. *Jean Caron (1833–1905) and Marguerite (Dumas) Caron (1843–1937) with granddaughters Emma and Marie and son Albert in front of their house at Batoche, ca. 1900 – Provincial Archives of Alberta, OB 3827.*

1.7. *Théophile Caron and third wife Lisa (Gervais) Caron with their children and Kokum Clémence (Boyer) Gervais, ca. 1915 – Parks Canada, donated by Walter and Marie Fidler.*

1.8. Ludger Gareau (1855–1954) and Madeleine (Delorme) Gareau (1868–1958) and their family in Pincher Creek, Alberta, ca. 1905 – Parks Canada, donated by Gérard Chamberland.

1.9. Boucher family of St. Louis, ca. 1915. On the wall are portraits of parents Jean-Baptiste Boucher and Caroline Lespérance. Standing left to right: Baptiste Jr., Rose-Délima, Charles-Eugène, Salomon, Frédéric, Élise and Joseph. Seated left to right: Sara, Caroline, Marguerite, Emma (Grey Nun), Marie-Rose, Alvina (« La Pie ») – Parks Canada, courtesy St. Louis Historical Committee.

Voyageur and ancestor Jean-Marie Boucher (1793–1870) – Courtesy of Réal Boucher.

hence the latter's nephew. There were thus several kinship ties between the two families. In 1887, Jean Caron Jr. married Virginie Parenteau, daughter of Moïse and Véronique. The bride and groom were second cousins. There were five other marriages between the two families. Dispensations for marrying a first or second cousin were frequently granted at the time. Several such dispensations were recorded in the Batoche and St. Laurent parish registers. It seems that there was disapproval of marriages between first cousins but that marriages between second cousins were accepted, if not encouraged. What made this practice dangerous from a hereditary point of view was the effect of double kinship between spouses and the persistence of this phenomenon until the third generation. For example, several children of Jean Caron Jr. and Virginie Parenteau, who were themselves cousins twice over, married their cousins. Frequent remarriages between sisters-in-law and brothers-in-law after the death of the first spouse reinforced still further the kinship ties between the children of these marriages. The third generation, who married between 1910 and 1925, was fairly limited in their choice of a spouse. The custom of marrying a Métis was nevertheless respected. Young people sometimes chose a spouse from among French Canadians, more often from among new French or Belgian settlers, but rarely from among Ukrainians. Religion, language, and the family network (in the broad sense) were important criteria. People felt a kind of fear of "outsiders." Sometimes, as for example in the Letendre and Dumas families, they re-established old family ties to Manitoba. It was only in the following generations (especially after 1925) that the Métis at Batoche began marrying outsiders, a practice that promoted assimilation and the loss of identity.

CUSTOMS AND TRADITIONS

Between 1870 and 1915, daily life at Batoche and surrounding communities was marked by the continuation or persistence of traditional customs. Certain social and economic changes modified the behaviour or role of each family member, but the family remained at the core of any activity. Life was generally characterized by sharing and by a certain equality between the genders at work, if not social activities. The interdependence between the members of a family extended to the community as a whole. This situation,

1.10. *Antoine Ferguson of St. Laurent with daughters Emma (left) and Ernestine (right), ca. 1915 – Saskatchewan Archives Board, R-A5225.*

combined with the restricted physical environment (at home) limited or even ruled out any possibility of private life or independent action.

Regarding inheritance, according to some wills[32] and oral testimonies, the family farm usually went to one of the younger boys after the parents' death, while the girls shared the cattle. According to the testimony of some women before the "Rebellion Losses Commission of 1885," brides received furniture, kitchen utensils, bedding, and animals as their dowry. The dowry was probably proportional to the parents' financial situation. Some elderly women stated that their trousseau had consisted only of their clothes and the wedding reception. Nevertheless, parents were always ready to help the newlyweds (with services, domestic production, etc.), and a very young couple often lived for some time with the husband's parents. Mutual aid and the community spirit extended also to neighbours, who were almost always cousins.

This did not mean, however, that Batoche was an idyllic society. On the contrary, social relations were charged with tensions, sensitivities, and intrigues. Members of the same family were often divided by jealousy. Parents tended to give more freedom and privileges to boys[33] and sometimes had a favourite. There were family quarrels that lasted for years.[34] At a time when separation of the spouses was condemned by the religious authorities and divorce was inadmissible or unobtainable, several people "borrowed" a spouse (or lived "common or customary law" with another person). There was the case of a father who brought his daughter back home when he found out she had been abused by her husband, but many women were left to fend for themselves.[35] There were also cases of *ménage à trois* where wives had to accept the presence of another woman under their own roof and were even forced to raise the children of that union. Métis society, however, was more open than European society and more ready to accept such "irregularities." "Natural" children were never rejected. They were integrated into the single mother's family or "adopted" by a relative.

Family homes were generally small,[36] consisting usually of a ground floor with an attic and, generally, a summer kitchen or other attached building. This did not favour intimacy, and in spite of a lifestyle centred on the community rather than on the individual, crowding was the source of family tensions. In certain large families or those including several generations, it often happened that the father or older children "got cabin fever"[37] and stayed away from home for long periods to work outside. Such a move, which was more open to men, sometimes served as a safety valve for an intolerable domestic situation.[38]

The oral and written descriptions of homes at Batoche between the 1870s and the 1920s shows that there were three types of dwellings. The spacious homes of Xavier Letendre, Salomon Venne, and Emmanuel Champagne illustrate the first type. These were log structures usually covered with boards and topped with a shingle roof. The Letendre house was built in two two-storey sections and measured about 9.75 by 13.4 metres (32 by 44 feet), and the interior walls were wood-panelled or plastered.[39] An average house consisting of one and a half storeys and measuring about 6.1 by 7.6 metres (20 by 25 feet) constituted the second type. The exterior walls were daubed with a clay mortar and plastered over with lime. The ground floor of this type of dwelling contained two rooms, a living room and a kitchen, while the attic contained a single room divided by curtains and sometimes a partition. When space was needed, an annex was added and connected with the main building by a corridor. "The houses were a series of rooms stuck together: they were added on one after the other."[40] The homes of Jean Caron Sr. (lot 52, built about 1890), Joseph Pilon Sr. (lot 67, built about 1888), and Charles Laviolette (lot 20, St. Laurent, built about 1900) were examples of this second type of dwelling. Quite a few people lived in more modest homes of the third type measuring 4.6 by 6.1 metres (15 by 20 feet) or less. During the 1880s there were some thatched roofs,[41] but these were later replaced by spruce-shingle roofs, with thatched roofs being confined to stables, sheds, and other outbuildings. The furniture in most dwellings was simple and homemade. Only the more well-to-do or those who were paid in cash (such as merchants and government employees) were able to buy home furnishings and decorations. Several families who had emigrated from Manitoba before 1885 had brought along such valuables as a clock, sewing machine, spinning wheel, weaving loom, four-poster bed, wardrobe, dresser, carpet, and even a silver teapot.[42] Among the traditional items listed in the 1885 inventories were: hooked rugs, quilts, violins, chests (trunks), belts, vests and "soft shoes" (moccasins) decorated with multi-coloured pearls and embroidery, arrow sashes, tobacco pouches, and hunting knives with a chiselled handle and decorated with various animals. The inventories also mention religious articles, and in particular images of Christ and the Virgin, crucifixes, rosaries, and prayer books.

From the 1870s on, most of the traditional mid-nineteenth-century clothes were replaced by European ones. Depending on place of residence, lifestyle, and social status, this change took varied forms. Some articles such as oxhide shoes, moccasins, shawls, arrow sashes, and animal-skin capes (made of racoon or other fur) were still worn by the old people in the 1920s.

Louis Schmidt (1844–1935) and Louis Goulet (1859–1936) left eyewitness accounts of the "outfits" worn by old Métis. According to Louis Schmidt:

> The voyageur, artisan or whoever wore only pants, a shirt, soft shoes and some kind of cap, or a hat or tuque to cover their heads. Socks or stockings were unknown to them. In the winter, they stuffed a rabbit skin or piece of woollen material into their shoes and put on a cape of unlined woollen cloth to protect themselves against the cold. Generally, they wore a sash over the [hooded] cape, but many young people let their sash hang down in front and used it only to hold up their trousers. Nobody wore suspenders, except for young children. Women's outfits were just as simple. Only their modesty demanded a little more care. Thus they wore a small shawl or big kerchief [often made of silk] on their chests, plus another one on their heads for going out, as well as a shawl [on their shoulders]. By way of stockings, they wore a kind of gaiters [mitasses]: small woollen leggings trimmed with fringes. They wore the same kind of shoes as men.[43]

According to Goulet,[44] the Métis were proud and always well-dressed, even though the winterers (the people in the hunting and trading camps of the North-West) did not dress the same way as the people of Red River, who dressed according to the latest Montreal or St. Paul fashions.

> The winterers still wore soft shoes, plain closely woven cloth suits, the thick flannel shirts of the Hudson's Bay Company, arrow sashes and gaiters. In the winter, they wore their hooded capes of fine woollen cloth, their *craint-rien* (very warm) capes and their old bonnets. A so-called *craint-rien* cape was a kind of short fur-lined overcoat.[45]

He added that shirts were usually made of grey flannel or brightly coloured cotton, while trousers were made of English cloth, most often navy blue, and sometimes of corduroy. Many winterers wore pants that opened on the hip, which were called *culotte à la bavaloise* (Bavarian breeches).[46] Like his compatriot Louis Schmidt, Goulet described women's costume as being more conservative.

Besides covering themselves in kerchiefs and shawls:

1.11. *Christine (Dumas) Pilon and daughters Octavie Lépine (left) and Adélaïde Pilon (right), ca. 1920 – Parks Canada, Omer Ranger Collection.*

... they wore a long dress skirt down to their feet and over it a kind of jerkin called a basque, with puffed-out sleeves between elbow and shoulder which tapered off to a point at ear level. The most common fabric was velvet.[47]

Several changes in dress were noted in Batoche between 1872 and the 1920s. Photographs show that men dressed more in the European (or North American) manner: they often wore "the arrow sash of the old halfbreeds," but on Sundays the freighters, farmers, and day-labourers wore "French" shoes, which merchants, officials, and other businessmen wore every day. According to some accounts, the cowboy outfit became popular among young people, beginning in the 1890s. Several young Métis who raised cattle or hired themselves out to the ranchers wore "crimped breeches," a kind of pants tight-fitting on the thighs and legs and bell-shaped above the shoes. They also wore a tall hat with a very wide straight brim.[48]

Inventories of merchandise in Batoche stores in 1885 and later lists of purchases at Mitchell's in Duck Lake indicate that all clothing fabrics and sewing articles were locally available. Few people bought ready-made clothes, except perhaps for the wealthier. Métis women were skilful with needle and thread and made clothes at home. One child's clothing served several brothers and sisters, and "we weren't difficult: we wore what we were given."[49] Among the fabrics for sale in the stores, there was printed calico (cotton), which came in yellow and red, in variously coloured squares (plaid) and in stripes. Batiste (cambric), fine cotton, wincey, flannel, and cashmere, especially in black, blue, and red, and ribbons, lace, and assorted buttons were much in demand. Among ready-to-wear clothes, there were mainly duffle coats (lined cloth coats), black capes, felt hats, kid gloves, leather boots and shoes, and rubber overshoes. Women also bought hats, fine cotton stockings, and jewellery such as earrings and brooches. Knitwear, especially scarves, tuques, bonnets, and mittens, was made at home. The same was true of underwear, except for the infamous corset.

Around the turn of the century, women's usual costume consisted of a skirt, blouse, and apron. Given the means, they would make themselves a fur coat, but more often it was made of cloth. They also began wearing hats to church. Well-dressed men wore a top hat, cape, and ankle boots for important outings. In short, while the traditional voyageur's dress continued to exist in some form or other until the turn of the century, the Métis adopted more and more the costume of the period and differed less and less in appearance from the people of Eurocanadian origin.

At the time of the winter camps and in the first communities along the South Saskatchewan River, the main diet consisted almost entirely of bison meat, as well as "roots" (vegetables) and wild fruits gathered while travelling or in camp. When "there was no cow [bison]," they hunted big game (caribou, mule deer, white-tail deer), duck or prairie fowl, or they went fishing.[50] Usually the only food they bought was flour, but on some occasions they also bought bacon, salt pork, and tea. Flour was essential for preparing bannock (a flat round bread), another important staple in their diet. This unleavened bread was made of flour, water, and fat, to which some added baking powder, before baking either directly over the embers (in the form of small cakes placed on sticks arranged around the fire) or in a big cast-iron pot, which served as an oven during their travels.[51] In long-term homes, it was baked in a casserole dish, either on the stove or in the oven.

During the 1870s, the Métis still subsisted mainly on bison. Fresh meat was preferred, especially tongue, hump, rump, and the two sides (rib steaks between the shoulder and the haunch). The meat was cooked, smoked or dried, but most often transformed into pemmican. Louis Schmidt described the preparation of *taureau* (pemmican) as follows:

The lean parts are used to make what is called *taureau,* or what the English call "pemmikan," which is a corruption of the Cree word "pimihkan" (meaning a mixture containing fat).... They spread a battering skin on the ground. They fashion a flail as for threshing wheat, and they beat the meat to reduce it almost to powder. It is then called *viande pillée* [pounded meat]. They then mix it with hot fat in big containers, and the *taureau* is ready. They put it in big well-sewn leather bags, and it is then ready to be shipped and sold.[52]

Dried or crushed fruit was often added to the meat.

Bison fat called *graisse de moëlle* [marrow fat] replaced butter and other fats in food preparation. When there was no meat, the Métis had recourse to fish, preferably broiled, for it seems that they hardly appreciated boiled fish, "that awful mush."[53] During the lean periods, they also ate barley soup and even wild cabbage soup.

In Red River during the 1850s and 1860s, and later on in the St. Laurent Settlement in Saskatchewan, the food was more varied and reflected both Aboriginal and French-Canadian traditions. In the 1870s, bison was replaced by so-called "wild" meat, including deer, bear, prairie chicken, pheasant, and duck. People also ate jackrabbit and more rarely, especially on meatless Fridays or during Lent, smoked fish (e.g., pike and sturgeon). Those who raised domestic animals harvested them in the fall. Pork was used to make blood pudding, sausages, and head cheese, and in the winter people ate salt pork and beef (mainly minced and in stews). During the spring thaw, the remaining meat was cut into strips and dried on wooden racks.[54] At the turn of the century, chicken or other fowl was stuffed and roasted in the oven on Sundays and on special occasions.[55] This dish was much appreciated, "a real treat," but relatively rare, as most people preferred to keep laying-hens. There were, in addition, various other foods, mostly of French-Canadian origin. Comparative studies (using documentary and oral sources) of traditional French-Canadian and Métis food reveal many similarities between the two. The following are some examples:

Tourtières (meat pies): a preparation of minced meat covered with pastry dough.

Les boulettes: ground pork or beef meatballs boiled in a browned-flour sauce or rolled in a batter and fried. These *boulettes* or *avrignoles*[56] were served as a main dish on feast days.

La piquette: a home-made wine made with various fruits such as rhubarb, dandelions, or cherries.

Cretons or courtons: very finely chopped pork meat, with fat (suet) added to it.

Among the most typical Métis dishes were the following:

Rababou:[57] a kind of fricassee of fowl, deer, or beef.

Taureau or pemmican: a variant of the traditional dish, with beef or venison replacing bison meat. The meat was pounded into a pulp and fat and dried fruit (saskatoon berries, currants, or raisins) were then added to it.[58]

Feuillet or fayet (omasum) and *panse* (paunch): the third and first stomachs of the bison or other ruminants, which were eaten boiled and seasoned.[59]

Flan: milk taken from the second milking of a cow which has just calved and then baked in the oven.[60]

Glissantes (dumplings): spoonfuls of dough boiled in chicken bouillon or other meat broth.

Poutine glissante (dumpling pudding): a thick pastry cut into squares and boiled in water and served with molasses or syrup. This pastry could be poured over compote of fresh or dried fruit and then baked in the oven. It was eaten with "a lot of good fresh cream."[61]

A favourite dessert was a twisted or braided doughnut that is still made in Batoche and surrounding communities. A similar dessert called *croquignoles* was eaten in Quebec at the end of the nineteenth century. According to one account:

> ... people loved to try the *croquignoles* that the young women of the house would make for Christmas and New Year's Day. While kneading the dough on the upturned cover of the dough trough, the women, all covered with flour, would invariably offer those browning delicacies to the young lads ... so they did

their best to make them turn golden brown as they twisted and turned capriciously in the foaming, boiling fat.[62]

People in Batoche also ate *ferlouche* pie (a mixture of molasses and flour), *tire-liche* (a kind of stew made with slices of pork, onions, pumpkin, or squash, and molasses) and "virgin soup" (a milk soup with white cabbage and eggs).

Gathering wild fruit was both an economic and a social activity. Families went out together and often used the occasion for a picnic and for camping out. Among other things, they gathered black and red wild cherries, currants, gooseberries, bunchberries, and especially saskatoon berries and cranberries. Cherries were crushed between two rocks and dried. Some people made little rounds of dried fruit. "In the winter, they boiled them in water to make tarts and cakes or to eat them with cream."[63] They also gathered nuts and dogwood (kinik-kinik), which they smoked like tobacco.

Vegetable gardens were an important factor in nutrition. The Métis grew large amounts of potatoes, carrots, rutabagas, cabbage, turnips, parsnips, pumpkins, onions, beans, cucumbers, and lettuce. Multicoloured corn (Indian corn) was very popular in the past. During the summer, fresh corn was roasted on a grill, and in the autumn it was dried and pounded into a powder or flour to add to soups and stews.[64] Corn flour, ground barley, and oatmeal were also used for bannock and bread. The latter gradually replaced the former as a daily food, especially when dry yeast became available commercially in the early 1900s.

After the fall harvest, root vegetables were stored in a cellar in the basement of the main dwelling or outside:

> The "roots" were put in outside or inside cellars. There was usually a trap door leading to the cellar underneath the kitchen or summer kitchen or lean-to floor. They also put straw in it.[65]

The root vegetables could be preserved in the cellar until July.[66] A Sister from a convent in Prince Albert gave a detailed description of a big cellar built by Métis:

> It [the cellar] is indispensable here so as to preserve vegetables for winter use, for everything freezes in the ordinary house

cellars. Our root-house was constructed, by a very experienced Métis, in the following manner. An excavation of eight feet by eight, and twelve feet deep was made on the side of a slope in the most sheltered part of our wood in front of the house. The excavation was entirely lined with boards and a slanting roof made of heavy blocks of wood covers the inside. The entrance has two doors, twelve feet distant from each other, a passage five or six feet deep separates them. It is covered with planks thus forming a kind of tunnel. This passage is filled with hay so that when the inside door is open the frost cannot get in. To complete the construction, the whole exterior is covered with manure to the depth of about three feet so that nothing can be seen except the outside door.[67]

Meat preservation was also a concern at a time when there was no electricity and when canning techniques were not yet well known. There were many smoke shacks in the Batoche area well into the 1950s. Beef, pork, and game were smoked. Pork especially was salted (and eaten as "grilled salt pork"). Besides salting, drying, smoking, and freezing (in the winter), the methods of food conservation were cooling in a well and burying.

When people slaughtered an animal, they went from house to house and sold meat. Everybody had a well. Some attached a bucket to a cable and lowered the meat to the bottom of the well. This preserved the meat for about ten days. Others kept the meat all summer packed in sawdust, while others used wheat instead.[68]

More established families, such as the Vennes and Boyers cultivated small fruit trees such as apple and cherry. The custom of planting bushes and flowers was fairly recent among the Métis as people had little leisure time to tend flowers and yards. The emphasis was on vegetable gardens, which were an important source of food and were often decorated with flower beds. Flowers and herbs (such as chives) were also grown near the house.

During the holidays and at weddings, Métis families prepared another series of special dishes. Those who had the means roasted a hind of beef or a choice piece of meat for meatballs. It was also a time to make "fancy desserts." One of these cakes was prepared in the following way:

1.12. « Sur le cou de ma bouteille » (Good Cheer) at Batoche, ca. 1914. Seated Louis Letendre at left and Alexandre Parenteau; standing Joseph « Caton » Pilon Jr., a Dubois – Parks Canada, Omer Ranger Collection.

> The women boiled nice raisins (bought in the store for the occasion) with sugar and water to make a fairly thick syrup. They made a nice dough with flour, fat, sugar and milk. When the raisin syrup had cooled, it was poured into a dripping-pan. The raisins were covered with the dough. This was then put in the oven.[69]

According to account books from the Mitchell store in Duck Lake during the 1890s,[70] the more well-to-do families bought mainly brown sugar [but little white sugar], flour, raisins, dried prunes, canned sardines and salmon, "fancy" soda biscuits, oatmeal, rice, Rogers' corn syrup, and maple-syrup bars (candy). Cocoa (chocolate) was a fairly rare and expensive delicacy. During the holidays, some people purchased candies and apples and, more rarely, oranges. Some spices, like cinnamon, ginger, nutmeg, cloves and red pepper, as well as salt and pepper were in common use. People also bought baking powder, baking soda and washing soda in order to make soap.[71]

The Métis drank large amounts of black tea, homemade "coffee" such as barley coffee (roasted barley grains), and homemade wine or *piquette*. A "home brew" or whisky made from rye or barley was a popular drink among men. A number of homes had stills hidden in a farm building where the men would meet for a *pchi-coup* (a drink).

Milk and milk products were an important part of the diet. On several farms, there was a dairy house close to the house, often near a well. The women went there both to work and to get out of the kitchen. Mrs. Ti-Jean Caron (Virginie Parenteau) had a dairy house of which she was particularly proud. According to her daughter-in-law:

> The dairy was lined with boards and covered with a shingle roof. There was a door on the north side. It was whitewashed both inside and out. The dairy was very clean and frequently washed with lye to prevent odours. There were also shelves from one wall to the other and a big table in the middle, as well as milk containers and a cream jar. We often went there to relax and talk.[72]

The fresh milk was taken there in buckets to be poured and separated from the cream. The family kept the milk and cream for the family or to sell and

1.13. *Family gathering on occasion of 50th wedding anniversary of Jean-Baptiste Arcand and Nancy McKay at Maskeg Lake, 1914 – Provincial Archives of Alberta, OB 3804.*

gave the sour or curdled milk to the calves. Women were quite competitive in their butter-making skills.

> To preserve butter in the winter, people filled small tubs, covering the butter with a white cloth topped with a good layer of coarse salt, and then poured some brine with an egg in it over and put back the cover, closing it very tightly. For everyday use, butter was made in small lumps, pressed into a mould and then placed on a big flat dish on the well.[73]

The hard work, pain, and hardship of everyday life were fortunately lightened by celebrations and by visits with parents and friends. People gathered and socialized on the church steps after mass every Sunday and on religious holidays. When it came to going out, however, men and women did not have the same opportunities. According to one lady's testimony, "we girls went out little, and even on Sundays we had to be back home at six o'clock to milk our cows. The boys, though, did go out."[74]

Weddings were occasions for getting together and having a good time. Many people got married in the winter, between Epiphany (January 6) and Lent (mid-February), though, at the turn of the century, more couples got married in the spring or fall, preferably on a Tuesday or Wednesday, and always very early in the morning. Wedding celebrations lasted two days and sometimes longer.

> In the home of Martin Lavallée, on of the greatest wedding-makers of them all, I have seen weddings start on Tuesday and finish only on Saturday, with time off on Friday.[75]

The suitor in his Sunday best had to formally ask his beloved's father for her hand. The engagement was short, and before the wedding, the marriage banns were published three times (on three successive Sundays) at the local church. On the wedding day, the religious ceremony was sometimes followed by a buggy ride that took the newlyweds all over the parish. Then came the festivities: a plentiful meal and dancing until late at night, as well as on the following days, with different relatives taking their turn as hosts.

Spending an evening in company at one home or another was another way to have a good time. "During the winter we often danced every night."[76] According to witnesses, each community had its own social evenings, and people from other towns or villages were not usually invited. At these evenings, young people sang and danced, while old folks sat and talked, told stories, or tapped their feet and clapped their hands to the rhythm of the music. Men often took advantage of the occasion to have a little drink, which women never did in public.

The people at Batoche loved to have a good time, and it was customary to be generous and hospitable. There could be no social evening without musical instruments: violins, accordions, mouth organs (harmonicas), drums, guitars, as well as such percussion instruments as spoons, plates, and bowls made of wood or tin, etc. They danced reels, jigs, step dances, cotillions, quadrilles (square dances), *châtises*, and even minuets, especially the old-timers. Their dances were called "two-step," "seven-step," *châtise*, "drops of brandy" (*danse du crochet*), "reel o'cats," "eight-hand reel" (*reel à huit*), "handkerchief dance" (*danse aux mouchoirs*), "pair of fours," and "rabbit dance" (*danse du lièvre*), the last one accompanied by little cries.[77] There was almost always a "caller" who indicated the figures the dancers were to execute. "Formerly, it was customary to remove the bride's moccasin at the wedding." The groom then had to look for it.[78] Men especially liked to "jig." St. Louis was famous for its singers (both male and female), while Batoche was known for its dancers (of either gender). But in general, everybody sang or played some musical instrument. The most outstanding singers were Charles-Eugène and Frédéric Boucher, Patrice Parenteau, and Charles Nolin. The holiday season (from Christmas to Epiphany) opened with a series of *bals à l'huile* (dancing through the night by oil light).[79] According to an 1889 account in a Prince Albert newspaper, "At Batoche, during the holidays, balls are the order of the day. Two were held last night, one at Pilon's and the other at D[aniel] Charette's and youngsters had all the chances they wanted of shaking themselves up."[80]

Among the traditional song titles reported, some are known in their entirety, others have survived only in part, and still others have come down to us in other forms.[81] The "Chanson de Louis Riel," composed by him on the occasion of his sister Henriette's marriage in 1883, was known to the older people, and, interestingly enough, the version widely known in Saskatchewan differs from the Manitoba one. The popular repertoire included: "Deux p'tits oiseaux avec le bec pointu" (sung by Patrice Parenteau), "J'ai fait une maîtresse" (sung by Raoül St. Germain), "Courtisan malheureux ou Riche marchand malheureux" (sung by Antoine Ferguson), "Le matin quand je me lève" (A. Ferguson), "Une chanson du temps des élections" and "Buvons mes chers amis" (composed by Charles-Eugène Boucher), "Sur le cou de ma bouteille" and "Du temps ou j'allais voir les filles."[82] There were also religious hymns: "J'irai la voir un jour" (Alexandrine Nicolas) and "Le voici l'agneau si doux" (Adélaïde Ranger). People sang in Cree, Michif French, and French. The tunes were often those of old French Canadian and Cree songs.[83]

Those who did not dance or sing were able to play cards: *quatre-sept* and euchre (called *à l'écarté*) were said to be popular games.[84] People sometimes played dice (poker) for money, much to the displeasure of the priest. Men were very fond of billiards. There were five billiard tables in Batoche in 1885: in the homes of George Fisher, Jean-Baptiste Boyer, Gabriel Dumont, Joseph Vandal, and Xavier Letendre. However, billiards was prohibited on Sundays on pain of a fine.[85] Other games were target shooting, "Recule-toi de là," "Madame demande sa toilette," "Trois pas d'amour," and "On fait son testament."[86]

The Métis observed religious and civil holidays in their own distinctive ways. At the turn of the century, Christmas had a purely religious character, the real festivities being reserved for New Year's Day: "On Christmas Eve, we went to midnight mass, and when we got home, we ate a little, drank some tea and went to bed. The presents were for New Year's Day."[87] Another person remarked: "we did not have Christmas gifts, only candies, apples and pastry."[88] Some families, like those of Jean Caron Sr. and Barthélémi Pilon, had a *réveillon* (celebration) after the midnight mass, but it seems that this custom was more French Canadian than Métis. The New Year's Day tradition included paternal blessings, hugging and kissing all around, and passing around a little gin, whisky or homemade wine, accompanied by meat pies and desserts. The atmosphere was festive, for "woe to those who weep on New Year's Day: their eyes will still be red on Christmas Day."[89] On New Year's Eve, children hung their stockings from the foot of their bed, and the following morning they found them stuffed with little treats, according to their parents' means.[90] Father Fourmond described a paternal blessing in 1878:

> These good people have a very touching custom: as soon as they come in, they kneel down before their priest and ask him for his blessing. Similarly, when they get up on the morning of that day, children customarily ask their father to bless them.[91]

Louis Schmidt, a Métis nationalist and fervent Catholic, blessed his children by reciting the following prayer:

> Blood of my blood, sons (daughters) of my race,
> Who are today gathered under my roof,
> Follow in the footsteps of your ancestors,
> Remain obedient to the faith,
> Preserve the customs
> Left by your ancestors,
> And above all, keep your language.[92]

New Year's Day was spent with one's family, and the noon meal was taken at the grandparents' home.

In the nineteenth century, nationalism and religion were closely linked and Métis feast days had a strong religious character. The *fête nationale* (national feast day) inaugurated in 1884 was first called St. Joseph's Day in honour of the patron saint.[93] A citizens' committee was responsible for organizing the festivities. Xavier Letendre presided over the committee between 1888 and 1890 and was succeeded by Moïse Ouellette. The day commenced with a mass, during which the banner of the St. Joseph Association was displayed. This was followed by a country fair with sports events, music, dance, and camp fires, as well as craft competitions and sales. The festival was held in Batoche at a place described as *la jolie prairie* (beautiful prairie). During the first few years, the organizers chose an open piece of land near the river, south of Emmanuel Champagne's (lot 45) and north-east of the village, but later on, they preferred a location east of the village, uphill from lots 45 to 47.

The celebrations brought together all the Métis from the surroundings. An account in a newspaper from the area describes the 1889 festivities:

> The French Halfbreeds yesterday celebrated the 24th of July, the feast of St. Joseph's. Parties were arriving all day from all parts of the country. Sports commenced about noon, commencing with horse racing, pony races: trotting races and slow races. There were tugs of war, foot races and other games.[94]

In the early 1900s, the feast day still started with a mass in church,[95] but according to one witness:

> ... one of the biggest attractions was killing a steer in the field, the way they used to kill buffaloes. They shot arrows and drew knives. They made a big fire. The steer was prepared on the spot and roasted on the embers. Everybody ate of it. Everyone got a piece for nothing. It was a real feast.[96]

Elder Moïse Ouellette had donated the animal on this occasion and many others.[97]

This ritual was followed by a picnic, buggy races, children's games, raffles, as well as an arm-wrestling competition and firearm shooting for the men. The women exhibited their needle or crochet work, lace, embroidery, quilts, hooked rugs, and arrow sashes. Some also tanned leather and made moccasins (soft leather shoes), Indian boots (harder red leather), and embroidered or pearl-studded vests and belts. Others tended the tables where oranges, candies, cold drinks, and pastries were sold. The Métis feast day kept its Michif French spirit and tradition until the 1930s. According to some accounts, after that it became "more of a drunken brawl" or lost its original character.[98]

Duck Lake also held a country fair in July and a farm show in October which attracted Métis, French Canadians, English and other groups in the district. Prizes were given out for the best products in the following categories: horses, cattle, milk products, threshed grain, vegetables, smoked meat, jam, leather (deerskin, moccasins, fur-lined gloves, coats), oil paintings, water colours, and charcoal or pencil drawings. There were also prizes for "ladies' work," which included embroidered shirts and pillow cases, pin cushions, knitted quilts, cushions and slippers.[99]

The pilgrimage of Our Lady of Lourdes at St. Laurent de Grandin was another important celebration. This annual event, which started around 1884, was formally consecrated in 1906.[100] Brother Célestin Guillet restored Brother Piquet's ancient grotto and built a chapel. To the small statue of the Virgin of Lourdes given by Charles Nolin in 1885 in gratitude for the recovery of his wife Rosalie Lépine was added another bigger statue, gift of a French benefactress. The pilgrimage illustrated the strong faith of the Métis, many of whom walked to St. Laurent a distance of over twenty kilometres or more. They came for a miracle that would heal both physical and mental suffering. An eye-witness gave the following report of the pilgrimage of 16 July 1906:

> From the previous day on, many pilgrims arrived in St. Laurent.... The following day, starting before dawn, a long line of carriages crisscrossed the fields to get there ... around 10 o'clock when the solemn mass would be celebrated ... there were a dozen oblate and secular priests, prostrate before the small chapel. There were more than 600 pilgrims gathered near the grotto ... singers from different parishes formed a choir and with genuine enthusiasm performed Dumont's beautiful royal mass.... In the afternoon, all the pilgrims were back near the grotto and getting ready to go in procession to the old mission cemetery.... After the benediction of the Holy Sacrament ... this beautiful day ended with the consecration to the Holy Virgin, followed by the singing of the beautiful hymn, "J'irai la voir un jour."[101]

A man who had a hernia declared that he was miraculously cured:

> When he got back from the altar, the good Métis felt better, and the swelling which a few moments before had impeded his walking had disappeared, so he stood there and dissolved into tears of joy, and after the mass he told us: "I don't feel my ailment anymore, I now walk without pain, and I feel like I can work like a young man of twenty."[102]

Another Métis pilgrim proclaimed his joy and fervour: "How good it feels to pray here."[103]

People at Batoche believed in the power of dreams, which often took on spiritual dimensions. Elders in the 1970s told stories from the past described as "old wives tales," legends, and prophecies (predictions of luck and misfortune). Death was the main theme of several of these accounts. One woman said that after her father's death her mother told her that she should never go to bed without reciting the prayers she had promised him. When she forgot (which did not happen very often), she felt someone pulling at the covers of her bed.[104] Another woman testified that she was told of her absent husband's death: "the flesh below my eyes twitched for three weeks."[105] She added that her father had also been forewarned of her mother's death:

> He was travelling on a train from Winnipeg when he felt a cold hand on his face. He knew then that things were not going well at home. My brother had gone to get him, and when they came back, she was lying on the floor. My mother was already dead.[106]

The sick were traditionally treated with herb teas and dressings. Among the aromatic and medicinal plants, there was white elder, sarsaparilla, chicory, couch grass, and "larch" (red spruce or tamarack). The women cultivated herbs and gathered them in the woods, often with the help of daughters and relatives. They also prepared purgative infusions of pine gum. The seneca root, also known as "snakeroot," was gathered for personal use and sale. It was used in the preparation of remedies for pneumonia, whooping cough, croup, rheumatism, and respiratory and digestive disorders. Store accounts, however, show that people also bought commercial medicines such as St. Jacob's oil, Mother Sygel's pills, "painkiller" vitriol, "electric oil," "pain destroyers," smelling salts, peppermints, castor oil, and spruce seeds.[107]

There were also traditional healers who used "Indian medicine," therapies based on Aboriginal traditions.[108] There was not much faith in Western medicine. People saw a *ramancheur* (bonesetter) rather than a doctor for the treatment of a fracture. In the 1930s and later, most people at Batoche sent for the doctor only when they were gravely ill and rarely went to the hospital, or only to die.[109] This may have also been due in part to the cost of getting a doctor as there was no health insurance, but there was also a certain fatalism or acceptance of death.

Métis men and women smoked a mixture of chopped dogwood bark called "kinik-kinik" and commercial tobacco called "plugs."[110] The kinik-kinik was kept in a deerskin pouch. Women smoked the pipe, an Aboriginal custom that was considered strange and unfeminine by outsiders.

> This odd habit of smoking has spread even to old women. I have often felt sorry that I am not a photographer, so I could send you a picture of our old cook sitting gravely in the midst

of her pots and pans and inhaling long draughts of smoke from her peace pipe.[111]

Smoking was an intrinsic part of everyday life. "Without the pipe, nothing is possible: no good dinner, no conversation, no business."[112]

Michif French and Canadien French were the main languages spoken in Batoche and surrounding communities. In the early years or until around the early 1900s, many people also spoke Cree, Ojibwe (Saulteaux), and the Siouan languages of their ancestors. The dominant language, however, was Michif (or Mitchif) French, which has been described as a mixture of old voyageur French with Cree syntax.[113] The memoirs of Louis Schmidt and Louis Goulet provide vivid examples of the written texts that incorporate words and structures of the spoken language. The following are some expressions that were used by the Métis elders at Batoche in the 1970s and 1980s:

- *Les Canayens* [Canadiens] (French Canadians)
- *Les Anglais* (English Canadians)
- *Savez-vous tu* (do you know that …)
- *Que viens-tu cri* (what are you looking for)
- *Agreillez-vous* (get ready)
- *Nous nous sommes fait galvauder* (we were pursued and mistreated in the context of the armed conflict of 1885)
- *On les mouchera* (they will be destroyed – said within the context of 1885)
- *Ça dit ça* (that's what they say)
- *Faire apala* (to have a meal along a prairie trail)
- *Aller rôder* (to go visiting)
- *Garnir les besaces de cartouches* (to fill the bag with bullets, in speaking of a bag with two pockets)
- *Être trop au blanc* (to be too few soldiers)
- *Coucher quelq'un ou un animal* (to kill a person or animal)
- *Aller aux graines* (to go and gather wild fruit such as the little wild pear)
- *Camper* (to sleep outside while on the road or to stop to make tea)
- *Piller* (to steal)
- *Jongler* (to think)
- *Wow Boy* (stop!)

- *Un terrain en déclivité* (a sloping piece of land)
- *Une corvée* (a piece of work)
- *Une musique* (a musical instrument such as a harmonium or harmonica)
- *Des mèches* (matches)
- *Une échore* (a small outbuilding, usually in the form of a lean-to)
- *Un rababou* (a meat stew, as well as something useless and ineffective, as for example in speaking of Gatling gun in 1885: "the rababou which made a lot of noise missed its target.")
- *Le barda* (personal effects)
- *Enfirwâper* (to be taken in, literally from the English expression "in fur wrapped")
- *S'écarter* [s'égarer] (to get lost)

Michif French was spoken at home, French was taught in school, but English became the primary language of instruction in Saskatchewan schools in the 1920s. Since most children had only six to eight years of schooling, neither French nor English was spoken fluently. Many Batoche families worked and visited relatives in North Dakota, Montana, and southwestern Alberta, where English was more widely spoken. There was also some prejudice towards French but some families remained very attached to it. According to Louis Schmidt's granddaughter: "My grandfather had been raised in French. So I can assure you that we had to speak it correctly."[114] Schmidt was very active in French-language associations in Saskatchewan and passed on his values to his children, whom he educated in French. However, because of discrimination against Michif French in particular and French in general, and in an effort to identify with the majority, most Métis opted for English. According to a former teacher:

> At that time, [the 1920s and 1930s], they had no objection at all to learning French, but had not yet spent much time outside St. Laurent and Batoche. They did not know that they had a jargon [*sic*] of their own. Once they became aware that they did not speak French like the others [the French and the French Canadians], that they had many peculiar expressions, they decided to take up English. Nowadays, they speak more English than French.[115]

After Mlle Dorval's departure in 1914,[116] Batoche, St. Laurent, and the other small country schools in the vicinity had difficulty recruiting bilingual teachers. Duck Lake and St. Louis had private convent boarding schools but only a few Métis families attended those schools. One important point is that the first generation of Batoche women who were born in Red River had attended Grey Nuns' convent schools in St. Boniface, St. Norbert, or St. François-Xavier. According to a descendant of Marie (Pagé) Montour: "grandmother Montour [was] well educated: she knew French and Latin and wrote very well."[117] In subsequent generations, the level of schooling and the value attached to it seemed to vary with the social and economic status of the families. For example, Xavier Letendre's boys went to St. Boniface College and two of his girls went to St. Ann's boarding school in Prince Albert. His son John was a teacher in Fish Creek during the 1890s. Salomon Venne's family included one music teacher (Elmire) and a notary (David). Louis Marion and Maxime Lépine Jr. became farming instructors on the Kàpeyakwàskonam (One Arrow) and Kàmiyistowesit (Beardy) reserves. The first generation of the Boucher family in St. Louis and the Fisher family of Duck Lake and Batoche may have had no formal schooling, but they ensured that some of their sons had high school in order to enter politics, the priesthood, or continue the family business.

The use of *sobriquets* (nicknames) was widespread among the Métis. It was an ancient custom that had its origins in France, particularly Normandy, and was imported into New France (Quebec) and Louisiana. During the seventeenth and eighteenth centuries, it was customary to "blazon" both people and animals.[118] A nickname was indicative of a person's way of walking, faults, qualities, physical appearance, and social and economic condition:

> In our ancient language, to blazon means to say both good things and bad things, to praise and to curse; but the popular blazon finds its inspiration more in satire than in eulogy. It is the counterpart of the knightly blazon. The popular blazon embraces all the vernacular expressions sanctioned by usage to describe an individual, group or people.[119]

Marius Barbeau, an early twentieth-century Canadian ethnologist, stated that popular genealogical and geographical *blazons* arise spontaneously:

> They have significance. Le Corbeau (the Crow) is generally dark-skinned.... They also reveal historical facts and observations about local mores and characteristics. Animals are often named after the colour of their fur or after their physical deformities and, it seems, sometimes also in order to ridicule a neighbour.[120]

Among the Métis population, there were several examples of nicknames attached to first names. The exact meaning is not always clear and may be subject to several interpretations. As a general rule, "le vieux" or "la vieille" indicated an old man or woman but spouses also addressed each other affectionately by the terms "son vieux" and "sa vieille." Some nicknames such as "Bonhomme" or "L'Homme," "Garçon," "Tchi-Père," "La Fille," and "Fillette" seemed to have no special significance and were applied to various people. Many nicknames were of Cree origin: "Mosóm" (grandfather), "Kokúm" (grandmother), "Wabash" (the blond one), "Catchou" (the dark-skinned one), "Sisíp" (duck), and "Pezzan" (little squirrel). Several were of uncertain origin and were probably derived from the popular language, as for example "Dodet," "Châlins," "Bidou," and "Cotit." Other expressions, such as Ti-Jean-Vieux-Jean (Caron), Louis-Louison (Letendre), Pascal-Pasquette (Fleury), Baptiste-Baptisens (Parenteau), Pierre-Pierriche (Parenteau), distinguished between father and son, or in the case of the Parenteau clan, for example, between two large families: Pierre Parenteau (ca. 1818–1910) and Pierriche Parenteau (ca. 1814–93).

Some nicknames were flattering: "Beau-Blé" Laverdure and "Brillant" (André) Sansregret, while others were not: "Trois-Pouces" Carrière, "Ti-Laid" Parenteau, "La Pioche" Vandal and "Cincennes" Ledoux. Women seemed to have fewer nicknames. There was "La Boiteuse" (Henriette née Letendre), "La Pie" (Alvina née Boucher), "La Bichonne" (Justine née Branconnier), and "La Fille" (Emma Ferguson). Others were more common derivatives: Caroline "Câline" Dumont (née Montour), Marguerite "Gigitte" Caron (née Dumas), and Rose "La Rose" Boucher (née Ouellette).[121]

The custom of attaching a *nom dit* (so-called) to the family name was followed in provincial France and subsequently in French-speaking Canada until the early twentieth century. This was a way of distinguishing different branches of the same family. Subsequently, some branches adopted the alias, while others kept the original name. In the course of time, these names were altered or the pronunciation changed. Among the French family names and aliases recorded in Batoche were: Letendre *dit Batoche* (from *batêche, baptême,* or *bâtard: jurons* or swear words meaning "chucks," "baptism," or "bastard"), Beaugrand *dit* Champagne, Schmidt *dit* Laferté, Chevalier *dit Lépine,* McGillis *dit* Giroux, Beaubrillant *dit* Sansregret, and Lafournaise *dit* Laboucane.

Some names of English or Scottish origin acquired a French pronunciation and sometimes a new orthography: Ferguson or Farquarhson (Fercusson), Fid(d)ler (Fideleur), Bruce (Brousse), Fisher (Fischer), McDougall (McDoub), and Henry (Hennerie).

SOCIAL ISSUES

« *Prendre un p'chi coup c'est agréable* » (a little drink is a source of comfort)

The use of alcohol (*la boisson*) was perceived as a general problem in the North-West by both the Mounted Police and the Church. The missionaries remarked that when the settlers arrived they set a bad example for Aboriginal peoples. In French Canadian society, drinking was part of the mores and was accepted when done in moderation. By way of contrast, Canadians of English and Protestant origin tended to preach prohibition. Certain cultural groups that consumed no alcohol, such as Mennonites, saw it as a sign of degeneracy and tended to regard the Métis as "a gang of drinkers and idlers."[122]

In the nineteenth century and thereafter, Eurocanadians regarded the Métis as having a propensity to drink. Studies have shown, however, that the proportionately higher incidence of drunkenness among Aboriginal peoples was the reaction of an oppressed people to imposed social and economic change.[123]

During the 1870s and 1880s, there were no regulations governing either the production or sale of alcohol in the Territories, except for First Nations living on reserves. The first ordinance establishing a system of sale by permit was issued in 1888,[124] but these regulations did not discourage either domestic production or excessive consumption. Like most other communities, Batoche had a number of enterprising homebrewers and bootleggers. The 1915 prohibition officially "closed drinking establishments," but it, too, failed to put an end to "clandestine production."[125] Among those who had a liquor license in Batoche during the 1890s and early 1900s were Xavier Letendre, George Fisher, Auguste Lenglet, and the Venne brothers (Napoléon and David). Philippe Garnot, E. Lemieux, and a Fidler from the Fish Creek area reportedly had their own stills. According to an 1891 report by policemen Lasker:

> ... there are suspicions that Philippe Garnot is brewing some kind of beer from barley ... also one E. Lemieux in the vicinity of Fish Creek has rented a small house some six miles from here where he lived all alone since last fall. He is doing nothing and owns only a small pony. I cannot see any of his means of existence.... He got [sic] a two gallon permit, early last fall but could not get any. He has the reputation of a whiskey smuggler and dealer.[126]

Corporal Lasker added that the Venne brothers sold liquor in excess of the quotas allocated to them.

"Alcohol abuse" turns up frequently in the files of the North West Mounted Police, but those responsible were primarily outsiders, especially land speculators, who made the Métis drink only to exploit them more easily: "We were checking liquor permits here [Batoche]. All quiet except Land Speculators giving liquor to the Métis."[127] Political meetings and celebrations are mentioned as two occasions for drunkenness and fighting. However, the organizers of the July 24th national feast day tried to control the use of alcohol. In 1890, the committee president Xavier Letendre collaborated with the Mounted Police. Inspector Huot reported:

> I gave instructions that no kind of beer was to be allowed on the ground while the sports were going on. Mr. Batoche who has a license for selling 4 percent beer consented to this.[128]

In 1892, however, the celebration was held on the west bank because the fair ground on the other bank was too close to the village liquor outlet.[129]

There were many prejudices on the subject of alcohol use by Aboriginal peoples. Inspector Huot stated: "as in my opinion an Indian or a Halfbreed will get drunk even on strong tea, I also prevented the sale of hop beer."¹³⁰ The 1889 celebrations led to a fight, which made the headlines in a Prince Albert newspaper. Charles Nolin, who was intoxicated, attacked a policeman, and Jean-Baptiste Parenteau took on Xavier Letendre. According to the newspaper report:

> The French Halfbreeds yesterday celebrated 24th July, their feast day. Parties were arriving all day from all parts of the country. Sports commenced ... races and other games but they were delayed by a furious pugilistic encounter, which resulted in the arrest of Charles Nolin our future member. It appears Nolin was on the committee for sports, but owing to the amount of beer and ginger ale indulged in, the gentleman was more capable of raising a rebellion than looking after the sports. The police were there, however, to do their duty, which Nolin resented. He was told to be quiet or go away, but instead of doing so he started to fight the police and abuse them, but he got badly left: they were too many for him. The darbies were put on his wrists and he was given a free ride to police barracks.... There was one more arrest. Jean-Baptiste Parenteau, for assaulting and striking Mr. Batoche on the nose.... He also tore one of Mr. Batoche's sleeves off.¹³¹

Increased alcohol consumption was related to the marginalization of the Métis after 1885. Several people interviewed confirmed this view. Liquor provided an escape from the sad reality of broken families, a dislocated economy, and the discrimination of outsiders. The case of Xavier Letendre, who drank increasingly in his advanced years is particularly tragic and revealing.¹³² Letendre enjoyed much prestige both inside and outside the community. He was a successful merchant but his debts accumulated by the late 1890s. He also suffered many personal misfortunes: the premature deaths of several of his children and the inability of his sons to find their place in "new order." The first generation of Métis to reach adulthood in the first decades following the armed conflict experienced severe tensions and hardships. For example, John Letendre, son of Xavier, born in 1876, who had a college education and became a teacher, went through a personal crisis in the early 1900s. There are several references to his drinking bouts and aggressive behaviour. An account by a former student at the Batoche school in 1909 provides a glimpse of Letendre's despair and resentment:

> John Letendre was as drunk as a dog, lying in front of the rectory. Mlle Dorval [the teacher] found him there. She stood next to him and said: "What do you think, John?" She said, "Drinking like that, what kind of life is this for you? And when your time comes, how are you going to die? You drink so much!" John replied: "Those who can survive will, Mlle Dorval. As for me, I don't give a damn!"[133]

John later moved away to Battleford, where he became a successful cattle rancher and respected community leader. His younger brother, Manuel [Emmanuel], however, was unable to overcome his problems. He lived with his widowed mother on the Letendre ranch at Alvena, where he set the house on fire and wasted her meagre financial resources. He died alone and dejected in the Alvena hotel in the 1950s.[134]

When beer parlours were closed during the 1920s Prohibition, drinkers got together secretly, either at a private location, such as a place the reproachful Father Myre had nicknamed "Sodom and Gomorrah," or south along the trail leading to Gabriel's Crossing, a site the Métis themselves called "Devil's Lake."[135]

Several studies have shown that disease was one of the disastrous consequences of contacts between Europeans and First Nations. The Métis were better immunized than First Nations against European diseases because of their heredity. Most Métis in the North-West escaped the smallpox epidemic, which decimated the Cree population in 1870. In fact, reports from St. Laurent and Fort Carlton show that there were only about twenty victims of the epidemic in Petite Ville and other local wintering camps. But the Lac Ste. Anne community to the northwest and the Wood Mountain colony to the southwest were more seriously affected.[136]

The population of Batoche and vicinity was decimated by other diseases common at the time. Between the 1870s and the early 1900s, there were a number of deaths due to the *la grippe* (influenza), diphtheria, appendicitis, "tumours" (cancer), and "consumption" (tuberculosis). Serious flu epidemics occurred in 1889–92, 1900–01 and 1903. According to one witness: "The flus were pretty nasty, but people never went to see the doctor. They treated themselves with infusions and mustard poultices."[137] The disease took various forms and struck families and especially young people. According to a 1903 witness:

> ... death of young Baptiste Deschamps's child, his first and only one, at about 1 o'clock in the afternoon. The disease reigns in almost every house. It's a kind of complicated flu.[138]

Several women died in childbirth or as a result of it: "They died young, many between twenty and thirty years of age, often without medical care; they bled to death and died as martyrs."[139] Women were especially prone to haemorrhages during childbirth, and certain midwives left a lot to be desired as far as hygiene was concerned. Men died primarily of work-related or hunting accidents, overwork (hernias), and heart attacks, while young children often succumbed to suffocation, intestinal and respiratory diseases, diphtheria, and whooping cough.

The main cause of adult deaths at Batoche until the 1940s, and even later, was pulmonary tuberculosis, commonly called "consumption" or "inflammation of the lungs." The parish registers, family histories, and accounts of the period testify to the large number of cases of this disease. Even though it was present in all ethnic groups, its main victims were Aboriginal peoples, and others who were most disadvantaged economically.[140] The disease has social and economic antecedents such as anxiety, tension, fatigue, overwork, lack of cleanliness, as well as a restricted diet and poor housing. These unfavourable living conditions were very widespread in the late nineteenth and early twentieth century and were present at Batoche. Tuberculosis generally affected several members of the same family. In the early 1900s, little was known about this disease, which was often identified as the flu, emphysema, "inflammation" of the lungs, or "red blotches," especially in its early stages. The first stage of tuberculosis might last several years, or worse, the affected person might escape the more obvious and deadly stages of the disease and yet remain contagious. The disease struck especially young people (15–35) and old men.[141] At first, tuberculosis patients were not isolated, which helped to spread the disease more rapidly. There was no effective treatment of tuberculosis prior to 1945. By that time, entire generations had been affected by it. Several Batoche families still felt its disastrous consequences during the fifties or were still predisposed to the disease.

The crimes committed in the region were relatively minor or primarily a way of "fighting back." There were incidents of drunkenness, "irresponsibility," vagrancy, assault, theft, fraud, perjury, and "madness," which was considered a dangerous and reprehensible condition at the time.

Deserting one's family may have been a way to escape an untenable domestic situation. It may also have been due to financial pressures. Some men left home to look for work, hoping to rejoin their families as soon as they had made some money. But some men did abandon their families. One example was Joseph Parenteau, who left his wife, Julie Ross, and their two children in 1898. His father-in-law, John Ross, filed a complaint with the North West Mounted Police in Duck Lake, who reported:

> John Ross, a halfbreed farmer living about six miles southeast of Duck Lake, complained that his son in law Joseph Parenteau had left his wife and two young children without support and had gone to Medicine Hat. Ross said that Parenteau was a drunken dissolute character and had sold a waggon, a mare and five head of cattle which he (Ross) had given him. Parenteau went out on last Monday's train and is supposed to have gone to Medicine Hat. He told some people he intended to stay away three years. Parenteau's wife and two children are staying with Ross. Ross wants the husband to do something to support his wife and family as they have no means whatever. Parenteau left here without the knowledge of his wife or her relations.[142]

Parenteau's side of the story is not known, and neither is the outcome. But this was not the only incident of the kind. William Bruce's family in St. Louis was in a similar situation. His wife, Marie, reported: "I am or was his wife. In 1895, he left me and family and joined the police and went off to the Klondyke [sic] and for eight years he has sent me no support ... deserted me."[143] In 1900 he sent her $10 through a friend from St. Louis who was returning from the Klondike, but Mr. Bruce never returned home, and his wife died in 1914. However, her sons François and John came to the aid of their mother and raised their young brothers and sisters. There was also the case of Clémentine Lévesque, whose husband had left her. She reported that he had lost his mind.[144] However, Mrs. Lévesque was luckier than most women in her situation: being a teacher, she was able to support herself.

Among other court cases involving residents of the area (Batoche, Duck Lake, St. Louis) and heard in Prince Albert, there was that of Moïse Charette of Duck Lake, who was charged with perjury. Charette had testified against Garnot at the Garnot vs. Malfaire trial.[145] The dispute was about a contract between the two about cutting and transporting forage. In 1895, Ambroise Richard appeared before the justice of the peace in Duck Lake for stealing wine from the St. Louis mission.[146] He was sentenced to two months of forced labour in the Prince Albert prison. The following year, a resident of St. Laurent was charged with defrauding the government of the Territories in connection with a $700 road construction contract.[147]

The charge of "madness" brought against Jean-Baptiste Rocheleau Sr. in 1888 was particularly sad and evoked the anguish and despair of the Métis following the armed resistance of 1885. Mr. Rocheleau's son attributed his father's behavioural problems to two things that happened to him during the resistance: his imprisonment and the loss of all his possessions, as well as the debts he was forced into afterwards.[148] Mr. Rocheleau was not the only one to succumb to post-1885 pressures. Between drinking and gambling, some committed petty crimes or applied themselves to annoying the police and administrative authorities. This seems to have been at least part of the motive behind the mail theft (a mail bag),[149] a crime committed between Batoche and Saskatoon in September 1888. Following his arrest, the accused appeared before the justice of the peace in Prince Albert in June 1889. There was no trial, and the accused was discharged for a lack of sufficient evidence and probably also due to the favourable testimony of Father Moulin, the Batoche postmaster. This incident, in which the so-called friends of the accused testified in a contradictory or incriminating manner, reveals the presence of intrigue, jealousy, and fear within the community. It is impossible to decide whether the accused did in fact commit the theft or whether his compatriots who had been called to testify wanted to be seen siding with the police in order to improve their own situation. The North West Mounted Police was a major employer: it hired Métis as guides, interpreters, and workers in the barracks, and it gave out contracts for supplying animal feed and providing animal care.

RELATIONS WITH FIRST NATIONS

There were two Cree reserves near Batoche and Duck Lake: Kàpeyak-wàskonam (One Arrow) and Kàmiyistowesit (Beardy).[150] In the South Saskatchewan River area, contact between the Cree and the First Nations (primarily Gros-Ventres [Atsina], Dakota Sioux and Cree) and French Canadian and Métis voyageurs took place around the end of the eighteenth century. From 1840 on, there were more frequent encounters, since the Red River Métis freighted regularly on the South Saskatchewan River. Intermarriage and common economic interests, including hunting and the fur trade and the need for trade goods, made for ongoing interaction between the two groups. However, a new era began between 1871 and 1877 with the signing of seven treaties by First Nations of the Canadian prairies and the establishment of reserves by the government. Several Métis acted as interpreters and witnesses to the signing of Treaty No. 6 with the local Cree at Fort Carlton in 1876. The Métis prided themselves on being intermediaries between the First Nations and the government. Some even thought themselves superior to First Nations in that they were more independent and integrated into the lifestyle of Eurocanadians. Other Métis, who were closer to First Nations in their way of life, wanted to live near them. In general, Métis accounts and actions reveal ambivalent feelings, or sometimes harmonious and sometimes tense relations with First Nations. One example was the 1885 Métis Resistance, when the Cree on the Beardy and One Arrow reserves were divided over whether or not to support the Métis. Michel Dumas from Batoche, farming instructor at One Arrow and one of the resistance leaders, put pressure on the Cree to win them over to the Métis cause.[151] The precise number of Cree from the area who took up arms is not known, but there may have been about fifty.[152] The Métis also tried to win the allegiance of bands living to the north and west, but few came to fight with them at the couli des Tourond (now called Fish Creek) and at Batoche. The Cree who joined the Métis set up camp on the west bank of the South Saskatchewan River in Batoche. The Dakota under Chief Wahpahissco (White Cap) from the Moose Hills Reserve (southern Saskatchewan) and the Wahpeton from north of Prince Albert came in much larger numbers. The Dakota from Moose Hills had kinship ties with the Métis of Prairie Ronde. Their leader Charles Trottier, who was a friend and relative of Gabriel Dumont, and some twenty Métis and Dakota fought at the couli and at Batoche. Two Dakota died in battle at the couli and one at Batoche, and a number of them were wounded. The Dakota had set up camp on the east side of the river in Batoche, in a small prairie close to some Métis families, but on the opposite bank from the Cree, their traditional rivals. First Nations support was important to the Métis, but during the armed conflict, it was uncertain and unpredictable.

1.14. L–R: *A.M. Frigon, Indian Agent, Maxime Lépine Jr. and Marguerite (Boucher) Lépine, "Farmer-Instructors" at One Arrow First Nation, ca. 1915 – Parks Canada, Omer Ranger Collection.*

Fear of reprisals and loss of annuities induced many to leave before the last battle at Batoche. Nonetheless, Beardy's band did not receive its rations for a number of years after 1885, and its chief was relieved of his authority by the government.[153] Chief One Arrow and White Cap were both arrested, tried in court, and received harsh sentences. The Cree of One Arrow were deprived of their rations, suffered severe hardships, and some were forced to leave the reserve.

The Almighty-Voice (Kisimanitowewew) incident in 1895–97 is another illustration of the friction between the Batoche Métis and their Cree neighbours. Gabriel Almighty-Voice, a young Cree from One Arrow, was charged with "stealing" and slaughtering an ox from the reserve without the permission of Louis Marion, the farmer-instructor (an employee of the Department of Indian Affairs). After being arrested and imprisoned in Duck Lake, Almighty-Voice escaped and found refuge in the Minichinas Hills near the Venne ranch east of Batoche.

The Cree of One Arrow subsisted on mixed farming and meagre annuities. The Department of Indian Affairs controlled all their activities, including the freedom to leave the reserve to hunt, trade, and visit relatives. They received cattle but were forced to farm communally and return most of their profits, if any, to the government. The living conditions on the reserve were miserable. A few Cree were hired as labourers in the Mounted Police barracks in Batoche and Duck Lake; however, Métis were generally preferred for jobs as guides, interpreters, and suppliers. This situation caused some resentment among the Cree. The Department of Indian Affairs added to the tensions by recruiting farming instructors, teachers, and reserve supervisors among the Métis. There were kinship ties between the people of Batoche and One Arrow, and they helped each other in times of need, but the actions of outsiders, and sometimes even their own people, were a cause of tension and division.

It was within this context of these strained social relations that the Mounted Police tried to recruit Métis in Batoche to "capture" Almighty-Voice. According to a police report: "Inspector Wilson had enrolled 30 Métis in Batoche, but they changed their minds and did not turn up."[154] Thanks to the actions of officer Odilon St. Denis from Duck Lake and to the intervention of local politician, Charles-Eugène Boucher, the police did succeed in rounding up enough volunteers to form a contingent. They then organized the manhunt. The police set up one of its bases of operation on the Venne ranch, and Napoléon Venne served as a guide. The fugitive's entrenchment was finally attacked in June 1897. The capture of Almighty-Voice and two of his companions caused several casualties on both sides.[155] To the people of One Arrow, however, Almighty-Voice had died a martyr and a victim of the White Man's justice. The collaboration of the Métis with the police was especially disheartening.

The Métis also played an assimilating role in education on neighbouring reserves. Between 1888 and 1918, they supplied the teachers at the Indian schools in Duck Lake and One Arrow. Several Métis teachers experienced difficulties and found it hard to be accepted.[156] The Cree resisted an educational program that condemned their language and culture and was centred mainly on teaching "domestic sciences," labour trades, and the Roman Catholic faith. There is some evidence however, that some Métis teachers and workers, especially the women, were compassionate and tolerant and at times tried to protect their charges from harsh government policies and regulations.[157]

RELATIONS WITH SETTLERS

The first French Canadians to settle in the North-West after 1870 were often regarded as a cause of discord and corruption by religious authorities:

> For some time we have had strangers here who drink, and already there is disorder as a result of drunkenness ... causing us much pain. They are Canadian compatriots who do us this dishonour ... we fear that easier communications will attract a lot of riffraff who will destroy our cherished peace.[158]

The same was true of the French, Belgians, and other immigrants, who began arriving in the South Saskatchewan River area in the late 1880s. Government and religious authorities had hoped that these compatriots would serve as models and support for the Métis group. In the Church's view, the two groups would consolidate and ensure the continuation of the French Catholic culture in the Canadian West. But some of them were disappointed, for from the very beginning, it was the Eurocanadians who became integrated with the Métis and adopted their lifestyle and culture.

> Strange to say, we have here some Frenchmen from France, Belgians and Canadians ... and I must say that they, too, are not free from the faults with which we reproach our poor Métis.... And yet, we have such a great need of good Catholics to provide our people who are still half savage with a good example of hard work and a Christian life and to prevent the good lands in these parts from falling into the hands of Protestants.[159]

Several French Canadians had come to Batoche as freighters and clerks for local merchants and decided to settle there. Ludger Gareau, his brothers Azarie and Napoléon, and their cousin Philippe-Charles Chamberland emigrated from Quebec between 1878 and 1881. Octave Régnier, originally from Quebec but living in St. Francois-Xavier, Manitoba, since 1878, moved to St. Louis in 1882 with his relatives, the Lépine family. Another French Canadian, Philippe Garnot, also came via Manitoba. They were soon followed by some Frenchmen, among them Ferdinand Ladret, Louis Riguidel, and Paul Schley. These people all intermarried with the Métis. In Batoche and St. Louis, there were also some "old" French Canadian families, such as the Nault, Landry, and Dumas families, who had come to Red River in the 1850s and were already intermarried with the Métis when they arrived in Saskatchewan. They were an example of integration and solidarity between the first generations of Métis and Canadiens.

Between 1881 and 1885, many French Canadians supported the Métis in the defence of their rights. In some cases, it was the revolutionary French immigrants who were the most militant. In 1884, Louis St. Louis de Gladiou, an Alsatian who had recently arrived in the country did not hesitate to openly declare his allegiance to Riel, impressed by the latter's leadership and the justice of Métis grievances.[160] Most francophones, however, were in favour of protest but against taking up arms. Besides differing in their opinions about politics, some francophones were uncomfortable with Louis Riel's religious views and Gabriel Dumont's militancy. Moreover, they had little affinity with First Nations, and feared the consequences of an alliance between the two groups. In this they were encouraged by other francophones in the service of the federal or territorial government and the North West Mounted Police who supported the government position and thus fomented fear and intrigue in the community in 1884–85. Nonetheless, feelings were divided, which caused Lieutenant-Governor Dewdney to remark that he could not trust French Canadians to support the government.¹⁶¹ Finally, during the 1885 resistance, most French Canadians and Frenchmen in the area tried to maintain a position of neutrality. Riel, for his part, called for unity and advocated a common front for his people, whom he called "French Canadian Métis." He was hurt by the lack of sympathy by some who considered the Métis to be inferior,¹⁶² and he accused the clergy of working against the Métis.¹⁶³ In spite of differences over the armed resistance, there was a general sympathy and support between French Canadians and Métis, which would last until the mass arrival of settlers and "colonizing priests" in the early 1900s.

The Métis reacted with some sensitivity to Eurocanadians' general lack of sympathy for their Aboriginal or "Indian" heritage and their prejudices against them. On the other hand, the pride and sensitivity of the Métis annoyed many Eurocanadians, especially those who thought themselves superior and wanted to dominate them. The Métis reacted either by isolating themselves or by putting on an air of indifference to avoid an unpleasant situation, or more rarely, by confronting their opponents. In this context, there was the example of George Fisher, who was subjected to the prejudices of the new anglophone bourgeoisie in Duck Lake before he obtained an alcohol licence and opened a hotel in that town. A local businessman who befriended Fisher wrote to a business colleague:

> As for George Fisher I respect him very much but I do not think it would be fair for him to come over from Batoche and run us out who were here first, and I do not think his Mrs. [Amélie Poitras] is fit for the business. In the first place she can't talk English and in a very short time it will be the English peoples' trade that would keep the Hotel and not the French halfbreed trade at all as I know from experience that there is nothing in them.¹⁶⁴

Francophone settlers who arrived during the 1890s and in the first decades of the twentieth century had different attitudes than their earlier counterparts. According to some witnesses, the French, Belgians, and Swiss had fewer prejudices,¹⁶⁵ being less conservative in religious matters and more open to the various political and "racial" ideologies of the time. By contrast, French Canadians were said to hide behind the official position of the clergy, who often lacked sympathy for the Métis. It has also been suggested that the heterogeneous population centres of Duck Lake, St. Louis, and Bonne Madone exhibited fewer prejudices than the homogeneous villages of Bellevue and Marcelin.[166] Those attitudes varied in different families as well. On the one hand, according to an English settler at Duck Lake, the French from the old country were more clannish, whereas the Métis and French Canadians were more sociable.[167] On the other hand, a Métis woman who had grown up close to the two francophone communities stated that "the French Canadians who had come from Québec considered the Métis to be inferior. This was very harmful to Métis progress."[168] The Batoche, Duck Lake, and St. Louis parish registers support the latter statement since they record more marriages between French and Métis than between French Canadians and Métis in the early 1900s and the following decades.

The plans for the francophone colonization of the South Saskatchewan River region were being directed mainly by the clergy, who had succeeded in getting the government to appoint priest-colonizers. The general aim was to make sure that the West would be colonized by francophones and Catholics, by attracting colonists from Quebec and repatriating French Canadians who had settled in the United States. The Métis communities would serve as rallying points. In the beginning, certain Métis, especially politicians and officials, supported the project.[169] In 1890, when Father Morin visited Batoche as an immigration officer delegated by Bishop Pascal, a meeting was held to form an immigration committee, which would encourage and come to the aid of new colonists. Father Fourmond was elected president, Charles Nolin, vice-president, and George Fisher, secretary. The Métis offered to put up French Canadians temporarily and help them choose and work their lands. According to a witness at the assembly: "This committee appears very well disposed to Canadian immigration in our midst. It recognizes the pressing need for it, to support our institutions and all the interests of the French race on the banks of the Saskatchewan."[170] But the Métis were divided on the merits of the project and many felt they were being exploited by the authorities. After sending some colonists off to Edmonton, the Batoche Métis ended their direct involvement in francophone colonization of the area and the clergy was left on its own.[171]

French immigration from Europe also had its share of difficulties. The Canadian government recruited immigrants through officers stationed abroad who knew nothing about the North-West, and better-off new arrivals were more attracted to the United States.[172] Many such immigrants had little aptitude for or interest in farming and headed for the urban centres. The Métis helped several French and Belgian settlers adapt to the new country.

> There are a few small Métis missions all around Batoche, which have acted like points of attraction for French-speaking Catholic colonists. Almost everywhere they have gone, the sons of the prairie have served unwittingly as scouts of French Catholic colonization.[173]

The Métis and the new settlers were also both subject to prejudices on the part of Anglo-Canadians, who viewed the Métis and French as one people with the same attitudes. According to Dr. Stewart of Duck Lake:

> ... they are as poor as poverty itself, that they are not good farmers; that indeed they are not even energetic or willing workers, and that they drop quite into the Half-breed habits of living.[174]

Francophone immigration to central Saskatchewan was limited and the arrival of immigrants from Eastern Europe such as Poles, Ukrainians, and Mennonites put an end to the hopes of a francophone majority in the region. It is interesting to note that the Métis in turn harboured certain prejudices against Eastern European immigrants. They deplored the presence of "Galicians" in Fish Creek and described some of their customs and practices as "primitive," and they even went so far as to notify Brother Guillet in Fish Creek that they did not want "Galicians" to dirty their chapel or attend their mass.[175] Most of the Métis around Fish Creek left the area in the early 1900s. This exodus was partly due to the presence of so-called "foreigners" but primarily to seek new economic opportunities. Families headed for Batoche, Carrot River, Aldina-Leask, and Battleford.

Between 1910 and 1914, several articles about immigration in the local French language weekly, *Le Patriote de l'Ouest*, advanced the thesis that Eurocanadians would replace the Métis, who were "doomed to assimilation" or would take refuge up north looking for "new frontiers." A French journalist who visited Batoche in 1911 saw little cause for optimism. The Métis did not appear to have many future prospects. The new generation lacked motivation and was losing its traditions: "the vestiges of the past hardly last in this country which constantly produces youngsters heedless and scornful of the past."[176]

At the beginning of the twentieth century, the Métis and French Canadians co-operated on a few projects. L'Association Canadienne-Française, founded in Duck Lake in 1912, had the support of the Union Nationale Métisse St. Joseph du Manitoba and the St. Louis local. The president, Roger Goulet, worked in collaboration with Louis Schmidt, representative for St. Louis.[177]

The social problems in several Métis communities observed by Marcel Giraud in 1935[178] were due to several factors. One of them was rejection and lack of support from their francophone compatriots. This isolation increased pressure to integrate into the anglophone community. Increased contacts with other ethnic groups, lack of social networks, and the suppression of their Michif language contributed to a "hidden" and suppressed identity. Starting with the 1911 census, the Métis identified themselves more as "French" or "English," according to the origins of their family names. During the 1930s the more acculturated Métis in Batoche, Duck Lake, and St. Louis were more closely associated with the Catholic clergy and the francophone elite, causing further estrangement and divisions within the general Métis population.

2

The Métis and the Roman Catholic Church

> *La Providence qui prévoyait ce mouvement miraculeux avait préparé cette église pour nous servir de forteresse et St. Antoine allait devenir célèbre dans l'histoire comme le lieu d'où allait sortir l'émancipation du Nord Ouest.*[1]

CULTURES IN CONFLICT

There have been a number of recent studies of the relations between the clergy and the Métis, more specifically, with the Oblates of Mary Immaculate,[2] and the sometimes ambivalent relations between the two groups. The Métis were genuinely attached to the religion of their voyageur forefathers but sensitive to the fact that missionaries wished to eradicate their Aboriginal beliefs and practices. Just as Métis culture was a blend of European and Aboriginal traditions, which came together to form a new culture, Métis spirituality was syncretic or incorporated elements from both parent cultures. The Métis believed in God and the Great Spirit and in miracles or divine intervention, as well as in spirit helpers and foretelling. The Roman Catholic clergy (in this case, the Oblates of Mary Immaculate,[3] who were the main missionary group in the North West in the nineteenth and twentieth centuries) believed they were ordained by God to export a western European model of Christianity. They believed in Christianity's superior spirituality and Western society as the highest form of civilization. They imposed these beliefs and values on "their flock" in a patriarchal and often dictatorial and intolerant manner. They were imbued with the missionary zeal of their order, and many were devoted and willing to endure much hardship for what they believed were the betterment and salvation of the people they evangelized.

The French and French Canadian Oblates who came to the North West in the nineteenth century promoted an ultramontane and conservative Roman Catholic ideology that proclaimed the supremacy of the Church in both spiritual and civil matters. The Church championed French-language rights, "western" justice, settlement of the West, and the transformation of Aboriginal peoples, in this case the Métis, into a sedentary people. The Oblates held the Métis in higher regard than First Nations, as being partly "civilized" and recruited them as auxiliaries in their work. In particular, they sought the support of the women who were the educators and transmitters of culture in the home and had the most influence on the children or future generations. It was also primarily the Métis women who taught Aboriginal languages to the missionaries.

The Church's missionary work with the Métis began in Red River in 1818 with the founding of the mission of St. Boniface. A number of missions were founded and priests, such as Fathers Belcourt and Laflèche, supported the Métis in their claims against the Hudson's Bay Company. This advocacy continued in the 1869–70 Resistance, when Father Noël-Joseph Ritchot, and to a lesser extent Bishop Taché, an Oblate, supported the Métis in their representations to the government. In the ensuing years, others tried to intercede on behalf of the Métis and to "protect" them against the Anglo-Protestant "enemy."

In 1843, Father Thibault left St. Boniface for the North West as an itinerant missionary to visit HBC posts in the Fort Carlton and Fort Edmonton region. He was led by Métis guides and interpreters:

> I started from Red River on April 20, having with me a Métis by the name of Jean-Baptiste Laframboise who was to serve me as a guide … the day before the Lord's Day, we reached the big Gros Ventres forks [near present-day Batoche] at about ten o'clock … we were expecting the shepherds from the Mountain

from one day to the next ... while waiting, I kept myself busy instructing the women and children and a few Savages. I did twenty baptisms and blessed two marriages.[4]

Between 1845 and 1855, the Oblates established missions at Lac Ste. Anne, Ile à la Crosse, and St. Albert, where many French Canadian and Métis voyageurs wintered. During the 1850s and 1860s, these missions served as bases of operation for visits to Métis seasonal camps on the North and South Saskatchewan rivers. A religious order of women, the Sisters of Charity, known as Grey Nuns, opened a day school and a boarding school at Lac Ste. Anne and St. Albert.[5] Although these institutions were relatively successful, reports by priests and sisters reveal a life of hard work marked by loneliness and deprivation. There were also conflicts between priests and sisters, which hampered some of their work.[6] However the evangelizing and educating of "the free people" was a relatively easy task as the missionaries usually enjoyed the support of the Métis, who provided them with food and assistance. However, the imposition of the French language met a fair amount of resistance, and the missionaries reported that after several years of instruction the Métis of Ile à la Crosse persisted in speaking only Cree. The missionaries were intolerant of Aboriginal practices and beliefs and the persistence of certain rituals among the Métis. They noted, for example, that the Métis believed in the immortality of the soul as well as some "form" of the body and that "the two would go to the happy hunting ground."[7] Customs such as serial monogamy, polygamy, conjuring rituals, and casting of spells practised by the Métis were condemned as "pagan" and "savage."

By the 1870s, several Grey Nuns of Métis descent worked in missions such as St. Albert and Ile à la Crosse, which facilitated interaction and acceptance. These women missionaries were held in high esteem by the Métis. The sisters helped to improve the status of Métis women, who suffered from the prejudices against Aboriginal women, and they often worked together as teachers in the schools, teaching catechism and artwork.

The Oblate missionaries at Ile à la Crosse, Lac Ste. Anne, and Lac Caribou (now Reindeer Lake) were among the earliest to visit the winter camps on the South Saskatchewan River near present-day Batoche. In 1861, Father Valentin Végréville established a mission dedicated to St. Paul in the vicinity of Fort Carlton. This mission, intended mainly for the Cree who lived in the district, also served the Métis employees at the fort and the "free people," including the McGillis and Pagé families.[8] Father Lacombe, who visited the mission regularly in the 1860s, reported: "Fort Carlton is full of people: French Canadians, Métis, Indians, Englishmen.... Let us try to do something for this place."[9] During these years, Fathers Julien Moulin and Alexis André accompanied the Métis on their hunting trips on the prairie and wintered with them. In 1870, Father Moulin wrote:

> I received the Bishop's order to go to the Gros Ventres Fork where I am to spend the winter.... [I]t seems that there are very many people in this place. They are all Métis from Red River.[10]

During the following years, two other itinerant missions, St. Joseph and St. Sacrement, were set up in the vicinity of Fort Carlton. The former did not last long, but the St. Sacrement mission, halfway between Stobart[11] and Fort Carlton, near present-day Duck Lake, received many visitors from the growing number of Métis who came to the area during the 1870s.

The missionaries were anxious to gather the Métis into settlements, so as to make it easier for them to adopt a sedentary lifestyle and practice the Catholic faith. To this end they supported the Métis of St. Laurent de Grandin in their plan for a local self-governing council. Gabriel Dumont was chosen president and Father André as spiritual leader.[12] Relations between the missionaries and the Métis were positive in those early years and the next year plans were laid out to build a mission church and residence. But things did not go according to Father André's wishes and he soon complained about the frequent departures of the Métis to go hunting and the difficulty of getting them to work and contribute to the construction of the St. Laurent mission. Deploring his parishioners' lack of enthusiasm, he wrote in 1875:

> For the hundredth time, they have failed to persevere and have left the work unfinished ... these unfinished institutions [St. Laurent and St. Sacrement in Duck Lake], as well as their own houses built here and there on a vague impulse to settle down and then almost immediately abandoned, are so many sad monuments to the laziness, heedlessness and inconstancy of this Métis group who to this day have failed to recognize the

devotion of those who look after their material well-being as well as their spiritual interests.[13]

The Métis did not have much cash and were often in transit so church construction was not always their priority. Other testimonies attest to their generosity and support in other instances. Father Fourmond, who visited the hunters from St. Laurent on the prairie in August 1876, reported that: "A very kind Métis had dislodged his family from his big tent and put them up wretchedly under the carts, in order to leave me as suitable a rectory as was possible under the circumstances."[14] At the St. Eugène mission founded in 1880 near Carlton, Father Végréville found a generous benefactor: "A kind and very devout Métis laid the foundations of the new church ... built a small chapel at his own expense...."[15] In August 1882, Father Julien Moulin[16] came to Batoche to establish the parish of the St. Antoine de Padoue founded by Father Végréville a year earlier. It was expected to be the largest parish on the South Branch of the Saskatchewan. But he had some difficulties getting the support of all the Métis because of a dispute with the superior Father André, whom some people disliked because of his authoritarian character. In 1887, a new mission was established by Father Lecoq at a place called Boucher, about twenty kilometres north-east of St. Laurent, on the east bank of the South Saskatchewan River. It was dedicated to St. Louis.

Other conflicts arose between the missionaries and the Métis, caused to a large extent by cultural, social, and even religious differences between the two groups. The missionaries' culture and ideology did not facilitate communication and exchange of ideas between the two groups. In fact, the clergy's objectives generally ran counter to Métis traditions. This explains at least in part the tension and distrust between the two groups, though in practical or everyday matters the relations were generally more friendly. The clergy's primary objective was to "civilize and christianize" – a policy implying that the people in question were inferior and not true Christians. Among the most severe criticisms levelled at the Métis was their "rather uncivilized and un-Christian tastes for hunting and moving from place to place, their stubbornness and laid back attitude which they interpreted as laziness."[17] In 1876, Father André reported that "the winterers are always tempted by the smell of buffalo and the prospect of an easier life on the prairie ... however, some of the latter have acted wisely and taken plots of land."[18] The missionaries did not recognize that hunting, freighting, and trading were basic to the Métis economy and that full-time farming was not very profitable. The sandy soil in many areas should have acted as a warning against adopting cultivation as a general practice, but they wanted the Métis to settle down on their lands to establish ownership.[19] The missionaries believed that farmers and merchants were the bourgeoisie or the best class of people among the Métis,[20] and that it was absolutely necessary to get the "wandering" group to adopt European customs and lifestyle to avoid the fate of the "poor Indians."

The missionaries deplored the use of alcohol and recreational activities such as gambling, playing billiards, and dancing, although a number of them were unfaithful to their vows and had drinking problems. They recognized the good qualities of the Métis: their kindness, generosity in times of need, friendliness, and hospitality. The local people at various missions often worked diligently and at little cost to assist the priest or the teacher.

For their part, the Métis regarded these representatives of a distant Church somewhat like intruders. They could count on the support of the clergy as long as they were submissive and their activities were peaceful and legitimate.[21] The missionaries reacted fairly severely to their insubordination.

> The poor Métis: if they could only understand the charity of the good shepherds who would gather them at any price under their beneficent shepherd's crook, to help them find in the true practice of religion and in a serious hard-working life the happiness they are looking for in vain far from the cross of the mission or the parish church![22]

The distrust of the Métis of any undertaking initiated by the clergy and their lack of enthusiasm for rigidly structured organizations were also illustrated by the events preceding the founding of the St. Antoine de Padoue mission in Batoche in 1881–82. In 1881, Father Végréville was invited to found a mission among the people already settled on the east bank of the river about twelve kilometres south of St. Laurent. As in Duck Lake and St. Laurent, the missionary initially enjoyed the people's financial support and co-operation. The Batoche Métis were also favourably impressed by Father Végréville's friendly and conciliatory attitude, compared to the inflexible André, the district superior. They also sided with the former in his

2.1. *St. Antoine de Padoue Parish, Batoche, ca. 1897 – Saskatchewan Archives Board, S-B6756.*

constant quarrels with his superior. Father André's intransigence almost compromised the establishment of the new parish.[23] The first dispute was about two riverlots reserved unofficially since 1877 for the planned Batoche mission. Father André reported that Mr. Sauvé and Jean Caron[24] were trespassing on the mission lands. He wrote an angry letter to Mr. Caron ordering him away in no uncertain terms:

> As superior I therefore protest against your intention to take this land away from us. We were the first to take possession of this land. I do not want to give up our rights to this land, all the more so because you will sell the land as soon as you get a chance, and we will have a neighbour who will be an embarrassment to us. If you stick to your claims, you will ruin the mission … I never gave you this piece of land, and now that I find out that it is beside the mission, I forbid you to go on working this land.[25]

When the land issue was finally resolved, another difficulty arose: that of raising funds to build a church and rectory. On Xavier Letendre's and Gabriel Dumont's initiative, a committee was formed to assemble the materials using a *corvée* (building bee) and to receive gifts and pledges to buy and transport lumber and other supplies. In the meantime, Father Végréville was the guest of Xavier Letendre, who gave him room and board for a year. The building committee's statement of accounts in May 1882 indicated that the logs were in place, that several items had been bought, and that gifts valued at about $55 had also been received.[26] However, Father Végréville complained about the small sum he received from the district funds and that Father André would not give him his rightful share of the Holy Childhood and Propagation of the Faith allowances. He added that he lacked what he needed for his own support and that he was reduced to begging.[27] When Xavier Letendre "offered to give an additional one hundred dollars on condition that the Bishop give $500,"[28] Bishop Grandin reminded him that setting up a parish was mainly the responsibility of its inhabitants. Although he responded favourably to Letendre's pleas, he sent the money to Father André, who refused to deposit it directly into the Batoche building fund, either out of resentment towards Father Végréville, whom he disliked, or to exercise his authority and control.[29]

2.2. *Father Julien Moulin and parishioners, St. Antoine de Padoue, Batoche, ca. 1902 – Parks Canada, donated by Justine (Caron) St. Germain.*

Whatever the circumstances, they had unfortunate consequences for the population of Batoche. Father Végréville reported bitterly to Father André that it had taken much perseverance and tact to obtain the good-will and contributions of the parishioners: "Not everyone wanted to give everything to the church.... In fact, immediately after the reading of your letter [of remonstrance], one of the members of the assembly said: I promised to give such and such a thing, but now I will keep it for myself."[30] Father Végréville was re-assigned to St. Laurent, and due to lack of support, the church was built only two years later in 1884 and with a $2,000 loan. The parishioners also refused to give free room and board to Father Moulin, Végréville's successor.[31]

Father Moulin had to put up with lack of enthusiasm on the part of rather distrustful parishioners, especially after 1885, and dip into his own funds (teacher's and postmaster's salaries, family money) for the construction and upkeep of the rectory built in 1883 and the church in 1884. He later claimed that the Métis had given in total only what was needed to pay for the foundation of the church.[32] However Brother Célestin Guillet, who assisted him at Batoche, reported that père Moulin was miserly and always complained about lack of support he received from the community.

Father Moulin opened a school in the rectory in the fall of 1883, and in January 1884 he became postmaster. The church plan was modified and the interior was unfinished when the armed conflict of 1885 broke out.

« *Père Caribou* » was very frugal. He lived alone, or with the occasional assistant, did not own a horse or carriage, and travelled on foot up and down his parish, which extended up to twenty-five kilometres. He slept on a *paillasse* [straw pallet] and his diet consisted of wild meat and bannock supplemented by garden vegetables. His clothes were ragged and he washed infrequently but he was a hard worker.[33] In 1892, he gave an update of his difficulties and accomplishments to his Superior General:

> With the money which I receive for my school and which comes from the government ... I was also able to build a tower surmounted by a steeple [on the church] ... I also built a loft [*jubé*] in which to put a harmonium which cost me 750 francs. All the improvements I made in my house [rectory] did not cost the parish one cent. I no longer receive an allowance. In addition, I have deposited 2500 francs in the Prince Albert bank with Bishop Pascal's consent.[34]

The parish council tried to control the priest's activities and sometimes even went against his decisions.[35] Father Moulin for his part did not hesitate to use religion as a means of intimidation. However, during his thirty-year term, a deep mutual affection developed between the Métis and the father, who declared that "despite their faults, my dear Métis give me enough satisfaction."[36]

Schools were a subject of conflict between the Métis, the Church, and the government. From the missionaries' perspective, there was never enough money and commitment on the part of the Métis. Father Fourmond described the situation in St. Laurent in 1883:

> Our school, the only one in the district which functions on a regular basis with some government help, is staying afloat only with great difficulty because of the apathy and lack of generosity of our Métis, whom one can never seriously count on when it comes to making sacrifices to found a church or school.... [I]t's sad, but everything has to be done free of charge.[37]

From the point of view of the Métis, they wanted to control their schools, but their mobile lifestyle, limited finances, and especially their preference for a traditional and practical education rather than formal schooling put them at odds with the Church's views.

Government regulations were also an impediment. The "North West Territorial Act" of 1875 granted to the Catholic minority the right to organize separate schools. However, it was only in 1877 that school boards were authorized to collect taxes in order to subsidize their schools. The first school in St. Laurent, founded in 1875, survived in the beginning exclusively on private funds.

In 1877, the trustees decided to move the school, which was located in the mission on the west bank, across the river to the east bank where most people lived and to take over its direction. The clergy opposed this move: "This school was first given to the mission by the people of St. Laurent and then, at the instigation of Mr. Moïse Ouellette, taken back again and transported to the other bank at public expense because the people wanted to have a school of their own directed by themselves."[38] For lack of funds, the plans fell through after a year, and Father Fourmond resumed control of the school, which was partly subsidized by the government from 1880 on.

According to the school ordinances for the North West Territories passed in 1880 and 1884, each school received a subsidy that had to be matched by taxpayers of the school district. The 1884 and 1885 ordinances established a Board of Education composed of a Catholic and a Protestant section. Each section controlled its own schools, whether public or separate. A public school could be either Catholic or Protestant, depending on the religion of the majority of taxpayers in the district. The religious minority, whether Catholic or Protestant, then had the right to form a separate district. The first district formed was always "public" and the second "separate." The Catholic separate school of St. Laurent, founded in 1881, was subsidized by the government, but the Métis were not able to supplement this grant.

The Tertiaries of St. Francis, lay Sisters in the service of the North-West missions, took over from the Fathers as teachers in the district until the turn of the century. In addition to teaching, they did domestic work in the Batoche, Duck Lake, and Battleford parishes, mostly without a salary.[39] For two years, between 1883 and 1885, the Sisters Faithful Companions of Jesus directed the school and a boarding school in St. Laurent.

This religious community, founded in Brittany had become established in England during the 1870s and the sisters were bilingual. Unable to obtain enough sisters from the various Canadian communities, Bishop Grandin had appealed to foreign communities. Eight Sisters, four of them bound for St. Laurent and four for Prince Albert, arrived in the fall of 1883. But lack of financial resources and support soon forced them to leave St. Laurent in 1885 and afterwards Prince Albert. According to Father Fourmond:

> Our good Sisters ... have already worked miracles. Mlle Dorval, the pious French Canadian Tertiary who had preceded them, had undoubtedly smoothed the way, but all her devotion had not been strong enough to overcome *all the prejudices against the Sisters* [emphasis added]. The beginning was therefore a painful trial period for the latter. Despite our entreaties, the children came to school only rarely if at all.... The Reverend Mothers multiplied their efforts and let the cup of kindness overflow – all to no avail: the children stayed away. Added to these difficulties born of prejudice and novelty, there was, for some of them, the difficulty of crossing the Saskatchewan River ... [but] after some painful trials charity was bound to prevail.[40]

The Métis resented the fact that their children who boarded at the mission school had to do a lot of domestic chores to earn their keep. They also missed their children and felt that the school program was rudimentary. Another important factor was that parents asked for instruction in English in addition to French, a demand the clergy interpreted as a lack of conviction about language and faith. The Faithful Companions of Jesus taught English and French during their short stay at St. Laurent. In 1886, the term "confessional" as applied to school districts was revoked in the Territories, and in 1892, the education offices were replaced by a "Council of Public Instruction," two of whose four members were supposed to be Catholics. English became the language of instruction, and French was authorized only at the primary level.[41]

In Batoche, the Catholic public school, officially established in 1884, became the first public school of the "District of Saskatchewan" in 1887 with an annual subsidy of $250. Father Moulin was the teacher from 1882 to 1896, but there was some local resentment on his control of this position for which he was only partly qualified while some Métis

2.3. First schoolhouse at Batoche (1894–1917), ca. 1907; standing at far left is teacher Mlle Onésime Dorval and at right, Father Moulin with school children – Saskatchewan Archives Board, R-B1771.

2.4. Sisters Faithful Companions of Jesus and boarders at Duck Lake Industrial School, 1900 – Saskatchewan Archives Board, S-B6759.

were fully qualified.[42] However, teaching remained under clerical control until 1914. Mlle Dorval, a lay Tertiary Sister of Saint Francis, took over as a teacher at the Batoche school from 1896 to 1914. She was a very devoted teacher, who was much appreciated by her students, some of whom still remembered her fondly in the 1970's.

Instruction by religious orders was only partly successful at Batoche. Their focus was religious instruction with little emphasis beyond the thee R's. Attendance was irregular due to seasonal and other work priorities, and few students achieved grade eight level, the highest level of schooling available until the 1940s. But perhaps the most serious impediment to schooling was the cultural gap between the Métis and the missionary teachers, which is reflected in the following statement by Father Moulin:

> They [the Métis] are generally little educated … most of them do not know how to read or write and see no use for it.… As most of our Métis and settlers live very far from one another and it is difficult for them to send their children, these children often miss school and as a result make little progress, especially since we are obliged to teach English and French. Most of these children understand neither the one nor the other.[43]

After Mlle Dorval's departure in 1914, there was a succession of young lay teachers, most of whom stayed only for one or two years. A new, larger one-room school with a teacherage was built in 1917, but the school board was unable to attract qualified teachers, who preferred more amenable conditions in neighbouring communities such as Bellevue, Hoey, and St. Louis. Few of the teachers who taught after 1940 were bilingual. Among the most fondly remembered by former students were Rena Hobbs, Marie-Louise Ethier, and Thérèse Mylymok, the last principal of the two-room modern school built by the Wakaw School Unit in 1958, and which closed in 1966. The last school offered secondary education. After its closure students were bused to Wakaw, a predominantly Ukrainian community.

2.5. *Prophet and Politician Louis Riel (1844–1885), ca. 1880 – Library and Archives Canada, C-86500.*

1885: THE RIEL FACTOR

Métis protests against the government in 1884–85 gave rise to increased tensions, discord, and resentment between the clergy and the Métis. The irreconcilable differences were tabled in subsequent publications of Father Jules Le Chevallier, OMI, who defended the actions of the clergy as "hapless victims" and condemned those of the "rebellious" Métis: "a simple people with little education who were duped by the mad schemes of the infamous Riel."[44] Father Le Chevallier failed to give a critical analysis of the clergy's behaviour and actions in 1885. He also made no mention of other testimonies that might have qualified or even contradicted some of his allegations. According to his contemporary Marcel Giraud, in *Le Métis Canadien*, however, it was inevitable that the clergy would oppose Riel and the armed "revolt" of the Métis:

> Their [the clergy's] defence of the principle of authority made them turn away from any alliance with men who did not respect strictly legal tactics.... Finally, they acted out of fear of appearing to favour a movement for which they would be held responsible and of compromising the cause of the Church and the French group with the government.[45]

In his 1996 study of the Oblates, Raymond Huel, argues that:

> In the end, the impatient and frustrated Métis rejected the Oblates whom they regarded as too closely associated with the government and turned to Riel ... whose creative doctrines had succeeded in indigenizing the Christian message and presenting it in a form that was meaningful and relevant to the Métis and the crisis they were facing.[46]

During the years preceding the armed resistance, the missionaries' position on respect of "legitimate authority" had been clear and consistent. The Métis had the support of the clergy, especially in their petitions to the government.[47] However, the priests saw themselves as leaders and chief counsellors of the community, and, as long as people obeyed their rules and code of conduct, there was harmony between the two groups. The missionaries tried to stay clear of political struggles as their mission was to ensure the spiritual and moral well-being of the community they served and the propagation and maintenance of the Roman Catholic faith and doctrine. However, as they had more formal education than most Métis and saw themselves as their spokesmen with the government, they were inevitably involved in their protests. The fact that the clergy agreed to join the Métis in their "peaceful" demands but shrank back before the prospect of an armed resistance was bound to arouse some animosity towards them. Suspect in the eyes of the Métis, the missionaries were, on the other hand, perceived by the government as being in collusion with them. Their position was indeed difficult and they were ultimately literally caught in a crossfire.

Relations between the clergy and the Métis were strained in the winter of 1883–84. The missionaries were annoyed at not having been consulted, nor invited to the "secret assemblies" to study various tactics to force the government to act. Riel's arrival in July 1884 aroused apprehension among the missionaries of the district, but they remained conciliatory and tried to win his good will. Riel for the most part was respectful but distrustful, having learned from his Manitoba experience. According to Louis Schmidt, eyewitness to these events:

> Riel did not have much confidence in the clergy ... especially in politics ... because priests by their very nature fawned upon governments. In Manitoba he accused Bishop Taché of being servile towards the government and then of being partial to French Canadians to the detriment of the poor Métis.[48]

On the other hand, Riel sought not only the tacit approval of the clergy, but their active participation: "because, he said, the clergy has a great influence on the people."[49]

At first, Riel's speeches and objectives were conciliatory, but the missionaries seemed uncomfortable with his hold over the Métis and even jealous of it. According to the Father Fourmond, who liked Riel:

> Notwithstanding his nice protestations, he repeatedly found himself in opposition to the clergy, and he did not show them enough respect in his public speeches. But when we called him to order, he always accepted our reprimands and counsel with submission and humility, protesting always that he was working

above all for the glory of God and would use only peaceful and legal means to demand the rights of his nation.[50]

In August, Father André, superior of the St. Laurent district, met Riel at the home of Xavier Letendre *dit* Batoche. Riel explained to him his dream of a distinct nationality for the Métis and maintained that he had a special divine mission to fulfil it. In September, there were several meetings between the Métis and Bishop Grandin in St. Laurent and Batoche. Despite frictions and suspicions on both sides, ties between the two communities were reaffirmed when Bishop Grandin supported the latest Métis petition and agreed to their request to adopt St. Joseph as the patron saint of the Métis nation.[51] This was an important moral victory for Riel in the eyes of some Métis, who said: "he made the Bishop give in, so he must be right."[52]

During the winter, relations deteriorated rapidly. In December 1884, Father André reported that "Riel began to rave,"[53] and both he and Father Végréville began to fear and resent his ascendancy over the people:

> Riel flew into a rage against the head of government and against spiritual authority.... I was angry, but this was not the time to reply, since I was all alone in the midst of a frenzied crowd determined not to listen to reason.[54]

Riel then began to reveal his prophetic mission and his plans for religious and political reform. He declared he was sent by God to restore the Métis nation to grandeur and reform the Church, thereby challenging the supremacy of the pope and the infallibility of the Church. The Oblates were appalled at his unorthodox and rebellious plans "to found an independent nation of which he [Louis Riel] would be the absolute monarch with its own religion of which he would be the supreme pontiff."[55] They denounced Riel as an apostate, a heretic, and a dangerous spirit of Satan. Opinions differed on his state of mind and the real meaning of his actions. Father Fourmond, who was initially more sympathetic than his fellow priests, attributed "his lapses in conversation and his fits of anger to past moral sufferings and misfortunes."[56]

Throughout this time, Riel remained very pious and fervent. He regularly attended church services, which earned him even more respect and devotion from the Métis, to the frustration of the clergy: "Our people ...

in their simplicity, seeing this singular person and a Métis like them pray almost day and night ... had a blind confidence in him and took him for a saint."[57] Unable to reconcile Riel's "heretical declarations" and profound religiosity, the clergy concluded that he was either insane or was putting on an act and wore "the mask of the most refined hypocrisy."[58] Resentful of his ascendancy over the Métis, offended by his refusal to submit to their authority, and apprehensive about the future, the missionaries resolved to denounce Riel and the "ringleaders" Gabriel Dumont, Maxime Lépine, and Charles Nolin.[59]

Father André worked with the North West Mounted Police and with D.H. Macdowall, the territorial representative for the District of Lorne (which included Batoche and St. Laurent) to persuade Riel to leave the country. These little schemes, which were unknown to most Métis but came out little by little, aroused much anxiety. Riel's political adversaries argued that he was looking for an indemnity or political appointment and that he was ready to sacrifice the interests of his people to his own pride and ambition.[60] During the winter of 1884–85, Riel was thinking of returning to Montana. He was poor,[61] the government had several accounts to settle with him, and he saw an opportunity to negotiate his departure, but the Métis persuaded him to stay. Riel knew that some officials were plotting against him, and Father André's open condemnation increased his distrust of the clergy and strengthened his conviction that the priests had "sold out to the government."

An assembly organized by Riel at Batoche on 24 February 1885 and attended by Fathers Fourmond, Moulin, and Végréville confirmed the split between the Métis and the clergy. Riel advocated abandoning political resistance because it was ineffective. But in March he was still hopeful for a negotiated settlement with the government and a reconciliation with the clergy. Father Fourmond responded by calling a public novena and agreed to baptize Riel's secretary William Henry Jackson.[62] He was reprimanded by Father André, who reported:

> I blame the good Father Fourmond for letting himself be influenced by Riel. The latter was continually at the mission, entertaining the good Father with his religious and political plans. He completely dominated Father Fourmond, who tolerated things of which I strongly disapprove.[63]

In the following weeks, however, relations deteriorated and Riel's ascendancy increased:

> The people ... regard him [Riel] as a saint or victim of persecution and us as ancient Roman slaves unable to understand the great and infallible insights of *His Spirit*, as people who have sold out to the government, as traitors and as enemies of our people.... It was not a good idea to treat it as a laughing matter or tell them the truth too bluntly.... We were made to feel unwelcome when we offered even the slightest criticism of his words or deeds.[64]

The Métis were somewhat divided in their attitudes towards the clergy, but nobody felt comfortable being faced with the threat of being refused the sacraments.[65] This was the clergy's position if the population rose up against "established authority." On 19 March, the Métis established the "little provisional government of Saskatchewan," formed a council called the *Exovidate*, and took over the church and rectory at Batoche. The Métis and the clergy were now estranged.

Deprived of Church services, the people established their own religious house or sanctuary in the village, where many went to pray and seek comfort during the armed conflict. The sympathetic Father Fourmond visited the little chapel, which held many Métis religious icons and cultural symbols and reported:

> Riel had made a small chapel in a second-floor room of Jean-Baptiste Boyer's home. People met daily in this 20 by 25 foot room to pray. The religious services had been moved to that room after being held for a few days upstairs in the empty Batoche store.... To sanctify this profane place, they had, on the Exovedate's [provisional council] orders, placed at one end of the room a big picture of Our Lady of Lourdes representing Bernadette at the Virgin's feet. Above the picture, they had attached a Christ without the cross, the kind people carried into battle. Below and to one side, there was, attached by a brooch, the benediction which Lord Bishop Grandin of St. Albert had given to all the Métis at Riel's invitation during the big assembly in September. On the other side was a letter ... written to Riel

by Bishop Bourget of Montreal. Riel treasured this letter, read it to everyone and based his mission on it: "you have a mission to fulfil...." To get back to the service in that improvised chapel, it must be said that the soldiers and partisans of the New Church came to pray there morning and evening and very often during the day and even, during the battle, all the time that there was fighting going on. It was even said that some young girls carried their zeal for their new religion so far as to sing hymns before the picture of the Virgin.... On the right [west] bank of the river, there was no chapel to the new cult. The image of Our Lady of Lourdes had been attached to an old aspen near the camp, and at any hour of the day, people came there with a rosary in their hands to pray in turn to the Holy Mother to have pity on her children and protect them in their present danger.[66]

During the armed conflict, between 26 March and 12 May, the missionaries of the district were placed under house arrest and supervised by the Métis council. Even though Oblate Fathers Le Chevallier and Morice[67] accused the Métis of imprisoning the priests in their writings, it is more accurate to say that they were kept under surveillance. Local Oblates, Fathers Végréville, Moulin, Fourmond, and Touze were in the rectory at Batoche during the battle. The Métis could not count on their neutrality, and it seems they were at least partly justified in their actions as events of the battle unfolded. The priests were in communication with government agents; they had withdrawn religious services and could not be trusted. The Métis also stated that they could not guarantee the priests' safety in case of an attack if they did not watch over them.[68]

In contrast to the Oblates, the four sisters of the order of the Faithful Companions of Jesus from St. Laurent, who were brought to Batoche on 17 April, had nothing but praise for the tactful and respectful treatment they received from the Métis:

> Riel said that he had the highest regard for us, that he wanted nothing better than to protect us, but that this would be difficult if not impossible from then on if we did not move closer to his camp. He advised us to go there [Batoche] as soon as possible if we could and, above all, *if we wanted to* [emphasis added]. Upon our arrival Alex Fisher offered us his house for

the night.... [The Métis] sent us cooked meat and milk. On Riel's order, the men led us to the most beautiful house in the place, that of Mr. [Xavier] Batoche.... The [Gabriel] Dumont woman [Madeleine Wilkie] served us as best she could.... Riel came to see us.... Mother Mary pointed out to him ... could we not retire to the St. Antoine mission.... Riel replied that he perfectly understood our wishes, that we would be perfectly safe at the mission and that he wanted nothing better than to see us there.[69]

THE GENERAL AND THE PRIESTS

On 9 May, the North West Field Force under the command of General Middleton attacked the St. Antoine de Padoue mission, located about two kilometres upstream from Batoche village.[70] The church and rectory were riddled with bullets, and when Father Moulin saw the machine gun aimed at his house, he came out with a white flag to negotiate a truce.

> When they saw me, they said that we had nothing to fear. The general advanced with his staff and shook our hands. *After gathering some information* [emphasis added], they moved towards the Métis who were in their trenches.[71]

This account confirms that the missionaries exchanged information with General Middleton and the Canadian army. Father Moulin admitted that he was willing to pay any price to save his mission, which had cost him so dearly.[72] The same day, the wounded soldiers were transported to the church, where the sisters gave them first aid and, following Father Moulin's orders, something to eat.[73] In the evening, when the soldiers retreated, Dumont and the Métis came to the rectory and accused the priests of betraying them. The clergy had been caught in a crossfire but had also given information to the Canadian forces about the number of Métis combatants and the location of their defences.

Two days later, Father Moulin was struck by a stray bullet in his thigh as he was looking for something he needed in the attic of the rectory.[74] Once

2.6. *General Middleton, Father André, Indian Agent R.S. Mackenzie and Chief Beardy (seated with hat) at Duck Lake, 1885 – Library and Archives Canada, C-18951.*

again the priests called on the soldiers, who came to get Father Moulin and brought him to the military camp for surgery, where he stayed until 13 May, the day after the battle.[75] Father Le Chevallier subsequently stated that it was the vengeful Métis who had shot Father Moulin.[76] However, none of the priests or sisters who witnessed the accident supported this charge.

The true nature and consequences of the exchanges between missionaries and Canadian soldiers are shrouded in ambiguity, but Father Végréville's correspondence confirms that Middleton's army received information on Métis defences. Shortly after the end of the conflict, he wrote: "It seems pretty obvious to many people here that the lives of eighty Métis and two hundred government soldiers were spared due to my mediation and reports."[77] The priests may have acted out of sympathy for all, but they were also afraid for their personal well-being and that of the Church.

The priests also refused to administer Church sacraments to the Métis fighters and their families and may also have buried the dead in unconsecrated ground. The burials were registered in the parish registers of St. Laurent and Batoche, which suggests they were buried in consecrated ground. However, the mass grave in Batoche was isolated from the other burial sites, and, to this day, many Métis claim that the victims of 1885 were buried outside the cemetery.[78]

In the aftermath of the armed conflict, the clergy's actions remained ambivalent and contradictory. They acted as official intermediaries between the Métis and General Middleton. Father Végréville tried to reassure the people of the peaceful intentions of the North West Field Force and transmitted the general's message to the effect that "those who returned home would not be arrested, nor bothered by the troops."[79] This was not the case. Many arrests followed, even among those who had not taken up arms. Indignant at the conduct of the Canadian soldiers, who burned and robbed mercilessly even after the battle was over, Father André became critical of the government in letters and articles that were published in various newspapers.[80] The priests had made an abrupt about-turn in their judgment of the Métis:

2.7. *Monument in honour of Métis, Cree and Dakota who died in the 1885 Resistance erected in the Batoche cemetery in 1901 – Provincial Archives of Alberta, OB 60.*

> Our poor Métis have shown a degree of bravery and skill of which we did not think them capable ... by way of excusing our poor people, it must be said that they did not intend to spill a drop of blood or to start shooting, no matter how serious the provocation.[81]

They stated that the real guilty ones were Riel and a few "ringleaders," such as Gabriel Dumont, Maxime Lépine, and Philippe Garnot. But gradually, as Riel's trial proceeded in Regina and he reconciled himself at least outwardly with the Church, the priests began to feel sympathy for him. Father André, his spiritual director, reported that Riel remained true to his prophetic mission, but he also acknowledged his sincerity and commitment to the Métis cause:

> Riel is in several respects one of those remarkable men, if a little cracked in matters of religion and politics ... [N]ow that I see him I am persuaded that he does not play the fool or hypocrite ... [H]e is convinced that the divine spirit tells him all its secrets, and he regards himself as a prophet who has been given a special mission to fulfil.... The poor man inspires much compassion in me and deserves the interest being taken in him.[82]

In Batoche, however, the Métis continued to distrust their missionaries. Father Moulin felt much sympathy for his parishioners and succeeded in making peace with some of them, but he never totally regained the confidence of the people. In 1887 he reported to his superior:

> The unfortunate Riel who paid for his rebellion and apostasy with his head has done much harm among our Métis, who no longer have the same confidence in us they once had. Some of them have still not gone to confession since the rebellion.[83]

RELATIONS AFTER 1885

The clergy was careful not to get involved in political issues after 1885. Consequently, when Lawrence Clarke, the former territorial representative (1881–83) and mission benefactor, asked Bishop Grandin to intervene personally during the federal election campaign of 1886, the latter refused. Clarke and the local conservatives had been particularly hurt by Liberal Philippe Garnot's statements against the government and asked Bishop Grandin to get Quebec conservatives to demand a public retraction: "A letter of this kind signed now by the Métis would have immense weight and would be gratefully remembered by the government and would benefit the Halfbreeds [sic] materially."[84] Bishop Grandin replied that he did not want to compromise the interests of religion and the Métis. His response also confirmed the deep mistrust and dejection of the clergy following the events of 1885:

> I do not think that I should do it: it would be to intervene in an issue which is too exclusively political.... Privately I am a Conservative, but as a Bishop I am nothing. However, I could see myself more specifically sponsoring whichever party would give us more freedom and show us more sympathy, but I confess that nowadays I am wondering which one of the two is better for us.... As you know, these poor people are set and biased against us, and the mere fact of intervening in this issue would be enough to arouse their distrust.[85]

Contrary to expectations, however, the parish of St. Antoine de Padoue expanded and even flourished in the late 1880s and 1890s. In 1889, Father Moulin reported that his big parish extended to thirty or forty kilometres.[86] He also had completed renovations to the church, which was "one of the most beautiful in the country."[87] In 1895, a schoolhouse was built, and an annex was added to the rectory to provide living quarters for the new teacher, Mlle Dorval. Brother Guillet who assisted the priest at Batoche during those years commented on the stability of the parish despite the lukewarm attitude of the Métis towards the Church.[88]

The neighbouring parishes of Duck Lake and Bellevue grew more rapidly than Batoche in the early 1900s, due to immigration and the presence of teaching sisters and resident priests. Father Moulin's departure from Batoche in 1914 marked the end of a period of continuity and stability for the parish. The Oblates of Mary Immaculate turned over the parish to the diocese of Prince Albert, and there were no resident priests between 1915 and 1924. The diocese then sold most of the mission lands (riverlots 50 and 51), except eight acres, to a neighbour Jean Caron Jr., who wanted to establish his sons. Secular priests from Bellevue and Rosthern visited the parish weekly. The Métis protested that they wanted a resident priest, but the diocese claimed that there was insufficient financial support from the parishioners. Nonetheless, a resident priest was appointed in 1925. Fathers Belleau and Laplante, who were at Batoche in quick succession in 1925–26, were very popular with the Métis. Father Belleau was a musician, artistic and easy-going, but his youth and inexperience made him vulnerable to errors, and he was soon recalled by Bishop Prud'homme.[89] In response, the parish council led by Barthélémi Pilon and Pierre Caron promised the Bishop to pay off parish debts, renovate the rectory, and make more financial contributions. Another parish priest, Father Laplante, was also suddenly recalled, much to the disappointment of Albert Caron and other parishioners who petitioned in his favour:

> The people, they are all for Father Laplante who told us: I leave my suitcases and I hope to be back. This is why we are working so hard to have him ... we would like to have him for our bazaar. If you want, we will give $1200 dollars a year. He is so likable, so good to us and he shows us how to live. But the Batoche parish, we do our duty. It's not our fault ... we are poor ... the people are very unhappy.[90]

The promises of renewed support and "submission" did not bring Father Laplante back, and the appointment of Reverend Pierre-Elzéar Myre was received with apprehension. The parish council sent another memorandum to the bishop:

> Up to now, we have got along well with Fathers Belleau and Laplante. As for Father Myre, we have known him for a long time, and we can say without fear of contradiction that he is very difficult to get along with, he would like to manage everything, the finances, in his own way. He is very unpopular.... Many parishioners have told us that if Father Myre came to Batoche, that they would not pay their tithes and give nothing for the church ... [however] with a priest who has a little patience and tact, the parishioners would continue to make efforts and even sacrifices to have a priest among them.[91]

Reverend Myre, a priest-colonizer who had been a parish priest in Marcelin and then in Bellevue, was an enterprising man with a fiery temperament and sharp tongue. He was also prejudiced towards the Métis, whom he called degenerates, drunkards, sluggards, and liars.[92] The Métis for their part were deeply offended and reacted strongly to his abusive words and disdainful attitude. They did not accept this stranger (a French-Canadian secular priest) and evoked the memory of "dear Father Moulin." Over fifty heads of families signed a petition demanding that Father Myre be recalled.[93] Taken aback but somewhat impressed by the Métis' fighting spirit, he replied to the bishop: "They are liars, and yet I like them and they interest me; they are so shrewd, and their latest exploit was cleverly staged."[94] He added that Batoche had been controlled by the same clique for forty-five years, and it was mainly these people with their relatives and friends who were asking for his resignation.

From a careful reading of the correspondence between Father Myre and Bishop Prud'homme, it seems obvious the former was insensitive to the problems of the Métis. The community was in the midst of a social crisis. Several families were destitute and some had become discouraged and abandoned their farms. Others sought refuge in alcohol, belligerent behaviour, and even petty crime. Reverend Myre attributed the Métis' defiant behaviour to their predominantly "savage" character: "The savage is shrewd and cunning, and the Métis has more of the traits of the savage than of the white man."[95] He considered the Métis inferior to 'whites' and reported that several families asking for financial aid "were well off for Métis."[96] Finally, he was convinced that they could only be "rehabilitated" by French Canadian settlers. This unfavourable comparison with their French Canadian compatriots deeply offended the Métis. Father Myre started a personal colonization campaign in Batoche and vicinity. He bought more than 1,600 acres of land on which he hoped to settle French Canadians and "good" Métis families, in order to "save" Batoche.[97] To this end he organized a French-language convention which he advertised in the Duck Lake weekly, *Le Patriote de l'Ouest*, of which he was co-founder and shareholder.[98]

Reverend Myre became less intransigent during the last years of his ministry at Batoche in the early 1930s. He collected enough funds through whist drives and bazaars to repair the church and pay off the parish's debts.[99] According to a former parishioner, who remembered him in the 1970s: "Yes, he was hard on us, he was mean that one, but he accomplished something."[100] His legacy was a stable and relatively prosperous parish. When he left due to illness in 1932, his successor Father Robert (1932–36) inherited a well-organized and united parish. The latter enjoyed being in Batoche and remarked "that in general the people are very respectful and very charitable towards the priest."[101]

Batoche was again administered by Oblates from Duck Lake after 1936. Father O. Allard, who was resident parish priest between 1938–44, was remembered by former parishioners in the 1970s as a kind and gentle man who was very independent and self-sufficient. He grew a large vegetable garden and raised rabbits to support himself.[102] One of his successors, Father Léo Bossé (1946–51), was also very frugal. He did not have a

2.8. *Father Georges Roussel with Adélaïde (Pilon) Ranger (left) and Marie (Caron) Parenteau (right) in front of rectory in 1977 – Diane Payment.*

truck until the last years and used to get around the parish on his bicycle. During the 1940s and 1950s the church and rectory were in disrepair and there was little revenue. The parish was supported by bingo, bazaars, and bake sales, and the main floor of the rectory, which served as parish hall, was rented for weddings and socials. Father Denis Dubuc, who was parish priest between 1951 and 1963 also left his mark. He was a driving force behind the purchase and creation of a museum in the historic rectory by the Historic Sites Branch of the Department of Indian Affairs. He shrewdly exploited the general public's interest in mementos of 1885 and was an avid genealogist and amateur historian. The museum brought some revenue to the parish, but Father Dubuc was unable to get the caretaker appointment, due to competition from local residents who also wanted (and needed) the job. After his departure, the parish again reverted to diocesan priests who visited from St. Louis. Parks Canada acquired and took over the church as a historic site in the mid-1970s, and a new parish church-hall was built a few kilometres south. Due to low attendance, shortage of priests, and easy access to services in neighbouring Wakaw and Bellevue, the parish closed in 2002.

During the 120-year parish history, there was often friction between the clergy and the Métis. The latter, always vigilant and critical, did not accept the unilateral approach sometimes taken by certain priests and jealously guarded their independence. However, their interventions were sometimes malicious or exaggerated. The wounds of 1885 never completely healed.

It is only in the last decade or so that profound changes have taken place in the views of the clergy towards Aboriginal cosmology. The Catholic Church has developed a more open attitude towards Aboriginal spirituality and integrated indigenous traditions in its ministry. Métis priests, such as the Oblate Guy Lavallée, have celebrated Métis spiritual values and culture in prayers and rituals that are meaningful.[103] Riel has also been recognized as a prophet, and his legacy has been celebrated rather than condemned or belittled as in the past. The historic church and rectory of St. Antoine de Padoue remain as a testimony to a rich past and are interpreted to visitors in a manner that reflects both the positive and negative aspects of the relationship between the Métis and the clergy. The bell in the church tower tolls on the feast of St. Joseph and the national Métis feast day, and a traditional mass and other celebrations are held in the church. Inculturation has replaced acculturation, and the Métis and the Church are entering a new phase of dialogue, renewal, and, hopefully, reconciliation.

3

Political Activism

> *Batoche de batoche, les Michifs ils onvaient droit, les Michifs ils onvaient raison! (The Michifs, they had rights; the Michifs, they were right!)*

Métis law, which evolved in the Prairies in the early 1800s, was based on the hunt and the harvest. Custom required the captain of the hunt, with the assistance of adjutants or "soldiers," to look after the maintenance of order and the respect for established laws.[1] The process was democratic in the sense that a chief or leader of the hunt or a wintering camp was chosen by the community, who then had to abide by its rules. Laws that were passed on orally over the years were usually ratified or changed at public meetings. Regulations also governed activities such as trading, the establishment of new communities, land exchanges, and respect of personal life. Traditions such as respect and authority of elders, care of the sick and infirmed, the adoption of children, and the "turning off" of spouses were also subject to moral persuasion and community control. Punishment for serious crimes, such as fights resulting in serious injury or death, was usually corporal punishment and on rare occasions a death sentence, while the casting of bad spells and control by an evil spirit or "Wendigo" were punished by shunning or banishment from the community.

One of the first instances in which the Métis of the prairies of the North West declared and defended their traditional rights was in response to conflicts between the North West Company (NWC) and the Hudson's

Bay Company (HBC) at Red River in 1815–16.² In the ensuing years, the Métis were appointed and elected to the HBC-sponsored Council of Assiniboia and protested restrictions on their right to trade independently and live according to their customary laws. In 1849 the Métis challenged the trade monopoly of the HBC at the trial of Pierre-Guillaume Sayer, and another Métis, Alexander Isbister, petitioned the English Colonial Office regarding the inherent rights of Indians and Métis and requested a representative government with control over lawmaking and the administration of justice.³

ST. LAURENT COUNCIL AND TERRITORIAL GOVERNMENT ERA

During negotiations regarding the creation of the Province of Manitoba in 1870, the Métis had expressed their disappointment at the exclusion of the North West Territories, in particular the districts of Alberta and Saskatchewan. The population of St. Albert, Qu'Appelle, and Ile à la Crosse communicated their desire for the confirmation of their laws and rights to the missionaries and the HBC.⁴

In the 1870s increasing numbers of Métis left Manitoba for the South Saskatchewan River region. Disappointed at their loss of political power in the Province of Manitoba, they now sought a place to live independently and exercise their rights. The hivernant camps of the 1850s and 1860s evolved into new communities, which made it even more critical to elect a self-governing council. In 1871 the elders of the seasonal camps met and laid the groundwork for a new Métis community called: "St. Laurent Settlement" on the South Saskatchewan River.⁵ The first public assembly was held on December 10, 1872, at the new parish, St. Laurent de Grandin. The St. Laurent Council elected Gabriel Dumont as its first president and appointed eight councillors: Alexandre and Baptiste Hamelin of Carlton, Baptiste and Pierre Gariépy of Gardepuis' Crossing, Abraham Montour, Isidore Dumont Jr. and Jean Dumont Jr. of St. Laurent, and Moïse Ouellette of Batoche's Crossing. The council was to act as an administrative, military, and judicial body during the annual hunts as well as during periods of residence in the colony. It was to serve as a judicial tribunal to settle disputes by way of arbitration. It also confirmed the multilingual tradition of the Métis and legality of contracts written in French, English, or Cree syllabics.[6]

Twenty-eight laws were updated and codified at assemblies between 1873 and 1875. They governed activities and behaviour such as the bison hunt, theft, inviolability of contracts between employer and employee, prevention and control of prairie fires, and respect of young women. In case of violation, the penalty could be confinement, restitution, or a fine, more commonly the latter. In 1874, the council set out regulations for ferry service and riverlot farms and confirmed the traditional usage of rights of common for woodlots and hay. Provision was made for a school levy in 1875.[7] This form of local government among the Métis was unique in the North West Territories. Councils were also organized in the Qu'Appelle district and in St. Albert, but neither enjoyed the authority of the St. Laurent council. According to historian George Stanley, it confirmed the independent and political maturity of the Métis.[8] The council was the sole local authority in the area during those years and it also acted as parish council.[9]

The rights of the Métis were soon challenged by the HBC and Canadian authorities. The distrust of the North West Mounted Police and the territorial administrators for a form of Métis government reminiscent of the provisional government of Red River soon erupted into conflict. A confrontation occurred in the spring of 1875 when some Métis hunters, led by HBC employee Peter Ballendine, violated the rules of the St. Laurent constitution and left for the annual hunt in advance of the main caravan. With the assent of the general assembly, the president, Gabriel Dumont, and his captains imposed fines and sanctions on the offenders. To avenge himself, Ballendine complained to HBC officer Lawrence Clarke, who was also the local magistrate. The latter then asked the local NWMP to intervene. According to Father André, who witnessed the incident:

> As soon as they arrived at Fort Carlton to sell or barter their provisions, they complained of having been mistreated, robbed and almost killed. Moreover, they knew whom to complain to, for they chose people who took a jaundiced view of the establishment of laws and colonies in which they had not had the honour to take part.[10]

What followed was an expedition of fifty policemen led by Colonel French to pressure the Métis to give up any attempt to exercise local power. The Métis sent out emissaries anxious to inform the governmental authorities of their good intentions but were forced to submit to the pressures exercised by the HBC and the NWMP. The colonial authorities resented Métis law and, with the support of Father André, pressured the Métis to abandon the enforcement of their customary laws and reimburse the offenders. Dumont and the council did so peacefully, but the authority and prestige of the council was seriously undermined. The HBC and the Territorial government had taken advantage of divisions within the Métis community to intervene and check its power.[11]

Deprived of all real power except moral persuasion and legislating mundane activities such as bartering, the council was soon reduced to inaction, a development which caused resentment against the Church and the Canadian government in the St. Laurent Settlement.[12] Faced with lack of control over key economic activities such as the hunt and the fur trade, it soon lost its raison d'être. A NWMP post was established at Duck Lake, symbolizing the extension of Dominion law and the denial of Métis local self-government and customary justice.

During the 1870s, the Métis had no voice in the Territorial government. From 1870 to 1876, the Territories were administered by the lieutenant-governor of Manitoba and his councillors, who were appointed by the federal government. Only a few were French Canadian or Métis. The South Saskatchewan River Métis, who constituted the majority of the population, were not represented on this council, which in any case had only consultative powers.[13] Councillor Pascal Breland,[14] a Métis from St. François-Xavier, Manitoba, who was appointed to the Territorial council in 1872 following pressure by the Métis to appoint one of their own, did not effectively represent the inhabitants of the South Saskatchewan River district. The latter identified for the most part with Riel and endorsed the platform of the provisional government of 1869–70, whereas the partisans of Breland, who were conservative and associated with the Hudson's Bay Company, represented what was commonly called the anti-Riel faction.[15] Others from Manitoba were appointed in 1873, namely Joseph Royal, Pierre Delorme, and James McKay, but they were also unable or unwilling to defend the interests of the western Métis.[16]

Revisions were made to the North West Territories Act in 1875 and 1877,[17] including the transfer of the seat of government from Winnipeg to

Battleford. There were also proposals to create electoral districts and, finally, to elect representatives from those districts starting in 1881. However, there was still no South Saskatchewan River Métis on the new council, a decision Lieutenant-Governor Laird himself deplored. In a petition delivered 1 February 1878, the St. Laurent Métis reiterated their demand for a representative.[18] But contrary to the petitioners' wishes, the federal government renewed the term of "the amiable non-entity," Pascal Breland, claiming that the Saskatchewan Métis were ignorant and incapable of assuming political responsibilities.[19]

Moreover, at the first council meeting in Battleford in March 1877, the council adopted many of the regulations of the council of St. Laurent to control the harvesting of bison. It also created a system of permits and charges to facilitate the operation and maintenance of river crossings. The council granted the French language the same status as English in court proceedings and council deliberations, thus responding to other Métis demands. The council's ordinances and deliberations would be printed in both French and English.[20] These measures appeased the Métis a little, but without weakening their resolve to obtain a representative on council. In 1879, during meetings at Duck Lake and St. Laurent, the Métis population rose up against the rumoured transfer of the seat of government back to Winnipeg and supported demands for a Territorial legislature.[21] It was not until 1881 that the electoral district of Lorne was created and that the Métis obtained a representative in the person of Lawrence Clarke. He defeated Captain Moore of Prince Albert due to Métis support, but Clarke was mainly the clergy's choice, in preference to Moore, who wore "masonic colours."[22]

The Lorne district was composed of the communities of Prince Albert, Carlton, Duck Lake, St. Laurent, and Batoche; that is, areas with French or Scottish Métis majorities, yet their elected representative was an officer of the HBC and an Englishman. Clarke remained in office until 1883.

The 1870s also witnessed several confrontations between the Métis and the government and police, the latter being usually insensitive to the way of life of the Métis, whom they referred to as vagrants. The Métis were often harassed and pursued for "hanging around" and being destitute. In 1879, a young man was sentenced to three months' imprisonment for allegedly slaughtering an ox belonging to the Hudson's Bay Company. The authorities reportedly misinterpreted the situation or failed to understand the testimony, and the conviction stirred up part of the population of the St. Laurent area:

> Believing that he had been unjustly convicted, they wanted to go and release him by brute force. Several hotheads had promised to join in, and their boasts made even the most peaceful waver.... Father André ... succeeded in calming down the angriest by promising to go to Battleford with a delegation of them to see the governor, who received them well.[23]

An issue of particular interest to the Métis during this period was that of the treaty concluded in 1876 between the federal government and the Cree population of the Fort Carlton area (Treaty No. 6). Most Métis of the South Saskatchewan River did not identify as "Indians," but the question of Aboriginal rights was a great concern to them. They had staked out and occupied riverlots in the region for several years and had become aware of the need to obtain precise guarantees concerning their lands. As a group, the Métis were familiar with Eurocanadian attitudes towards land ownership and carefully observed the negotiations intended to get the Cree to share their lands. Several Métis were even called upon to take part as interpreters and witnesses.[24] The role of the Métis as intermediaries during treaty negotiations is unclear. It is not known to what extent they supported the First Nations, nor what real impact the treaties had on their own claims during the following years. On the other hand, it is clear that some Métis of the Fort Carlton area urged the Cree to take a relatively firm stand against Lieutenant-Governor Morris and the treaty commissioners. The authorities complained about the distrustful attitude of the Métis, especially those of the St. Laurent council, and about their influence on Chief Kàmiyistowesit (Beardy) of Duck Lake. The St. Laurent Métis had several relatives among the people of Beardy's band, as well as with Kàpeyakwàskonam's (One Arrow) people.[25]

The Duck Lake group was the most persistent in its negotiations: "it showed at first the greatest reluctance and made the most exorbitant claims."[26] Chief Beardy demanded measures to stop the overhunting of the bison. He also wanted to rent his lands for four years rather than hand them over for good to the government. But lacking the support of other First Nations in the area, he did not obtain these conditions.

Could the Métis who attended the deliberations have insisted more on these conditions, or were they – like some Cree – coerced to the government's side by clever tactics? Some Métis were convinced of their ascendancy over First Nations and were eager to please the government with the hope of confirming their own rights. Moreover, the prestige and authority of the Métis council had been seriously shaken by Colonel French's intervention in 1875. The government skilfully exploited the divisions among Aboriginal peoples of the North West. Several Métis leaders were among the witnesses who signed the treaty on 23 August 1876.[27]

During the years preceding the armed resistance of 1885, the Métis defended their rights in a series of petitions to the Canadian government. Batoche and other communities along the South Saskatchewan River were part of the Territorial constituency of Lorne from 1881 to 1888.[28] This electoral division was not fair to the Métis, for the outcome of the elections was decided by the people of Prince Albert, most of whom were anglophones from Ontario. Neither the Prince Albert *Times* nor the Battleford *Herald* supported the Métis position. These two papers tended either to ignore their presence or to take sides against their claims, which they considered too radical and not representative of "white interests."[29]

From 1878 to 1882, there was a marked increase in the Métis population of the South Saskatchewan River. In 1883, the number of Métis within a radius of forty kilometres around Batoche was estimated at 1,500.[30] By 1884, Batoche was the business and social centre of the district, but it continued to be represented by members of the HBC or Prince Albert anglophone commercial interests. Lawrence Clarke of the HBC was succeeded by D.H. Macdowall (1883–85) and by O.E. Hughes (1885–88) of Prince Albert.[31]

In 1881, Edgar Dewdney took over from David Laird as lieutenant-governor of the Territories.[32] Dewdney, a partisan of John A. Macdonald and his policies, paid little attention to Métis interests. As a result of this indifference perhaps, the Métis made many representations to the government in the early 1880s. The Territorial council was one of the few forums where they could address their demands. Lacking federal representation, they nonetheless sent petitions to the Canadian government directly or indirectly through the clergy and supporters. From 1882 to 1885, they sent at least five such documents to Ottawa and Regina (the Territorial capital from 1883).

3.1. Louis Schmidt dit *Laferté (1844–1935), politician and land agent in Prince Albert – Archives of Manitoba, N10414.*

The first petition from "the inhabitants of St. Louis de Langevin," drafted by Louis Schmidt,[33] was submitted to the Minister of the Interior in Ottawa through Joseph Royal, member for the federal constituency of Provencher in Manitoba in 1881.[34] According to Schmidt, whose testimony is supported by Father Végréville, neither Royal nor the deputy minister of the Interior, A.M. Burgess, acknowledged receipt of this petition until the intervention of Lawrence Clarke, territorial member for Lorne. The main issue for the Métis was the surveying and resurveying of the land in riverlots. The petitioners and their intermediaries met with no success. In 1882, the inhabitants of Batoche sent another petition, signed by all the leaders of the community, including the parish priest, Father Moulin.[35] They received a negative reply. At that point, Father André, who was district superior at St. Laurent, wrote to Ottawa on behalf of the Métis,[36] and Bishop Grandin also agreed to speak to the prime minister of their behalf. All replies were vague or non-committal. The clergy also tended to confuse matters by presenting their own priorities to the government. For example, the Métis petition requested the appointment of a Métis or bilingual Dominion lands agent in Prince Albert. Louis Schmidt, who wanted the appointment, lobbied with Father André and Bishops Taché and Grandin. The other candidate, Philippe Garnot,[37] was disliked by the clergy for his lifestyle and lack of religious fervour. Schmidt was appointed deputy officer at the Lands Office in May 1884[38] to the delight of the clergy, but other Métis demands were sidelined or forgotten.

Under the influence of leaders such as Charles Nolin, Philippe Gariépy, and Maxime Lépine, the Métis of Batoche and vicinity had supported Macdowall rather than Dr. Porter's candidacy in the Territorial election of 1883.[39] In return, the elected representative contributed $100 to the building fund for the Batoche church and promised to plead the Métis cause personally, but he too was unsuccessful or lacked enthusiasm for the Métis cause. These failures discouraged the Métis and increased their impatience with the Canadian government and its representatives. During the winter of 1883–84, Nolin and Lépine organized a committee to bring together all the Métis of the district but did not invite the local clergy.[40]

Increasingly suspicious and resentful of government agents and the clergy, the Métis held several "secret meetings" in early 1884.[41] Participants discussed ways to claim rights, drew up lists of grievances, and proceeded to elect a committee to study those grievances. Meetings were also held at the home of "English Metis" in the Prince Albert area. A number of settlers also supported the Métis. It was at one of those meetings, at the home of Isidore Dumont, Gabriel's father, in April 1883, that participants voted against a resolution to send a delegation to Ottawa and opted instead to bring Riel back from Montana.[42]

Riel's arrival in July consolidated the resistance movement and the adoption of a more militant stance. Numerous meetings were held in the Métis communities throughout the summer and fall of 1884. In July, there was a local meeting at Charles Nolin's and an important meeting between Riel, the "English Metis," and settlers in Prince Albert.[43] In August, a meeting took place at Xavier Letendre's, where an unsuccessful attempt was made to win the clergy's active support. Earlier in June, 1884, Bishop Grandin had tried to intercede with Prime Minister Macdonald. The petition presented to Macdonald incorporated all the claims and grievances of the South Saskatchewan River Métis. Among other things, they demanded the status of a province with a responsible government, the granting of titles and the resurvey of their lands, and the official recognition of Louis Riel's leadership through his appointment to the Territorial council or the Canadian Senate.[44] They protested above all against lack of Métis representation in the territorial and federal governments, against the appointment and employment of newcomers rather than Métis, and finally, against the lack of response from the government to their petitions.

3.2. *Louis Riel and Mistahimaskwa (Big Bear) at Duck Lake, 1884 – La Liberté et le Patriote, 21 septembre 1951, p. 13.*

The inaction and incompetence of the territorial government were well known and deplored by all. On this point, the clergy were in agreement with the Métis:

> It is time for the government to take some steps to organize this vast district. The country is really without a government and without an administration, and it is scandalous to see how government officials carry out their functions.... [M]ost are incompetent or corrupted and inspire neither respect nor confidence. Everybody seems tired of this system.[45]

On the other hand, the clergy collaborated with the government in its campaign against Riel and the more militant Métis. A plan was developed to try and get Riel to leave the country:

> Judge Rouleau and Indian Commissioner Mr. Hayter Reed, both members of the North West Territorial Council, arrived here to see with their own eyes how things were going around here.... Mr. Rouleau saw Father André about Riel and asked him for information about his activities and what could be done about him.[46]

At that point, the government also tried to divide or appease the Métis by offering them certain positions. Michel Dumas was appointed farming instructor on the One Arrow Reserve, and Louis Marion obtained the same position on the Beardy Reserve. The government also flattered Charles Nolin and Maxime Lépine by offering them contracts for installing telegraph poles but they did not accept the enticing offers.[47]

Local politicians D.H. Macdowall and Lawrence Clarke also mounted an active campaign against Riel. In December, Macdowall wrote to Governor Dewdney to ask him to obtain a few thousand dollars for Riel "so he could leave the country and leave us in peace. Father André will also write to you to that effect."[48] The latter informed Dewdney that Métis such as Philippe Garnot, Norbert Delorme, Michel Dumas, and Damase Carrière were hotheads and needed to be controlled.

3.3. Remains of a picture of Our Lady of Lourdes which was pinned on a white flag flown by the Métis during the 1885 Resistance. Below is a prayer by Louis Riel and the names of his children, Jean and Marie-Angélique – Library and Archives Canada, C-15527.

3.4. 1885 flag in custody of Nault family of Ste. Rose du Lac (Manitoba) – Diane Payment.

A NATIONAL FEAST DAY, A FLAG, AN ANTHEM

Batoche was the birthplace of the Métis movement to obtain a patron saint and national feast day distinct from those of the French Canadians, who celebrated St. Jean Baptiste Day on June 24. Louis Riel promoted the idea with the clergy and his compatriots. In a speech given in Prince Albert in August 1884: "He explained his vision of a distinct nationality for the Métis. He wanted French Canadians in the community to identify with the Métis and the latter for their part to become one with French Canadians."[49] The idea gained momentum the following month when a crowd gathered in the St. Laurent church to make a formal request to Bishop Grandin. Moïse Ouellette, Gabriel Dumont, and Louis Riel made speeches to that effect, followed by a symbolic alliance:

> Ludger Gareault [a French Canadian], Paul Schley [a Frenchman] and Louis Riel [a Métis] together approached Bishop Grandin. The bishop accepted their request and asked them to place their trust in God and ask for the protection of a saint.[50]

Riel chose St. Joseph as the patron saint and Saint John the Baptist as a secondary protector.[51] The Métis celebrated their National Day for the first time on September 24th in 1884 and afterwards, from 1886 on, on July 24th.

They also founded the St. Joseph Society to promote the religious, political, and social consciousness of the Métis. The society adopted a banner showing "on the one side St. Joseph carrying the infant Jesus and on the other Saint John the Baptist as he is represented on the banners of the St. Jean Baptiste Society."[52]

In March 1885, Louis Riel and his council adopted a flag that underscored both the national pride and religious spirit of the Métis people. The primacy of religious symbols illustrated the theocratic nature of Riel's provisional government in Saskatchewan. Eyewitness accounts of the flags suggest various representations of the Virgin Mary on a white background. According to a description by Father Fourmond:

Louis Riel raised the standard the day before St. Joseph's Day [March 18], calling the revolt the holiest of actions and placing it under the protection of St. Joseph and Our Lady of Lourdes. As a flag he chose the white flag of ancient France [with a royal blue shield bearing three golden fleurs de lys], saying that he was called to renew its ancient glories. On it he placed a large image of Mary's immaculate heart.[53]

In another account, he described it as: "the flag of St. Louis, which they already had in 1870, with the hearts of Jesus and Mary on the other side."[54] The Métis flag was raised on the council house in George Fisher's home in the village.[55] Taking into account all visual and written descriptions, the main flag of the Métis at Batoche in 1885 was in all probability a white flag with an image of Our Lady of Lourdes fastened to it. This standard has not survived intact as the flag was taken by the soldiers as a souvenir after the battle. Part of the image was torn but the artefact is now conserved in the Library and Archives of Canada. The following poem, signed by Louis Riel, is inscribed on the back of the image:

> You are rightly called Our Lady of Lourdes
> You whose Son went through such heavy sufferings
> O Virgin whose heart was pierced seven times
> By the most bitter pain
> Mother, whose soul suffered so much from cradle to cross!
> Since you have chosen the Kingdom of France
> In which to give free rein to your great sweetness
> Chase from this country the deep darkness
> Of ... desolate.... May its deliverance
> be accomplished by you
> whose heart is so sweet
> Our Lady of Lourdes
> Our sufferings are overwhelming and heavy
> Deliver us from evil, we beg of you
> [Be so good as to favour] our noble undertakings
> [Be so good as to] make them succeed
> Let us triumph over evil and its excesses
> Pray for us so that God may deign to sweeten

Those who are evil strike them down and even [subjugate] them
Under his beneficent law.
Pray to our good Master
Jesus Christ to prove today to mortal men
That he alone is Lord, Emperor, King, Monarch,
President, Czar, Premier; pray to him to mark me
With the Seal of the Elect at the foot his altar.
Pray to Jesus for me! Pray that I may support
The Church with all my might
Make me stronger than other people
[That] I may forever remain faithful to my duty.
Louis "David" Riel[56]

The Métis also adopted a national hymn with a religious theme for the Resistance. The text was recorded by Father Fourmond:

> Air:
> Holy Spirit Descend on us
> Refrain:
> Heart of Jesus protect us (repeat)
> In life in death we are (repeat) all yours

First Stanza:

> Heart of Jesus, our hope,
> Hear our chants and our vows,
> To our suffering country (twice)
> Give unity and constancy
> Give happy times

Second Stanza:

> Heart of Jesus our love our glory
> In our battles for salvation for honour
> Guide, o guide our steps to victory,
> Be, o be our liberator

Third Stanza:

> O St. Joseph, Patron Saint of the Church
> John the Baptist, protector of French Canadians
> Save the French and Métis race
> By your conquered love[57]

THE LAST STAND: ARMED RESISTANCE

In the spring of 1885, positions hardened on both sides. Riel, together with his most fervent supporters, drafted a new petition.[58] It set out the same principles as the preceding ones but adopted a more urgent tone. The government's response in January 1885 was extremely disconcerting: it did not want to negotiate with Riel and would consider the demands presented to it at the proper time and place in the future.[59] Louis Schmidt, Maxime Lépine, and other leaders would later declare that this response precipitated an armed resistance.[60]

When he received the government's negative response in early February, Riel declared: "Forty days from now Ottawa will have my reply" [translation].[61] During the following weeks, he was particularly distraught, and, believing he had failed his people, he spoke of going back to Montana. Dumont, Lépine, Ouellette, and Nolin urged him to stay, and from this moment on they were committed to defending their rights by the force of arms, if necessary. On 19 March, the "little" provisional government of Saskatchewan was established, and Pierre Parenteau Sr. became president, Philippe Garnot secretary, and Gabriel Dumont adjutant-general. Riel also set up a people's council or *exovidate* composed of eighteen or so members or *exovedes*. The first battle of the armed conflict took place at Duck Lake on March 26 when Gabriel Dumont's small army forced the North West Mounted Police from Fort Carlton and Prince Albert to retreat. Only then was the government forced into action, and it responded by mobilizing Canadian forces against the Métis.

On April 24, the Métis fought the North West Field Force under the command of General Middleton at la couli des Tourond (now Fish Creek). The engagement ended with a Métis victory. The Métis then pulled back to Batoche, where they dug trenches and laid ambushes, waiting for the Canadian offensive to resume. On May 9, Middleton and his army of some eight hundred men attacked Batoche. The government forces succeeded in penetrating the Métis defences only on May 12, the final day of the battle. For three days, Dumont and some 250 poorly armed combatants were able to hold the Canadian army in check.[62]

The *guerre nationale* sowed discord and even created a split among the Métis. On the one side

3.5. *Adjutant-General Gabriel Dumont (1837–1906) – Union St. Jean Baptiste, Woonsocket, Rhode Island, Mallet Collection.*

were the partisans of Dumont and Riel and on the other those who opposed a resort to arms. The strong hold of the two Métis leaders naturally attracted many of the undecided. Those opposed to Riel tended to stay on the sidelines or discreetly left the area. After the shock of defeat, however, the divisions came out into the open and grew more pronounced. The loss of life, the arbitrary arrests, and the denunciations provoked a hardening of conflicting positions or an "every man for himself" attitude. In order to avoid further persecution, several Métis now denied any affiliation to, or participation in, the resistance movement. For the same reason, some also testified openly against their compatriots.[63] The humiliation and constraints of defeat also led to a kind of psychological withdrawal within the population. The political expression of this withdrawal was for some a

3.6. *"So much sadness, so much fear"*: Métis in chains in front of Regina prison, 1885: L-R Ignace Poitras, Johnny Sansregret, Pierre Parenteau, Pierre Gariépy, Philippe Garnot, Albert Monkman, Pierre Vandal, Baptiste Vandal, Toussaint Lussier, Maxime Dubois, James « Timous » Short, Patrice Tourond and Emmanuel Champagne – Saskatchewan Archives Board, R-B714.

formal disavowal of Dumont's party and his *rouges* (radicals)[64] and affiliation with the conservative faction and the party in power.

Following the fall of Batoche on May 12, many Métis left and took refuge in the United States, along the Canadian border in North Dakota and Montana. The Canadian government, suspicious of their activities, especially of Gabriel Dumont and Michel Dumas, set up a spy network to watch over them. One of the agents, James Anderson, reported on the comings and goings of Dumont in the fall of 1885:

> About thirty Halfbreeds arrived here from the South Saskatchewan some few weeks ago, fifteen stayed here and others went on to Sun River ... at Lewistown: Gabriel Dumont, wife, 1 child, Edouard Dumont, wife, 2 children, Jean Dumont, Parenteau, wife, 3 children. Gabriel Dumont is living with his brother in law, David Wilkie and others are building small

houses for the winter. They arrived here with twenty horses and very little money. I had a long conversation with Dumont.⁶⁵

The authorities feared an uprising or a coalition with the First Nations to the south, particularly the Dakota and Blackfoot. It was rumoured that Dumont would come back supported by a fair number of them, as well as by the Métis who had settled in the United States. An agent along the Canadian-American border reported:

> Yesterday an intelligent and respectable half-breed Charles Pruden called in my store in a state of semi intoxication.... On the Riel question he said there would be "big trouble" next spring; Dumont would be their leader; and when the Halfbreed nation called, they would all go and fight, and they would clear all the white men out of this their country, and take their property.⁶⁶

Several Métis refugees also campaigned to mobilize their compatriots. Alex McKay, a Métis working for the government, who passed through the Turtle Mountain area in early 1886, reported: "Michel Dumas has all the Sioux to join him ... given people to understand he was Gabriel Dumont."⁶⁷ He also said that there were rumours of a big uprising up north the following spring, as the Métis were very bitter because Riel was hanged and angry at the English Metis for not supporting them.⁶⁸

Reports from Montana confirmed that the Métis travelled back and forth along the border, and, in particular, visited the various centres inhabited by their relatives. The Nault brothers (Napoléon and Elie) regularly travelled between St. Vital, Manitoba, St. Joe (North) Dakota, and Billings, Montana. They visited the Dakota Sioux and other bands who were angry at the government and wanted to fight.⁶⁹

The feared uprising of First Nations and Métis never materialized. The leaders of 1885 were dispersed. Norbert Delorme was in the Battleford area, Dumas and Dumont were in the United States, and the others were in prison at Stony Mountain, Manitoba. In a conciliatory but calculated gesture, the authorities released the Métis prisoners Maxime Lépine, Philippe Gariépy, and Philippe Garnot in the fall of 1886. The "more respectable" exiles such as Jean-Baptiste Boucher Sr. in Fort Assiniboine and David Tourond and Alexandre Venne at Turtle Mountain were also invited to return home.⁷⁰ Finally, a general amnesty was granted in the fall of 1886. This gesture, as well as the wretched condition of the refugees, and the Métis in general, ruled out any plans for a new resistance. However the rumours persisted in 1887 and an Oblate brother at Batoche reported that the Métis said they had the support of the Blackfoot and the Dakota (Sioux) and were sending emissaries to the Cree reserves.⁷¹ Dumont was unable to consolidate the First Nations and Métis forces in 1887, and, henceforth, the Métis would act alone and take the political rather than the military route.

Riel's execution on 16 November 1885 had important political consequences. On the national level, the Liberals did not miss the opportunity to accuse the Conservatives of injustice and murder. Not all the Métis immediately renounced *les pendards* (the conservative "hanging" party), but traditional ties were severed. In Quebec, the Nationalists under Honoré Mercier launched an *appel à la race* (nationalistic outcry) and assembled at the Champ de Mars to condemn the martyrdom of their compatriot. The French Canadian Nation had been wounded; one of their own had been killed:

> Public subscriptions provided for Riel's defence at the trial, and after the sentence, press and platform demands for his pardon grew more insistent.... And in any case, Riel and the people he had championed were kinsmen.... It was in vain that every priest on the Saskatchewan wrote publicly and privately denouncing Riel as the arch-enemy of the Church, an anti-Christ.⁷²

On the other hand, French-language newspapers of the period reveal that, initially, French Canadian public opinion (based primarily on the views of the clergy and the political elite) was opposed to the resistance and condemned Riel. There was a battalion of French Canadians in Middleton's army and some unknowingly fought the Métis at la couli des Tourond.⁷³ However, during and after the battle, public opinion changed dramatically due to accounts in the press. There is no denying that Mercier and his partisans took advantage of the situation to further their political ambitions, but Mercier personally came to the aid of the Riel family in the 1880s. Public opinion in Quebec was more favourable to the Métis than in Manitoba where the Conservative clergy had complete control. One of Riel's former friends and colleagues, Joseph Dubuc, now a judge, refused to come to Riel's aid or to hear his appeal at the Court of Queen's Bench.[74]

The Métis did not give up, however. Despite the defamatory and discriminatory policies that followed, the military defeat of 1885 acted as a catalyst and hardened their resolve to resist the government. While Métis political action was often isolated and sometimes marked by deep internal divisions, it was all the more resolute.

MÉTIS RIGHTS AFTER 1885

No Compensation for Those "who were party to their own losses."

In February 1886, the government set up the "Rebellion Losses Commission" to inquire and determine compensation for people who had suffered losses as a result of the armed conflict (see Appendix 2). Three categories of victims were established. The first one included those who were able to prove that they had supported the government, while the two others disqualified the claimants for "complicity with the rebels" or disloyalty to the government.

The official response of Métis families who had suffered losses was that they had been drawn involuntarily into the conflict, either by ignorance or by Riel's intrigues. Several spouses of combatants also tried to prove in vain that they had individual claims to property by virtue of their dowry. But their applications were not accepted unless they had been widowed before March 1885. The Métis argued that they were victims of injustice who had been forced to defend themselves against government forces. Furthermore, the combat had been unequal and its consequences disproportionately devastating.[75] They were careful, however, not to express these views openly or to denounce the execution of Riel, whom they still honoured privately.[76]

The commissioners of the inquiry were of the opinion "that having contributed to their own losses, the Métis were not eligible for any compensation."[77] However, what aroused most resentment among the Métis was the frankly arbitrary and partisan manner in which the government

3.7. *Mme Josephte (Paul) Tourond (1831–1928) on her farm at Batoche, ca. 1920 – Parks Canada, Brenda (Boyer) Percell Collection.*

> Réclamation (Batoche)
>
> De Mme Veuve Tourond
>
> Veuve depuis deux ans — a un Homestead 40 arpents de terre cassée — Terre entrée au bureau de Prince Albert — Depuis 3 ans dans le pays. — maison — étable — hangard
>
> Réclame
>
> 1° Une maison de 30 pieds sur 20 détruite par Midleton estimation faite — 1000 $
> 2° 5 gros bœufs estimés à 100$ chaqu'un — " 500 —
> 3° 1 Cheval étalon estimé à — " 500 —
> 4° 2 Chevaux estimés — " 300 —
> 5° 2 gros poêles estimés — " 130 —
> 6° 2 Commodes — " 50 —
> 7° 1 Valise pleine de butin — " 150 —
> 8° 1 autre — " 100 —
> 9° 1 Machine à Coudre — " " 60 —
> 10 1 hangard de 20 pieds sur 20 — " 300 —
> 11 210 Minots de blé à 2$ le minot — " 420 —
> 12 105 sacs à 50¢ — " 102 —
> 13 1 faucheuse et son rateau — " 150 —
> 14 1 crible — " " 70 —
> 15 1 horloge — " " 15 —
> 16 3 Couchettes tournés — " " 45 —
> 17 3 lits de plume — " " 15 —
> 18 Différents articles, ustensils de cuisine, mobiliers — " 400 —
> 19 un Cochon pesant environ 300 livres — " " 50 —
> 20 20 poules — " "
>
> 4,5 [illegible]

3.8. *"Mme Veuve" (Widow) Tourond's claim to the North-West Rebellion Claims Commission — Library and Archives Canada, RG 15, Vol. 914, No. 21.*

3.9. *Charles Nolin (1837–1907) and Rosalie (Lépine) Nolin (ca. 1850–1927) of St. Laurent de Grandin and Onion Lake – Provincial Archives of Alberta, OB 3810.*

dealt with the issue. It invited denunciations, which created much anxiety and division within the population. Most Métis were discreet, but some were less scrupulous and did not hesitate to implicate their neighbours in order to serve their own interests.[78] Several merchants in Batoche succeeded in having their claims accepted, for they had influential witnesses and were avowed Conservatives. But the indemnities granted to Xavier Letendre, George Fisher, or even Mme Tourond, who was widowed and had lost three sons in 1885, did not cause much animosity in comparison to those granted to certain individuals who had been actively involved in the resistance at some time. These included Baptiste and William Boyer, and especially Charles Nolin.

Nolin was one of the known leaders of the resistance movement. Until May 1885, he had been active within the provisional government. He fled to Prince Albert during the battle at Duck Lake and tried to rehabilitate himself in the eyes of the authorities by agreeing to be one of the principal witnesses for the prosecution at Louis Riel's trial.[79] His conduct as well as his subsequent compensation aroused much indignation. According to Philippe Garnot, secretary of the Provisional government, who had been arrested and convicted: "as soon as he smelled gunpowder, he thought it was time to escape. And yet, if you had known Nolin as I knew him before, you would have taken him for bravery itself, the way he went around intimidating those who were weaker than he."[80] Speaking of Baptiste Boyer, he added "… a councillor [Boyer] also deserted, but he had more of an excuse because he went in the direction of Lake Qu'Appelle and had never been one of those who had led people."[81]

For the population in general, whether directly involved or not, there was no compensation at all, even though several had good grounds as their property had been destroyed or stolen by the North West Field Force after the battle. Emmanuel Champagne, for example, was a known and avowed participant in the resistance. In a court declaration supported by witnesses, he declared that his furs, merchandise, and his prized grey mare had been stolen by General Middleton after the battle.[82] But as a known liberal, he received no indemnity for his losses, evaluated at $13,310. Philippe Gariépy, another liberal, also received no compensation.[83] Moreover, none of the claims of freighters and farmers were accepted, except in the case of a few widows, elderly people, and the clergy. The bias and injustice in the administration of the claims aroused much resentment and left the poorest to their fate.

"Party Politics:" Unity, Patronage, and Land Rights

After 1885, deep resentment caused most Métis to turn away from their traditional support of the Conservative party or its candidates.[84] The Liberals or *rouges* of the South Saskatchewan River were in contact with Honoré Mercier and the Nationalists in Quebec. At an assembly in Batoche, Philippe Garnot introduced a motion of support for "a letter he had sent to one of his friends in Lower Canada to thank the liberals who had managed to get him and his comrades released from prison and Alex Fisher supported him in a virulent speech against the government."[85] The clergy was outraged and complained that the malcontents threatened the unity of the French Catholics in the district against the anglophone majority in Prince Albert. The Métis were in fact divided as some now distrusted the so-called "ringleaders" of the resistance: Lépine, Nolin, and Garnot.[86]

In the Territorial election of 17 September 1885, Owen E. Hughes, a Prince Albert merchant, defeated Dr. Porter by a majority of eight votes in the Lorne constituency.[87] But this election was relatively inconsequential for the Métis of the district in view of the unrepresentative nature of the Territorial council. In 1886, Saskatchewan obtained for the first time a representative on the federal level; the election set for 15 March 1887 was therefore particularly important. The candidates were the Liberal David Laird, former lieutenant-governor of the Territories, and the Conservative D.H. Macdowall, former territorial representative for Lorne. The clergy and Métis "bourgeoisie" supported Macdowall and the government,[88] but a public meeting held at Batoche showed that the general population did not:

> Since most of them could not resign themselves to supporting a government against which they had so many grievances, they went over to the Liberal side. They were supported in this move by two French Canadians [including a Mr. Campeau and Mr. Préfontaine] who had come specially to relight the fire smouldering under the ashes.[89]

As the majority of Métis had voted for the Liberals, Macdowall's victory cost them the favour of the government and coveted patronage appointments. The Métis distrusted Macdowall, a scrip dealer and avowed supporter of Prime Minister J.A. Macdonald, who served two terms before Wilfrid Laurier and the Liberals came to power in 1896.

The Métis of Batoche and surrounding communities persisted in the defence of their rights through numerous petitions in the late 1880s. The first one was presented at an assembly in St. Laurent de Grandin on 24 February 1886.[90] Signed by Jean Caron, president, and Octave Régnier,[91] secretary, it received the support of the majority. This temporary alliance between the Conservatives and the Liberals put the Métis in a stronger position. The eleven resolutions addressed primarily the difficult economic conditions and recommended ways to come to assist the population. The tone of the petition was moderate in the hope of gaining the confidence of the authorities who still distrusted them. The Métis did not want welfare assistance that would indebt them to the government but programs that would promote economic recovery and self-reliance.[92] The government's response showed little sensitivity to the harsh circumstances of the Métis. The reply stated that, considering that the Métis had been guilty of "rebellion," they should not expect any consideration from the government.[93]

In May 1887, the people of Batoche petitioned Territorial Lieutenant-Governor Dewdney for exemption from customs duties on imported cattle to enable exiles to come back with their herds.[94]

They received a favourable response, which enabled a number of Métis to return to the North West Territories.

Slighted by the federal Conservatives, the population of Batoche addressed a petition to Laurier and the Liberal party in the hope of winning that party's support. The leaders, Maxime Lépine, Alex Fisher, and Philippe Garnot, who had just been released from prison, formed a committee and held meetings throughout 1887. They communicated with Gabriel Dumont, who had been given amnesty but was being watched by the authorities and was afraid of returning to Canada, especially to the North West Territories.[95] During this interval, he corresponded with former associates, including Maxime Lépine, who surreptitiously passed on the letters to the North West Mounted Police.[96] Dumont informed them of his speeches in New York State and Quebec and meetings with high officials sympathetic to the Métis cause. He incited the population to claim their rights, such as compensation for losses suffered in 1885, and apply for the scrip certificates that the government had promised. The contents of the letters were not incriminating, but Lépine's actions illustrated the fear and divisions in the community and intimidation tactics employed by the police.

3.10. *Maxime Lépine (1837–1897) member of Manitoba legislature 1874–78 and councillor of Métis Provisional government of 1885 – Archives of Manitoba, N10909.*

Dumont, the military leader and former combatant, had succeeded Louis Riel as political leader. Even though Dumont was still an advocate of a solution by force of arms rather than by compromise, only the political arena remained open to him in 1888.[97] Dumont, too, gave himself a "mission," that of justifying the actions of his leader Louis Riel:

> Riel is dead and I am anxious to speak for him in the name of those for whom he laid down his life. I have always worked to place on a solid basis our religious, civil, and political institutions, as well as the social [sic] of the North West, my country, and I regret to say that I and mine have been badly rewarded by the Government for this.[98]

The events surrounding the petitions sent to Wilfrid Laurier in 1888 testified to intense political activity in the Métis community. The members of the drafting committee came mostly from the ranks of avowed Liberals, such as Lépine, Garnot, and their extended families, but they were joined by moderates and former Conservatives like Jean Caron.[99] A preliminary communication sent to Laurier on 17 December 1887 outlined the main grievances or points to be elaborated in the petition: recognition of the Aboriginal rights of the Métis people, the granting of titles to their lands, and an impartial adjudication of claims for losses suffered during the 1885 Resistance.[100] The petitioners attributed the responsibility for the armed conflict to the Conservative government and denounced the punitive policies of the government since then. The members of the committee also deplored the lack of French institutions and services, as well as the lack of Métis representation in the government.

In the spring of 1888, Alex Fisher advised Laurier that Maxime Lépine and Philippe Garnot had "left the committee and parted company with us."[101] He described the nature of the split in a letter to his mentor Gabriel Dumont:

> The Métis of Batoche suspect Mr. Max L'Épine [sic] to be in league with Mr. Charles Nolin, and you know that the Métis have an aversion to the said Charles Nolin. You also know that there are some Métis here, such as Nolin, the Boyer brothers [Baptiste and William] and Xavier Letendre [known as Batoche] who are against everything we do, as are the Batoche and

Venne families. These are all people who were paid by the government, and they are all at the service of the government.[102]

Nolin and Lépine,[103] who were related through marriage, were now associated with the conservative faction, which was drawn primarily from the local bourgeoisie, including Xavier Letendre, the Fisher brothers (George and Ambroise), and the Boyer and Venne families. This group enjoyed governmental patronage, especially in the form of public works contracts. Several had been paid compensation for losses suffered in 1885. Lépine's crossover to the Conservatives can probably be attributed to the prevailing climate of political instability and general distrust. Having been only recently released from prison, he was unemployed and may have hesitated to get involved in any action that could have negative consequences for him. Meanwhile Garnot, who was unpopular since the 1887 election campaign, remained on the sidelines. Nonetheless, neither Lépine nor Garnot signed the petition drafted by the Conservatives in December 1888.

Deprived of their support as well as that another former Liberal, Philippe Gariépy,[104] who had recently been enticed into the Conservative camp with a contract, the Liberals now relied on Alex Fisher, Jean Caron, and Emmanuel Champagne[105] to work on the memorandum. Fisher, who had some schooling and was fluent in English and French, drafted the petition which was submitted in March 1888. The document has not survived in parliamentary records, but the points were probably similar to the preliminary draft of 17 December 1887.[106] The Liberals had a great deal of difficulty drafting this document. Fisher constantly referred to betrayals and intrigues of the committee. Two petitions had been drafted in February, one by Maxime Lépine and one by Fisher. According to Fisher, his draft had been accepted by the committee, but Lépine's petition had been substituted for his own. Fisher informed Laurier, who returned the petition to him requesting a copy of the official one.[107] All these actions showed the division among the Métis, which threatened to weaken them politically. In a letter to Dumont, Fisher summed up the actions of the Métis as follows:

> And so, my dear Gabriel, you'll know where you stand. You know all the Métis around here, most of whom are very decent people, but we are sorry to say, there are also some pretty bad schemers.[108]

Fisher also responded to a request by Wilfrid Laurier for a Métis perspective of antecedents and events of 1885.[109] Fisher wrote a personal and lively account in Michif French, which was naturally critical of the Conservative government. It contradicted the government military accounts in several instances. For example, Fisher, who was the ferryman at Batoche in 1885, claimed that the Métis never lowered the ferry cable, which broke the smokestacks on the steamer *Northcote*. This had not been necessary as the boat, which was travelling along the east bank, got caught in the cable, which was quite low at that spot.

The Conservatives in Ottawa made fun of Alex Fisher's claims and refused to recognize that government injustices were responsible for the armed conflict. A colleague of Superintendent of Lands William Pearce wrote to him:

> I think you will smile when you read it. The proposition of children born between 1870 and 1888 [sic] getting something is definite but presumptious, and all the foregoing is so vague and so untrue as to make it difficult to deal with.[110]

The Conservatives of Batoche and the neighbouring communities were quick to respond and send their petition to the prime minister, Sir John A. Macdonald. The principal members of the committee were Charles Nolin (president), Xavier Letendre, and Baptiste Boyer. Father Fourmond of St. Laurent, who had been advised by Bishop Pascal to stay out of politics, openly supported the Conservatives. Several of their resolutions were similar to those of their Liberal fellow citizens. They demanded assistance programs to alleviate the harsh poverty of the district and the establishment of a North West Mounted Police barracks, a telegraph office, and a technical school at Batoche. They reiterated the request of the Liberals for land grants to Métis born in the North West between 1870 and 1885. Concerned about their power base, the petitioners deplored the unfairness of the electoral boundary of the new Territorial constituency of Batoche created in 1888. The Métis and French Canadian population had been split into two by the exclusion of St. Louis and the inclusion of Saskatoon, an anglophone community.[111] Revision of the constituency boundaries was crucial if a Métis, francophone, and Catholic majority was to be obtained. Xavier Letendre went to Ottawa in February 1889 and personally delivered the petition to Sir J.A. Macdonald.

The petition was understandably more successful than the Liberal one, as it had the advantage of the support of the party in power. On the subject of redrawing the electoral boundaries, the federal government deferred to the authority of the territorial assembly, but some of their other demands were granted.[112] Moreover, the Métis were assured that the telegraphic service connecting Batoche and Duck Lake since 1886 would be permanent, and a North West Mounted Police post was established at Batoche later that year. At first, the police occupied Baptiste Boyer's buildings and then moved into Xavier Letendre's house, which it bought in 1895. The post provided some local employment, but the much-desired economic assistance was tied to so many conditions that few citizens took advantage of it.[113]

It was in this contentious atmosphere that the first election for the new legislative assembly of the Territories was held in June 1888. This election was particularly important for the new constituency of Batoche with its Métis and francophone majority. The candidates were George Fisher Jr. of Batoche and Hillyard Mitchell of Duck Lake.[114] The winner was Fisher, the Métis Catholic candidate, but Mitchell contested the election, claiming that there had been irregularities (blackmail, double voting) at the Batoche polling station. As the secret ballot was not introduced until 1894, voting was done openly at the time, which tended to encourage fraud. The population was in turmoil. The Métis had united behind Fisher, who had even succeeded in rallying his rival, Charles Nolin. But this common Métis front was unable to overcome the English establishment. Father Fourmond reported:

> The much-desired union took place to everyone's satisfaction. It gave the victory to the French party, despite all the efforts of the English. There was general rejoicing when we learned of the election of the good Mr. Fisher, a peaceful man if there ever was one, and fluent in both French and English. However, our joy was of short duration.[115]

The returning officer, Rodolphe Ouellet,[116] an employee of Mitchell, reportedly deceived the voters of Batoche. Pretending to support Fisher and his compatriots, he then stated that certain voters had misrepresented themselves and subsequently declared Mitchell the winner.[117]

The disappointed Métis prepared a counterattack. During their National Day celebrations on July 24, they held meetings in Batoche to work out a plan of action. Charles Nolin and Louis Schmidt worked together on a petition demanding that Fisher's election be confirmed and that the "traitor" Ouellet be punished.[118] The participants agreed to send this memorandum to Lieutenant-Governor Joseph Royal. The petition was presented to the Territorial assembly during the fall session. In its report to the assembly on December 5, the elections committee for its part declared that the petition did not conform to the rules.[119] Fisher, a mild-mannered and conciliatory man, had not gone to Regina to defend his cause and had refused to deposit $500 to lodge his appeal. The report concluded by recommending that "the controverted Election Ordinance No. 7 of 1884 be amended so as to cover the case of the petitioner against the return of H. Mitchell."[120] However, this motion was defeated by a vote of 14 to 5, and Mitchell's election was confirmed.

Father Fourmond took a strong stance against the legislative assembly's decision. He stated that the authorities had done little to help the Métis, who were disadvantaged and destined to assimilation by a government controlled by anglophones. He particularly deplored the inaction of Lieutenant-Governor Joseph Royal, a French Canadian and past Métis supporter, whose functions gave him control over the assembly.[121] It is probable that Royal was insecure about his position and did not want to intervene, as he was unpopular with the predominantly English-speaking assembly.

After his election had been confirmed, Mitchell was appointed to the lieutenant-governor's advisory council, where he supported the claims of the Métis in his constituency concerning land grants, scrip, and compensation for losses suffered in 1885.[122] Mitchell, a prosperous businessman and astute politician, did in fact have the support of several Métis, especially in the Duck Lake area. But he opposed French-language rights in the Territories and did not have the support of the Métis of Batoche and St. Laurent.

The demographic situation of the French-speaking population had changed since 1875, when the Métis and French Canadians together made up about half the population. In the Saskatchewan of 1885, they were in the minority. Moreover, after the 1885 Resistance, Canadian public opinion became polarized against the Métis, who constituted the majority of that francophone population.

3.11. *Charles-Eugène Boucher (1864–1926), member for Batoche, Legislative Assembly of the North West Territories, 1891–1898 – Parks Canada, donated by Boniface and Agnès Fidler.*

The MP for the Saskatchewan district, D.H. Macdowall, stopped in Batoche during his election tour at the end of 1889 and returned in 1890 to present a plan for establishing a Métis reserve.[123] The clergy favoured the plan but the Métis saw in it an attempt on the part of the government to isolate them: "to treat the Métis like Indians."[124] Above all, it was an assault on their pride and independence. They wanted scrips that could be exchanged for land or cash and associated the reserve plan with the government's immigration policy, which was to encircle the Métis and "free" the surrounding lands for settlers. The question was debated at several assemblies in the district. The St. Laurent committee, under the influence of Father Fourmond and Charles Nolin, supported the plan, but it was rejected in Duck Lake and, more resoundingly, in Batoche. Among the strong opponents of a Métis reserve in the district was the new Territorial representative for Batoche, Charles-Eugène Boucher[125]

Macdowall was mainly preoccupied with his re-election and with keeping the Macdonald government in power. An astute politician, he outwardly supported the claims of the Métis population of his constituency, whom he considered "a political factor," but he did not believe in Métis land rights. He reported to Sir J.A. Macdonald:

> In urging you to take steps for the settlement of this question [the land question, or that of granting scrips to the Métis born between 1870 and 1885], I do so, not because the halfbreeds are legally entitled to such a settlement but in the interest of peace and good government.[126]

Macdowall kept his seat in the federal election of 1891, defeating the Liberal candidate by a majority of almost three hundred votes.[127] But he had lost the general support of the Métis.

The 1890s were years of rivalry and triumph. The Territorial election of 1891 provoked another heated debate. The candidates in Batoche were Charles Nolin and Charles-Eugène Boucher, both Conservatives. Nolin had considerable political experience, but he was from the "old guard" and had lost the confidence of many people. Boucher was young and dynamic and came from a prominent and respected family. Nolin was defeated but successfully contested the result with the lieutenant-governor and the assembly. The election campaign and the events of the following months created conflict and divisions in the community.[128] Nolin occupied the seat during the first session, but an appeal lodged by Boucher was followed by an inquiry, which ruled in his favour.[129] George Fisher's similar experience a few years earlier had served as a lesson. Boucher, the son-in-law of Xavier Letendre, benefited from the support of the merchant community, the younger voters, and a personal friend of Letendre, Lieutenant-Governor Joseph Royal.

As one of two French-speaking representatives in the Territorial assembly, Boucher tried in vain to maintain the use of French in the government and the schools. In 1892, the official use of French was abolished in the Territories, and the following year, an amendment to the school act revoked bilingualism and made English the only language of instruction.[130] These measures, which had negative consequences for the expansion of the French language and the preservation of the Michif French community, were part of the anglicization policy that Boucher fought against. He also brought forward many other issues of concern to his fellow citizens. In 1893, he introduced a new resolution demanding just compensation for the losses suffered by the Métis during the armed conflict of 1885, arguing that:

> In respect to property destroyed or confiscated by the Canadian militia at the close of the rebellion which has been refused by Government of Canada on grounds that such persons were rebels, at the time of such destruction or confiscation all hostilities had ceased and rebellion was entirely at an end, and said persons were living quietly and peaceably at their homes.[131]

Boucher's resolution was adopted by the assembly and sent on to the Canadian government, but the Métis affected were never compensated. He also tabled a motion supporting the extension of the right to scrip to Métis born after 1870.[132] Boucher was re-elected in 1894 with twenty-five votes more than David Venne, notary and postmaster of Batoche. The two candidates were related through marriage, and there was no report of heated rivalry and cabals as in 1891.[133] This election was also held by secret ballot, nicknamed "the Oliver ballot" after representative Frank Oliver, who had proposed that the legislative assembly adopt such a voting method.[134]

In 1897, the executive council became responsible to the legislative assembly in the North West Territories. In a sense, the Territorial government acquired ministerial responsibility. Boucher was not particularly involved in this question. He saw no advantages in it for his compatriots, but rather for F.W.G. Haultain and his partisans, such as Hillyard Mitchell, opponents of the francophone minority, who were coming into power.[135] Boucher sat on the advisory committee on agriculture. He also dispensed patronage in his constituency, especially in the form of construction and public works programs.

The federal election of 1896 brought important changes in representation and ushered in the Liberal era. Batoche was no exception and the Métis were described as "red like fire."[136] The Liberal candidate T.O. Davis was opposed by the Conservative James McKay.[137] Davis was the mayor of Prince Albert and a popular figure in Batoche, while McKay an English Metis and lawyer was disliked by many Métis because of his pro-government position during the 1885 Resistance. However, it was the Liberal leader Wilfrid Laurier, uncertain of his election in Quebec, who ran in place of Davis with the latter's consent in the Prince Albert West constituency. In the election of June 1896, Laurier won over McKay by 988 votes to 944.[138] Having also been elected in his Quebec East constituency, the Liberal leader gave up his Western seat, and Davis won the by-election in December by a majority of 175 votes. He kept his seat until 1904. The Liberals had worked hard during the campaign to attract the Métis and francophone vote.[139]

Charles "Le Marquis" Fisher[140] of Duck Lake was the Liberal candidate for Batoche in the Territorial election of 1898. He won over his compatriot, Jean-Baptiste Boucher Jr., brother of Charles-Eugène, and a provincial rights or Conservative candidate. The rivalry between the two candidates never reached the intensity of the Boucher-Nolin fight. They had more or less the same platform; that is, scrips and increased economic development for the district.

Despite the internal rivalries, which lessened its impact, the Métis population of the Batoche exercised considerable political power between 1888 and 1908. However, after the turn of the century, their power declined slowly but surely. William F. Grant,[141] a Batoche merchant, was the Liberal candidate at the first provincial election in December 1905. He received 983 votes to Boucher's 120, the largest majority ever given to a member of the Territorial legislature. Grant was married to Catherine Henry, a Métis from Vandal (present-day Gabriel's Crossing) and supported Métis interests. In 1907, he offered his seat to the new attorney-general, Alphonse Turgeon,[142] stating that he did not hesitate to resign in favour

3.12. *Charles "Le Marquis" Fisher (1865–1907) member for Duck Lake, Territorial and Saskatchewan legislature, 1898–1905 – Parks Canada, donated by Justine (Laviolette) Pambrun.*

of a French-speaking Catholic. Turgeon was elected in the city of Prince Albert in December 1907 and in the general election of the following year in the new constituency of Duck Lake, which included Batoche.

After 1908, there was a rapid decline in the political power of Batoche and the neighbouring communities. The southeastern part of the Duck Lake constituency lacked political organization, and for this or other reasons it did not receive its share of patronage. The turn of the century witnessed the relocation of several Métis in northern communities. Immigration from eastern Europe also reduced its numbers and influence. The arrival of Galicians and Poles (around present-day Fish Creek) and Mennonites (present-day Rosthern area) isolated the Métis. Efforts to increase the francophone population met with some success: a few hundred French, French Canadians, and Belgians settled in Duck Lake, Domrémy, and Bellevue. But the Métis and the francophone population was too diverse, disparate, and isolated to unite politically.

4

> *Batoche ... is a charming spot. The Métis there are busy farming, hunting, and fishing with the occasional freighting.*[1]

The Métis, who were primarily hunters, freighters (carriers of merchandise), interpreters, farmers, and labourers, attached different values to work than Europeans. For the Métis, work was generally related to an immediate need for food or personal resources. They assigned little importance to accumulating goods; in fact, custom required that anyone who had a good hunt or good harvest shared it with his family and friends. This tradition of sharing and not profiting, described by Manuel and Posluns in *The Fourth World: An Indian Reality*,[2] was the general rule in the nineteenth century and first decades of the 1900s. However, there were exceptions, especially among the merchants who accepted the increasingly invasive Western capitalist system. These people adopted the culture of Europeans or Eurocanadians and the practice of accumulating goods and investing income. Their lifestyle went hand in hand with a permanent home, a network of commercial contacts and financial interests, and more time devoted to work.

Eurocanadians looked down upon the slower rhythm of Métis life, which varied with the seasons and was based on the principle of "living in the present." Missionaries, explorers, and other agents of "progress" saw these people as lazy, improvident or unconcerned about the future, and "wasteful" or too fond of having a good time.

Before the immigration of the 1890s, Eurocanadians did not seriously threaten the lifestyle and values of the Métis. However, other economic realities constrained the "free people" and forced them to diversify and change their way of life. The demise of the bison and the end of hunting expeditions around 1878 precipitated a crisis. The transition from hunting to farming had to be made very quickly. Lacking farming techniques and ploughing implements, as well as markets for their produce, the Métis were nonetheless forced to adopt it, especially if they wanted to remain in the area and live off the land. Some invested in cattle raising or mixed farming. Between 1870 and 1930, the majority of Métis, practised "subsistence" farming combined with other seasonal work. They went hunting and fishing for food, cut cordwood, gathered "roots" (senega), or if they were fortunate got contract work from local merchants and government agencies. They became "a class of poor people"[3] living marginally on the fringes of the capitalist economy of the Eurocanadian society that had displaced them.

THE EARLY COMMERCE: FUR TRADE, BUFFALO HUNT, FREIGHTING, AND OTHER ENTERPRISES

The commercial activities of the Métis in the South Saskatchewan River region go back to the eighteenth century. At the time, the territory was the centre of activity of the Gros Ventres (Haaninin) and Blackfoot (Siksika), but the Assiniboine and Cree also hunted and traded there. The Cree were migrating to the prairies during the period from about 1740 to 1820. Coming from the wooded areas north and west of Lake Superior, they were drawn more and more to the west and southwest by their rapidly expanding role as intermediaries in the fur trade. The Métis presence in the area also probably originated during that period. A number of French Canadian voyageurs came to the North West ("the Western Sea") in the 1730s.[4] Between 1750 and 1756, the French put up a series of posts on the Saskatchewan River: Fort St. Louis (Nipawin), Fort à la Corne, Fort des Prairies, and Fort la Jonquière.

The period 1770 to 1820 witnessed an increase in the western fur trade. More voyageurs came to work as *hivernants* (winterers) or for the

North West Company and other Montreal trading firms. Others came as peddlers and freemen. During the 1780s, the NWC and the HBC competed with each other and erected two trading posts on the South Saskatchewan River. The "South Branch Houses" were situated near the future Gariépy (Gardepuis) Crossing, about twenty-five kilometres downstream from Batoche.[5] This place was the scene of an intense struggle between the Gros Ventres, the main hunters and inhabitants of the district, and the new arrivals, the Cree and the Assiniboine. The Gros Ventres were especially angry that European traders should favour their enemies. In 1794, they attacked the NWC post, which Nicolas Montour and Louis Châtelain were barely able to save, and destroyed the HBC post.[6]

Between 1805 and 1810, commercial activities resumed once more in the area. The HBC established Carlton House on the left bank of the South Saskatchewan River, near the future St. Laurent Crossing, about twelve kilometres downstream from Batoche.[7] Very close by, the North West Company built "South Branch House II" but soon abandoned this location for another, "La Montée," situated on a more favourable supply route on the North Saskatchewan. "Carlton House II" (HBC) and "La Montée" (NWC) became important supply centres for pemmican. In 1819–20, there were about seventy French Canadians and Métis plus seventy women and children living around the post, each of whom produced three hundred to four hundred pounds of pemmican during the winter.[8]

The voyageur Jean-Baptiste Letendre *dit* Batoche,[9] (grandfather of the future founder of Batoche) was in the vicinity of Fort à la Corne around 1810 and built "Batoche Post" on the North Saskatchewan, about five kilometres west of the junction of the two branches of the Saskatchewan River.[10] An HBC employee who came to this place in 1825 noted the presence of French Canadian and Métis hunters with their families.[11] Continuing his trip, he arrived in the vicinity of Fort Carlton, where he met a number of independent Métis hunters, among them Lavallée, Sayer, Plante, Primeau, and Parisien, who traded with the Company.

> Baptiste and Laventure Parisien joined us. They are freemen, halfbreeds. Their families are encamped in the Islands above and they left the Fort ten days ago. The people at the Fort are well.... These halfbreeds though free have always been stationary at the Fort from where they hunt both large animals and occasionally furs and they always live well without encumbering

the Company. They often provide the Fort with fresh meat and I allow them to return to remain there during the winter.[12]

During the following years and especially after 1849, when the HBC tried in vain to tighten its monopoly by restricting the activities of free merchants, more Métis moved to the Saskatchewan River district.[13] Some sold their furs to the Company, while others sold them on the American market, using as intermediaries such merchants as Narcisse Marion, Antoine Gingras, and Norman Kittson at Red River and St. Paul.[14] In 1850, there were numerous Métis hunters and traders in the English (Churchill) and Saskatchewan River area. The HBC reported:

> [We are] troubled with a strong opposition in the neighbourhood. Escapot [Isidore Dumont], Louis Batoche, Joseph Dauphinais, Emmanuel Champagne, Hyacinthe Parisien, Abraham Bélanger.... Here [at Carlton] have traded a large quantity of provisions and traded 50 horses.[15]

In the 1860s, the *hivernements* (wintering camps) on the South Saskatchewan River began to take on a more permanent character. Prairie Ronde (near present-day Dundurn), led by Charles Trottier, and Petite Ville (across from present-day Fish Creek) led by Gabriel Dumont, were the largest. Several hunters and traders also congregated at smaller winter camps such as Grosse Butte (present-day Humboldt) and St. Paul (close to present-day Carlton).

The first missionaries in Red River, including Fathers Belcourt and Laflèche, wrote detailed accounts of the buffalo hunt.[16] Another contemporary, Alexander Ross, described various aspects of these expeditions.[17] The hunt was subject to a hierarchical paramilitary structure and was governed by precise regulations and controls. The hunters chose ten captains with ten soldiers each. One of the captains, usually known for his skill and prestige, became leader of the expedition. During the years 1840 to 1850, Jean-Baptiste Wilkie and Jean-Baptiste Falcon of St. François-Xavier successively held that position. The caravans from White Horse Plains (St. François-Xavier and Baie St. Paul) and St. Boniface usually met on the Pembina River. The expedition consisted of men, women, children, and a considerable amount of equipment. The caravan was subject to a series of regulations to prevent discord and make sure everyone got a fair share.

There were two big hunts of about two months each: one in June and the other in September. According to a report by Father Laflèche in 1845:

> In mid-June, almost all the Métis with their families and about 800 to 1000 wagons and 400 riders left as a group and headed for the Souris River, a branch of the Assiniboine, while others headed for the Missouri, though they did not usually reach the river. The riders did the hunting proper, and only the women or the Indians who had been hired to dry and wrap the meat were left behind in the carts.[18]

Women played a key role in the bison economy. They were responsible for processing the meat and treating the skins.

From the 1840s on, the caravans had to go further south and southwest. In 1845, Father Laflèche reported: "In Red River, the bison hunt has diminished considerably over the last few years. The settlers have been obliged to go 80 to 100 leagues, and still it often happens that they do not find enough to load up their carts."[19] Natural factors as prairie fires, floods, and snow storms reduced the number of bison. But the systematic harvesting of females, who were preferred for their meat, and of bulls, who were prized for their coats, prevented the herds from reproducing naturally. As a rule, there was also much waste. Much of the meat or the less-tender portions of it were often left behind on the prairie.

> The Red River colony alone destroyed 25 000 of them every year. It takes ten animals to make a load, or a thousand pounds of dried meat.... It is not rare for one family to eat one cow a week.[20]

The expeditions were also exposed to other risks. During the chase, rifles often exploded, and hunters were often crushed by bison. Father Belcourt described one particularly tragic accident:

> Three years ago, another young man wrapped himself inside a steaming hot skin he had just taken from the animal he had killed, when he realized that he would perish. The poor chap had not foreseen that, once the skin had frozen on him, he would be entombed within it, unable ever to get out of it.[21]

In the early 1860s, a strong demand for coats from the United States increased the frequency of winter hunts. This practice precipitated the gradual extinction already underway. An eyewitness account in 1871 showed how serious the situation was:

> The hunters still have (almost) nothing, and the animals are rare and skinny … one can no longer rely on the hunt. From Wood Mountain to the Little Rocky Mountains, we did not even see 3,000 bisons, and it would take at least 15,000 to load up the camp.[22]

During their first years in the South Saskatchewan River region, the hunt was still the main occupation of the Métis who went on yearly expeditions. They had good hunting in 1873 and 1877, interrupted by periods of scarcity and hard times. In 1873, a traveller in the district mentioned the prosperity of several Métis, in particular, Xavier Letendre: "The previous year had been one of plenty, buffalo had once more appeared on the prairies of the Saskatchewan; wolf skins, robes and pemmican had fetched high prices, and Monsieur Batoche was rich and prosperous."[23]

Increasingly aware of the imminent destruction of the bison, the Métis asked the government to introduce controls on the hunt.[24] However, when the North West Territorial Council promulgated a law to that effect in 1877, the Métis of the Cypress Hills stated that they had been put at a disadvantage with respect to the First Nations, who were subject to no restrictions and could also take full and exclusive advantage of the winter season when hunting was most profitable but generally prohibited.[25]

According to Gabriel Dumont, leader of the South Saskatchewan River caravan, the bison had become extinct in the area in 1878.[26] This scarcity pushed up the price of pemmican. It rose from 14 to 25 cents a pound between 1878 and 1880.[27] But few hunters were able to meet the demand. In fact, those who persisted in this occupation had to go north in search of other pelts to eke out their income. According to 60 homestead declarations in Batoche, St. Laurent, and la couli des Tourond (Fish Creek) in 1884 (45 of which reported occupations), no Métis claimed to be living only on the hunt. Most had two occupations: 23 (51.1%) were freighters and farmers, 10 (22.2%) were only farmers, and the other 12 (26.7%) combined various different trades with farming.[28]

Although they often had to spend part of the year up north in the Cumberland House, The Pas, and Lac la Ronge areas, several local Métis were successful trappers during the 1890s and 1900s. The skins of the badger, fox (red and silver), skunk, lynx, muskrat, beaver, wolverine, mink, and marten fetched good prices on the Winnipeg, Montreal, and London markets. These furs, usually sold by auction, enabled Batoche merchants to make considerable profits. At the Winnipeg auction in 1889, Salomon Venne's furs sold for $1,700, and George Fisher's for $3,131.[29] In 1891, Fisher obtained $4,371 for 930 skins, including 300 marten, 102 bear, and 200 muskrat skins.[30] Venne and Fisher even made more profits on the London market than did Hillyard Mitchell of Duck Lake.

From the 1840s on, the freighters between Red River and Fort Edmonton followed a route that crossed the forks of the Gros Ventres (South Saskatchewan River) in the vicinity of Fort Carlton (La Montée). The number of freighters increased during the 1850s and peaked around 1860. Until 1891, freighting was at least a partial source of income for about a third of the population of Batoche, St. Laurent, and St. Louis.[31] The freighters worked either for the Hudson's Bay Company or on contract to local merchants. The main merchants, Xavier Letendre, Salomon Venne, George Fisher Sr., Jean-Baptiste Boyer, and Emmanuel Champagne, hired men to take merchandise to their northern posts and bring back furs. The furs then had to be taken to the major trading centres, particularly Fort Garry (Winnipeg) and St. Paul (Minnesota). This is how several adventurous young men from Quebec, such as Ludger Gareau and Philippe Garnot, came to Batoche.[32] The place was at the centre of a network of trails: the Carlton trail from Winnipeg via Qu'Appelle to the northwest, the Elbow trail from Cypress Hills and Wood Mountain to the south, the Prince Albert and Montreal Lake to the north, and the Cumberland trail to the northeast. In addition, there were local trails linking Batoche with Battleford, Meadow Lake, Green Lake, and Ile à la Crosse, where there were important trading posts. After 1882, when the Canadian Pacific Railway was built, most merchandise arrived by train in Troy, a station located about twenty-five kilometres south of Fort Qu'Appelle. Freighters from Batoche came with their oxen, horses, and carts to load the goods and deliver them to their destination.

Many witnesses testify to the skill of the Métis freighters. According to HBC agent Lawrence Clarke at Fort Carlton: "as carriers for the northern districts, they are a reliable source and as settlement increases in

4.1. George Fisher Sr. (1830–98) merchant of St. François-Xavier (Manitoba), Fort Qu'Appelle and Cypress Hills (Saskatchewan) - Parks Canada, donated by Authur Fisher.

population, so will competition arise amongst them for fuller employment in this, their favourite occupation."[33] The HBC saw the Métis as a plentiful source of cheap labour and therefore easy to exploit, but not only did the posts depend on them for their supplies, but all commercial activity in the area was dependent on them.

Among freighters with a *pied-à-terre* or residence in Batoche during the years 1870 to 1880, there was "Dodet" (Joseph) Parenteau, the Nault brothers (André and Napoléon), "La Moëlle" [Daniel] Gariépy, Norbert Delorme, and Abraham Montour.[34] The latter went regularly to Fort Pitt on his own account or on contract to Xavier Letendre, while André and Napoléon Nault worked mainly for private individuals and went back and forth between Winnipeg and Fort Carlton until 1882, when they settled for good in Batoche. Philippe Gariépy, a local resident since the early 1870s, and Maxime Lépine, who moved west in 1878, owned carts that regularly went to St. Albert and Ile à la Crosse.[35] Louis Goulet of St. Norbert (Manitoba), a freighter who came to Batoche in 1883, recalled in his memoirs:

> I arrived in Troy [Qu'Appelle]. While I got rid of my trade returns [goods received in exchange], I decided to go and look for my brother Roger. He was with André Nault who like my brother had come from Batoche, the trading post of a man named Letendre known as Batoche. They had both come to look for freight for the Batoche and Duck Lake traders. I joined them, at that time met Dolphus Nolin [son of Charles], Michel Dumas (called the Little Rat). I bought another wagon – loaded – and left for Duck Lake. My brother Roger lived four miles south of Batoche at Gabriel Dumont's Crossing. I stayed with my brother Roger while taking freight from Prince Albert to Troy and vice versa. In October 1883, I joined my brother to take freight from Prince Albert to Battle River. I spent the winter with him.[36]

Frédéric St. Germain,[37] travelled regularly between Qu'Appelle, Carlton and Duck Lake during those years, and Patrice Fleury,[38] whose family had been in the West since 1858, freighted goods to Green Lake. Abraham Bélanger and his sons, who had come to the couli des Tourond in 1880, had a big business. The father owned a store in Battleford and travelled regularly to Winnipeg and in Dakota and Montana, thus establishing a trade network between the Métis in that region and the Métis in Saskatchewan.[39] Bélanger and sons also freighted for the North West Mounted Police between 1886 and 1900.

Freighting was a risky economic activity. The rigours of the winter, fluctuating demand, and road accidents often forced a contractor or employee to work at several jobs. Employers usually paid their workers in kind, rather than in cash. The year 1884, for example, was a bad one: the workforce was large, the demand was weak, and the South Saskatchewan River Métis were forced to accept starvation wages. In 1885, the rate was only about three to four dollars per hundred pounds of merchandise.[40]

The years following the 1885 Resistance were particularly harsh:

> Freighting is no longer enough to pull our poor people out of their misery, for many of them hardly earn enough to buy the flour they need for their families. The Métis have tried to obtain freight but the merchants and the Company have lowered the freight rates, now that they can have their merchandise shipped cheaply by the Steamship Company.[41]

The records of the HBC for the Carlton district during the 1890s indicate that the freighters of Batoche, St. Laurent, and Duck Lake continued to ply their trade, but not anywhere, nor at any price. A Duck Lake agent reported:

> I was all through Batoche and St. Laurent yesterday but could not get anybody to take freight for Montreal Lake. I saw Philip Gardepuis [sic], William Boyer, Daniel Charette, Toussaint [Laplante] and others. [Emmanuel] Champagne said he would take some freight but have not yet heard from him.[42]

He added that the independent Métis "were afraid of bulldogs and bad roads."[43]

Freighting remained an important source of livelihood in the 1890s. The Gervais brothers, Norbert Bélanger, Isidore Dumont Jr., Daniel Hamelin, and Edouard Laframboise carried an average of six thousand pounds of merchandise to Qu'Appelle during the summer of

1891.[44] Another group, including Toussaint Lussier, Gabriel Parenteau, Cyrille Lafond, and Corbet Fayant, went regularly to Green Lake.[45]

Freighting to the north continued to be marginally profitable until the turn of the century, which encouraged several young men to migrate seasonally to Carrot River, Fishing Lakes, Jackfish Lake, and other centres. However, mechanization gradually displaced these freighters and forced them into other employment.

MERCHANT TRADING

In 1884, there were six merchants in the village of Batoche. Xavier Letendre's village had expanded rapidly since its foundation some ten years earlier. The small store and modest home he had built in the early 1870s had been replaced by buildings that were "the nicest west of Winnipeg."[46] Letendre's neo-gothic house was valued at $6,000 in 1885.[47] Xavier Letendre and his family lived comfortably. In Batoche, his returns, including furs, provisions, and general merchandise, were estimated to be more than $25,000.[48] His commercial network extended to Fort à la Corne, Stony Creek, Frog Lake, and Fishing Lakes. He hired freighters, some of whom were "family," such as Moïse Parenteau, Châlins Thomas, William Letendre, and Édouard Dumont.[49] From 1884 on, he had clerks in his Batoche, Frog Lake, and Fort à la Corne stores, including his son-in-law Charles-Eugène Boucher, and Philippe Chamberland.[50] Xavier Letendre also employed teams of salesmen. They visited the Cree and bought their furs in exchange for food and manufactured articles. Mr. Batoche managed one of the biggest businesses in the North West informally but effectively: "I never took stock of my goods, I always made my own business. I have no education for such purposes and had to depend on my memory."[51] He had to spend several months each year outside Batoche, either to visit his warehouses or to buy and sell in Winnipeg and sometimes Montreal. His main suppliers were the Hudson's Bay Company, Carscadian and Peck, Thibaudeau Frères of Winnipeg, and Caswell of Qu'Appelle.

Letendre was ambitious and innovative. He had big plans for his village, whose virtues he praised in an account he dictated to Father Fourmond:

4.2. *Batoche merchants in Winnipeg, 1878: standing left to right, Baptiste Boyer, Xavier Letendre; seated, left to right, Alexandre Boyer, George Fisher Jr., William Letendre and François Gingras of St. Joe (now Walhalla), North Dakota – Parks Canada, donated by Beatrice (Boyer) Gervais.*

> Let us come to our future city of Batoche.... [M]y place will become the population centre as well as an important business centre. I will make places available for well-disposed people.... From next year on, we hope to see five or six stores display their wealth to the eyes of the public including a flour mill, sawmill and a forge, establishments for which we feel an urgent need.[52]

Around 1883, he put up a village blacksmith shop, and, in 1884, he sold a lot along the row of stores, called "Batoche Avenue" (lot 47, see maps, chap. 5: Land Claims on the South Saskatchewan River), to Richard Tees of Prince Albert, a farm implements dealer for David Maxwell, Manitoba Dealers and Implement Works. Xavier Letendre acquired a steam-driven threshing machine, which he rented out to farmers, a sign of the prosperity of the community.[53]

Letendre's flourishing business also benefited the St. Antoine de Padoue mission as well as the whole district. He himself received many travellers, bishops, and politicians, including the governor general of Canada. Serving in turn as justice of the peace and president of the school council, he was a man of law and order who supported formal education and training.[54]

Despite heavy losses in 1885, Letendre maintained his businesses. In fact, he even undertook new initiatives. He renovated and redecorated his house in Batoche and opened a new store. He remained the main merchant of the district and planned to open another store in Duck Lake but decided to focus his efforts on his northern posts, which were his most profitable operations.

In 1895 he established a ranch in the Minichinas Hills (present-day Alvena area), about twenty-five kilometres southeast of Batoche, where he raised cattle and horses.

A relative, Jean-Baptiste Boyer, also opened a store at Batoche in 1882.[55] Although Boyer had owned a farm in St. Laurent since 1874, he was primarily a merchant trader. He had been travelling in the West for twenty years, either on his own account or in association with his brother William and his brother-in-law George Fisher Sr. of Fort Ft. Qu'Appelle. His Batoche store stocked a variety of merchandise such as fabrics, blankets, clothes, toilet articles, and canned and dried food for local sale and trade at his stores in Green Lake and Ile à la Crosse.[56] His business was smaller than Letendre's, and his stock was assessed at about $9,000 in

1885.[57] There was only friendly competition between Letendre, Boyer, and their neighbour George Fisher Jr.

The store opened by George Fisher Sr. in the summer of 1883 was run by his sons George Jr. and Joseph. The business was a branch of the Fort Qu'Appelle store but stocked a variety of merchandise, furs, firearms, ammunition, and provisions.[58] Fisher sold household articles retail, and, like Letendre, had a liquor licence. His establishment was both a commercial and a social centre. People came there to smoke a pipe, to have a shot of liquor, and to play cards or billiards.[59] Fisher's main suppliers were Stobart & Sons, the Hudson's Bay Company, and Lyon Mackenzie & Powis. In 1885, the store had $7,000 worth of merchandise and $18,000 worth of furs.[60] During the 1890s, Fisher took turns with Father Moulin and Salomon Venne serving as postmaster, and he also held the position of justice of the peace for the district. He opened a store in Duck Lake in 1892 and kept his Batoche store until around 1905.

Letendre's brother-in-law, Emmanuel Champagne,[61] who had been at Batoche since 1878, had warehouses for merchandise and furs on his lot (44), just north of the village stores. He stored provisions and household articles, which he traded with First Nations. In 1885, he assessed his stock of furs at $10,000 and his merchandise at $4,000.[62]

When Salomon Venne,[63] another prominent trader, opened a store southeast of the village (on lot 55) in 1883, he had already spent over thirty years in the North West as a successful fur trader. His store in Batoche was a relay point for his employees who transported goods from Winnipeg and Qu'Appelle and brought back furs from the North. His sons Alexandre, William, and David were in charge of his posts at Fort à la Corne, Green Lake, Meadow Lake, Canoe Lake, and Ile à la Crosse. Venne's commercial "empire" was comparable to Letendre's both in the number of posts and in turnover.[64] In Batoche, Venne sold groceries, clothing, and hardware. During the 1890s, the store also had a liquor outlet, which served as a post office during certain years. It remained one of the main stores in the district until the departure of Napoléon, the founder's grandson, around 1925. Patrice Parenteau, nephew of Xavier Letendre, also operated a store in the village between 1894 and 1904.[65]

At various times, a few outsiders also opened stores in Batoche. In 1882, the F.G. Baker firm of Prince Albert set up shop on the left bank of the river, at the junction of the Carlton and Prince Albert trails. The Batoche branch was managed by a partner, Harry Walters, and was based almost entirely on barter. The business relied mainly on government contracts for supplying First Nations, including One Arrow First Nation near Batoche. The Walters & Baker store at Batoche hired local freighters Louis Marion, Paul Grézaud, and William Boyer to transport their merchandise. The firm also bought local furs and farm produce, thus providing competition to the Métis merchants. The store suffered heavy losses in 1885, and, even though Walters & Baker were paid compensation, they decided to concentrate their activities in Prince Albert.[66] The partnership was dissolved in 1889, but Fred Baker continued to operate a store in Prince Albert until 1907.

Brothers George and John Kerr[67] also had a store at Batoche in 1884–85. Nicknamed "Little Canada" by the Métis, it was situated next to Venne's. The Kerr brothers were primarily barterers: "We bought everything in their home, such as potatoes, grains of all kinds, horses, cattle, furs, feathers, silk, wool, etc."[68] It was the only firm to provide such a vast outlet for local production.

The store was the first to be seized by the provisional government in March, 1885, on the basis that the Kerr brothers were reporting to the government on Métis activities.[69] A few years later, Pierre Guillemette[70] took it over before opening a store at Fish Creek around 1900.

By 1898, George and William Grant of Duck Lake rented the Letendre store, and, in 1915, Joseph Branconnier bought the firm. He was the last owner of the store, which was destroyed by fire in 1923. Its disappearance marked the end of commercial activity in the old village. The other stores had already been abandoned or moved to the east and southeast, along the road between Gabriel's Crossing and Batoche. Among the new merchants in that area in the 1920s were Gustave Parenteau and Raphaël Boyer.

To sum up, the Métis merchants enjoyed a viable and at times flourishing economy until the turn of the century. To be sure, the great losses and destruction suffered in 1885 caused a major setback. However, several unrelated factors also affected economic growth, such as isolation as regards transportation of local merchandise, a Canadian tariff policy unfavourable to Western economic activity, and the discriminatory attitude of Canadian institutions (governments, companies, banks) towards the "Halfbreed rebels."[71]

4.3. *Batoche and Duck Lake businessmen in front of Massey-Harris office in Duck Lake, 1894: seated, left to right, Charles-Eugène Boucher, Xavier Letendre and W.J. Pozer; standing, left to right, George Fisher Jr., Damase Racette, Gustave Fournier, W.S. Urton, L. St. Louis de Gladiou, Patrice Parenteau and R.S. Mackenzie – University of Saskatchewan Library, C55/2/10.5M.*

THE LATER YEARS

"Before 1885 we were not rich, but we all enjoyed modest comfort"[72]

The armed conflict took place in the midst of an economic and social crisis: low farm output due to disastrous climatic conditions, a shrinking volume of freight, and an expansionist Canadian economy, which isolated the Métis. A prosperous community was suddenly torn apart and destroyed by war. Middleton's soldiers who expected to see a bleak country inhabited by "savages" commented on the prosperity of the community:

> They have a fine settlement, comfortable houses, with plenty of horses and cattle; as compared with other settlements they are well off. The land on which the rebels are located is one of the most fertile and beautiful localities North West of Manitoba ... at Batoche we found some of the nicest houses in the country.[73]

The battle and military defeat caused much destruction. There was general loss and destitution. Emmanuel Champagne reported: "When I was captured, I did not even have a coat, and my wife and children had only what they were wearing."[74] The Letendre children and others ran to the hills northeast of Batoche, where they lived on dog meat.[75] Some elders and ill people died of exposure, and "consumption" and the "flu" assumed devastating proportions in the following years. Sadly, much of the pillaging and destruction was committed after the capitulation of Batoche. Canadian soldiers reported that: "empty houses were ransacked. We captured over forty head of cattle and each man has some loot he intends to keep as a relic: knives, saddles, violins and beadwork."[76] The church bell, "Marie-Antoinette," was also stolen and was taken to Ontario as a war trophy.[77] A friend of merchant George Fisher who came to assess his losses in May, 1885, wrote: "I found all the houses for about three and half miles down burned, the place looked very desolate.... The sight it represents now is pitiful and the people are scattered."[78]

In the aftermath, the government distributed food through the missionaries of the district. The destitute or women whose fathers or husbands were in prison or in exile were forced to accept government relief. Able-bodied men were required to do menial jobs such as cutting firewood in exchange for provisions. After a few months, however, stubborn pride and fear of the government induced the population to refuse charity. Many men were forced to leave the community and find jobs. It took many years for the community to recover.

The South Saskatchewan River Métis communities had its small group of government agents, doctors, insurance agents, notaries, and school teachers. The North West Mounted Police maintained a sub-post in Batoche between 1888 and 1921. There were usually three policemen, who contributed to the local economy and social life. Quite a few people in administrative positions came from the outside and their stay in Batoche was often short. This group received regular salaries and injected at least a little money into an economy limited basically to barter. Among the government officials at the Lands office, there were Louis Schmidt of St. Louis in the Prince Albert office, Jean-Baptiste Boucher Jr. in St. Louis, and Baron Huysmans de Neftal in Duck Lake.[79]

Other government positions included farming instructors at the One Arrow and Beardy First Nations (reserves). They included Michel Dumas, Ferdinand Ladret, Louis Marion, Maxime Lépine Jr., and Charles-Pantaléon Schmidt. Their wives, in particular Mme Marion (Andronique Ross), Mme Lépine (Marguerite Boucher), and Mme Schmidt (Rose-Délima Boucher), were responsible for bookkeeping and teaching First Nations women the three R's and domestic skills. In some instances, they were actually hired by the government along with their husbands, although they were not paid an individual salary. Several Métis men and women who had a high school education (grade ten level at the time) were school teachers. Octave Régnier, Norbert Turcotte, and (John) Letendre taught in local schools during the 1880s and 1890s. Louis Schmidt and George Fisher were justices of the peace at various times, while Father Moulin, Francis Tourond, Raphaël Boyer, and Napoléon and David Venne were postmasters. David Venne was also a notary. Many of these men's wives actually served as postmistress, officially or unofficially. Georgine d'Amours Lenglet, originally from Batoche, became postmistress at Duck Lake upon the retirement of her husband in the 1920s.[80]

The few medical doctors at Batoche were from France and Quebec. Little is known about Dr. Pascal, who was in Batoche in 1902, or about Dr. Gautier de Rues, who arrived in 1895, except that the latter, who was divorced and estranged from the Church, was disliked by Father Moulin. Drs. Bourgeault and Touchet, who came from Quebec became long-time residents of Duck Lake and made calls to neighbouring villages. More important in terms of health care, however, were the traditional healers and midwives.

North West Mounted Police officers at Batoche were generally posted for short periods. Sergeant St. Denis and Inspector Bégin, who remained in the area were well respected in the community.[81] Inspector Huot[82] also befriended local families, but there was less interaction between the Métis and English-speaking officers. The NWMP was less favourably disposed towards First Nations. The confrontation with Almighty-Voice at One Arrow and other incidents suggest that there was some complicity between the police and the Métis in the "control" of First Nations.[83] The police barracks were a source of prestige and employment for the Métis. Philippe Gariépy, David Venne, and Gilbert Breland worked as guides and interpreters, and Charles Laviolette and William Bruce served briefly as policemen. The force also hired carpenters and gave out contracts for supplying wood, hay, oats, barley, and beef.[84] Access to contracts and government positions was limited. Favouritism, nepotism, and patronage governed the choice of candidates, but in 1899, 1891, and 1898, for example, all the surveyors' assistants were local recruits.

Several jobs enabled the Métis to eke out an income from farming or at least to earn their living. Some jobs, like carting field stones to a building site or delivering firewood, were seasonal and not very profitable. The annual deer, duck, and prairie chicken hunts brought in some income but more importantly provided food for the family at little cost. Besides fishing, the Métis also collected senega root, which brought in about 20 to 25 cents a pound in 1894.[85]

The community also had carpenters, ferry operators, and blacksmiths and millers, whose skills were valued by the community. This group included the builder Ludger Gareau, the carpenter Jean Caron, and ferrymen Barthélémi Pilon and Jérôme Racette.

Around 1890, the railway became the biggest source of employment. The construction of the northern line of the Canadian Pacific, the "Qu'Appelle, Longlac and Prince Albert" (between Regina and Prince Albert), caused quite a stir in the community. People pushed for recognition of Batoche's central location and called a meeting to request that the railway pass through their locality.[86] Old rivalries between Duck Lake and

4.4. North West Mounted Police Barracks (former Boyer store and house), Batoche, 1891. Interpreter and scout Napoléon Venne is standing in the centre, arms crossed – Parks Canada, Fort Battleford National Historic Site Collection.

4.5. Road construction gang near Batoche, ca. 1925 – Parks Canada, courtesy of Marguerite (St. Germain) Caron.

Batoche came out into the open. But since Batoche was on the east bank of the South Saskatchewan River and about eighteen kilometres east of the planned route, the authorities preferred to build near the "settlement belt" between the two branches of the South Saskatchewan River, more to the west. As in 1881, when the Canadian Pacific Railway had planned to build a transcontinental route across the parkland near Batoche, the village lost out again in 1890. Railway construction was nevertheless a small economic boon for the Métis. They were hired by contractors Ross, Keith and Madigan & Robinson to cut and transport ties:

> Luke Madigan, tie contractor is getting out ties. He is letting out small contracts at the rate of $7.50 per hundred ... 75 teams and 125 men will be put on. It is said wages will be $26 and board per month for good men. It is expected that a force of 1500 men and teams will be employed to push the completion [of the railroad] to Prince Albert as soon as possible.[87]

Between 1889 and 1893, several Métis from Batoche gathered bison bones between Qu'Appelle and Saskatoon. They put 800 to 1,200 pounds of bones in an ox-cart that brought in $3 a load.[88] This work lasted only a few years, but it paid well because of the strong demand from fertilizer and chemical manufacturers in Chicago and St. Louis.[89] The coming of the railway to Saskatoon led to the creation of a major bone depository. During the Boer War, the Canadian government hired Métis to make pemmican for the troops.

Between 1899 and 1901, the Klondike Gold Rush attracted several young men from the area. Among them were Jean-Baptiste Boucher Jr., Maxime Lépine Jr., and William Fidler. Most returned home after a few years with a few nuggets but little money in their pockets.

One of the biggest merchants and ranchers in the area was Hillyard Mitchell,[90] who sold supplies to Batoche merchants X. Letendre, P. Parenteau, and G. Fisher. He also hired Métis locals as clerks, freighters, cowboys, and labourers for his store and ranch. Mitchell was a generous but demanding employer and his contracts were very detailed. He generally paid his employees wages in merchandise from his store instead of cash. He distrusted Métis workers and regarded them as prone to laziness and unruly behaviour. Ambroise Fisher worked for him for a long time: in 1885, he started as a clerk and interpreter at $25 a month, and he kept

4.6. *Pile of buffalo bones and skulls waiting for shipment in Saskatoon, 1890 – University of Alberta Archives 74169/15/93.*

this position until about 1910.[91] In 1892, "Dodet" Parenteau tamed horses on Mitchell's ranch at the rate of $3 a head. Patrice Fayant mowed and gathered hay there at $1.25 a day in 1893 and $1.25 a ton at the turn of the century. Patrice Fleury also regularly worked for Mitchell. Between 1892 and 1902, he signed contracts for delivering wood "pickets" and "poles." In 1902, he was paid $5 a hundred for cutting and transporting 2,000 pickets.

Another local Métis, Jérôme Ledoux, was hired as a labourer for one year at Mitchell's farm. The contract, including board and room, was $182 a year. He also received a bag of flour, two pounds of tea, and thirty pounds of bacon a month.[92] Métis who worked with their own teams of horses received $2.50 a day. During his term in the Territorial assembly, Mitchell provided construction jobs on roads, bridges, and crossings to his supporters.

Agricultural Activities

The main purpose of the "St. Laurent Settlement," founded in 1871, was to promote farming and the adoption of a more sedentary lifestyle. As the founding elders put it themselves:

> Our children must do like other white men, cultivate the ground or they must live and die like Indians.... The young people cannot not [sic] lead the same lives as their fathers. The country is opening out to the strangers and the Métis must show his white blood and not be crushed in the struggle for existence.[93]

The Métis were aware of the oncoming settler economy and did not want to be left on the fringe like the First Nations who were being forced onto reserves. They were not destitute: "They are far from being poor men, they are rich in horses, and have all, more or less money at their disposal."[94]

The lands the Métis chose in Batoche and St. Laurent were specially adapted to mixed farming. There was plenty of water, wood, and fertile soil – though swampy in some places, especially on the left bank – and a network of trails, as well as other resources:

> The trees, generally aspen, grow in clumps to provide firewood and fence stakes as needed, and beyond those clumps are meadows suitable for ploughing, and lower-lying places yielding hay.... The idea of a waterway 300 yards wide on the average might arouse fear of flooding. But our Saskatchewan [River] is digging itself a bed, putting all the people out of danger.[95]

During the 1870s, farming was seen as way of life complementary to hunting, trading, and freighting. As long as these three activities were profitable, even marginally so, it was possible to make a living. Otherwise, the Métis found themselves in a precarious position. At the time, there was no established agricultural economy in the Canadian West. The only market for farm produce was an unpredictable local one. Farming amounted mainly to growing cereals and animal feed and cultivating a vegetable garden. Bad weather could easily reduce all that labour to nothing. In addition, there was the risk of infestation by insects, rodents, or weeds. In general, the 1870s were good years, the drought of 1876 being an exception.

Few Batoche Métis devoted themselves mainly to grain farming and ten to fifteen acres of cultivated land was the norm by 1884. On the west bank, Abraham Montour cultivated sixteen acres in 1876, and the Bélanger brothers fifteen in 1879. On the east bank, no farm equalled Xavier Letendre's. Before 1880, his farm already covered fifteen acres on lot 47 and ten acres on lot 48. In St. Laurent, Gilbert Breland, Jean-Baptiste, and William Boyer were dedicated farmers. Similarly, in the Fish Creek area, Gabriel Dumont, Charles Carrière, and Isidore Villeneuve cultivated an average of twelve acres in 1881. Since most Métis who took up some land at the time earned their living mainly by other means, they were often absent from their farms (up to five months a year) and were able to devote only a limited amount of time to ploughing and raising crops. Among the part-time farmers were Elzéar Parisien, Baptiste Parenteau, Emmanuel Champagne, and Corbet Gervais, each of whom cultivated about five acres.[96]

The St. Laurent de Grandin mission served as a model farm during those years. Father Fourmond and a few hired hands cultivated the mission lands; they had several animals and a big garden, which fed almost the entire staff. Others imitated it, especially the elders. The mission chronicle of 1879 recorded that:

> Isidore Dumont Sr. harvested 190 bushels of wheat and thanks to the hard work and care of his wife, his garden is more beautiful every year and the richest one in the country. Joseph Ouellette, another patriarchal figure, already four of his children have become the most prosperous farmers, and one of them has the most beautiful herd of cattle in the parish.[97]

If most Métis had small fields, they used much of their land as pasture for horses, horned animals, milk cows, pigs, and even sheep. The 1870s were the transitional years between two lifestyles, one essentially migratory and the other increasingly sedentary. Father André summed up the economic activity of those years as follows:

> While travelling on the prairie ... or to Red River to sell their pelts and make their purchases, the true colonists gradually increase their ploughed fields.... Moïse Ouellette has ploughed an immense area and sown some thirty bushels of barley on it, without counting other kinds of grain.[98]

The 1880s were promising years. According to sixty homestead applications in 1884, 64 per cent of the Métis were already engaged in activities related to farming in 1884. The Stobart and Eden Company near Duck Lake put up a flour mill, which saved the Métis a long trip to Prince Albert. In their petitions to the government,[99] the Métis had asked several times for ploughing implements and seed grain. They never succeeded in convincing the authorities that they needed help and training to make the change to a farming economy. In general, the 1880s were difficult. Climatic conditions went from extreme drought to hailstorms and early frosts. The harvest was fairly good in 1881 and still better in 1882. But 1884 was particularly difficult, and there was general misery throughout the area. Father Fourmond nevertheless managed to harvest 300 barrels of potatoes, 50 barrels or bushels of turnips, two bushels of carrots, and 50 cauliflowers.[100]

About twenty families arrived from Manitoba in 1882–83, and all the lots on the east bank of the South Saskatchewan River were now occupied. According to the owners' homestead declarations in 1884, the cultivated portion averaged only about ten acres on a 160- to 190-acre lot.[101] This area was small for a 160- to 195-acre lot, but enough for domestic consumption. The Kerr Brothers of Batoche offered producers the following prices in 1885: *wheat*, $1.75 per bushel; *barley*, $1.25; and *potatoes* $1.[102] Almost all farmers also raised cattle. A herd of twenty to thirty head was not uncommon, and some, like Xavier Letendre, Emmanuel Champagne, Salomon Venne, and George Fisher, had more than fifty animals.[103] In 1884, Télesphore Demers, a prosperous cattle-breeder from Montana, established a ranch on his brother-in-law Philippe Garnot's land. He kept more than a hundred horses on it, including two Percherons worth $250 each, and set up a local cattle-breeding business.[104]

Few of the farms on the west bank were cultivated. The soil was not suitable for farming, being generally sandy and rocky, especially near the river. The difficulties the Métis had were similar to those encountered by Eurocanadians: "Many are not well enough equipped with draught animals and especially farming implements, and they have no experience at all."[105] Families relied heavily on garden produce, especially potatoes, onions, and carrots, to supplement a diet consisting essentially of meat and bannock. Some also planted rhubarb, and some even tried to cultivate sugar maple, though with little success. Gathering wild fruit was a seasonal ritual, and the preparation of several of their dishes depended on it. The Sisters in St. Laurent reported that wild fruit saved the community, following the bad harvest of 1884:

> A lot of fruit was found at Eagle Creek. Métis to the number of a hundred went together in a band to gather the fruit (strawberries, raspberries, cranberries, stone fruit, currants and gooseberries). They found four miles of country absolutely black with the wild pear [saskatoon berries].... Some gathered as much as sixty bushels each and each bushel would sell as much as $3.[106]

The years following the 1885 Resistance were particularly difficult for farmers. The fields were not seeded in the spring of 1885 so there was no harvest. In July 1886 a hailstorm destroyed the few fields under cultivation. There was a moment of respite in 1887 after the first real harvest in four years. The following yields were reported in the Saskatchewan district: *wheat*, 25 bushels an acre on 831 acres; *barley*, 30 bushels an acre on 1,559 acres; *oats*, 35 bushels an acre on 1,602 acres.[107]

But the drought returned in 1888 and 1889. From 1886 on, the government came to the aid of the neediest by supplying them with seed grain. Though seemingly beneficial, the program carried several restrictions. After the harvest, the farmer had to return twice the amount of seed he had received, and his farm was mortgaged. Several Métis either hesitated or declined to take advantage of the program; they were especially afraid of the consequences of farm liens. The population of Batoche raised their objection to this mortgage clause in their petitions of 1886 and 1888 and demanded its removal.[108] The government denied their request, assuring the Métis that they would be treated with the greatest indulgence and compassion if, as a result of a bad harvest, they should be unable to meet their payments.[109] The other requests – for draught animals and ploughing implements (to be financed by a system of loans) – were also rejected on the ground that the Métis did not have special status and had to look out for themselves. However, in hindsight such assistance would have encouraged the farmers and possibly prevented many from abandoning their lands or leaving the community. For example, Cléophas Champagne and Daniel Gariépy left their lands without having obtained title because they were unable to meet their financial obligations. Among those who took some land at the turn of the century, Louis Letendre Jr. and Pierre Caron found themselves forced to abandon theirs.[110] Others managed eventually to pay off their debts. Jean Caron Sr., who borrowed seed grain on several occasions between 1886 and 1896, paid his debt and obtained title to his property in 1903. Another farmer, Jean-Baptiste Gervais, was grappling with similar difficulties, but died before he was able to meet his obligations, and it was not until 1930 that his son Moïse managed to free the family property of debts. All in all, few Métis accepted seed grain or took social assistance during the 1880s and 1890s. They were an independent and wary people. In the words of a local North West Mounted Police officer: "They have not asked for seed grain and very few have availed themselves of the offer of work made by me."[111]

In spite of all the difficulties, most Métis were engaged in some type of farming between 1885 and 1925. Out of 135 homestead applications during this period, 108 (80%) declared that they were working in occupations related to farming. Of this number, 85 (63%) identified themselves specifically as farmers. But the markets for farm produce were still limited and largely regional. For example, most grain (or flour) was shipped north in exchange for furs. Prices remained low. In 1890, the price of hay was

4.7. *Baptiste Larocque's steam threshing outfit at Duck Lake in 1908 – Saskatchewan Archives Board, R-A8248(1).*

only $5 a load.[112] In the 1890s the Métis were making the transition to farming but the lifestyle did not appeal to all. They did not like to be tied down to the land. According to a policeman stationed at Batoche:

> Called at some local farms and found them in moderately good circumstances but a quantity of grain was still standing in the fields ... cattle and horses in good health ... most of the people are busy hauling grain to the grist mill at Duck Lake but if the Half-breeds would think more of farming and less of sport they would be better off. The white settlers seem to prosper fairly well but the majority of Half-breeds are always behind.[113]

There were three population movements within the farming community at Batoche. First, several young Métis bought some land, thanks to scrips granted to children born between 1870 and 1885.[114] Several sons inherited lands from their fathers or purchased lots that had been abandoned in 1885. Finally, families from Manitoba came to join their relatives, and a number of French and Belgian immigrants took up lands on the west bank of the river. In the immediate vicinity of the village (lots 1 to 71 on the east bank and 1 to 24 on the west bank of township 43-1-3), about fifteen properties were claimed between 1895 and 1913. Of the fourteen new properties on the west bank, eleven were taken by Métis.[115] Louis Letendre's sons, Baptiste, Joseph, Eugène, and Louis Jr., each claimed some land between 1904 and 1910. Their farms were well-suited for raising cattle. In 1910, Baptiste Letendre had a herd of twelve head, plus five horses and ten pigs. He also cultivated thirty acres of his property, which was better than average for the area.[116] Some of his neighbours, including Joseph and Jean Pilon, had a lot of difficulty because their lands were swampy and unsuitable for cultivation. On the east bank, where the soil was more fertile, the young farmers were more successful in their efforts. But even there, the number of acres under cultivation rarely exceeded twenty-five. The emphasis was on cattle, the average being twenty-five to thirty head.[117]

The situation was similar in St. Louis. Jean-Baptiste Boucher and his sons Baptiste and Salomon took a second homestead. At the turn of the century, the acreage under cultivation in St. Louis averaged twenty-five, but some, like the Boucher family, Maxime Lépine Jr., and Charles Ferguson, cultivated between thirty and fifty acres.[118] Several people had herds of fifteen or more cattle. In St. Laurent, conditions were generally poorer, but between 1895 and 1910, Moïse Ouellette had an average of fifty acres under cultivation, whereas the average for the area was only fifteen. There was good farmland in the vicinity of Fish Creek, but that area was the first to be abandoned by the Métis under pressure from immigrants. Two of these, Abraham Bélanger and Daniel Charette, had thirty acres under cultivation, hay fields and pastures, and a large herd of horses and cattle in the early 1890s.[119] They freighted goods to Battleford and Jackfish Lake, respectively, and relocated to those communities, where they became big ranchers.

The years 1886 to 1900 were years of change in the Métis communities along the South Saskatchewan River. Families wanting to remain in the area tended to regroup, while others left. This tended to consolidate farms and manpower. The Fidler and Carrière families, who had settled south of Gabriel's Crossing during the 1880s, moved north, closer to their relatives in Vandal (between Gabriel's Crossing and Batoche). In 1886,

Isidore Dumas of St. Louis took a second homestead, lot 69, in Batoche. His brother-in-law Joseph Ladéroute (married to Geneviève Dumas), who was still in Manitoba, joined him in 1901 and claimed lot 56. Louis Letendre, husband of Angélique Dumas, had been living nearby, on lot 59, since 1886. Finally, in 1896, Mme Josephte Tourond[120] from la couli des Tourond took a second homestead on lot 58 in Batoche. Her daughter and her son-in-law Raphaël Boyer joined her on the neighbouring farm, where they also opened a general store around 1915. Mme Tourond was an enterprising rancher and farmer. She had a herd of forty head in 1896, and her neighbouring relatives had almost as many.[121] One of her neighbours at the coulee, Marie Vandal (née Primeau), also took a homestead as the widow of an original homesteader. She received patent to her land in 1906, and it was passed on to family other members, who were still on the land in the early 1930s. Another enterprising matriarch, Marguerite Caron (née Dumas) took up a second homestead in the Fish Creek area after the death of her husband, Jean Caron, in 1905. Her youngest son, Albert, followed suit in 1913. Mme Caron was trying to provide her large family with more land to raise cattle. Emmanuel Champagne of Batoche actually transferred one of his lots to his wife, Marie Letendre, which she used to graze her herd of cattle.

Some families in the area decided to go into cattle and horse ranching on a larger scale. In 1890, Salomon Venne and his sons, Napoléon, David, and Bruno, set up a ranch near the present village of Wakaw, about twenty kilometres southeast of Batoche. The family kept its main residence and store in Batoche but diversified its farming and business activities. Another major operation from 1892 on was Xavier Letendre's ranch near Alvena: Letendre had more than two hundred head of cattle and some thirty horses.[122] His son-in-law Charles-Eugène Boucher, who lived near Gabriel's Crossing, also kept prize herds, which he brought from Montana. Other prospective ranchers headed for the open grasslands of southeastern Alberta. Among them were Ludger Gareau, Norbert Delorme, and Corbet Gervais. Calixte Lafontaine and Édouard Dumont, who had sought refuge across the border in 1885 were able to obtain custom exemptions on the import of live animals and returned with their herds.[123] Quite a few local ranchers either wintered further north with their herds or rented pastures in the vicinity.

The Métis of the region had petitioned the government for the establishment of an industrial school to provide technical training in 1888–90.

The school, subsidized by the government, would have at its disposal modern farming implements, enabling the Métis to familiarize themselves with new techniques. It is difficult to judge whether such a school would have benefited the Métis. In retrospect, industrial schools did not provide farming skills or opportunities to the Cree who attended the school at Duck Lake.[124] On the other hand, the Métis at Batoche were interested in mechanized farming and trades, and it is possible that, if they had had access and control of such institutions, they would have benefited from the training. Both the government and the clergy were against the establishment of a Métis industrial school.[125] As a result, many felt that they had been discriminated against or were the worse off: "The Indians had tools because the government had given them some. The settlers had enough money, or more than enough, to buy land and implements, but the Métis had nothing."[126]

A quantitative analysis of the homestead files for the South Saskatchewan district illustrates the nature and extent of Métis agricultural activities from 1884 until about 1925 (see Appendix 3). They were persistent and innovative, which disputes the argument that they were unsuited to farming. Although the results were modest, the Métis had cultivated their lands since the 1870s.

According to 58 declarations in 1884, 28 individuals had cleared 1–12 acres, 9 had cleared 13–21, while 4 had cleared more than 21 (see Table 1).

Table 1. Number of acres under cultivation from date of settlement to date of declaration, according to the Métis homestead files in 1884 (Appendix 3: codes 1, 2)

Acres	Farmers	
	Number	Per cent
0	17	29.3
1–3	7	12.1
4–6	7	12.1
7–9	7	12.1
10–12	7	12.1
13–15	3	5.1
16–18	2	3.4
19–21	4	6.9
over 21	4	6.9
Total	58	100.0

Missing cases: 2.

After 1885, the gap between Métis and Eurocanadian farmers was not as wide as some have supposed. According to six categories of declarations, 101 out of 131 (77%) of the Métis and 19 out 28 (67.6%) of the Eurocanadians took from zero to three years to clear their lands. On the other hand, none of the 28 Eurocanadians took more than nine years, whereas 7 Métis took from seven to twenty-seven years.

The Métis cultivated a little less land than their French Canadian, French, and Ukrainian neighbours. But if 17 (28.8%) of the Métis did not cultivate their lands in 1884, after that date, 88 (56.8%) cultivated between 16 and 30 acres, and 26 (16.8%) between 31 and 60 acres. There are also more differences between the Métis themselves than between Eurocanadians (see Tables 2 and 3).

Table 2. Number of acres under cultivation at time of declaration, for all Métis applications in 1884 (Appendix 3: codes 1, 2).

Acres	Farmers	
	Number	Per cent
0	17	28.8
1–15	32	54.2
16–30	9	15.3
31–35	1	1.7
over 35	–	–
Total	59	100.0

Missing cases: 1.
Note: The only declaration by a non-Métis in 1884 is for a farm of 1–15 acres.

Table 3. Number of acres under cultivation by ethnic group, for all registrations after 1884 and until about 1925 (Appendix 3: codes 3, 4, 5, 6).

Acres	Farmers			
	Métis	Non-Métis	Number	Per cent
0	2	1	3	1.6
1–15	38	3	41	21.7
16–30	88	18	106	56.1
31–45	22	11	33	17.5
46–60	4	1	5	2.6
over 60	1	–	1	0.5
Total	155	34	189	
Per cent	82.0	18.0		100.0

Missing cases: 3.

Until about 1915, the number of acres under cultivation at the time of application for title to the property was from 16 to 30 acres for the two groups, Métis and non-Métis. But after 1915, the non-Métis gradually gained over the Métis (see Table 4). These figures support the argument, during their first decades as farmers, the Métis were as "successful" as Eurocanadians.

Table 4. Acres under cultivation at the time of applying for title (Appendix 3: codes 4 and 5)

(a) Métis

Acres	Before 1885 to 1897	1898 to 1915	1916 to 1933	Farmers Number	Per cent
0	–	–	1	1	0.7
1–15	20	14	3	37	27.4
16–30	17	45	11	73	54.1
31–45	1	14	5	20	14.8
46–60	–	1	2	3	2.2
over 60	–	1	–	1	0.9
Total	38	75	22	135	100.0

Missing data: 1 case.

(b) Non-Métis

Acres	Before 1885 to 1897	1898 to 1915	1916 to 1933	Farmers Number	Per cent
1–15	–	1	1	2	6.5
16–30	2	11	3	16	51.6
31–45	–	8	3	11	35.5
46–60	–	1	–	1	3.2
over 60	–	–	–	–	–
Total	3	21	7	31	100.0

Missing cases: 1.

The Métis also took more time to cultivate their lands or to meet official requirements (30 acres during the three years between registration and application for title): 42.4 per cent of the Métis took more than seven years and some even over twenty-five years. On the other hand, 50 per cent of the non-Métis obtained their titles after six years (see Table 5).

Table 5. Number of years of cultivation between date of registration after 1884 and date of obtaining title (Appendix 3: codes 4 and 5).

(a) Métis

	Farmers	
Years	Number	Per cent
0	1	1.0
1–3	32	29.6
4–6	29	27.0
7–9	17	15.7
10–12	6	5.5
13–15	5	4.6
16–18	3	2.8
19–21	5	4.6
22–24	2	1.8
over 25	8	7.4
Total	108	100.0

Missing data: 28 cases.

(b) Non-Métis

	Farmers	
Years	Number	Per cent
0	1	3.3
1–3	8	26.7
4–6	15	50.0
7–9	6	20.0
over 10	–	–
Total	30	100.0

Missing cases: 2.

The Saskatchewan Métis were stock farmers rather than grain farmers. Between 1885 and 1925 or so, they had an average of five to ten head of cattle and one to five horses. However, the number of animals reported probably does not reflect the real situation, for most of their cattle were destroyed in 1885. At that time, some moved temporarily to other areas or

Table 6. Head of cattle and horses declared by the Métis after 1884 (Appendix 3: codes 3, 4, 5).

(a) Cattle	Respondents	Per cent
0	21	16.3
1–5	30	23.3
6–10	34	26.4
11–15	19	14.7
16–20	13	10.1
21–25	4	3.1
26–30	2	1.6
31–35	1	0.8
46–50	1	0.8
51–55	2	1.6
over 55	2	1.6
Total	129	100.0

Missing cases: 12.

(b) Horses	Respondents	Per cent
0	11	8.5
1–5	13	10.0
6–10	95	73.1
11–15	5	3.8
16–20	2	1.5
21–25	2	1.5
26–30	1	0.8
31–35	1	0.8
over 35	–	–
Total	130	100.0

Missing cases: 11.

were forced to sell their herds. It was not until the 1890s that cattle-raising resumed in full force in the area (see Table 6).

The inherent difficulties in farming before the First World War – particularly the lack of frost-resistant seed grain, the presence of such diseases as blight, and ignorance of such farming techniques as crop rotation, fertilization, and mulching – meant the Métis managed to survive but not to prosper. Quite a few of them were therefore forced into other jobs to supplement their income.

The method of cultivation used in the Batoche area was a traditional one. The fields were ploughed in narrow strips separated from one another by deep furrows. Each field was usually bordered on one side by a deep ditch and enclosed by a fence made of wooden stakes. In 1910, the farm equipment used by the Métis was still essentially non-mechanical, or oxen, plough, and scythe. Threshing machines and harvesters were rare.

During the 1880s and 1890s, farming was closely associated with the northern fur trade. In the absence of world markets, grain was often taken to the northern posts by freighters and traders. It was also used as a means of exchange for manufactured goods. On the whole, any agricultural activity was limited in scope and relatively unprofitable. A resident of Duck Lake in the 1920s recalled the farming situation in the following terms:

> Not much value was attached to land in terms of farming value, by both Métis and whites. Twenty-five acres was a big farm. There was wheat, oats and a little barley. But all we could do with it, was to take it to the mill and grind what we needed. The rest we fed to the chickens. The Métis, they preferred other things, a few fish, a few furs. But they were successful with ponies. Farming was too big a gamble.[127]

Impact of Newcomers

The 1890s marked the arrival of settlers into the region. French and French Canadians began arriving in Duck Lake and Bellevue area, while Mennonites, Ukrainians, and Poles settled in the Rosthern and Fish Creek. This immigration created apprehension among the Métis. They were afraid of the favouritism generally shown to Eurocanadians by the government and church. In general, immigration tended to push away the Métis who, because they felt threatened and vulnerable, tried to consolidate their position by settling elsewhere. In 1893, Father Moulin reported "that some of them want to leave the place."[128] Between 1890 and 1915, there was a general exodus from Fish Creek. Some of these departures were temporary or people moved back and forth trying to make a living in various communities, but for many it was a permanent relocation.

Most of the families who left the area after the military defeat of 1885 took refuge in the United States, particularly in North Dakota and Montana. After some time, many exiled families returned to Canada but not necessarily to Batoche. Some went back and forth between Lewistown, Selby Junction (Hill), and Kalispell in Montana and the area around Medicine Hat, Lethbridge, and Pincher Creek in Alberta. In the 1890s, the Montana residents included Ambroise Dumont and his son in Malthy; Pierre Ouellette, his wife Marguerite Gingras, and their family in Lewistown; Alexandre Venne in Sweet Grass; and Urbain "Pezzan" Delorme Jr. in Kalispell. In 1900, François Champagne, son of Ambroise, was in Havre, while Charles-Eugène Boucher, the former representative of Batoche, stayed in the Musselshell (Coquille) River area from 1898 to 1908. Afterwards he returned to St. Louis. In 1898, Patrice Fleury Jr. was living near Helena, while Abraham Montour and Isidore "Wabash" Parenteau were in Hill. Patrice Fleury Jr. returned to St. Laurent around 1905, while Montour and Parenteau settled in the vicinity of Medicine Hat. Other families went to live in the vicinity of Belcourt, Walhalla, and Dunseith in North Dakota. They included Jean Desmarais and his family between 1885 and 1887, as well as Napoléon Nault and Michel Dumas around 1885 to 1888. Afterwards, Desmarais and Nault headed for Medicine Hat, while Dumas moved to Ebb and Flow on Lake Manitoba. Finally, in 1900, Napoléon Nault and his family were in Dunseith (North Dakota), his brother André Jr. in St. Vital (Manitoba), while another brother, Élie, went to the Battleford area in Saskatchewan. Roger Vandal of Fish Creek rejoined his relatives in St. Jean-Baptiste (Manitoba).

The families who left the South Saskatchewan River district for the long term were motivated by economic and social factors. There was a great demand for young cowboys to train and ride horses on southern Alberta ranches. Those who went there, included Xavier Pagé, Athanase Falcon, Joseph Dumas, Dodet Parenteau, Frédéric St. Germain, and Théophile Caron. They all eventually returned to the Batoche area. Cuthbert Gervais, Ludger Gareau, Norbert Delorme, and Jean-Baptiste Fidler settled down for good at Pincher Creek, where they established ranches.

A larger number of families headed north. The North was especially attractive to freighters, fur traders, fishermen, trappers, and interpreters. There was also open range land for cattle. The Battleford area, including Jackfish Lake and Meota, received the largest number of South Saskatchewan River expatriates. The following families relocated there by the mid-1890s: Elie Nault (Marie-Anne Charette), Baptiste Boyer Jr. (Virginie Nolin), Abraham Bélanger Sr. (Marie-Anne Versailles), Norbert Sansregret (Irène Monet), William Sauvé (Marie-Rose Sansregret), William Letendre (Mélanie Fayant); Jules Marion (Véronique Boucher), François Fidler (Josephte Laplante), Joseph "Dodet" Parenteau (Julie Houle), Isidore Dumont Jr. (Marie Cayen), Daniel Charette (Marie-Anne Bélanger), George Ness (Élise Delorme), and William Venne (Florence Mannix). Bachelor Napoléon Venne also lived there for some time before returning to Batoche.

Baptiste Boyer Jr. first settled further north at Onion Lake and William Venne at Meadow Lake and Green Lake. Other families went to Aldina, Leask, and Marcelin. They were: Philippe Garnot (Florestine Arcand), Magloire Ledoux (Élise Parenteau), Alexandre Venne (Aldina Lalonde), Jonas Moreau (Caroline Desjarlais), Gilbert Breland (Émilie Boyer), and Chrysostome Boyer (Alexandrine Ouellette). Finally, many families headed for the Carrot River district northeast of Batoche. This area included Crooked Lake, Kinistino, Birch Hills, and Crystal Springs. Frédéric Rocheleau (Françoise Dubois) and Azarie Pilon (Virginie Letendre) went to Crystal Springs; Maxime Dubois (Pélagie Parenteau Carrière) settled in Kinistino, while Albert Marion (Sara Boucher) and Ambroise Dubois (Angélique Caron) settled in Bonne Madone. Another group, consisting mainly of the family of Modeste McGillis and Isabelle Poitras, headed for Willow Bunch, where they had relatives.[129]

These families regularly visited their relatives on the South Saskatchewan River. Some came back to die and be buried in the little cemetery on the hill. Their descendants always claimed that, while they were pushed out by newcomers and racism, Batoche, "the promised land," always remained home in their hearts.[130]

5

Land Claims on the South Saskatchewan River

"[Their] birth-right was sold for a mess of potage."

CUSTOMARY LANDHOLDING AND THE MANITOBA PRECEDENT

The Aboriginal peoples of North America, although involved in intertribal conflicts over hunting and camping territory, did not pursue a tradition of owning land individually or permanently. The arrival of the European in the seventeenth century gradually challenged and eventually encroached upon Aboriginal communal and migratory patterns of land tenure. The newcomers grouped in settlements and, as they became more numerous, demanded more land. Initially welcomed by the Indians (First Nations) to share the land, Europeans soon began to displace them by force. According to René Fumoleau:

> The Indians were soon regarded as an embarrassment, since what was being taken belonged to them. Depending on time and place, different methods of handling the Indians were tried. Often they were treated benevolently, sometimes

enslaved, frequently massacred, occasionally annihilated, or systematically assimilated as individuals or tribes. When all else failed they were banished into the hinterland to await the next advance of civilization.[1]

During the French colonial period (ca. 1608–1763), the right of indigenous peoples to their ancestral lands was vested in the "benevolent power of the sovereign." The principle of Aboriginal land rights was reaffirmed by the British in the Proclamation of 1763, which also set aside "western lands" as a "reserve" for First Nations. The British system was adopted by the Canadian government in 1867, but the conflicting concepts of European land ownership and Aboriginal landholding remained. The treaties and land concessions, which were negotiated in Western Canada beginning in 1871, were attempts to extinguish Aboriginal land rights.[2] Although in these agreements the First Nations were the losers, treaties provided a measure of protection against unofficial encroachment and acknowledged the existence of Aboriginal rights.[3]

The rights of the Métis as an indigenous people of the North West were not acknowledged by the colonial authorities: the Hudson's Bay Company and the Canadian government until the Provisional Government of Red River secured some guarantees in 1869–70. The Manitoba Act recognized the principle of Métis land rights by setting aside 1.4 million acres (566,560 hectares) for their use. The Métis were excluded, however, from the federal Indian Act of 1876, which provided for various fishing and hunting rights as well as social and economic benefits. Treaty No. 3 (North West Angle) in 1873 was the first to recognize that both First Nations (Ojibwe) and Métis of the region had inherent land rights. But the commissioners also stipulated that only those Métis who lived with or as "Indians" and did not occupy lands like Eurocanadians could benefit from treaty provisions. This principle was reiterated by Lieutenant-Governor Morris during the negotiations for Treaty No. 6 at Fort Carlton in the Saskatchewan district in 1876.[4] Notwithstanding the fact that many Métis acted as interpreters and brokers during treaty negotiations, few wished to identify themselves as Indians in order to benefit from the treaty.

The Métis of the North West claimed their rights by virtue of their Aboriginal parentage and early occupancy. They had begun to use or occupy lands along the Red and Assiniboine rivers around 1800.[5] Their presence in the area, intermittent at the beginning, increased after the establishment of the mission of St. Boniface in 1818. Most Métis only wintered on their farms, which comprised a vegetable garden, some cattle, a field of oats and hay, and perhaps a small wheat field. Cultivation, however, did not really expand until around 1850s. The Métis occupied riverlots an average of six to twelve chains wide and up to two miles deep. This custom had been brought to Red River and other western settlements by their French Canadian fathers or forefathers. There were also other distinctive landholding customs. The land at the rear of their farms, known as "the outer two miles" (*bouts de terres*), was reserved for hay and woodlots. In the case of small lots known as *emplacements*, in the parish of St. Boniface, some common property or *la commune*[6] was reserved for the inhabitants.

These customs as well as the Métis' flexible approach to individual land ownership and exchanges were not respected by newcomers. The Métis and the French Canadians who took up lands informally "according to the custom of the country," or without registration or title, were identified as squatters. When the Hudson's Bay Company conducted a survey of property in the Red River Settlement in 1836–38 and proceeded to make an inventory of all lands granted, sold, or exchanged, it encountered strong resistance on the part of the Métis and found it impossible to resolve the situation.[7] Contemporary accounts suggest that the Métis informed Company officials of their land transactions only when it was necessary to establish a claim to obtain collateral. There was a general mistrust of Company regulations and a conviction by the Métis that the land was theirs as original occupants. Concurrently, Company surveys and administration of lands in the first years of the Settlement were sporadic and inefficient. The result was an incomplete and often inaccurate record of land occupation and exchange, as illustrated in Register "B."[8] Father Belcourt, an ardent defender of Métis rights, described the HBC landholding system as utter confusion or a *galimathias*, in 1842:

> The counsel for the defence [in the land case pleaded] got the upper hand. It is a tacit admission of their [Hudson's Bay Company] helplessness since those who are on the land without contracts are masters just as those to whom they were given (the bourgeois) [*sic*]. It is an admirable hullabaloo [galimathias] in the holding of land: those who were well enough off to pay for their land before leaving the service possessed these lands against their better judgment. When, upon seeing them, they

did not find them to their liking, it was in fact their fault, since they purchased them without seeing them, blindfolded. Those who, more astute, wanted to see the land before purchasing, arrived at Red River, paid an old settler for his house, his finished stable, this old settler would give up his place and go get another piece of land; sometimes they spoke about it, sometimes they said nothing; my man went about his business seeding and harvesting. Some have a small unwitnessed note from the governor, others have old papers from Lord Selkirk. All of them, just as all those who have no documents, saw the lines of their lands drawn several times: some saw their fields cut crosswise, other were dumbfounded to suddenly see their house in the field given to their neighbour.[9]

Métis lands in Red River extended southward along the Red River to St. Boniface, St. Vital, and St. Norbert, and westward from the forks of the Red and Assiniboine rivers to the White Horse Plain (St. François-Xavier). Until the 1860s, there was no urgent need to register these riverlots or occupy them year-round. By then though, the increasing presence of newcomers in the Settlement alarmed the Métis, and they were increasingly sensitive to Canadian government claims to the lands of the North West (present-day Manitoba, Saskatchewan, and Alberta). In 1869, the HBC, by virtue of its colonial charter of 1670, negotiated the sale of the territory and all its lands to the Government of Canada. Both parties showed little or no concern for indigenous rights. As a result, the Métis protested and negotiated the terms of the Manitoba Act, which formally recognized their custom of landholding.

Section 31 of the Manitoba Act (1870) set aside 1.4 million acres for the Métis, and Section 32 guaranteed them and all other occupants possession of the lands they occupied. In spite of these provisions, the numerous changes made to these sections of the Act between 1872 and 1880 greatly reduced these rights.[10] For example, in 1873, an amendment excluded heads of family from a share in the land. The following year, another amendment restored this right but in the form of scrip. Scrip was a certificate worth $80, $160, and $240; it was redeemable in land, issued by the federal government. Scrip was granted to the Métis of Manitoba, and later of the (pre-1905) North West Territories between 1876 and 1901, as a means of extinguishing their Aboriginal rights. Conditions of the complex and confusing system varied over the years; at the outset of 1871, scrip could only be exchanged for land in the name of and for the bearer. It was initially granted only to the children of the heads of families, but money scrip was later issued to heads of families and as part of a Supplementary Issue. The 1899–1900 issue in the North West Territories was redeemable in land or money.

Despite some legislation established to protect the rights of Métis children, most of their claims passed into the hands of speculators through powers of attorney or assignments.[11] Inquiries have revealed that few Métis children ended up exchanging their scrip for land and fewer in obtaining title to it.[12] Heads of families were not any more successful. The land offered was not divided into riverlots and assignment was determined by lottery. Notwithstanding the disadvantages and, in many cases, the impossibility of meeting increasingly strict government requirements regarding occupancy improvements, most Métis hastened to register their claims allowed under Section 32 in 1873 and after. Recent research has indicated that the land granted to Métis in Manitoba between 1876 and 1887 amounted to less than 600,000 acres.[13] The plunder was not attributed solely to the federal government and its collusion with real estate agencies. Manitoba laws and judicial illegalities after 1878 contributed as much as federal policy to the creation of an intolerable situation and provoked a massive relocation.[14] While the Métis constituted the majority of Manitoba's population in 1871, numbering about 10,000, by 1885 they represented about 7 per cent.[15] The vast majority had headed northwest to the district of Saskatchewan.

Surveys and Homestead Entries between 1878 and 1885 (See Appendix 3)

The Métis began to leave Manitoba soon after the debacle of the 1870s. Most of the people were already familiar with the Assiniboia or Saskatchewan districts and had claimed riverlots informally demarcated according to local custom at places such as Batoche, Willow-Bunch, and Qu'Appelle. Land claims along the South Saskatchewan River extended along both banks between Gabriel's (Dumont's) Crossing to the south, passing through Batoche's Crossing, St. Laurent de Grandin, and as far as Gardepuis' (Philippe Gariépy's) Crossing, an area of about forty kilometres.

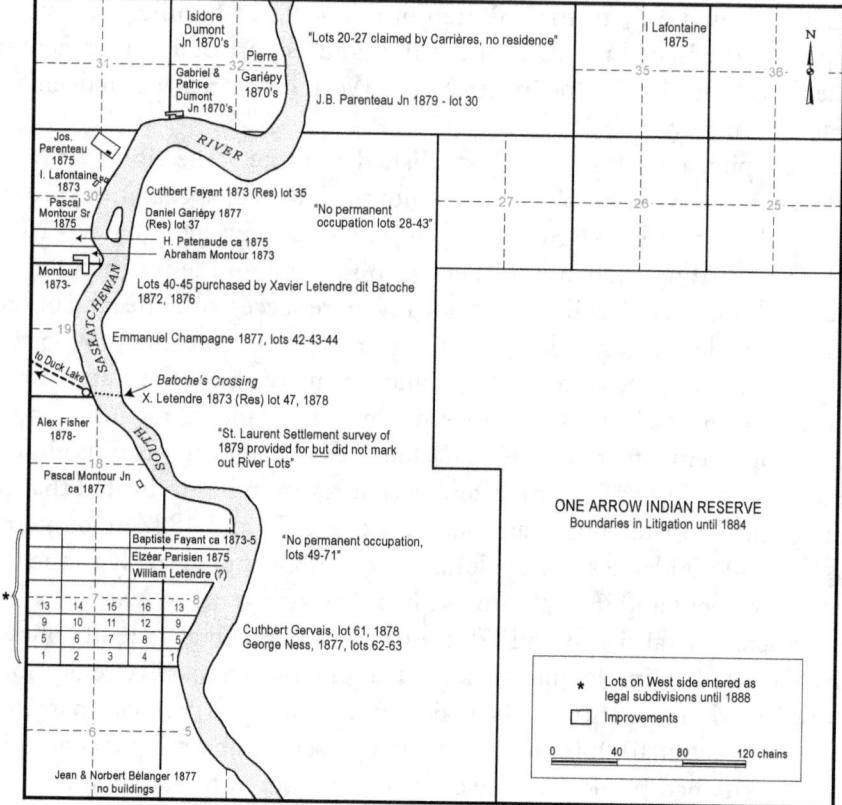

5.1. *Land Claims at Batoche in the 1870s* – Parks Canada, compiled from Saskatchewan Archives Board, Homestead and Lands Branch files and Surveyors' notebooks.

The Canadian government had not surveyed the lands along the South Saskatchewan River. It was only in 1875 that surveyors began laying out the village of Prince Albert and surrounding lands. In the beginning, the Métis living at the various crossings to the south were not too concerned about these developments. They left regularly to hunt and trade on the Prairies and their land was used primarily for pasture and vegetable gardens. However, the unfortunate experience of many compatriots in Manitoba prompted an increasing number to conform to Dominion Lands regulations or take up formal residence on their lands by erecting buildings and fences. The signing of Treaty No. 6 in 1876 with the Plains Cree in the Fort Carlton area also persuaded the Métis that it was time to reach an agreement with the government and to obtain titles to their lands. The treaty signalled the imminent arrival of immigrant settlers and the eventual displacement of Aboriginal peoples. Encouraged by the experience of their compatriots at Qu'Appelle, the Métis of the South Saskatchewan River asked the government for a survey of the "St. Laurent Settlement."

In 1878–79, Mr. Aldous and Mr. Reid were sent to the district with instructions to do a preliminary survey.[16] These two surveyors were both English-speaking and could not understand the Métis they met in the fall of 1878. They also interpreted the absence of many inhabitants as proof on non-residence. They adopted the township surveying system (six square miles subdivided into 36 sections, each a mile square or 640 acres; further subdivided into four quarter sections or homesteads approximately 160 acres each) on the west bank of the river, even though the layout of properties was in riverlots. About twenty families had established a *pied-à-terre* or a more permanent residence on the west bank between Gabriel's Crossing and St. Laurent de Grandin after 1873.[17] Most of them, except for Joseph "Dodet" Parenteau and Alex Fisher, were freighters and hunters, which would of course explain their absence when the surveyors came. A block of about twelve miles along the east bank, identified as the "St. Laurent Settlement," was surveyed into seventy-one riverlots.[18] However, since Mr. Aldous and Mr. Reid saw few residences, they drew only a few lines and staked some pickets at the boundaries of each section of the block. According to a later account by Father Végréville, the surveyors used their township system of square lots without regard for the Métis riverlot system:

> The intention was to take the lands in river lots 10 chains wide and 2 miles deep. In the first surveys, five years ago [1878], only a few miles were surveyed, but like the rest of the country, in squares. A line was drawn to serve as a basis for several other miles but not one piece of land was surveyed, its borders demarcated.[19]

A report from the Department of the Interior in 1885 stated that "all lands *found in occupation of half-breeds* [emphasis added] at time of survey of St.

Laurent in 1878 were subdivided into lots having 10 chains river frontage and running back an average of two miles."[20] It neglected to specify, however, that only the general boundaries of the block of land *set aside* for riverlots had been marked. In effect, only a few individual lots had been demarcated or surveyed. A map signed by Aldous in 1879 confirmed this. In his notebook he reported only ten inhabitants on lots 1 to 19. He also indicated that he numbered the lots but added that it was not necessary to trace the lot lines for lands south of lot 25: "Lots number 20 to 29 inclusive are only claimed by the Carrières; they are not at present in occupation."[21] He did not report any occupants on lots 28 to 43 and added that lots 44, 45, and 46, as well as 49 to 71, were not occupied. André Letendre *dit* Batoche (in fact, it was not André but his brother Xavier) was reported as occupant of lots 47 and 48.[22] Nonetheless, according to declarations made to support their claims in 1884, a number of Métis occupied these lands at that time, among them Cuthbert (Corbet) Fayant on lot 35 since 1873, Emmanuel Champagne on lots 42, 43, and 44 since 1877, and George Ness on lots 62 and 63 also since 1877.[23]

The west bank was surveyed by J.L. Reid in 1879 according to the township system adopted for the Canadian North West. Although the inhabitants, more numerous than on the east bank during the 1870s, had divided their properties into riverlots, Reid ignored this fact. It was later claimed by the government that the Métis had settled there after the survey.[24] However, a review of the land applications made by the Métis in 1884 confirms that there were at least eight families on the west side at Batoche's Crossing by the early 1870s. Reid's notebook also contradicted his official report. He noted some inhabitants on sections 31, 32, and 19, adding that "both banks of the river are settled by French half-breeds."[25]

At the beginning, few Métis complained about the irregularity of government surveys. It was not until the arrival of a group of compatriots from Manitoba in 1882 and the adoption of a more agriculture-based economy and lifestyle that the people were moved to assert their rights. Many disputed the size of their lots or the poorly defined boundaries. The area around Gardepuis' Crossing in township 45 (hereafter called Boucher and part of the later parish of St. Louis) was a particular source of dispute. It had been surveyed according to the township system in 1881 and 1882. Some of these lands were occupied by the Métis at the time of or shortly after the survey. But at least eight Métis had staked out claims before 1880, two of them as early as 1871–72. Mrs. Marguerite Ouellette, Louis

Schmidt, and Octave Régnier held disputed claims. The last two, who had arrived in 1881–82, were on lands already claimed by Hayter Reed and Philippe Gariépy. They could not make entry until the boundaries of these old claims were resolved. Maxime Lépine, Michel Dumas, and Louis Letendre, who had settled on T45-27-2 (township 45, row 27, west of the 2nd meridian) between 1872 and 1882, refused to make official entry until their lands were resurveyed into riverlots. There was a particularly controversial issue in T45-28-2. The area was claimed by the Bouchers, Bremners, Richards, Boyers, and others in 1882 and 1883. Rumours circulated that these lands were part of a tract that had been sold by the government to a colonization company. This situation created much apprehension and resistance among the Métis. It was generally believed that it was best not to make entry, pending an inquiry and a resurvey. All these disputes were the subject of a petition addressed to the Territorial government by the inhabitants of Batoche, Duck Lake, and Boucher in 1881.[26]

The same year Louis Schmidt and the inhabitants of the Boucher Settlement also sent a request to the Minister of the Interior through Joseph Royal. They implored the government to resurvey their lands in order to permit them to make entry and obtain titles.[27]

The opening of the Dominion Lands office in Prince Albert in 1881 had the effect of increasing requests for riverlot surveys and resurveys. According to a report by Father Végréville to the Surveyor General in 1884:

> Since the opening of the land office, these poor people have been asking that their lands be surveyed in order to be able to enter land claims. I wrote to Ottawa several times through Mr. Duck in Prince Albert with no luck and several discouraged Métis have left.[28]

He added that in February 1883 Father Leduc had also presented Métis demands to the federal government, which promised to act but did not do so:

> It was promised in writing that the occupied lands would be surveyed into river lots ... and that the surveying would be done next fall [1883]. But nothing has been done ... the people fear they will lose everything ... that straight parallel lines will cut across their fields, through their homes.[29]

The government did not want to resurvey the land into riverlots. It proposed, instead, to divide the sections into legal subdivisions,[30] arguing that the settler could claim the parcels required to make a riverlot.

> It is not the intention of the Government to cause any re-surveys to be made. Of course any subdivision differing from the regular survey they may desire, they [Métis] can procure for themselves when the lands come into their possession.[31]

In principle, this was possible, but it was often difficult or impossible to incorporate all fields or improvements. People who were settled on odd-numbered sections or on those reserved for the Hudson's Bay Company and the Crown could lose everything.[32] All in all, the Métis were suspicious of such a solution and resentful of the government's inflexibility.

The land agents in Prince Albert could not communicate directly with the Métis. Mr. Duck, the agent at the Land Office since 1881, understood a little French and Cree, but Michif French was the main language of the local population. When Mr. Duck and his assistant, Mr. Gauvreau,[33] visited the St. Laurent district in the spring of 1884 to take applications from the Métis who wished to register their land claims, they encountered a great deal of mistrust and apprehension. Accompanied by Father André, they gathered applications from most of the occupants that were there, about seventy in all (from 99, excluding Duck Lake), but met opposition from a determined and agitated minority. According to Pearce, in a report to the Department of the Interior: "the result showed the necessary of the Rev. Père's influence, as, even with it, about 15% of the claimants though visited by Mr. Duck at their houses, refused to make any application."[34] Other applications were gathered in the fall, about a hundred in the entire district. Opposition came mainly from those who had settled at St. Louis and on lands that had been surveyed into quarter-sections. The government eventually recognized that it had to address the issue of lack of communication, trust, and respect by appointing a Métis, Louis Schmidt, to the Land office, but he was unable to convince his superiors of the gravity of the situation.[35] In the interval, other disputes or conflicting claims had developed in the area.

One of these was the location and encroachment of the Kàpeyak-wàskonam (One Arrow) Reserve. According to the initial plan of the reserve, it encroached on several lots in Batoche, so that these lands were less than two miles deep. After lengthy negotiations, this issue was resolved in November, 1884. Only then did occupants of the "St. Laurent Settlement Survey" agree in principle to make entry for their lands. Other points of contention were pre-emption costs and requirements for residency and cultivation.

Surveys and land grants were the main issues of petitions addressed to the government in June and December 1884. The last petition, drafted by Louis Riel and his secretary, William Henry Jackson (alias Honoré Joseph Jaxon), reiterated all of the concerns and demands relating to Métis lands in the South Saskatchewan River area.[36]

Métis opposition to the survey system and the refusal of many to make applications for land in 1884 stemmed essentially from their firm conviction that they could not trust the government. According to the Superintendent of Lands, William Pearce, however, the refusal of the Métis to comply with requirements of the official survey system was due to their primitiveness, their ignorance, and their intrinsically malicious nature. In an official report in 1886, and later in his memoirs, he wrote:

> It is difficult for many to understand why they would not avail themselves of entry, but no more illogical than many of their actions. Many parties had in settling along the river, ignored the regular surveys and squatted regardless of the sections being odd or even-numbered.... An excitable, uneducated people like the majority of the French Halfbreeds of the Canadian North West naturally concluded that a similar action would prove a bonanza to them. There was a conspiracy not to make entry and if refused, the Government would issue patent without an entry fee being paid.[37]

Pearce continued to support the validity of the township survey system and government policy and to attribute the opposition of the Métis to a determination on their part to circumvent authority. The figures and examples he gave in an official report to this effect in 1885 reflected his prejudices, and, in some cases, he actually lied. For example, he reported that some Métis had received patents for their lands, but none were actually issued before the outbreak of the armed conflict in March, 1885.[38]

The applications of 1884 had been sent to Ottawa, and on 4 February 1885, the commissioner in Winnipeg told the agent in Prince Albert to inform applicants that they could enter their lands. The notices were sent to the Métis between 26 February and 7 March 1885. Copies of the notices have not survived in the Department of the Interior records. According to William Pearce's report, only one-third of the claimants (81 out of 258) were able to obtain the land requested. But only half of those had fulfilled the homestead residency requirements and less than a quarter had made "significant improvements." Furthermore, claimants outside the "St. Laurent Settlement Survey" were being pressured to abandon claims in odd-numbered sections and conform to the township survey by entering their lands in legal subdivisions. In addition, the Mr. Duck had not gone to St. Louis. The claims of the Bouchers, Richards, and others in T45-28-2, in conflict with the Prince Albert Colonization Company, remained unresolved or were only investigated in October, 1885.[39]

By March 1885, the Métis were tired of unfulfilled promises and delays. There was little doubt in the minds of most Métis that the government was still far from recognizing their rights. Philippe Garnot, secretary of the provisional government, wrote about the escalating situation:

> It is easy to see by that that they were further away from making the arrangements than ever. If there was something that was feared more than anything else: it was the promises, because for fifteen years, they had received nothing but promises and not a single one of them was ever kept.[40]

Government responses also indicated no recognition of Métis Aboriginal land rights and confirmed that they were to be subject to the same regulations as immigrants or homesteaders:

> *These people can found no claim upon being Halfbreeds* [emphasis added]. It is only as settlers that any indulgence can be shown them. Anyone who goes to the Saskatchewan district to settle, has just as much right to go there and enter on unoccupied land as those who went before them.[41]

The residents of the South Saskatchewan River area and other districts had defended their Aboriginal land rights in the North West in a series of petitions between 1878 and 1884. They also argued for the recognition for their custom of hay and wood lots, a right not specified in the Dominion

Lands Act. The principle of a direct Métis land grant gained some support at the Territorial level, but the federal Department of the Interior and the Dominion Lands Branch, in particular the policies and views of A.M. Burgess and William Pearce, were negative and uncompromising. This question remained unresolved on the eve of the armed resistance. A letter from Lieutenant-Governor Edgar Dewdney to Prime Minister Sir J.A. Macdonald in February 1885 suggests that the government intended to do something but that the measure was only a preliminary phase in a long-term assessment of Métis claims:

> I have the following telegram from Sir David Macpherson. Government has decided to investigate claims of the Halfbreeds and with that view has directed enumeration of those who did not participate in the grant under the Manitoba Act. No representations were received lately.[42]

Dewdney added that he did not dare to forward the notice to the local member of Parliament as it stood, fearing to provoke the Métis:

> On receipt of the above I wired Macdowall as follows: Government has decided to investigate claims of the Half Breeds and with the view has already taken the preliminary steps. I feared to send the Telegram as worded by Sir David as it would seem to the bulk of the French Half Breeds who are making demands that they have nothing to expect. They would at once work on the English Half Breeds to help them, start a popular agitation which could make it more difficult to carry out the views of the Government than if the announcement is made later on. You will gather from my letter of yesterday that I would like any action in regard to the Half Breeds to be taken in the spring when they would be occupied with their own business and they would not be so likely to interfere with our Indians.[43]

In retrospect, it would appear that Métis suspicions and interpretations of the government's policy regarding Dominion Lands surveys and their inherent land rights were well-founded. It took an armed resistance to force the government to respond or take their concerns seriously.

Resurveys and Homestead Entries: 1885–ca.1925

In 1888, the lots in townships 42, 43, 44, and 45 were resurveyed by the government.[44] This action reconciled a large part of the population. Leclerc, the surveyor, was sympathetic and hired local assistants. At Batoche, more specifically, the land along the west bank (beginning with sections 5, 6, 7, 8, 15, 19, and 30 of township 43-1-3 and sections 20, 21, 28, 32, and 33 of township 42-1-3 as far as Gabriel's Crossing) was divided into lots eight to ten chains wide and generally one mile deep.[45] The resurvey made it possible for many sons of families who were established there to take neighbouring lands. Surveyor Leclerc reported on the positive results of his work:

> I have the honour of submitting to you, in accordance with my instructions, a report for the subdivision into river lots requested by the Métis of Saskatchewan to which you agreed. I thank you on their behalf for granting them this survey, which they desired with great pleasure. [They] express their gratitude toward our governments. I found the entire Métis population well-disposed towards the government with a few exceptions, although uneasiness continues to prevail in some families. I concluded the work on the site after learning of all complaints.[46]

The following year (1889), other issues arose. The survey work of the previous year, done in winter, was already in the process of being destroyed. The surveyors had not erected mounds, and the wooden posts had disappeared with the spring floods. The Métis requested new iron posts to demarcate boundaries under dispute, but this was not done. In 1891, surveyor Reid erected new posts here and there in the district when he surveyed the trail between Fish Creek and McKenzie's Crossing (St. Louis). However, the survey lines and posts remained a source of difficulty in the area. In 1893, Inspector Wilson, in charge of teams at Batoche and Duck Lake, reported: "that he has had a thorough search made for survey posts in the vicinity of Batoche. There is not a post or mound to be found except the iron posts on the surveyed trail, which had no marks."[47] In 1898, Mr. Reid was told to renew the posts, but he found no trace of the first ones. He nevertheless proceeded to mark some boundaries, and in many instances encroached on private property, which earned him the admonishment of his superiors.[48]

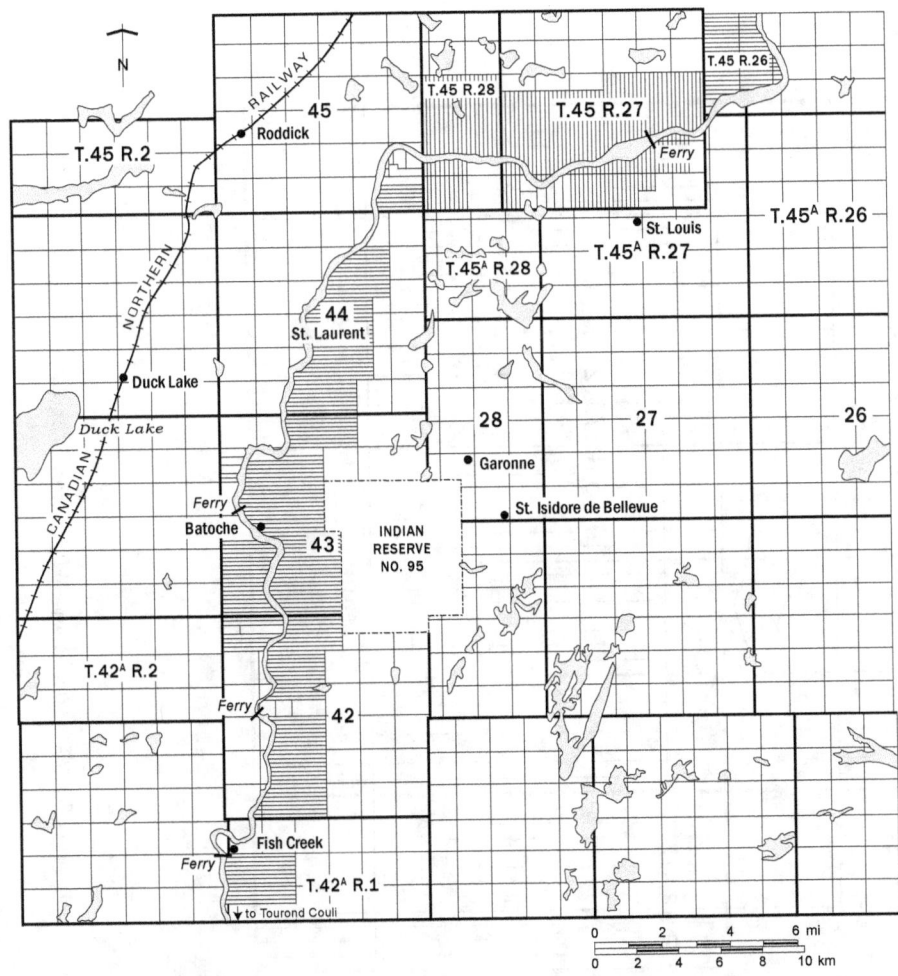

5.2. *Riverlot settlements along the South Saskatchewan River – Saskatchewan Archives Board, Prince Albert District Map [ca. 1900].*

These posts were removed, and it was not until 1908 that the original survey lines were retraced and corrected and iron posts erected.[49]

After the resurveys, the Métis were more favourably inclined to make formal land entries. Problems such as distance to the land office in Prince Albert, language barriers, and the inability to pay the $10 entry fee, however, discouraged or delayed many people.

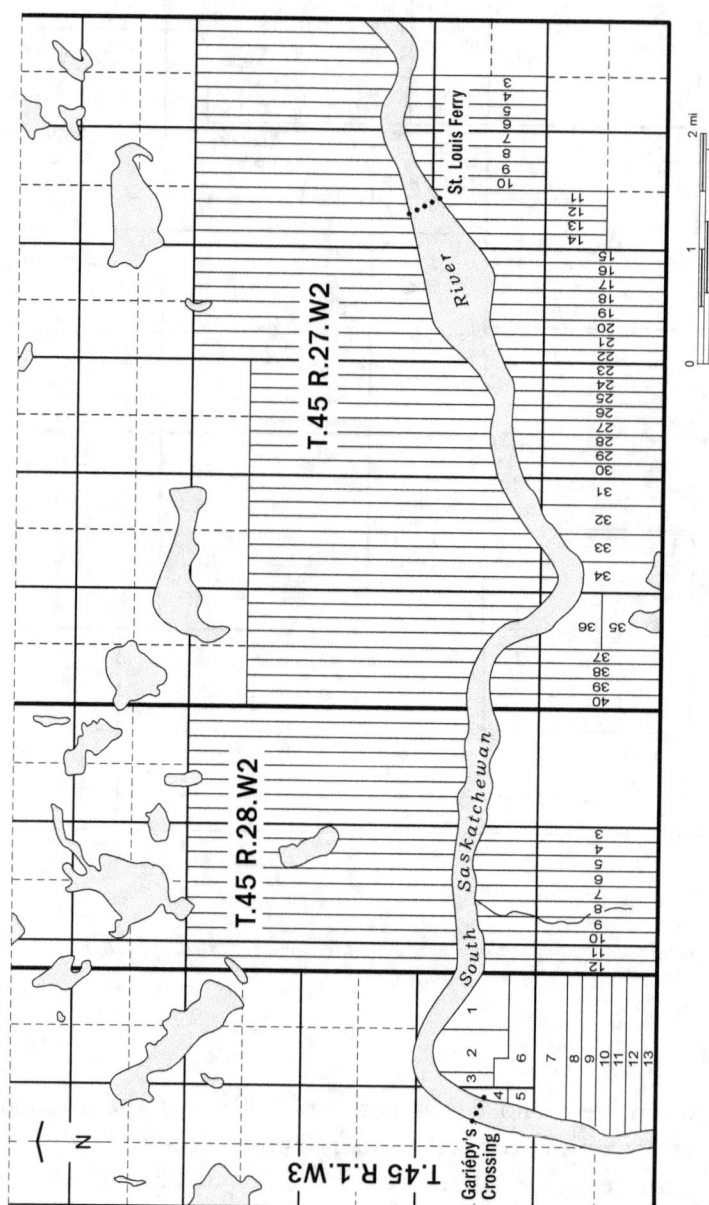

5.3. *Map and claims at St. Louis (de Langevin) after 1889–90 resurvey – Map drafted by Marilyn Croot.*

Table 5.3

T45-1-3

1. Octave Régnier
2. Marguerite Ouellette
3. Pierre Gariépy-Hayter Reed
4. Philippe Gariépy
5. Louis Schmidt dit Laferté
6. Philippe Gariépy– T. J. Agnew
7. Louis Schmidt dit Laferté
8. Justine Laviolette
9. James Short
10. Sedley Bird
11. W.H. Misener
12. Jules Boucher
13. Ernest Boucher

T45-28-2

3. Norbert Turcotte
4. Norbert Turcotte
5. Maxime Lépine Sr.
6. Maxime Lépine Jr.
7. Louis Letendre
8. Octave & Célestine Régnier
9. Jean-Baptiste Boucher Jr.
10. Patrice Lépine
11. Jean-Baptiste Boucher Jr.
12. Charles Ferguson

T45-27-2

11. Jean-Baptiste Boucher Sr.
12. Jean-Baptiste Boucher Sr.
13. E. Lecoq omi
14. Odilon St. Denis
15. Jean-Baptiste Boucher Jr.
16. William Bremner
17. Moïse Bremner
18. Franz Hauser
19. Magloire Boyer
20. Joseph Bremner
21. Jonas Laviolette
22. Edmond Lefebvre
23. Antoine Richard
24. Flora Fidler
25. Charles Laviolette
26. William & John Bruce
27. Ambroise Richard
28. Napoléon Boyer
29. Magloire Boyer
30. George Fidler
31. Alcide Légaré
32. Louis Schmidt dit Laferté
33. W half 33 – E half 34 Alexandre Bremner
34. E half 33 – W half 34 Pantaléon Schmidt
35. William Richard
36. ―
37. Pierrre Van Brempt
38. Frank Bruce
39. Antoine & William Richard
40. Jean-Baptiste Boscher

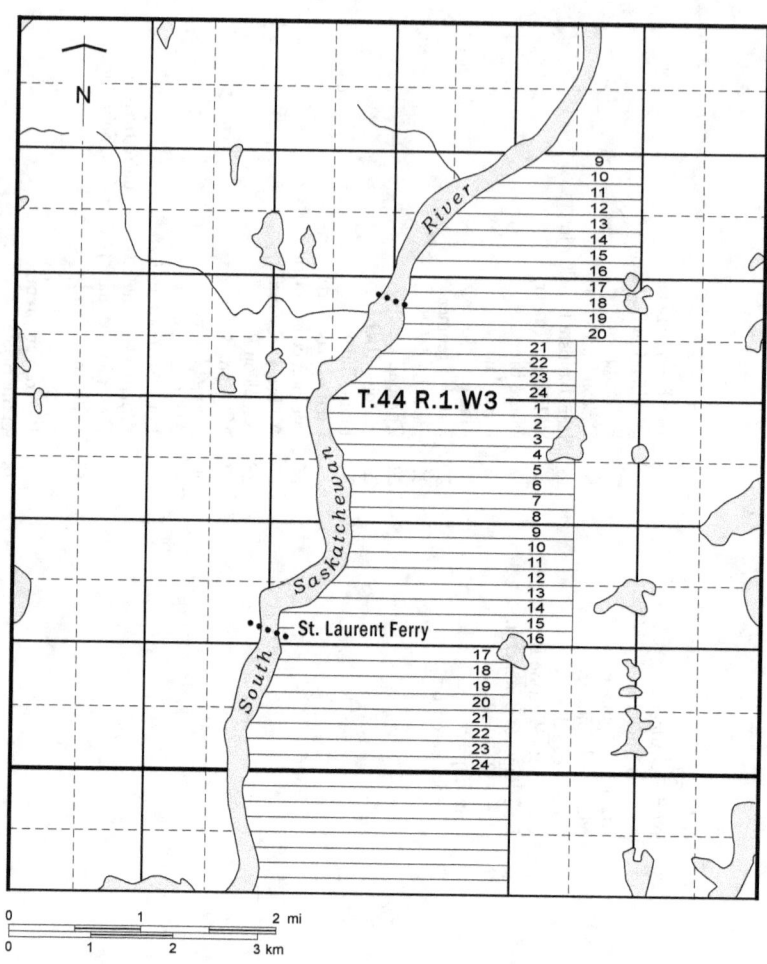

5.4. *Map and claims at St. Laurent (de Grandin) ca. 1884 to 1930 – Map drafted by Marilyn Croot.*

Table 5.4

T44-1-3

9 Domithilde Dumont (widow of Jean)
10 Domithilde Dumont (widow of Jean)
11 Maurice Hollinger
12 François Arcand
13 François Fidler
14 François Fidler
15 Chrysostome Boyer
16 Georges Ferguson
17 Harry Watson
18 Joseph Dorcey
19 Ernest Arcand
20 Charles Laviolette
21 James Taylor
22 Henri Pilon
23 François Dumas
24 Isidore Parenteau

"St. Laurent Settlement"

1 André and Catherine Letendre
2 William Ferguson
3 Léon Ferguson
4 Joseph Nolin
5 Jérôme and Hélène Racette
6 Baptiste and Élisabeth Boyer
7 Robert Venne
8 Gilbert Breland – Tobie Boyer
9 William Boyer
10 Damase and Mary-Jane Racette
11 Moïse and Élisabeth Ouellette
12 Moïse Ouellette Jr.
13 Moïse Ouellette Sr.
14 Moïse Jr. and Joseph Ouellette
15 Baptiste Ouellette
16 William Boyer
17 Baptiste Parenteau-Joseph Dumont
18 Alexandre Boyer
19 Antoine Ferguson Jr.
20 St. Pierre Parenteau
21 Pélagie Carrière-Dubois
22 Ambroise Gervais
23 Louis Pilon
24 Antoine Ferguson Jr.

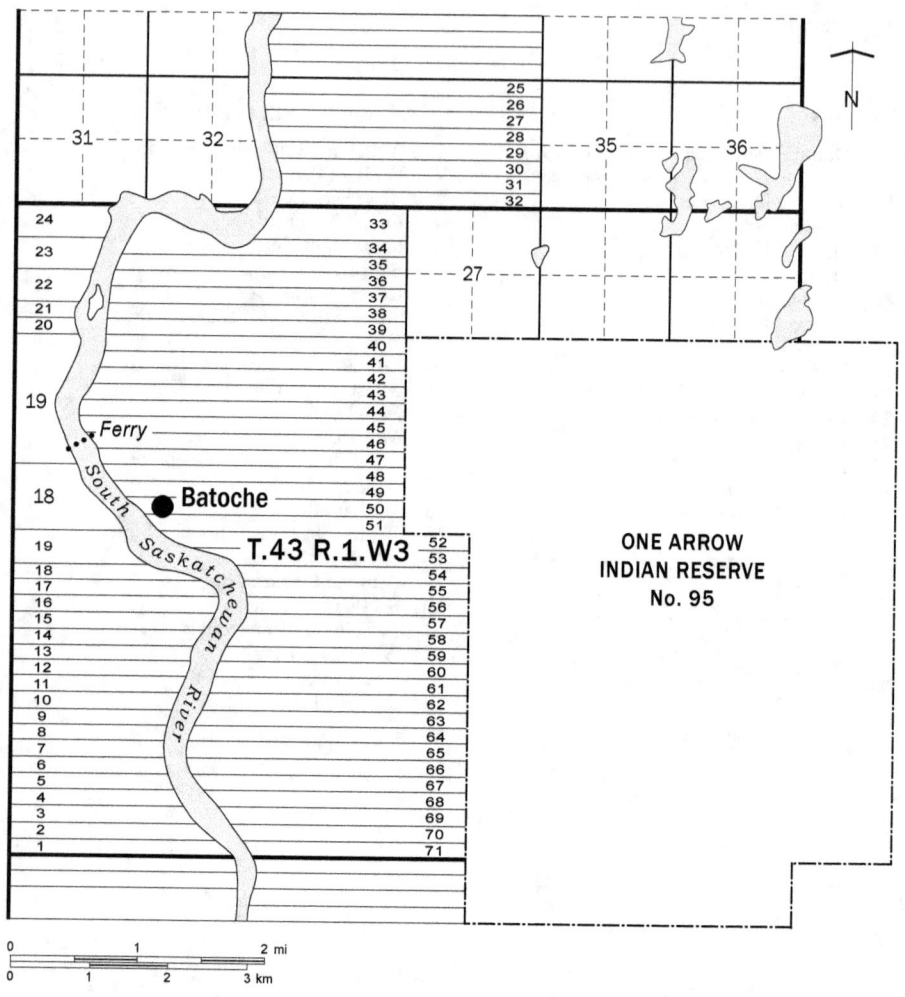

5.5. *Map and claims at Batoche, ca.1884 to 1930 – Map drafted by Marilyn Croot.*

Table 5.5

T43-1-3 (EAST SIDE OF THE RIVER): "ST. LAURENT SETTLEMENT" (BATOCHE)

25 André Nault-Joe Ferguson
26 Napoléon Nault- François Slater
27 Baptiste - Moïse Gervais
28 Alexis Gervais
29 Isidore Gervais
30 Baptiste Parenteau
31 Guillaume Laplante
32 Pierre Gervais
33 S half: Calixte Lafontaine N half: Joe Lafontaine
34 Alfred and John Fayant
35 Corbet and William Fayant
36 William and John Fayant
37 Daniel Gariépy and John Fayant
38 Edmond Gervais
39 Édouard and Sophie Dumont
40 Moïse and Véronique Parenteau
41 Pierre and Marie-Anne Parenteau
42 Ambroise Champagne-George Grant
43 Cléophas Champagne
44 Emmanuel Champagne
45 Xavier Letendre and Joseph Branconnier
46 Xavier Letendre
47 Xavier Letendre
48 N half: Xavier Letendre – S half: Charles Thomas
49 N half: Charles Thomas, J. B. Ranger S -half: Charles Pilon
50 OMI (St. Antoine de Padoue)
51 OMI (St. Antoine de Padoue)
52 Jean Caron Sr.
53 Jean Caron Jr.
54 Barthélémi Pilon
55 Salomon Venne
56 Norbert Delorme - Joseph Ladéroute
57 Raphaël Boyer
58 Josephte Tourond
59 Patrice Gervais - Louis Letendre
60 Modeste Parenteau
61 Cuthbert Gervais
62 George Ness
63 Pierre Caron
64 Jean Desmarais - William Pilon
65 Barthélémi Pilon
66 François Ladouceur – Joseph Pilon Jr.
67 Joseph Pilon Sr.
68 Patrice Caron
69 Isidore Dumas
70 Alexandre Pilon
71 Pierre Parenteau Jr.

SECTION 27:
N-W quarter: A. Gaudet
S-W quarter: R. Gaudet
N- E quarter: Jos. Dupuis
S- E quarter: E. Dupuis

SECTION 35:
S-W quarter : A. Lafontaine
N-E quarter: I. and Jos. Lafontaine

SECTION 36:
N-W quarter : Létournel and Leroy
S-W quarter : Baptiste Parenteau Jr.

T43-1-3 (WEST SIDE OF THE RIVER) BATOCHE

SECTION 31:
N-E quarter: André Vanpeteghen
N-W quarter: Bernard Montour
S-E quarter: Paul Géry
S-W quarter: Joseph Paradis

SECTION 32:
S-W quarter: Isidore Dumont Jr.

RIVERLOTS:
24 Joseph "Dodet" Parenteau
23 Isidore Lafontaine
22 Pascal Montour - Joannis Rousset
21 Hilaire Patenaude - Joannis Rousset
20 Abraham Montour

SECTION 19:
S-W quarter : Abraham Montour
S-W quarter parcel: Alexandre P. Fisher

SECTION 18:
N-W quarter: Alexandre P. Fisher

RIVERLOTS:
19 Louis Letendre Jr.
18 Eugène Letendre
17 Joseph Letendre, claimed by HBC 1884-91
16 Elzéar Parisien - François Lanovaz, claimed by HBC 1884-91
14 Claimed by HBC 1884-91
13-9 Transferred to HBC in 1891 and Saskatchewan government in 1930
8 David Slater
7 François Vandal
6 Normand Fidler
5 Alexandre Pilon
4 François Parenteau
3 Baptiste Letendre
2 Alexandre Parenteau
1 Norbert Bélanger-Clément Brun

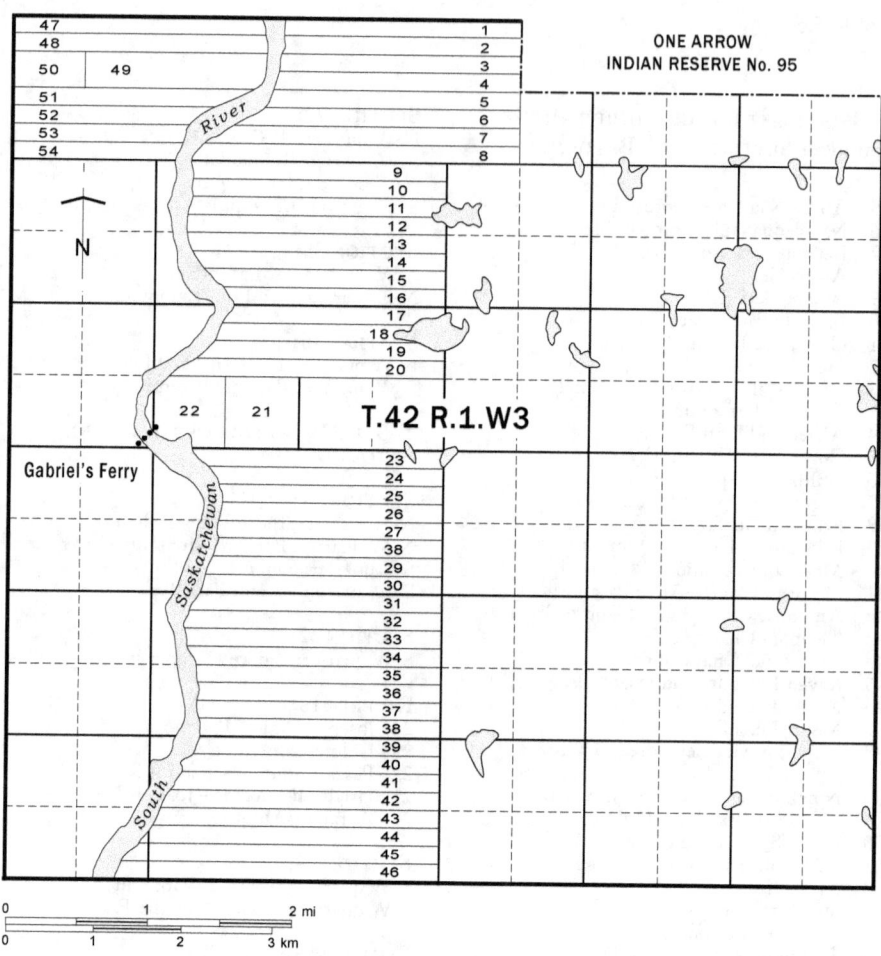

5.6. *Map and claims at Vandal and Gabriel's Crossing, ca. 1884–1930 – Map drafted by Marilyn Croot.*

Table 5.6

T42-1-3: Vandal and Gabriel's Crossing

1	Patrice Parenteau	28	Pierre Vandal
2	Frédéric St. Germain	29	Joseph « Cotit » Vandal-Clovis Nogier
3	Charles-Eugène Boucher	30	Pierre Henry
4	Louis Parenteau	31	Isidore Villeneuve
5	André Sansregret- Georges Parenteau	32	Charles Carrière
6	Maxime Dubois-Baptiste Parenteau	33	Joseph Branconnier
7	Pierre Ledoux-Alfred Carrière	34	Jérôme Henry
8	Ambroise Dubois	35	Antoine Vandal Jr.
9	Napoléon Parenteau	36	Baptiste Rocheleau
10	Maxime and Michel Poitras	37	Marie (Carrière) Rocheleau
11	Michel Poitras	38	Maurice Henry
12	Théophile Caron	39	Cuthbert Fidler-Peter Buhl
13	Ignace Poitras Jr.	40	Ivan Fediasz
14	Henri Poitras	41	Ivan Fediasz
15	Ignace Poitras Sr.	42	Modeste Rocheleau-Sofron Civik
17	Marie (Primeau) Vandal	43	William Rocheleau-Frank Boczar
18	Odilon Garnot-Wasyl Zamolski	44	Leoko Kozar
19	Philippe Garnot	45	Narcisse Henry-John Fidler
20	Philippe Garnot	46	David Desrivières
21	Gabriel Dumont	47	Jean Bélanger-Edmond Pilon
22	Gabriel Dumont	48	Abraham Bélanger Jr.
23	Joseph et Étienne Vandal	49	Abraham Bélanger Sr.
24	Isidore Villeneuve	50	——
25	Frank Buniak	51	Élie Nault-Albert Caron
26	Wasilena Kapacila	52	Marguerite (Dumas) Caron
27	Pierre and Norbert Henry	53	Albert Cadot
		54	Daniel Charette

An analysis of 253 homestead declarations (the "special" applications in 1884 and the formal entries or homesteads from 1885 and ca. 1925 (see Appendix 3) reveals that, contrary to widely held opinion, the Métis wanted their lands. The individuals who made entry persisted, although the interval between entry and patent generally exceeded the three-year term stipulated in the Dominion Lands Act. Similarly, the Métis usually resided on their land or occupied it "unofficially" for some years before making entry. In the St. Louis, St. Laurent, Batoche, and Vandal area, which was studied, there was no important difference between Métis and non-Métis (mainly French and French Canadians) in terms of age at time of entry, absenteeism, improvements, and persistence, at least not until the period of the First World War. Certain other trends can also be gleaned from the statistical analysis. Once the Métis resolved to make entry, they persisted until patent, but the interval between the two dates depended on what they intended to use the land for: if they intended to sell, they were more eager to apply for entry and patent. Moïse Ouellette at St. Laurent, applied for patent for one of his lots shortly before his death in 1911, the same year as his official entry but thirty-eight years after establishing residence.[50] The message that Mr. Ouellette and others wanted to give to the government was that they were an Aboriginal people and not settlers, and therefore they should have received a direct land grant and should have been subject to Dominion Lands regulations.

Another important aspect of Métis landholding was "absenteeism" or seasonal movements and the pursuit of other activities. Although there was probably a tendency by all claimants (Métis and non-Métis) to minimize absenteeism to authorities, half of those who responded to this question in 1884, were absent one to two months a year and the other half three to four months a year. This response was not surprising in a transitional period from a primarily hunting and freighting to a more agricultural economy. Little absenteeism was reported in post-1884 declarations, but it is known from other sources that most Métis pursued other occupations for essential complementary income.

The 1884 declarations were those taken by the local Prince Albert Lands Branch office in a special survey by agent Duck, who tried to get all Métis who had "settled" or claimed lands along the South Saskatchewan River to participate. As previously mentioned, no declarations were taken in the St. Louis district, especially not in the township where many residents refused to enter their lands as legal subdivisions or were intimidated by the claims by the Prince Albert Colonization Company. A number of unconvinced or absent claimants also refused to make declarations at St. Laurent and Batoche, while a number of Métis who had settled in the area of Gabriel's Crossing declared their lands in legal subdivisions. The sixty-one included in the sample of 1884 declarations used for this analysis do not include the ten originating in the Fish Creek area (specifically la couli des Tourond), who were not established directly along the river. The second series of applications was made up of those filing after 1884, a total 192 (see Appendix 3). In both cases, only the recorded entrants or persons who made official entry were used in the analysis. Unlike the 1884 declarations, the post-1884 ones provided some insight into the number of previous occupants (usually customary or unofficial):

Table 7. Total Non-Persistent Occupants per Lot. Post-1884 Métis Declarations. (Appendix 3: Codes 3, 4, 5, 6)

Previous Occupants	No. of Lots	%
0	60	45.5
1	49	37.1
2	16	12.1
3	5	3.8
4	1	0.8
5	1	0.8
Total:	132	100.0

Missing cases: 25.

Table 7 reveals that, of those who were queried about the number of previous occupants, mainly pre-1900 applications, 45.5 per cent said there were none and 54.6 per cent that they were not the first occupants. The number of previous occupants may have been withheld by some Métis who believed it was more prudent to be circumspect. Otherwise, some improvements might not be accepted by the agent or one of the previous occupants might later try to make entry.

In order to fully appreciate the Métis response to land entries and patents under the Dominion Lands Act, we must have some idea of the general principles and regulations governing the act.[51] The Métis were not granted any special provisions under this legislation. More specifically, their Aboriginal rights were to be dealt with by scrip or some other special grant and not through homesteads (see next section: Aboriginal Claims through Scrip in 1886 and 1899–1900). As early occupants, some would meet less stringent regulations than later arrivals, but the same duties were applied to both Métis and immigrant settlers. The object of the Dominion Lands Act, as set forth and administered by the federal Department of the Interior between 1870 and 1930, was to promote European immigration and settlement of the Canadian West. The regulations changed frequently in the early years, and a corrupt and inefficient bureaucratic web entangled Métis and Eurocanadian settler alike.

Homestead entry for one quarter-section or 160 acres was obtained by an adult male upon payment of a $10 fee. Until 1884, the residence requirement was six months out of every year for three years. For a short time afterwards, residence was waived, except for three months preceding application for patent, while the expense of entry could be replaced by cultivation, buildings, or stock. This system led to abuses and the three-year term was reinstated. Similarly, until 1889, the required acreage broken was fifteen acres; this was increased to thirty by the 1890s and fifty in 1922. There were exceptions where land was scrubby and hard to break, a condition that applied to the Métis who were living along the west bank at Batoche and St. Laurent. Upon fulfilment of the residency and cultivation requirements, the homesteader presented himself at the Dominion Lands office to make an application for patent. The sworn statement, corroborated by two witnesses, was verified by the local agent. Upon approval, a patent certificate was delivered to the homesteader and the land was registered at the Dominion Lands office. In 1874, the right of pre-emption (or purchase of an adjoining 160 acres) was introduced. The original fee of $1 per acre was raised to $2.50 in the 1880s. Pre-emptions were abolished in 1890, but those who had settled before 1881 retained this right. Few Métis, however, could afford to purchase the pre-emptions applied for in 1884. Amendments to the Dominion Lands Act in 1883 provided for a second "free" homestead entry. This privilege was likewise abolished in 1886 but was retained for an "old settler" who had made a first entry before 1889. He could obtain a second one after completing the three-year term on the first. Barthélémi Pilon, Xavier Letendre, Antoine Richard, William Boyer, and Baptiste Boucher Sr. were among the sixteen or so in the district who availed themselves of this privilege.[52] The right to pre-emptions and purchased homesteads without conditions at $3.50 per acre were revived for all in 1908. Lands in odd-numbered sections that had initially been reserved for the railway were also opened for sale by the government at $3 per acre. Although the latter did not affect the Métis who claimed riverlots, other policies did.

Riverlots almost always exceeded the grant of 160 acres. From a sample of 188 cases where lot sizes were recorded, only twenty-five (21.2 per cent) were the standard 160 acres, while others ranged from 95 to 203 acres. According to homestead regulations, the settler had to pay for any land in excess of 160 acres. If he had settled before 1880, the cost was $1 an acre; before 1889, $2 an acre; and after that date, $3 an acre. The government's unofficial policy during the 1890s and early 1900s was to apply pressure on the occupants of riverlots to pay for these parcels of extra land. In the meantime, title on the 160-acre homestead was withheld. According to accounts in government files, most of the Métis did not want to break up their farms and undertook to purchase any land in excess of 160 acres.[53] When they were unable to pay and interest accumulated, they were finally threatened with losing their land. Only upon proof of extreme poverty or being "first settlers" would the Department consider granting a property title or patent, and then only for the 160 acres. There is no doubt that this situation contributed to delays in the issuing of patent. The case of Jean Caron Sr. of Batoche is a good example. Caron occupied lot 52 in 1881. When he applied for patent to his land in 1888, he was informed that he must first purchase the excess twenty-three acres at $3 per acre (in fact, Caron should only have had to pay $2). He was confused and somewhat shocked and as a result, put the matter aside for the time being. He did not receive a further notice from the government on the matter. Finally in 1903, when Caron was seventy years old and it became obvious that he either would not or could not pay and in consideration of his status as an early settler, he received title to the westerly 160 acres of lot 52.[54] Other *bona fide settlers*, such as Jean-Baptiste Boyer on lot 6 of St. Laurent and Emmanuel Champagne on lot 44 at Batoche, encountered similar difficulties.

There were other factors peculiar to the Métis. They had chosen their lands for hay and wood lots as well as proximity to water, and not solely for cultivation purposes. There were good agricultural lands at St. Louis and Batoche, but the importance of being near family and community discouraged many from settling in adjoining townships, at least initially. Another issue, in contrast with the Eurocanadian settler generally, was the mistrust of the Métis towards the government. This attitude is illustrated by the concealment of information and by delays in complying with regulations. Other practices such as the custom of moving from one unoccupied lot to another or cultivating it confused and angered the land agents.

Amidst these difficulties and the maze of regulations that many failed to understand, the Métis who settled in the South Saskatchewan River district were persistent in establishing the claims to their lands. Tables 8–12 illustrate this fact and other features of Métis land settlement.

Table 8. Years between Residence and Entry Application by Métis as per 1884 and Post-1884 Declarations. (Appendix 3: Codes 1, 2, 3, 4)

	1884 Patent		Post-1884 Patent			
Years	Obtained	No.	Obtained	No.	Total	%
0–3	24	10	43	2	79	52.0
4–6	6	7	18	2	33	21.7
7–9	3	3	3	1	33	6.6
10–12	4	3	5	–	12	7.9
13–15	–	–	6	–	6	3.9
16–18	–	–	4	–	4	2.6
19–21	–	–	2	–	2	1.3
22–24	–	–	3	–	3	2.0
25–27	–	–	1	–	1	0.7
28–30	–	–	–	–	–	–
31–33	–	–	–	–	–	–
34–36	–	–	1	–	1	0.7
37–39	–	–	1	–	1	0.7
Total:	37	23	87	5	152	100.0

Missing cases: 11.

According to Table 8, sixty-seven declarations entered (24 entries in 1884 and 43 in the post-1884 period) by those who persisted until patent made entry within three years or less of establishing residence. For the post-1884 successful applicants, the interval between residence and entry extended up to thirty-nine years, although only 30 per cent took more than six years to make official entry. In all, 124 Métis (approximately 81 per cent of all Métis who made entry) obtained patent to the land. The interval between land occupation and entry was characteristic of their response to land registration.

For the non-Métis, the pattern was markedly different. Out of a sample of twenty-eight for 1884 and post-1884 declarations, twenty-four (85.7 per cent) were on the land three years or less before making entry.

The cross-tabulation of successful post-1884 Métis applicants with the year of application for entry revealed some interesting data on Métis settlement periods (see Table 9). Entries were most numerous in the periods 1885–90 and 1899–1914. The number of Métis respondents was ninety-six, of whom sixty-four (67 per cent) registered between 1899 and 1914.

For the period 1885–86 (Tables 8 and 9 and Appendix 3), there were thirty-seven entrants from 1884 and eleven from post-1884 who persisted for a total of forty-eight for the two declaration types. Those who didn't persevere numbered twenty-three in 1884 and three in post-1884 for a total of twenty-six. The rate of non-persistence was relatively high during that period, twenty-six (35.1 per cent) out of seventy-four. Perhaps more important were the number of entries in the post-1899 period, which coincided with the second generation Métis settlement. This period witnessed the entry of unsettled lands on the west side of the river at Batoche and north of the "St. Laurent Settlement Survey." It is possible, however, that the numbers also reflect the planned exodus of some Métis, as witnessed at Fish Creek at the turn of the century. It was usual to quickly apply for entry and apply for title just when a sale or move was likely.

Table 9. Year of Entry Application by Ethnic Background for Post-1884 Applicants Who Later Obtained Patent (Appendix 3: Code 4).

	1883–86	1887–90	1891–94	1895–98	1899–1902	1903–06	1907–10	1911–14	1915–18	1919–22	1923–26	Total
Métis	11	9	2	5	16	27	11	10	1	3	1	96
Non-Métis	2	–	1	2	6	6	8	4	–	1	–	30
Total	13	9	3	7	22	33	19	14	1	4	1	126

Missing cases: 2 Métis.

Table 10. Year of Application for Patent by Ethnic Background for Post–1884 (Appendix 3: Code 4).

	1875–86	1887–90	1891–94	1895–98	1899–1902	1903–06	1907–10	1911–14	1915–18	1919–22	1923–26	Total
Métis	6	9	4	4	3	21	15	17	8	7	4	98
Non-Métis	1	–	–	1	2	4	5	7	5	3	1	29
Total	7	9	4	5	5	25	20	24	13	10	5	127

Missing cases: 1 non-Métis.

The year of entry and application for patent can also be linked to ethnic background (see Tables 9 and 10). Although the sampling of Métis (96 and 98) was much larger than of non-Métis (30 and 29), the results suggest that the period of entry and patent was generally the same for both groups. More important, however, out of a total of ninety-six Métis who made entry between 1883 and 1926, fifty-four did so between 1899 and 1910. The same number (actually 53) who applied for patent during the subsequent three-year periods (1903–14), suggests that the 1900–14 period was one of the most persistent and successful in terms of Métis official land entry and application for patent.

The number of years between residence and patent for all post-1884 applicants (Table 11) reveal that 65 per cent of the Métis applied for patent within fifteen years of establishing residence. By that time, however, 94 per cent of the non-Métis had already obtained patent. Many Métis resided on the land for some time before making entry and applying for patent.

Delays in applying for patent varied between three years or less and thirty-nine years. According to Table 12, 83 per cent of the Métis obtained patent within twelve years of entry while 94 per cent of the non-Métis had obtained patent by that time. More significant, however, was the fact that two Métis were taking up to thirty-nine years while only two non-Métis took more than thirteen years.

Table 11. Number of Years between Residence and Patent for Post-1884 Records (Appendix 3: Codes 4 and 5).

Years	Métis	%	Non-Métis	%
0–3	5	4	3	10
4–6	31	23	11	36
7–9	18	13	11	36
10–12	17	13	3	10
13–15	16	12	1	2
Total	87	65	29	94
16–18	7	5	–	–
19–21	7	5	2	6
22–24	11	8	–	–
25–27	4	3	–	–
28–30	10	8	–	–
31–33	3	2	–	–
34–36	2	1	–	–
37–39	1	1	–	–
40–42	2	1	–	–
43–45	–	–	–	–
46–48	2	1	–	–
Total	136	100	31	100

Missing cases: 1 non-Métis.

Table 12. Year Interval between Formal Entry and Patent.

Years	Métis	%	Non-Métis	%
0–3	44	32.8	5	15.6
4–12	67	50.0	25	78.1
Total	111	82.8	30	93.7
13–21	20	15.0	2	6.3
25–39	3	2.2	–	–
Total	134	100.0	32	100.0

Missing cases: 2 Métis.

Absenteeism or the comings and goings of the Métis when they were not on their land was of particular concern to the land agent. To the Métis, it was a necessary by-product of their mixed economy. It is important to note in Table 13, however, that in response to the absentee question, almost half of the Métis (45.4 per cent) queried and just over half of the non-Métis (52.8 per cent) replied that they were not absent. There was no significant difference, then, between the two groups.

Table 13. Reasons for Absence from Homestead (Appendix 3: Codes 1 to 6).

	Métis				Non–Métis	
	1884	Post–1884	Total	%	Post–1884	%
Present	5	93	98	45.4	19	52.8
Absent						
With friends/family	7	16	23	10.6	3	8.3
Working elsewhere	40	26	66	3.6	8	22.2
Living on another homestead	1	12	13	6.0	4	11.1
Squatted elsewhere	–	1	1	0.5	–	–
Other reasons	–	8	8	3.7	2	5.6
No Reply	7	–	7	3.2	–	–
Total	60	156	216	100.0	36	100.0

Missing cases: 1 Métis.

Only twenty (7.9 per cent) of all land declarations and entries were made by women. Single women were not eligible for homestead entry. A widow with minor children could obtain entry and title, but only as a legal representative of her deceased husband. Otherwise, she would have to be legally designated as an heir. Examples of widowed women who obtained entry and patent as legal representatives in the South Saskatchewan River district were Hélène Racette, Marie-Rose Ferguson, Josephte Tourond, Marguerite Ouellette, and Véronique Parenteau. Emmanuel Champagne designated his wife, Marie Letendre, as heir to lot 44 at Batoche, whereas Marguerite Caron, widow of Jean Sr., obtained entry and patent for a second homestead, lot 52, at Vandal (near Gabriel's Crossing).

In addition to adherence to inflexible government regulations, other problems beset the Métis who wanted to obtain ownership of their land. Poverty forced many to take out seed grain advances in 1886 and subsequent years. As a result they mortgaged their farms. Title to the land was withheld until the liens were discharged. A settler who was able to reimburse the government within a year or deliver the equivalent in oats, wheat, or barley was relieved of his dept with a small (6 per cent in 1886) interest fee. Otherwise, the debtor had to pay double the amount due plus yearly interest. Although the initial lien was usually small, it was rarely paid within a year. Crops were generally poor in the 1880s and 1890s, and cash flow was limited. Interest on the loans accrued, and many Métis still had 1886 liens registered against their lands in the 1920s. This situation explains at least in part the delays in obtaining patent. Among those seriously affected were Jean Caron Sr. (lot 52, Batoche), Frédéric St. Germain (lot 2, Vandal), Abraham Bélanger Jr. (lot 48, Vandal), François Arcand (lot 12, St. Laurent), and Mrs. Célestine Régnier (lot 8, St. Louis).[55] Daniel Gariépy and Élie Dumont lost their lands through these liens, and the descendants of Pierre Parenteau Sr. and Jean-Baptiste Gervais did not manage to obtain title to their properties until 1926 and 1930, respectively.[56] The outstanding seed grain mortgage liens were finally discharged by the Grain Adjustment Board in 1932, the main reason being that many lands had been transferred and the present occupant was not directly accountable for the debt.

Many other factors contributed to the relocation of the Métis, a phenomenon that accelerated after 1915 and reached its peak during the Depression of the 1930s. The arrival of immigrants at the turn of the century tended to drive away the Métis. The exodus was not as massive as in the Qu'Appelle Valley, but it was clearly evident at Fish Creek and to a lesser degree at St. Laurent. In some cases, the elders died and the children who had long since left the district sold the land. On the other hand, there was a regrouping of families, particularly at Batoche and St. Louis. Undesirable features such as marshy and sandy lands, particularly along the west bank of the South Saskatchewan River, forced off both the second generation of Métis and the French and Belgian immigrants who attempted to cultivate it.

Reserved lands under the Dominion Lands Act also caused some confusion and disturbed some claims in the Batoche area. As part of the agreement of sale of its land claims to the Dominion of Canada in 1869, the Hudson's Bay Company was granted 1/20 of the land in the fertile belt of the North West. In each township, section 8 and three-quarters of section 26 (all of the section in every fifth township) were reserved by the Company. According to an 1884 regulation, this reserved area included approximately four hundred acres in sections 7 and 8 (T43-1-3) on the west side of the river at Batoche. The area corresponded roughly to riverlots 14, 15, and 16, originally surveyed according to the township system of 1878–79 and resurveyed into riverlots in 1888. The area corresponding to lot 16 had been claimed by Elzéar Parisien since 1873 and occupied by him until around 1885, while lots 14 and 15 were occupied by Thomas Lépine and Athanase Falcon between 1882 and 1885.[57] There is evidence that insecurity regarding these claims influenced their departure. But the conflict only came to a head when Alexandre Pierre Fisher, owner of the NW quarter of section 18 to the north, claimed lot 16, which he had purchased from Parisien around 1885. Fisher, who had settled around 1877, had obtained title to his first homestead in 1888. He was entitled to a second homestead and wished to enter lot 16, located in the immediate vicinity of his farm. On the basis of his early occupancy and possibly to placate an outspoken local Liberal leader, the government negotiated an agreement with the Hudson's Bay Company in 1891 by which it gave up lots 14, 15, and 16 in exchange for riverlots 9 to 13, which were unoccupied.[58] Fisher won his case after three years of negotiations and was granted the lot, but because of bitterness or disillusionment, he never registered his claim.

There were some isolated efforts by land agents and homestead inspectors to assist the Métis in obtaining entry and patent to their lands. By the turn of the century, Métis were employed as sub-agents at Duck Lake and St. Louis. Nevertheless, financial difficulties such as tax arrears resulted in the loss of lands. Many lots at Batoche and St. Laurent reverted back to the Municipality of St. Louis in the 1920s. Some of these difficulties were not peculiar to the Métis. Eurocanadian settlers experienced difficulties during this period. It is evident, however, that the Métis as a group were more disadvantaged or were less informed about policies regarding fee schedules, residence requirements, and improvement duties. An 1890 letter by Abraham Bélanger Jr. to land agent Louis Schmidt, from his wintering place at Grosse-Butte (near Humboldt) in 1890, suggests he wished to settle outstanding debts on lot 48 (T42-1-3) near la couli des Tourond (Fish Creek), but that he was waiting for the government to advise him.[59] The more informed Salomon Venne was also confused. When he applied for entry for lot 55 in 1884 and again in 1886, he believed patent would be delivered automatically as residence and improvement requirements had been met. It was only when he offered the land as collateral on a business transaction in 1890 that he came to realize that he had to make a formal application for patent.[60] He obtained legal counsel and the issue was resolved, but at some personal cost and humiliation. Inquiries and statements by Charles Nolin, Charles-Eugène Boucher, and Louis Schmidt, who were familiar with Dominion Lands regulations and government bureaucracy, also reveal some confusion over the interpretation of regulations governing land entries and patent requirements. School teachers, such as Philippe Garnot and Octave Régnier, were often requested to write inquiry letters for Métis seeking information or settlement of a dispute.

By the 1890s, the Métis were better informed about homestead regulations and willing to use the system. There is little doubt, however, that they remained convinced of the moral and constitutional precedence of their customary land rights over Dominion Lands regulations enacted for the benefit of Eurocanadian settlers.

ABORIGINAL LAND CLAIMS THROUGH SCRIP IN 1886 AND 1899–1900 (SEE APPENDICES 4.1 AND 4.2)

The government attempted to extinguish the land and resource rights of the Métis in the North West Territories through the issue of scrip. The Manitoba precedent served as a model and as a result similar problems and delays in administering the grant fostered dissatisfaction amongst the Métis. It has been convincingly argued that the delays drove down the price to that which speculators were willing to pay and induced more Métis than might otherwise have done so to part with their claims to speculators for cash rather than wait for their land.[61] The failure of section 31 of the Manitoba Act to assist the Métis delayed the enactment of a similar grant in the North West Territories. It was only in 1879, after several requests by the Métis and their spokesmen, that the government recognized the Aboriginal rights of the Métis outside Manitoba.[62] This principle was reiterated in 1883.

Initially, the federal government considered granting the Métis non-negotiable non-transferable (up to the third generation) scrip. Bishops Taché and Grandin and most of the clergy favoured the establishment of Métis "reserves" that would control the disposition of the lands. They argued that the Métis were unable to resist the enticements held out by the speculators and that their adaptation to the sedentary way of life depended on the success of a "block system" of settlement.[63] It was a paternalistic view and one which most Métis adamantly opposed. But it stemmed from some genuine consideration for the Métis and fear regarding French-speaking and Catholic settlement in Manitoba and the North West.

Bishop Taché, in particular, had been deeply involved in the disposition of Métis lands in Manitoba. He personally purchased many lands as well as some scrip through representations, actions which he defended on the basis of wanting to impede the dispossession of Métis lands to Protestant Ontarians or outsiders. He reiterated his deception and fears regarding scrip in a letter to Riel in late 1884.[64]

The Métis of the South Saskatchewan River area had begun petitioning the federal and territorial governments for lands pursuant to their Aboriginal rights as early as 1874. Some of them were "western" Métis, not eligible for the Manitoba grant. Others had left the Red River Settlement in the 1850s and 1860s. The question of land rights was raised by the Métis of Batoche and district in at least six petitions between 1878 and 1885. They requested that land be granted to heads of families and children who had not participated in the Manitoba allotment.[65] Most Métis, however, were strongly opposed to the idea of Métis reserves. Only a group from the Cypress Hills area spoke out in favour of a reserve or in a petition to the Territorial Council. The latter recommended to the federal government, however, that it grant a non-transferable land scrip of 160 acres to each family head and his children (when they each reached 18) and to residents of the Territories in 1870, with the stipulation that the land would remain the property of the Crown or that title would be withheld for ten years.[66]

When the federal government finally decided upon the issue of scrip in early 1885, it was guided by expediency, rather than the long-term interests of the Métis. The policy was not a negotiated agreement but was enacted through legislation and order-in-council. The National Policy of Western settlement and isolation of Aboriginal peoples was the guiding force of the North-West Scrip Commissions.[67] The order-in-council of 28 January 1885 only authorized the appointment of three commissioners who would ascertain the number of Métis able to participate in the Métis land grant, based on their residence in Manitoba or in the North West Territories as of 1870.[68] A subsequent order-in-council (adopted 30 March 1885 in the wake of the armed resistance), authorized the commissioners to proceed not only with the enumeration of eligible Métis but also to set aside land for the distribution of scrip.[69]

According to the amended resolutions, every head of family residing in the North West Territories or outside Manitoba on or before 15 July 1870 would be eligible to receive a homestead grant of 160 acres. If he did not already occupy any land, he would receive a scrip certificate valued at $160, which could be exchanged for land (or a number of acres of land) of equivalent value.[70] The children of these heads of families living in the Territories on 15 July 1870 would be entitled to 240 acres of land and, if they were not settled on any land, to scrip of $240, which they could exchange for land of equivalent value.[71] The commissioners soon realized, however, that the two types of land grants, one under the Homestead Act and the other through scrip to extinguish Aboriginal rights, were a source of confusion. As a result, provisions were made to distribute scrip as a distinct grant.

The 1885 Street Commission visited the Fort Qu'Appelle district in the midst of the armed resistance. It would appear, according to accounts from that era, that deprivation and intimidation guided the Métis to cash in their negotiable scrip or to quickly dispose of their land scrip. D.H. Macdowall, MP for Saskatchewan, reported that the Métis had been placed in an impossible situation:

> The Half-breed population was in a considerably disturbed state of mind. Some of their friends were killed, some expatriated, others they knew not where – so they took the scrip as it was given, and only afterwards, when they had time to consider, concluded that they had not received their due and that their birth-right was sold for a mess of potage.[72]

The ministerial order of 18 April 1885, made amendments to the issuance of scrip. Métis children would receive a certificate worth 240 acres. However, they preferred scrip for $240, and an amendment to the Act on 13 April 1886 enabled them to choose between scrip for 240 acres and scrip for $240. The order of March 1885 granting the heads of families scrip for $160 exchangeable for land was still in effect, but most chose money scrip.[73]

Métis commissioner Roger Goulet visited St. Laurent and Prince Albert to deal with claims in the South Saskatchewan River district, in the fall of 1886 and in the spring of 1887.[74] There were various types of claims – as heads of families, children of heads of families (born as of 15 July 1870), and heirs of deceased heads of families and children. Twelve or so claims had been settled at Batoche in June 1885, almost all by women who were elderly, widowed, or heirs.[75]

On the basis of a list of scrip issued to "children of heads of families" in Batoche and vicinity between 1885 and 1887 (see list, Appendix 4.2), no land scrip was claimed but then most of the Métis in that area were already settled on lands for which they could obtain homestead patent. The majority of the South Saskatchewan River Métis were from Manitoba, had already claimed scrip under the Manitoba grant, or were not eligible for scrip under the provisions of North West Territories grant of 1885. There were also some, particularly the men, who, fearing prosecution or reprisals as a result of the armed resistance, chose not to come forth.

Dire straights and unfavourable economic conditions immediately following the 1885 Resistance were the determining factors in the immediate cashing-in of scrip. According to Father Fourmond, parish priest at St. Laurent:

> They came from everywhere for eight days to receive these precious rights. They totalled roughly 16,000 dollars just for the district of St. Laurent…. This scrip, almost all of which was immediately sold, relieved many a misery without enriching anyone, except perhaps the buyers. Many of our poor people had already promised them to merchants in order to obtain staples and clothing. I was happy to see the joy of these poor people and to think that this providential help would relieve them of much misery and hardship this winter.[76]

There were other reasons why the Métis favoured money scrip. In a report to the Department of the Interior in 1890, D.H. Macdowall stated that the Métis generally opted for money scrip because it was negotiable at face value. He added that it was difficult for the Métis to opt for land as it cost at least $2 per acre; in other words, the recipient of scrip could purchase

5.7. *"Halfbreed Scrip Commission" at Batoche village, 1900 – Saskatchewan Archives Board, S-B9737.*

5.8. *"Halfbreed Scrip Commission" headquarters in former Letendre house now North West Mounted Police Post, Batoche village, 1900 – Saskatchewan Archives Board, S-B9738.*

5.9. *People waiting for Scrip Commission at Duck Lake, 1900 – Saskatchewan Archives Board, S-B9722.*

only 80 or 120 acres, not 160 or 240.[77] He would also have to choose a lot immediately, which did not give him the best choice nor the possibility of choosing land elsewhere: "Had this not been done every Half-breed would have taken land scrip as being more valuable and at the same time they would not have sold all their scrip, as part of the scrip only which each family got would have relieved their indebtedness."[78] There was also evidence that the majority of Métis did not perceive advantages in land scrip. They saw scrip as a means to ready cash, not as an investment. Some also confused scrip and land entries (homesteads) under the Dominion Lands Act as titles for both were distributed at the same office. Finally, the 1885–86 issue around Batoche involved a proportionately large number of older women, younger men and claims by virtue of inheritance, circumstances favouring a quick cash settlement.

In 1886, the Métis of Batoche and St. Laurent raised some of the irregularities and problems regarding scrip. One petition, asked that those who had taken up arms not be excluded[79] while the second deplored that Métis with no fixed residence had not been able to obtain scrip.[80] They also asked the government to grant scrip "to the children of parents married in 1870, so that there is no jealousy between the children of a single family,"[81] Another resolution demanded that the scrip registered in Manitoba for people now in the North West be granted in the North West.[82] The extension of scrip rights was again reiterated in 1888. Fisher, Garnot, and the Liberals requested that scrip "be granted to all children born between 1870 and 1885 in that way, the Métis of the North West would be treated in the same manner as those of Manitoba."[83] Xavier Letendre, Charles Nolin, and the Conservatives also agreed: "We insist that the rights of Métis children be granted until at least 1885 with the same privileges as those granted to the Métis children of Manitoba in 1870."[84]

The issue gained political momentum in the 1890s. The government, fearing trouble, asked the North West Mounted Police to keep an eye on the Métis. In a letter to his superior in 1889, Superintendent Perry reported: "The French Half-breeds are confidently expecting that the present Parliament will give them Scrip till 1885 and there is a feeling amongst them that Government has promised them."[85] That same year, A.M. Burgess, the assistant deputy minister of the Department of the Interior, visited the St. Laurent district in order to observe the situation in person. The issue was hotly debated. On one hand, there was the clergy, who opposed issued money scrip. On the basis of the Manitoba and 1885 experience in the North West, in which most of the Métis had lost or sold their scrip, the missionaries suggested establishing a Métis reserve instead. At a meeting in Duck Lake, the Conservative MP, D.H. Macdowall, spoke in favour of a reserve, which was supported, at least initially by the population of St. Laurent, which formed a committee to examine the proposal. At a subsequent meeting in Batoche, at the beginning of 1891, however, there was strong opposition. According to a biased observer, Father Fourmond:

> The key speaker [Boucher] who intended to run for the legislative assembly of Regina, and wished to become popular began to rail against the colony, which he unjustly confused and without taking notice of the committee's work with the Métis reserves, accusing the supporters of the colony of wishing to treat the Métis as Indians, adding that it was necessary to request scrip, nothing but scrip. All but eight asked for scrip.[86]

This opposition put an end to the reserve scheme. The federal Liberals, who came to power in 1896, supported scrip without restrictions. In 1899, under the Laurier government, an order-in-council granted scrip to all children born between 15 July 1870 and the end of 1885.[87] A certificate worth $240 enabled the recipient to exchange it for land worth up to the equivalent value or to take 240 acres of land available for homesteading.[88] The issue included claims for children of deceased parents and the assignment of scrip of minor children to their parents. Shortly after a last petition from the Métis of Duck Lake and district in January 1900, the government also recognized the rights of children whose parents had received scrip in Manitoba and granted parents the land rights of children who had died between 1870 and 1885.[89] The Walker-Côté Commission, which dealt specifically with Métis claims (as opposed to non-treaty Indians), was established in March 1900. Most of the claims in the Batoche and St. Louis were distributed between June and August. The Commission recognized powers of attorney or assignment with respect to money scrip, while land scrip was non-transferable, a policy that favoured the selection of money scrip.

A tabulation of claims for the district suggests that most eligible claimants came forward. There were numerous assignments by women and minor children to fathers and husbands. Claims of deceased parents were usually shared by the surviving children, while those of deceased children were usually claimed by the father or head of family. Although money scrip was more popular, there were a significant number of land scrip applications (see list, Appendix 4.2). A glance at these names suggests a link between socio-economic circumstances and the selection of land scrip.[90] For example, Charles-Pantaléon Schmidt, son of land agent Louis Schmidt, chose land scrip, as did Baptiste Jr. and Tobie, sons of merchant Baptiste Boyer. John Letendre, son of Xavier, and his cousins Louis Jr., Modeste Parenteau, and Victor Thomas also chose land scrip. "Children" of other more prosperous families – Salomon Venne, Ambroise Fisher, and Louis Marion – did the same. Some, such as Moïse Ouellette Jr. and François Slater, also chose land despite their financial difficulties. The selection of land scrip, however, did not preclude its disposition or sale. Most of these scrips were sold to real estate agents or other interests between 1901 and 1907.[91] The land scrip was generally located at some distance from the residence of the claimant, and, unless he wished to relocate or had some knowledge of the agricultural value of the claim, it was sold.

The case of John Letendre, son of Xavier Letendre, illustrates this point. He selected scrip for 240 acres and was awarded land (NE quarter

5.10. *Scrip certificates valued at (a) $160 in 1885 and (b) 240 acres in 1905 issued by the Department of the Interior – Library and Archives Canada, RG15, Vol. 1391, 1406 (C-132171 and C-13272).*

NOT TRANSFERABLE.   Form E., No. 413

DEPARTMENT OF THE INTERIOR, CANADA.

HALF-BREED COMMISSION.

Batoche 25th June 1900

Under the powers vested in us by an Order of the Governor General in Council dated 2nd March, 1900, WE HEREBY CERTIFY that John Letendre dit Batoche son of Xavier Letendre dit Batoche, a Half-Breed, has proved to our satisfaction that he is entitled under the terms of the said Order to Scrip to the amount of TWO HUNDRED AND FORTY (240) ACRES, such Scrip to be redeemable in Dominion Lands open for ordinary Homestead entry, by the above named person.

Ref. No. 599532   **DUPLICATE.**

Department of the Interior,
PATENTS BRANCH.

Ottawa, NOV 28 1902

To the Accountant
  Department of the Interior.

Scrip No.   Required the Issue of the following Scrip, viz.:—

John Letendre, dit Batoche, son of Xavier Letendre dit Batoche

Approved.
Cert. E. No. 413   240 acres
D.H.I.

Under the authority of an Order in Council dated the 2 March 1900
Received the above mentioned
Scrip this
                                                         WM. M. GOODE
                                                         Chief Clerk.

5.11. *Scrip awarded to John Letendre dit Batoche in 1900 – Saskatchewan Archives Board, Homestead files 989 and 671 (S-B8302 and S-B8303).*

and west half of NW quarter-section 6, T40-6-W3), located southeast of Rosthern, in a Mennonite settlement area. The claim was promptly assigned by Letendre to A.J. Adamson, who secured patent in 1902. Letendre, who resided at Batoche, subsequently made entry and obtained patent for a homestead (SW quarter-section 16, T42-24-2) at Bonne Madone. He was evidently interested in acquiring land, and he may have used his scrip income to establish himself at a more suitable location.

Land prices had risen since 1885, and the increase in immigration and the enlargement of farms pursued by Eurocanadian settlers made the selection and disposal of land scrip more financially attractive. Scrip buyers or speculators followed closely, as they had in 1885, and there is little doubt that some Duck Lake and Rosthern merchants made some profitable transactions. Many Métis were also indebted to these stores or businesses: Goodfellow Brothers and W. Tait of Prince Albert; I. & R. Friesen and D. Hoeppner of Rosthern; H. Mitchell, R.S. Mackenzie and J. McIntyre of Duck Lake; A. Marcelin of Aldina; the Corporation Épiscopale de la Saskatchewan; and a number of firms in Moose Jaw and Indian Head, where the Métis had also located lands. The largest dealer in Métis land scrip in the area, however, was A.J. Adamson of Rosthern, who bought either for his firm (Canada Territories Corporation) or for the account of the Saskatchewan Valley Land Company.

In sum, scrip was a complex and largely unregulated system by which the government proposed to dispose of Métis Aboriginal rights in Western Canada. The intentions of the government were not only to settle these claims, but also to free the land for Eurocanadian settlement. Speculation was considered an honourable pursuit by Eurocanadian business in the late nineteenth century. Scrip was the ideal device for these ventures. The Métis, on the other hand, were in a period of social and economic turmoil and found themselves on the fringe of the economic and social mainstream of the era. They viewed scrip as a form of immediate compensation or relief, and not as a substitute for land. The Métis of the South Saskatchewan River district had occupied their riverlot farms since the early 1870s. They believed they could enter these lands and confirm ownership under the Homestead Act. A homestead was not the direct or "free" grant, which was their inherent right, but it was preferable to the circuitous land scrip alternative.

Certain aspects of the scrip policy, in particular powers of attorney, assignments and scrip accounts accumulated by the speculators in order to control the buying and selling, facilitated fraud and misrepresentation. Finally, the whole system, as conceived and carried out by the government, was unfair to the Métis. They had not been party to its design and were its victims, not beneficiaries as intended. Member of the Territorial Legislature, Charles "Le Marquis" Fisher, himself a Métis, exposed some of its abuses and felt the government had a moral responsibility towards his disaffected people:

> I desire to draw your attention to a matter affecting the issue of Métis scrip which from my own personal knowledge is assuming most serious proportions in this district, with a strong hope that some steps will be taken by the Government to remedy the evil.... The Métis are being prevailed upon by agents or speculators to sell their interest in their own and that of their families scrip for a mere song; 240 acre scrips are being bought up for the paltry sum of $75.00 to $80.00, which is not only robbing the Métis but is also a serious prospective blow to the district, as it affects the well-being of these people. I understand that one party has secured a lien on at least seventy-five claims in this immediate neighbourhood. I trust the Government will see their way to protecting these poor misguided people from the hands of money sharks.[92]

6
Hard Times and Coming of Age: Batoche since the 1930s

> « On n'a mangé d'la galette pis on n'a bu d'la piquette! » *(We ate lots of bannock and we drank lots of home made wine.)*

This chapter is based primarily on oral history interviews I carried out for Parks Canada for and since the first edition of the book, published in 1990. For this edition, the Gabriel Dumont Institute generously provided access to all their interviews conducted in the 1970s and 1980s and shared other rich cultural resources. Métis writers have also made an important contribution to the literature in recent decades. Activists such as the late professor Howard Adams, probably the first Saskatchewan Métis to hold a PhD, wrote extensively on Aboriginal struggles and political issues and his own personal journey as a Métis "who came out of the closet." He also documented his tumultuous life and career, which were the basis of a biography published by friends and colleagues in 2005.[1] Other contemporary leaders and educators such as Murray Hamilton and Keith Goulet and historians such as Heather Devine, Brenda McDougall, and Darren Préfontaine have brought fresh insights into Métis history and inspired me to revisit previous interpretations. In stark contrast to the 1970s, when Métis history was largely "hidden" and forgotten, Métis studies are now "à la mode" and new work is being published regularly.

6.1. *Alexandrine (Fleury) Nicolas seated left with friends at Duck Lake picnic, 1983 – Diane Payment.*

This account is in many ways a retrospection. It has been a long personal journey since I first came to Batoche in 1976. I was a young historian full of energy and idealism about "rehabilitating Métis history," finding out why my grand-mother had denied her heritage and why my maternal aunts used to state emphatically « on n'i pas Michifs nous ôtes. »[2] Along with colleagues such as Anne Morin and Walter Hildebrandt, I was intent on vindicating Métis actions in 1885 but more importantly on telling the story of the community and its people who remained largely unknown and misrepresented at the National Historic Site. In the course of this "mission," which had its joys and sorrows, I made many special friends. Marguerite Perillat opened her house and her heart and introduced me to Métis families of Duck Lake. Alexandrine (Fleury) Nicolas and I shared many bottles of "Blue Nun" while retired Colonel Réal Boucher originally from St. Louis and Art Fisher of Regina shared stories and family history over the years. Many families kept in touch and continued to provide family photographs and accounts "for the book." Brenda Percell, a descendant of the Boyer, Ladéroute, and Tourond families, shared her family history, her experiences about growing up at Batoche in the 1960s and the more recent re-affirmation of her identity and culture.

This portrait of Batoche or its more recent history is based on "stories from within the community" and personal observations and experiences. As a result this chapter has a different narrative form from the previous chapters. It is culturally specific or a blend of oral discourse and written accounts; spontaneous, purposeful, and often indirect and open-ended. Some oral narratives were autobiographical, while others focussed on societal values and collective experiences. Some government, ecclesiastical, and other public records were consulted, but they often provided only partial or selective glimpses of the community. Because of their persistent oral tradition, limited schooling, and marginalization, the Métis themselves produced few formal written accounts for the public record until the 1970s. However, they are no longer historically voiceless. The recording of Métis history has challenged traditional white concepts of history and brought to the fore their own values, issues, and experiences.

Located in the parkland belt, Batoche was not subject to the same extreme drought conditions or economic hardships as southern Saskatchewan in the 1930s. Life continued much as before "on the fringe" of Western society or communities such as the Mennonites of Rosthern, the Ukrainians of Wakaw, and the French Canadians of Bellevue. The people of Batoche, St. Laurent de Grandin, and St. Louis along the South Saskatchewan River were closely related through marriage and culture, and interaction with neighbouring communities was minimal. The French Canadian community of Bellevue, which had grown and prospered in the 1920s, was increasingly insular and prejudiced towards its compatriots, which some referred to derisively as: « les batochiens » (the dogs from Batoche). It is a fact of history that a minority community is often harsh towards a parent minority. The francophone minority in Saskatchewan was subjected to increased restrictions on French and Catholic education by the provincial government, which resulted in retrenchment. In addition, French Canadians were often viewed as "bastardized French" by French and Belgian immigrants as well as English Canadians, which fostered an inferiority complex. The French Canadian nationalist views and policies of parish priests such as Reverend Pierre-Elzéar Myre, who was at Batoche and then Bellevue in the 1930s deepened the rift between the two communities. Unlike "old Father Moulin," who was paternalistic but sensitive towards Aboriginal cultures, l'abbé Myre, and some of the other priests who followed him were hostile and critical of the Métis and aggressively promoted French Canadian aspirations and lifestyles. People who expressed their Métisness or Aboriginal heritage were viewed as backward or inferior and isolated from the parish council and activities. As a result many cultivated their "Frenchness" to avoid discrimination.

"School got you nowhere"

Schooling was difficult for the Métis. Parents sent their young children to the local St. Antoine de Padoue two-room school, but few went beyond grade 8, which was the highest level in the 1930s and 1940s. Many children had to walk over four or five miles to school, which was too far or dangerous in the winter or when the roads were impassable in the spring and fall. The oldest children were often taken out of school to work in the fields or in the home. It was not that schooling was not valued, but it was considered something "for the rich" or parents who could afford to do without their children's labour. Most children had to leave school around the age of twelve to do chores for the family and some even had to make a living on their own because of family misfortune or break-up. Only a few families were able to send their daughters to the convent boarding school in Duck Lake or St. Louis for a secondary education. A few promising young boys were given bursaries by Church benefactors to attend seminaries and junior colleges in the hope that they would eventually become priests. One of these, Alfred Boucher, became a bishop, while one of his aunts, Emma, became a Grey Nun. They came from an influential St. Louis family, and, although they quietly acknowledged their Métis ancestry, they were part of the French Canadian elite in Saskatchewan. Some boys went to St. Michael's Industrial School in Duck Lake, which accepted some Métis students, but even though they experienced less prejudice than their Cree school mates, they also spent more time working than learning. In the classroom, the focus was on religious instruction and an "elementary" education.

For the Métis in general, the strongest impediment against school was prejudice and low self-esteem fostered by teachers. It was generally believed by most Eurocanadian educators that elementary schooling was good enough for Métis men who were destined to work as labourers or farmhands and Métis women who worked as domestics outside the home. Délima Parenteau (née St. Germain) who attended school in St. Laurent in the 1930s was told not to speak Michif French and was slapped by the teacher, Omer Courchesne.[3] However she acknowledged that she did learn to read and write and was able to help her parents with paperwork. There were few if any opportunities for those who pursued their education unless they identified or passed as "whites." There were some young men who returned from both world wars and sought to pursue their education and training, some at the university level. One man who trained as a civil engineer in the 1940s was forced to accept a lower-paying position once the company found he was "native." He could have hidden his identity or said he was Scottish as his name was Ross, but he chose not to. He eventually found work for which he was qualified with Indian Affairs, but they only hired him part-time, and he never did get any pension or benefits when he retired some twenty years later.

The government of Saskatchewan increased funding to public schools in the late 1940s. One of the motives for this initiative was to promote "betterment and civilization of Halfbreeds," as they were then called. The curriculum focussed on English instruction, which meant that the Métis could "fit in" and experience less prejudice as was the case in French schools. Michif French was still spoken in the home in the 1950s and 1960s and many youth refused to learn or speak "the other French" because of the persistent prejudice and cultural differences between the two parent communities.

Transmission of cultural values took place at home and generally was done by the grandmothers, or kokums, who were "the real teachers." Most elderly or widowed grandmothers lived with their children and grandchildren, sometimes "visiting" for long periods of time with each of their children. Children of single parents and orphaned children were usually raised by their grandparents. Rose Fleury (née Gariépy) stated that "everything I know I learned from my grandmother."[4] Kokum Élise Paul (née Trottier) taught her Cree, Michif Cree, and French and told her many stories about her past and life at Round Prairie (south-east of present-day Saskatoon). Story-telling was an important educational tool as there was traditionally a moral to a story to promote good behaviour and actions. Mémère Paul was strict but strong and supportive and instilled in Rose and her siblings the values of courage, enterprise, and self-reliance. Élise

6.2. *Kokum Mary-Jane (formerly Racette, née Ouellette) Charette besides Riel's grave in St. Boniface (Manitoba), 1935– donated by Marcel Giraud.*

Paul was paralysed in one leg and walked with difficulty but she never stopped. She prepared hides for moccasins and beaded clothing. Rose often accompanied her grandmother when she delivered babies, and together they gathered herbs for "Indian medicine." Kokum was a spiritual woman and a devout Catholic. She was also a Métis nationalist, following the tradition of her grandfather, 1885 leader Charles Trottier.

These women had agency. Their moral, emotional, rhetorical, and political resources were manifold. They were the bosses in the homes and were responsible for the education and survival of future generations. They got together to work at activities such as sewing, herb-gathering, and berry-picking. They also helped each other in core community and family functions such as health care and childbirth. There were usually at least two practising midwives in each community along the South Saskatchewan River. Women such as Albina "La Pie" St. Denis (née Boucher) were respected for their expertise with difficult births and saved the lives of many women in the 1920s and 1930s. But some midwives were to be avoided as they often took risks or "lost mothers and babies." The Catholic Church's position on childbirth until the 1950s was that the new life took precedence over the existing life or that the child should be saved before the mother. There is some evidence that Métis women resisted this Western patriarchal value, especially in the case of mothers with many young children to care for.

"On the Road Again": "A little bit of this and a little bit of that"

During the Depression years, people worried about food and shelter or the basics. In the words of Rose Fleury: "If you had more, you were rich." There was a reluctance among the proud Métis to accept welfare or handouts. Families were able to subsist by working at a variety of labouring jobs. The riverlot was the home base where men raised a few cattle and women grew large gardens and sold eggs and butter in neighbouring towns. According to Aimé Dumont: "we ate whatever had four legs, gophers, rabbits and even skunks."[5] One of the important social changes of that period was the extended absence of fathers and sons from home for work. The Métis had traditionally pursued a mobile lifestyle but as a family unit. But now the need for a cash income to supplement meagre harvests meant that men were away from home for extended periods. Joseph Vandale, whose

6.3. Joe Caron with horse team, ca. 1940s – Parks Canada, donated by Russell Porter.

6.4. Ferryman Napoléon Fayant at Batoche's Crossing, 1963 – Saskatchewan Archives Board, R-A22306-2.

father was absent for years at a time, started looking after his mom and brothers and sisters when he was twelve years old. Many men "rode the rails" in search of jobs at lumbering camps in northern Saskatchewan and British Columbia or as ranch hands in southern Alberta. Bella Arcand (née Vandale) thought that Métis men often got the dirtiest and lowest-paying jobs on railway and road construction crews.[6] Many men worked on threshing outfits and as "hired hands" on neighbouring Eurocanadian farms. Graham Adams of St. Louis worked as a farm labourer in the 1930s and 1940s: "rates were one dollar a day, sometimes less for haying grubbing and brushing and two to five dollars a month in the winter."[7] Hired men "bunked" in a heated shed adjoining the house. They were well fed but kept to themselves or were not allowed to socialize with the family, especially the young women. Local young men who left home in search of work often looked at it as an adventure: "you had to make it on your own during the depression years as the people were poor ... boy we had a hard time."[8] Maxime Parenteau started working part-time at fourteen years old to help his dad in the 1930s. He cut cordwood for fifty cents a cord. School for him and his friends became a part-time activity and he completed grade seven at sixteen years old. Walter Fidler also left school at fourteen to earn money to help his father, who was partly blind. He started by working for farmers and cutting cordwood, but in his early twenties he went to work in the sawmill at Montreal Lake and made enough money to buy a riverlot and farm near Gabriel's Crossing. He remained at Batoche, where he bought more land to raise cattle and horses, but some of his friends went to work in shops in the northern United States and stayed there.

Cousins Élie and Aimé Dumont were proud of the fact that they were continuously employed during those years and throughout their lifetime. They worked hard, ploughing fields with an ox before they got their own horse teams. They got a lot of personal satisfaction from their work and were sad when they weren't able to go out and work as hard as they got older. Élie eventually made enough money to "settle down" and purchase a horse ranch in Wakaw, east of Batoche. But, as Médéric McDougall and his contemporaries stated, the Métis work ethic was centred on work to enjoy life, not to save money: "We were a little different in our ways.... We worked but we believed in having a good time.... I used to take the day off to go the Batoche Sports Day on the 24th of July and the Duck Lake picnic. This French fellow I worked for used to kind of laugh at me for losing some dollars.... Today he is richer than me but not happier."[9]

Some families moved further north, to communities such as Green Lake and Buffalo Lake to trap and fish. Although these moves were regarded as temporary, they often resulted in permanent relocations in areas with better resources. There was also more unoccupied land available for cattle-raising or farming in north-western Saskatchewan. Although many people suffered hardship and deprivation, few went on social assistance, which was viewed as a last resort for the sick or handicapped. "People helped each other and took care of the old people" is an often-heard statement from those days.

There were a number of "successful" storekeepers at Batoche and surrounding communities: Alfred Boyer in St. Louis, Raphaël Boyer and son-in-law, Ferdinand Paulhus, and Avila Chénier at Batoche. The Nogier family, originally from France and intermarried with the Métis, were enterprising and prosperous farmers at Batoche in the 1940s–1960s. However they did not identify as Métis and associated primarily with English-speaking businesses in Duck Lake and Rosthern.

WOMEN'S WORK AND MORE

Women did other jobs for "expense money" in addition to the housework and regular farm work. They went out in groups berry-picking and to dig seneca root, which they sold for twenty-five cents a pound. It was a labour-intensive activity, which also involved drying and packing the root for sale as medicine. They also made quilts and knitted mittens and stockings and sewed clothing for sale in Prince Albert and Saskatoon. Many were expert dressmakers and could make couturier-class suits and dresses from pictures in catalogues. Alice Arcand (née St. Denis) recalled that sometimes she was able to use the remnants from those ensembles to make a nice dress for herself or her daughter.[10] Many young women also left home to work as domestics for families, cooking, cleaning, and taking care of children. There was a lot of demand for "hard-working Halfbreed girls" in Eurocanadian homes in Duck Lake, St. Louis, and Bellevue. Victoria Dumont (née Laframboise) earned seven dollars a month in the 1930s, including room and board and no time off except for Sunday Church services. She used to attend Mass in the morning and benediction and vespers in the afternoon to get some time off. No big chores such as laundry were allowed on Sunday but meals and dishes had to be done unless the family went out to visit. In one of the homes that she worked in, the mother who was paralysed was kind and generous. She taught her how to cook and embroider. But Victoria was forced to leave the family because one of the sons "was always trying to force her into a corner and fondle her."[11] She was ashamed to tell the mother and was afraid of the father, who was a hard man and abusive towards his wife.[12] Délima Parenteau (née St. Germain) started working out of the home when she was fifteen in 1937 and married at seventeen. Then she worked with her husband on the farm, milking the dairy cows and separating the milk and cream for shipping. She also raised chickens and sold eggs for five cents a dozen to buy luxuries such as tea and sugar. All the food was homemade. Meat was mostly wild meat, deer, partridges, prairies chickens, and rabbits, and all the vegetables came from the garden and fruits from the bush. The family purchased flour to make bannock and bread, a food staple, but other women reported that they had a grinding stone to grind their own wheat kernels, a time-consuming activity, and the flour was coarser and often of poorer quality. However, rye and other grains were crushed for cattle feed as the selling price was only ten cents a bushel. Women of those days were real "domestic scientists" in the sense that they knew how to make do with very little. Joseph Vandale recalled how his mother "was an enterprising woman. I don't know how in the world she managed to keep us fed, all the kids. You really had to pull and make things stretch to make it go." Mock recipes such as "apple" pie made with soda crackers instead of apples and « poutine chômeur » (poor man's stew or pudding) without meat or raisins were standard fare.

Being Métis meant being poor, especially for women. They had the responsibility for the home, which meant raising, feeding, and clothing a large, often extended, family. The Great Depression years were particularly hard when the men often worked away from home and they were responsible for running the farm as well. Single women and increasingly married women continued to improvise and work independently in the 1940s and 1950s. An increasing number had to support their family because they were single parents or widowed. Alexandrine Nicolas (née Fleury) worked on the farm with her husband while raising two families. During the 1930s, she milked fifteen cows by hand then separated the cream, which she prepared for shipping. She would get a maximum of $1.80 per five-gallon can, which was a lot of "spending money."[13] But bartering with her neighbour was more remunerative and she made a deal with her to exchange cream for butter. When she was widowed in 1945, she took in boarders from Child and Family Services. Her daughter-in-law, Rose Fleury (née Gariépy), who is still a going concern in her eighties, "never depended on someone to do something for me. I always worked to make my own living."[14] She was raised by her maternal grandparents and learned how to live off the land or harvest and conserve meat, fruit, vegetables, and medicinal herbs. Her grandmother instilled in her values of self-reliance and enterprise. Rose had a large family and raised many of her grandchildren. At one time, she had sixteen children in her home. Her husband was a supportive partner but times were hard in the 1950s and 1960s. "Not one to stay idle," Rose became involved in the Métis Women's Association and went back to school at forty years of age to get her high school diploma and become a social worker. A better-paying job gave her independence. She bought lots in Duck Lake, and she and her husband were able to have their own home. Rose remained a community activist and respected elder, committed to the revival and promotion of her Métis culture. She was the main force behind the establishment of a Métis museum and genealogy centre in Duck Lake.[15]

Family relationships changed quite dramatically during those years as more women went out to work outside the home, at least part-time, to supplement the family income. Whereas in the past orphaned children would always be raised or adopted by relatives, institutional care became more commonplace. Jeannette Gervais' (née Caron)[16] parents died when she was very young. Her elderly widowed Kokum Parenteau did her best to look after her, but she lived far from school, and Jeannette and her young brother were sent to St. Patrick's orphanage in Prince Albert. It was a very hard experience for the young children, who could not speak their own Michif French language and were forced to speak English. Food consisted of cold porridge every morning, and other meals consisted of soup, fried potatoes, and stale bread buttered with lard. There was very little meat and only the nuns and priests had fresh-baked bread, desserts, and fruit. The "orphans" looked forward to the summer months at their grandmother's, where there was care and nurturing.

People married young at Batoche, especially the women. They were encouraged to do so by their parents "before they could get into trouble" as customs were changing and people were going out more. Eveline Caron Boyer married a local young man who was in the service at seventeen in 1944. One of her sisters also married a local Métis man, but the others

6.5. *Wedding of Eveline Caron and Joe Boyer, Batoche, October 16, 1944 – Parks Canada, Derek Bodington Collection, courtesy of Annette Boyer.*

dated outsiders, which caused the parents some anxiety. One of her unmarried sisters had a son, who was raised as their own by his grandparents, Albert and Marjorie (Adair) Caron. There was social stigma and a double standard towards unmarried mothers at that time: "It was hard to find a husband if you had a baby. You were ignored and some men joked about you, or thought you were easy."[17]

Métis who married outside the community suffered from stigma and prejudice. Métis women were particularly vulnerable: "We were laughed at and had to hide our heritage." Marie-Louise Éthier, a French Canadian who came to teach at Batoche in the 1930s and married a local Métis, Ernest Caron, also experienced discrimination. She was very fond of her family; however, her husband died after only a few years of marriage, leaving her with two children. She then married a French Canadian, who she said looked down upon her children and made unkind remarks about her first marriage.[18] Another "white" woman who married a Métis man said she was cut off from her parents. She could only come alone to visit them and her children never knew their grandparents. When you crossed

6.6. *Children of Edmond Boyer and Berthe Ladéroute, 1930s – Parks Canada, Brenda (Boyer) Percell Collection.*

the lines of race and class, there was often a price to pay so "we stuck to ourselves."

Estelle Boyer, daughter of Edmond Boyer and Berthe Ladéroute, had a happy childhood at Batoche and St. Laurent in the 1940s and 1950s. But there were no career opportunities for young women at Batoche at the time, only domestic and seasonal farmwork that were hard and low-paying. Most of her friends married and stayed around, but she wanted some adventure and a career. Independent and adventurous, she went to St. Boniface (Manitoba) where she had relatives (the only way her family would let her leave) to complete grade twelve. She joined the Women's Army Corps in Winnipeg for a short time and drifted into various jobs. Life was exciting but difficult in "the big city." When her marriage broke down, she came back home with two daughters. The grandparents helped her out until their death, and then she was on her own as a single mom. The Catholic Church was harsh and punitive towards single mothers during that time, but fortunately Métis families accepted the children or did not discriminate against them as in most Western societies.[19]

OFF TO WAR

Many young men from Batoche and surrounding communities had joined up during the First World War. The main reason they had gone off to war in 1914 was for work and adventure, in particular to get away from the farm. But most of the Métis who had returned were sick or injured and never received the promised Soldier Settlement grants and job opportunities. Young men who went off to war again in 1939–40 cited unemployment and adventure as the main incentives. Some "boys" joined up secretly with their buddies without telling their parents because they were underage. Most Métis opposed conscription or compulsory enlistment. This may have been a legacy of their treatment at the hands of the Canadian government in 1885 as well as their French Canadian heritage. Both Métis and French Canadians had a tradition of resistance to British colonial wars. They also supported the Liberal party, which opposed conscription. Médéric McDougall said that he was a pacifist like many of his friends. They did not really see a reason to go and fight as it was far away and it was not as if they were defending their way of life. He

6.7. Standing left to right: Baptiste Primeau, John-Baptiste Letendre and seated: Azarie Letendre in 1914 before they left for overseas to serve in World War I – Parks Canada, courtesy Stella Parenteau.

recalled that he was a little more concerned when he read about the fall of France in 1940 and bombings in London. Reports of U-boats in the St. Lawrence River and the dislike of dictatorships were also a concern.[20] The main reason why Aimé Dumont, Emile St. Germain, Archie Nicolas, Claude Petit, and Léon Ferguson went to war was for "a steady income." The pay was $1.50 a day plus room and board when you enlisted, much better than cutting brush from daylight until dark for fifty cents a day.[21] Aimé Dumont mentioned that he wanted to do his bit and be accepted in society: "When I volunteered for active service I was treated as an equal or as a Canadian. We served our country and they didn't call us names like *mangeux d'galette* (bannock eaters)."[22] Edmond Boyer of Batoche, a veteran of the First World War, enlisted in 1940, but, due to his age, he did not go overseas and was assigned to kitchen duty in Regina. As a veteran, he was treated with consideration and respect by his "war buddies." War service also meant a steady income for his family and he was able to purchase a farm in St. Laurent.

David Dumont and Joe Fayant found their French useful in the army, especially in France and Belgium. Archie Nicolas was a member of the Royal Vingt-Deuxième or "Vingt-Deuse," the French Canadian Regiment, and felt quite at home: "they thought I was from New Brunswick [Acadian] with my Duck Lake French."[23] Métis soldiers were known for their expert marksmanship, scouting expertise, and ability to drive and fix any type of machinery. Some veterans mentioned that they had difficulty with the rigorous army discipline as they were used to being their own bosses, but they stuck it out in order to learn a trade and send money to their families. There was reportedly little discrimination between men in uniform, but it is not clear how many Métis soldiers acknowledged or talked openly about their Aboriginal heritage.

The Métis made up the largest component of Aboriginal peoples serving in the Canadian forces in the Second World War and the Korean War, but they received "less than a hero's welcome." Once the war was over and you were out of uniform, the old prejudices returned. Aimé Dumont of Duck Lake recalled that he went to see a politician regarding promised employment and vocational training: "He wanted our votes so he told us that the door would always be open to any soldier who needed help. I had been a driver mechanic in the army and like others I wanted to learn more about diesel engines.... We went to see him again but of course the door was always closed."[24] The general feeling among Métis veterans

6.8. *Edmond Boyer (1897–1966) veteran of two World Wars – Parks Canada, Brenda (Boyer) Percell Collection.*

after the Second World War was that they had been good enough to fight during the war but not good enough to get employment priority, as did returning white soldiers. Disability pensions were small, there were no rehabilitation programs, and many could not get jobs requiring physical labour because of injuries. Archie Nicolas returned to his hometown of Duck Lake on crutches in May 1945. He did not want to be discharged as the war was still on in Japan and he could earn $7.50 a month while still in uniform, but he had no choice in the matter. He was unable to get the support of Veterans' Affairs.[25]

For some, however, war had become a lifestyle and the army the only place they felt accepted. Léon Ferguson, for example, had a long career in the army. When he returned in 1946 he did not know what to do. He tried working in bush camps and in the mines but he didn't like civilian life and enlisted to go to Korea with this brother Ernest. He joined the Princess Patricia Regiment with Claude and Norris Petit. Claude Petit, who was in the army for fifteen years in Europe, Korea, and Alaska, felt that it was not worth it. Too many had died, and when he was discharged he was "on the road again," working in sawmills in Ontario, the bush in Manitoba, and eventually as a roofer in Saskatchewan. Léon Ferguson, on the other hand, remained in the army until his retirement as a sergeant in 1972, when he joined the Corps of Commissionaires. His army career was a positive experience: "The army gave me training and discipline. I've always been proud to be a Métis who served in the military. My great grandfather [Augustin Laframboise] was killed in the rebellion of 1885 at Duck Lake."[26]

Women also experienced suffering during the war. Alexandrine Nicolas had two sons, Archie and Robert, who went to war. Both survived but were wounded, while Marguerite Gervais lost a son, Émile. There is no evidence of local women who joined the service, although many supported the war effort by making clothing. One of the unfortunate legacies of the war for families was alcoholism. Almost all soldiers drank to ease the fear and stress of fighting and death of their comrades. Some were able to return to civilian life and deal with these issues, some joined Alcoholics Anonymous, while others never fully recovered.

One of the positive impacts of war service for the Métis was the schooling and training that they received during their enlistment. They saw how other people lived and became more aware of the need to defend their rights. The new political leaders of the late 1940s and 1950s, such as Jim Brady, Archie Nicolas, and Joe Amyotte, all credited their military experience as a training ground for subsequent political battles. Sixty years later, Métis veterans are still fighting for compensation and feel forgotten. In 2002, the National Council of Veterans Association filed a claim with the United Nations Human Rights Commission for financial and statutory benefits. It remains unsettled.

POLITICAL RESURGENCE AND GROWTH

"Fighting for Our Rights"

Batoche and surrounding communities had been very active politically in the 1880s. Louis Riel had founded the first Métis association, « l'Union Métisse Saint-Joseph », at Batoche in 1884. The following year, the Métis formed a provisional government, called « le petit provisoire de la Saskatchewan », to distinguish it from the larger provisional government of 1869–70 in Manitoba, and took up arms against the Canadian government to defend their rights. The « Union Nationale Métisse Saint-Joseph du Manitoba » (UNMSJM), founded in St. Vital (Manitoba), by Joseph St. Germain, Joseph Riel, and associates in 1887, was the first official "national" Métis association. Its main objectives were the defence of Métis rights, the rehabilitation of Métis history and the promotion of Michif French language and culture. The UNMSJM founded locals in a number of communities in Manitoba and southern Saskatchewan, and a local was

6.9. Elders of l'Union Nationale Métisse St. Joseph du Manitoba celebrating la fête nationale in Riel Park (St. Vital, Manitoba) in July, 1917: standing left to right: Alexandre and Joseph Riel (brothers of Louis), André Nault, Elzéar Lagimodière, William Lagimodière; seated: Paul Proulx – Parks Canada, donated by André Nault Jr. family of Meadow Lake, Saskatchewan.

6.10. *Damase Carrière (1848–1885) who died at the battle of Batoche on May 12, 1885 and was reportedly "finished off" by the North West Field Force in retaliation for Captain French's death and Pélagie Parenteau (1854–1920), married (1) Damase Carrière and (2) Maxime Dubois – Parks Canada, courtesy of Mrs. Jean Groat.*

quietly established at Batoche in the 1890s. In 1902–03, a historical committee from St. Boniface visited the community to interview veterans of 1885, including Gabriel Dumont, Moïse Ouellette, and Jean Caron. It is known through oral history that most families supported the Union, but it seems that the veterans of 1885 and their descendants met secretly in their homes to avoid public scrutiny. No minutes of these meetings, held until the 1920s, are known to have survived.

« *Le grand silence* » was the legacy of 1885. Political activism in Métis communities along the South Saskatchewan River was frowned upon and controlled by both government officials and the clergy. When Moïse Ouellette, one of the organizers of the local July Fête des Michifs set up a donation fund to erect a monument to the Métis and First Nations victims of 1885 in the Batoche cemetery in 1901, he aroused the suspicion of local Church officials. The Church, which had lost the support of many Métis since 1885, reluctantly approved the initiative in a gesture of reconciliation. A banner of the Union Nationale and its patron, St. Joseph, made by a local woman, Élise Boyer (née Tourond), was displayed in the church every July 24. The Batoche community reacted negatively to the erection of a plaque by the Historic Sites and Monuments Board of Canada commemorating the "Northwest Rebellion" in 1925 but otherwise remained silent out of fear of repression and retaliation by the government. Resistance was usually expressed in quiet actions such as the erasure of the offensive words on the government plaque and isolating themselves from mainstream communities.

There was a strong legacy of fear among the veterans of 1885, and they rarely spoke of the resistance outside their ranks or even to their children. Mme Josephte Tourond, who had lost three sons in 1885, and lived until the 1920s, remained a strong nationalist and passed on the torch to her extended family. In 1935, Patrice Fleury spoke cautiously of the events of 1885 to visiting ethnologist Marcel Giraud and members of the Prince Albert Historical Society. Frédéric St. Germain, who had fought in « la guerre nationale », told his family in the 1940s that he remained convinced of the justice of his actions but did not want to talk about it. Alfred Boyer whose grandfather Isidore died in battle said his grandmother Marguerite (née Bremner) and father Magloire used to speak about the events among themselves in French [Michif] but became silent when children were around, probably so they would not get hurt. The outcome had not been good and it was best to get on with life.[27] It was not customary to question elders, and it was considered disrespectful to pry into sensitive issues, but the message was clear. Both Alfred Boyer and Médéric McDougall were told that the "rebellion" occurred because the Métis were trying to defend their land and other rights. The Métis cause was just and yet the government put it down. To ease tensions, the elders would often tell "success stories" such as the strategic attack on the steamboat (*The Northcote*) and humorous accounts such as the misfiring of the Gatling gun or the « rababou », which made a lot of noise but could not match the marksmanship of the Métis. These and other stories were passed on and shared, but more controversial topics such as Riel's actions, Métis

6.11. *Patrice Fleury (1840–1941) veteran of 1885 Resistance in front of Batoche monument, 1935 – donated by Marcel Giraud.*

rights, and current politics were discussed at private gatherings away from the scrutiny of « les étranges » (strangers or outsiders).

The actions of Métis women in 1885 have only more recently come to light.[28] Women were very much present during the resistance, although they were left out as the battle was perceived as a contest between men. Mme Marie-Louise Boucher (née Bremner), who was hiding in the dugouts along the riverbank at Batoche during the battle, told her family the poignant story of the church bell taken by soldiers. They clumsily wrapped it in blankets and swore as they tripped and hurt themselves under its weight. She was quite scandalized as this was a blessed Church object, but she and others had not dared to intervene and risk the lives of their families.[29]

Marguerite Caron (née Dumas) persuaded Riel to send reinforcements to la couli des Tourond (now Fish Creek), and her sister Christine Pilon (née Dumas) was one of the leaders at *la loge des femmes* (the women's camp) along the riverbank, rounding up cattle, cooking, and caring for the sick. Marie Letendre Champagne protested vainly when the government soldiers started rounding up her horses and cattle but managed to hide sacks of flour and some meat from them. It was the women who made bullets out of melted lead during the battle and picked up the dead afterwards. Many of them were left alone to raise large families and rebuild the community as many of the men were sent to prison, were forced into exile, or left in search of work in the years following the armed resistance.

There was a long tradition of resentment towards « *la maudite police* » ("the damned police"), a term used to describe any enforcers of the white man's law, whether it was the military or the Mounted Police. This was another legacy of the armed resistance of 1885 and the police patrols and surveillance that followed. The prejudice that persisted in the government and police circles well into the 1950s also contributed to their attitudes and actions towards Aboriginal peoples. According to Médéric McDougall: "the police did not treat the Métis well. They treated us roughly … for just a little bit of trouble … there was a double standard." He recalled the incident when his son Butch went to the beer parlour and things got a bit rowdy. The police came over to his home to arrest his son, and when Médéric tried to talk to them and protect his son, they became aggressive. There was a scuffle and then the police drew their guns, ready to shoot. It was only Mme McDougall's timely intervention that prevented a serious incident.[30] Médéric's nephew, Métis leader Howard Adams, also wrote

6.12. RCMP constable Archie Lépine (1938–1962), who died on duty – Parks Canada, courtesy of Octavie (Pilon) Lépine.

about police brutality and their attitudes towards the Métis, whom they considered drifters and troublemakers.

Yet there were some positive experiences or evidence that the relationships were changing by the 1960s. Achilles (Archie) Lépine, a relative of Médéric and Howard, became a constable of the RCMP, to the delight of his parents and community. He was posted in British Columbia, where he was killed in an accident at the age of twenty-four in 1962, in the early years of his career. Réal Boucher, a member of the famous family from St. Louis, enrolled in the Air Force in 1957 and rose to the rank of colonel during a career of twenty-six years. He was posted throughout Europe and served in the diplomatic corps with much success, but he remained faithful to his heritage and prairie roots.

"Do Something for Yourself"

Métis associations established in the 1930s were mainly concerned with addressing economic conditions and land claims in the North. The Métis Association of Alberta and the North West Territories, founded in 1932, started as a francophone association supported by the Catholic clergy. The leaders included Jim Brady, Malcolm Norris, Joe Dion, and Peter Tompkins.[31] Brady and Norris were both middle-class socialists and intellectuals who visited Métis communities in Alberta and Saskatchewan but remained somewhat aloof or separate from the people they represented. They also opposed the Church's policy of assimilation and federal control and were soon branded as "radicals" by the latter, causing division and apprehension among the general Métis population. The Alberta association succeeded in bringing the Alberta government to action by drawing up a petition to address the issue of land tenure. In 1935, after intense lobbying, the government appointed the Ewing Commission to inquire into the health, education, and welfare of the "Half-Breed population." The Commission failed to positively address issues of Métis identity and culture but convinced the Alberta government to establish ten Métis colonies in northern Alberta. The Métis wanted a cooperative venture with the government but ended up as wards with little or no say in the administration of the colonies. Nonetheless, the Métis of northern Alberta were the first to obtain a land base in the twentieth century, an important achievement and a precedent.

In Saskatchewan, Joe Ross, Joseph Larocque, and other leaders who were based in Regina laid the groundwork for the Métis Society of Saskatchewan, established in 1938.[32] The Métis Association of Saskatchewan, led by Norris and Brady, also established locals in northern communities such as Prince Albert and Meadow Lake. Ross, who was blind, secured a government railway pass, which enabled him to visit communities throughout central Saskatchewan, including Saskatoon, Duck Lake, and St. Louis. Aimé Dumont and others remembered that he came up to try and organize locals. The organizations were having difficulty getting memberships and gaining trust during those years, perhaps because people were experiencing so much hardship due to the Depression but also probably due to the legacy of fear and suspicion of the post-1885 period. Other issues included differences in identity, lifestyle, and aspirations between northern and southern Métis. The Society was successful in getting a grant from the provincial government for a legal inquiry into Métis land claims.[33] The report was unfavourable. It acknowledged that the Métis had a moral claim against the federal government but that a land settlement claim had been eradicated through scrip. The report recommended that they seek welfare if they needed assistance and even went so far as to suggest that the Métis did not want to be educated or "civilized" (assimilated into white society). Médéric McDougall, a Batoche area Métis who remembered this period, felt betrayed by the bosses in Regina who had spent much needed money on a worthless report while most of the little people were landless and destitute.[34]

Things were quiet during the war and the rest of the 1940s. In the words of activist Pierre Carrière, who enlisted: "all young people were gone and the little locals that we built went down."[35] Initially, there was a certain complacency and disillusionment among those who returned to their communities. Euclide Boyer from St. Laurent felt that the Métis veterans never got the freedom and the rights that they fought for. However, many of the veterans had acquired invaluable experience in dealing with the bureaucracy, both military and civilian. Pierre Carrière, whose grandfather had moved from Batoche to Cumberland House in the early 1900s, recalled that people from the Batoche area and to the south had been "pushed around by the government and pushed out by newcomers" and, as a result, were marginalized and afraid to speak out.[36] But the descendants of the 1885 combatants had not lost their fighting spirit and soon began reclaiming a political voice. Many of the more outspoken and militant Métis

6.13. *Marie-Anne (Lépine) McDougall and Médéric McDougall on their 50th wedding anniversary, 1983 – Courtesy of Doris McDougall.*

of the period who were living in communities such as Battleford, Debden, and Green Lake traced their ancestry to Batoche area in the 1880s. Tom Fiddler of Green Lake and Joe Vandale of Debden organized their locals and set up local cooperatives to gain more control over trapping, hunting, and fishing. Many of the younger Batoche Métis were working in Prince Albert and Saskatoon where they became involved. R.O. St. Denis and Mike Vandale, who were originally from Duck Lake, both became president of the Saskatoon local in the 1940s. That generation also began to reject the traditional Liberal and Conservative parties. Joe Vandale recalled that his parents and grandparents had voted Conservative so they could get a few jobs cutting brush on the road or operating the ferry.[37] But his support went to the new party or the Co-operative Commonwealth Federation (CCF) because « ça travailli pour le p'chi monde » (the people without money or power.)

The CCF party under T.C. Douglas came to power in Saskatchewan in 1944. Douglas, who was premier of Saskatchewan, was guided by social welfare and humanitarian principles, but, like his predecessors, he was also inherently conservative and paternalistic towards the Métis. He met with fellow-socialist Métis leaders Jim Brady and Malcolm Norris to address ongoing issues of poverty and unemployment in many communities but pursued the former Liberal government's Métis colonies rehabilitation scheme. A small Métis "colony" was created in Duck Lake in collaboration with the local First Nations Industrial School operated by the Oblate Fathers.[38] It was essentially a make-work project for people on welfare who were offered farming jobs in a co-operative setting. This did not appeal to many local Métis who preferred independent wage-labour, and the project was boycotted or short-lived. Nonetheless, the working-class ideals and social reforms of the CCF inspired local leaders such as Médéric McDougall of St. Louis, who saw in the party a champion of the working class that could address the poverty of the Métis people. An avowed *tête chaude* ("hothead") who stood up for his beliefs, "Medric Mcdoub" (his Michif name) had a generous heart and true leadership qualities of tolerance and respect. He did not have much formal schooling, but he was a good judge of character and was familiar with political wheeling and dealing. I had the privilege to meet and talk to him many times in the 1970s and 1980s and considered him a true patriot who carried the torch of his famous forebears, Maxime Lépine, Charles Nolin, and Baptiste Boucher. Médéric recalled that it was not easy to be a Catholic and vote CCF in the 1950s: "You had to tell little white lies at confession and some family and friends thought of you as a Communist."[39] Although it initiated some important economic and social programs such as health care and housing that were a benefit to the Métis, the CCF government avoided controversial issues such as land claims and self-determination and did not acknowledge their special status. Ultimately, there were few government grants, and the provincial Métis Society and twenty-five or so locals continued to function mainly through small membership fees and money raised by women at social functions such as bingos and picnics.

The Métis associations were re-organized provincially in the mid-1960s with renewed attempts to unite northern and southern communities. The Métis Association under Malcolm Norris united the more militant and independent northern Métis in 1964. However, it was soon reunited with the south, and Joe Amyotte became the first president of the new Métis Society of Saskatchewan in 1967. Médéric's nephew, Howard Adams, a political activist and scholar originally from St. Louis, who was largely

6.14. "The man who would be bishop:" Monsignor Alfred Boucher (1901–1984) – Prince Albert Diocesan Archives.

responsible for the society's reorganization, became its second president in 1969. Duck Lake, St. Louis, and Batoche had active locals in the new association. According to Walter Fidler, things were pretty quiet at first. He attended some meetings in Saskatoon but still voted Liberal because the Church said it was against his religion to vote CCF.[40] Generally speaking, Métis in the Batoche area continued to vote Liberal federally while the provincial vote was split between the Liberal party and the CCF (which later became the New Democratic Party).

The Boucher family, a prominent francophone Métis family of St. Louis, was closely associated with the political and religious elite of the time. The family was related to Louis Riel, Archbishop Taché of St. Boniface, and (Saint) Marguerite d'Youville, foundress of the Grey Nuns of Montreal.[41] Jean-Baptiste Sr., one of the founders of St. Louis, supported the 1885 Resistance, but his eldest son, Baptiste Jr., did not. Another son, Charles-Eugène, served two terms as MLA for Batoche in the 1890s. One of the daughters, Emma, became a Grey Nun, and another, Rose-Délima, who married Indian Affairs farmer-instructor and later inspector Charles-Pantaléon Schmidt, was instrumental in his career advancement. The tradition of leadership continued in the next generation with William Albert "Boss" Boucher, the politician, and Msgr. Alfred Boucher, a prelate of the Roman Catholic Church.

Although many local Métis were involved in politics, few were elected to the provincial legislature or the House of Commons until the 1970s. One notable exception was "Boss" Boucher of St. Louis, a member of the francophone and conservative Métis establishment who followed his father and his uncle Charles-Eugène of Batoche into politics.[42] An entrepreneur and businessman, he owned a general store and a large farm in Hoey, south of St. Louis. Mr. Boucher first became active in municipal politics as reeve of St. Louis and was elected as Liberal MP for Rosthern in 1948, representing that constituency until 1953. In 1957, he was appointed to the Senate and chair of a special committee on agriculture by Prime Minister Louis St. Laurent, a personal friend. He remained an active and influential senator for nineteen years, until the early 1970s. His death in 1976 marked the passing of the "old guard" or more traditional Métis politicians who had gained acceptance and power by identifying more strongly with the Catholic Church and their francophone heritage.

"Boss" Boucher was succeeded by a more militant class of Métis politicians who identified more strongly with their Métis heritage. His nephew,

John B. Boucher, has been an advocate for Métis rights since the 1960s and more recently on the Métis National Council and the RCMP Aboriginal Advisory Board. He was appointed to the National Métis Senate in 1991 and became a member of the Order of Canada in 2002. Senator Boucher had the honour of presenting the Métis sash to Nelson Mandela on his visit to Canada in 1998. A respected elder and keeper of oral history, he remained committed to teaching and guiding Métis youth.

Alfred Boucher (1901–74) was ordained to the priesthood in 1927, and in 1948 he was appointed domestic prelate with the clerical title of Monsignor and Vicar-General of the diocese. His devout mother was very proud of this achievement. When his brother "Boss" made a speech that took on political overtones at a family celebration, she reportedly interrupted him saying: « Tais-toi, Boss; j'ai demandé au bon Dieu de me donner un prêtre et non un politicien. »[43] Msgr. Boucher was a university graduate and gold medalist, cultured and well-read, yet close to the land and his Métis roots. He was a long-time rector of Sacred Heart Cathedral in Prince Albert and was considered in line to become bishop of the diocese in the early 1950s. According to his family, he was denied that honour because of his Métis ancestry.[44] In retrospect, this is not surprising as there was racial discrimination and conflict in the diocese during that period. The few francophone dioceses in Western Canada (such as Prince Albert and Gravelbourg in Saskatchewan) were considered training grounds for bishops or aspiring cardinals from Quebec. Ironically, the Boucher family was instrumental in the removal of the bishop who was appointed in his place but was forced to resign in 1959.[45]

Self-described Red Power advocate and local Métis "guru" Howard Adams[46] chartered a new course for the Métis in the late 1960s. "Doing it our way" became the new motto. Adams was a self-described revolutionary leader whose provocative Red Power discourse offended some Métis and caused internal strife. As president of the Métis Society from 1968 to 1971 and then as an educator at the University of Saskatchewan and in the United States, he did much to raise the political consciousness of Aboriginal youth and combat racism in mainstream political and educational institutions. Adams was an advocate of union between Métis and Non-Status Indians in the struggle against government for recognition of Aboriginal rights. However, his association with the "intelligentsia" and his radical views were not well accepted by the rank and file, and he was ousted from the presidency in 1971. He was succeeded by Jim Sinclair, who established the Association of Métis and Non-Status Indians of Saskatchewan (AMNSIS) in 1976. During this period, there were government grants for housing, education, training, and health care. The economic situation of the Métis started to improve with these benefits, but other developments such as increased migration to urban centres, created urban ghettos where poverty and alcoholism became problems. In smaller predominantly Métis rural communities such as Batoche and St. Louis, people maintained their Métis culture, but in larger centres such as Saskatoon, schools became centres of assimilation. According to Marge Laframboise, who was raised in Saskatoon in the 1940s and 1950s, prejudice convinced many parents to hide their ancestry from their children or to not talk about their history. She remembers hearing her parents speak Michif French and some Cree, but they spoke only English with their children.[47] But things began to change and people "started coming out" in the early 1970s. Both St. Louis and Duck Lake had active Métis locals by that time. In Duck Lake, Leonard Pambrun, who was president in the early 1980s, and other activists such as Maxime Parenteau, Archie Nicolas, and Rose Fleury addressed issues such as education and vocational training. Women were more actively involved in politics, especially in the promotion of social welfare programs and education.

CULTURAL REVIVAL AND RENEWAL

Taking Hold

Métis culture also witnessed a revival in the 1980s due largely to the increased recognition and initiative of Métis locals who established friendship centres and arts and craft associations. The traditional « Fête des Michifs » or Métis Days, which had not been celebrated since the 1930s, were re-established as "Back to Batoche Days." The new name reflected change in Métis society, the need to reinstate a forgotten history, and the recognition of Batoche as a special place for all Métis in Western Canada. Some local people such as Adélaïde Ranger and Marie Parenteau did not like the new celebrations with the absence of the traditional Catholic Mass and Michif French and the emphasis on Indian (First Nation) music and cultural events.[48] But with the centennial of the North West Rebellion – Métis Resistance in the mid-1980s, Métis cultural activities and artistic expression again came to the forefront.

The creation of Gabriel Dumont Institute (GDI) in 1980 was a clear indication of the awakening and coming of age of Saskatchewan's Métis community. The educational and cultural organization honoured the memory of renowned and revered 1885 Métis leader Gabriel Dumont, who called Batoche his home and was laid to rest there in 1906. GDI's main mandate was to promote cultural renewal, pride, and dignity through education, a key element in economic development and self-government.[49] GDI carried out key research to document and rehabilitate Métis history and held annual cultural conferences that focussed on past and present traditions. The Institute built partnerships with local universities and established the Saskatchewan Urban Native Teacher's Education Program (Suntep) and technical programs. These initiatives had a strong impact on the local Métis youth, many of whom pursued their education and training and found professional jobs. One of the more recent initiatives of the Institute has been the recording and transmission of the Michif language and Cree, which were traditionally spoken in Métis communities but had only been passed on in a few families. GDI has developed an impressive library and research centre for the use of Métis and non-Métis alike. It has carried out ongoing oral history to record the life stories of elders and the experiences of its veterans in twentieth century world conflicts. The recordings and publications of artists and women's artwork have heightened a sense of identity, and other Métis-specific projects contributed immensely to cultural growth in communities along the South Saskatchewan River. In addition, GDI cross-cultural programs have fostered a better understanding of contemporary issues among other Canadians and helped address enduring social issues such as negative stereotyping of Aboriginal peoples and racism. Many Batoche-area youth have benefited from these programs.

Batoche National Historic Site of Canada and the Métis Nation

The federal government first commemorated the site of the "North West Rebellion" at Batoche with a bronze plaque in 1925. The unilingual English plaque text reflected the government bias and prejudices of the time, referring to the "capture" of Batoche and the defeat of the "rebels." It was the source of much controversy and resentment in the community, and the offending words were soon chiselled out, but it was only replaced by a more neutral bilingual plaque almost twenty-five years later, in 1949. Other than the plaque, the government (i.e., the National Parks Branch, predecessor of present-day Parks Canada) did not carry out any development at Batoche. In the early 1950s, the local parish priest, Father Denis Dubuc, a heritage activist and genealogist, lobbied with the Prince Albert Historical Society and local politicians, such as Walter Tucker and William Albert Boucher, to preserve 1885 sites at Batoche. Father Dubuc wanted to sell the dilapidated old rectory, built in 1883, so he could build a new one, but he also had a genuine interest in the history of Batoche, particularly in telling the Métis side of the story.[50] He also proposed that the government acquire the village site, the remains of the Métis trenches, many of which remained undisturbed, and develop a historic park at Batoche. It is not known if he had full community support for this project, and in discussions with him, this author had the impression that he was quite authoritarian in the patriarchal tradition of the clergy of the time. Liberal Prime Minister Louis St. Laurent visited Batoche and environs in 1951 and met with Father Dubuc and his supporters. The government purchased the site of Middleton's encampment and the rectory but did not act on the other recommendations, due to financial constraints or other issues that remain unclear. It was a Liberal government that promoted the preservation of Batoche and the "rehabilitation" of the Métis in the 1950s, but it was a Conservative government, led by John Diefenbaker, that was able to capitalize on the achievement.

John Diefenbaker, who had practised law in Wakaw before entering politics as a federal MP for Prince Albert in 1940,[51] gained the support of some Métis around Batoche. The Métis traditionally supported the federal Liberals since 1885, and, according to people interviewed, Diefenbaker appears to have received support primarily from families who had relocated to urban areas such as Saskatoon and Prince Albert. A Progressive Conservative and self-described spokesman for the "non-establishment," "Dief the Chief" was a popular and inspiring speaker who affirmed his prairie roots and supported social programs for the benefit of Aboriginal peoples. But according to Marge Laframboise, he was not very tolerant of non-English ways, and, like most politicians, he only thought about Native

6.15. *Prime Minister J.G. Diefenbaker at official opening of Batoche Museum, June 28, 1961 – Saskatchewan Archives Board, S-MN-B3101.*

people when it was time to get votes.[52] The prime minister presided at the opening of a museum in the old rectory on June 28, 1961. In his speech he paid tribute to Gabriel Dumont and soldiers on both sides, but he made no reference to Louis Riel. Local Métis such as Johnny and Patrice Champagne had worked on the restoration of the rectory, but period accounts and photographs of the opening ceremonies suggest that it lacked local involvement. There was community support for the new museum as many families had donated artefacts, but there was also division and caution. The Carons, Pilons, and Boyers supported Father Dubuc's initiative, but other families such as the Fidlers and Gervais' voiced their opposition and saw the development as another example of church-government collaboration and control.[53]

The Museum Era

In 1955, Parks Canada purchased the site of General Middleton's 1885 encampment or zareba on the Albert Caron farm and the old rectory and an adjoining parcel of land for parking and utilities.[54] The sale of the old village site (riverlot 47) did not materialize and most of the remaining Métis rifle pits in that area on the east side of the river were ploughed over by the owner for agricultural use. Parks Canada's focus at that time was the commemoration of government military sites. It was more concerned, for example, with protecting the gravesite of the soldiers buried along the river-bank on Caron's property. According to local tradition, however, the Caron family, which lived there since the 1880s had been tending the gravesite for many years. Albert Caron (1888–1971), whose father « Vieux Jean » and his older brothers had fought at Batoche, was an unofficial guide at the encampment and military gravesite on his property. He loved to tell stories of "the rebellion" and sometimes embellished them to entertain visitors in return for small donations. He invited tourists into his old home to sit in "Middleton's chair" and tell them how Gabriel Dumont had shot off Middleton's cap, although he could have shot him dead if he had wished to, as no one was a better marksman than old Gabriel. He would bring out his little collection of food tins, bullets, and other mementoes of the battle, which had been left on his property.[55] Albert had certainly heard many stories from his parents and his older brothers, who had participated in the armed conflict. One wonders whether he told the story of the looting and burning of the Caron home and many others by Middleton's soldiers en route to Batoche and the hardship the families endured. During those years, most of the tourists were "white folks" from Saskatoon and Prince Albert and descendants of the military from Ontario. Albert Caron and other old-timers kept certain stories to themselves or shared them only with trusted family and friends.

In 1967, Parks Canada purchased the old village site (riverlot 47) from local farmer Armand Nogier, and in the early 1970s adjoining lots 43 and 44 were acquired from the Nogier family. The original 1884 St. Antoine de Padoue church was purchased in 1970, and negotiations were carried out with the owners of the old mission site on lots 50 and 51, the Corporation Épiscopale of Prince Albert, Adélaïde Pilon, and Dmytro Hryciuk and his wife, Bernice (née St. Germain). The original mission lands had been divided into parcels since the 1920s. Parks Canada wished to acquire the lands for the development of a major national historic site with access roads and visitor and maintenance facilities as well as to protect historic resources such as the Carlton and Humboldt trails. The diocese retained ownership of the parish cemetery as well as an access road. However the Hryciuks did not wish to sell their land (116 acres on lots 50–51) and were eventually expropriated, an action that created resentment among certain local families. In the late 1970s, Parks Canada also acquired lots 48 and 49, completing its holdings or ownership of lands from the historic village (lot 47) to the Caron Sr. farm (lot 52) on the east side of the South Saskatchewan River. It also acquired lands on the west side of the river to provide uninterrupted views from both river-banks and to protect resources such as the old river crossing, west village archaeological remains, and 1885 Métis rifle pits. The lands on the west side of the river were mostly grazing and scrub lands or not prime real estate. On the east side of the river, the lands were purchased mainly from older or retired Métis farmers with little opposition.[56] The sale of the church, however, saddened many parishioners, especially the elders. There was also local concern about future government plans for the large land base. This was at a time before public consultations by government, and its past record at Batoche created some uneasiness. The Métis Society was not involved during this period, or there was no official organization to protect and promote Métis interests.

A Site Management Plan and Shifts in Interpretation

The 1970s ushered in a period of growth and expansion for Batoche, which was identified as the "the new Louisbourg" of western Canada. Parks Canada developed its first management plan for Batoche in 1972. It recommended the construction of a new Visitor Reception Centre (VRC) with interpretive facilities, the period restoration of the church and rectory, and the interpretation of the village site and battle site. The mini-plan, which was not implemented or was superseded by a more comprehensive one a decade later, confirmed an important shift in the historical interpretation at Batoche. The interpretation of the 1885 "rebellion" was to include "the Métis point of view":

The main thrust of our interpretation at Batoche must be towards showing the visitor the lifestyle of the Métis in the 1880s and what they were willing to fight to protect.... [W]e believe the visitor must be made to realize the basic causes of the actions that were taken [in 1885] and fully understand the Métis and their point of view.[57]

As a result, two themes were identified and eventually approved for Batoche National Historic Site: Métis Settlement and the North West Rebellion of 1885. According to a recent article and critique of the dominance of the "Métis point of view" at Batoche, "the formal acceptance of two themes [Métis and 1885 'Rebellion'] equal in importance was a significant innovation."[58]

These initiatives brought immense change to the local community. Canada was in a nation-building mode, and the creation and development of national historic sites was a key element of this process. It was an era of comparative prosperity and generous funding for Parks Canada. It was also a period of historical revisionism propelled by movements such as Aboriginal and francophone rights and Western Canadian nationalism. There had been some evolution in the historical interpretation at Batoche since the 1920s, but the story was being told primarily from the point of view of the victors of 1885. The exhibits and storyline in the museum, which were developed in the early 1960s presented a sympathetic portrait of the Métis, but it was a paternalistic and colonial view. The main message was that a "poor misguided people" had been defeated by government forces and as a result its culture had been destroyed. It was the story of "conflict of cultures," of the struggle between old and new ways of life and the victory of civilization over "savagery," essentially still a story of conquest and assimilation.

Contrary to popular belief, however, there was a very early Métis presence at Batoche NHS. Edward Bruce, a local Métis, became the first seasonal guide in 1961, was hired full-time in 1965, and worked at Batoche until the early 1990s, a career of over thirty years. In the beginning, he did both general maintenance and historical tours. He recalled how he was given four books to read by Superintendent Harry Tatro at Fort Battleford and was asked to develop a storyline for visitors.[59] He mentioned that there was nothing on Batoche in the references and the literature on the "rebellion" said very little about the Métis side of the story. To fill in

6.16. *Edward Bruce at work at Batoche National Historic Site of Canada, ca. 1995 – Parks Canada.*

the gap, he talked to local people, especially the "old-timers," and tried to incorporate their perspectives in his presentations. He was committed to telling the story "from both sides," although he felt he had to avoid controversy. During those days, most of the visitors at Batoche were locals or from the prairie provinces, and most were sympathetic toward the Métis. "Ed," as he was called locally, was a dedicated and respected employee at Batoche. He had a genuine interest in history and became an invaluable source of information to staff and visitors alike. A man who was quite circumspect and identified himself to outsiders as French Canadian in the 1970s, he became much more comfortable with his Métis identity and language and was often called upon to exercise his diplomatic skills as mediator between Parks Canada and the community at public meetings. He collected many local artefacts for the museum and salvaged many paintings and furnishings from the historic church, which had been cast off or stored in other parishes after the mid-1960s renovations fostered by Vatican II. After his retirement, he continued to be involved at the site as a respected elder.

Émile Parenteau, who started to work in maintenance in the early 1970s, also made an important contribution to the site. A diligent worker, he quietly passed on invaluable knowledge on the land and cultural resources at Batoche to archaeologists, historians, planners, and countless others who came to "study" the site. He was a gifted "diviner" who found a water source where engineers could not, and he also shared many stories about Batoche and its people.

The so-called new social history of the 1980s acknowledged cultural differences, and Métis history, which was being re-assessed by ethnohistorians, gave rise to the recognition and celebration of the new and free people of the Canadian northwest. When this author first arrived at Batoche in 1976, she observed a persistent legacy of fear and suspicion toward outsiders, in particular, "government agents." My cultural links and ability to converse with elders in French and some Michif French were definite assets. I was imbued with the idealism of youth and the "Métis cause," but I also felt a deep personal commitment to the community and telling its side of the story. I eventually made many friends and heard stirring accounts of their lives and those of their ancestors. The history of the community of Batoche was unknown, except in the hearts and minds of the people themselves. A few years earlier, when I submitted a master's thesis proposal on the Métis, I was met with skepticism and reactions such as:

"where are you going to get the documentation for your inquiry? ... Marcel Giraud wrote all there is to know about the Métis.... Batoche disappeared after 1885, the people all left!" I challenged those statements, and, in the course of my career, I met with criticisms from some colleagues who suggested that I privileged the Métis point of view and as a result the story of the 1885 Resistance is now told primarily from the Métis perspective, while the government side has been minimized.[60] In my view, Batoche is and remains primarily a Métis experience, that of a people who defended their homeland, their rights, and their culture. The armed conflict of 1885 was a dramatic and pivotal event in the history of the Métis people in general and Batoche in particular. The call for a renewed emphasis on the government side of the story, or "North West Rebellion," reflects a persistent and insidious 'white' Anglo-Canadian bias, which dominated Canadian history in the nineteenth century and persists until today.

The Era of the "Big Project"

The anticipated centennial of the "North West Rebellion" in 1985 precipitated the development and implementation of a comprehensive and ambitious development plan for Batoche. The two major site themes required extensive research as little had been written about the community of Batoche and even less on Métis perspectives of the battle. This author documented the structural history of the church and rectory and the village site and carried out archival research and oral history interviews with elders to document local Métis culture, lifestyle, and viewpoints, which culminated in the publication of *Batoche* in 1983 and *The Free People: Otipemisiwak: Batoche 1870–1930*.[61] In the meantime, a colleague, Walter Hildebrandt, undertook the equally challenging task of documenting the battle of 1885 from the perspectives of both the North West Field Force and the Métis. His work culminated in the publication of *The Battle of Batoche: British Small Warfare and the Entrenched Métis*.[62] There was support for telling "both sides of the story" in the Prairie regional office but less in the national office, which was suspicious of "regional interests." There was objection to the use of the term "resistance" in conjunction with Métis actions in 1885 and the possible downplay of the "rebellion" story.

Public consultations for the 1982 management plan revealed support for telling the Métis as well as the government side of the story of 1885.

6.17. Official Opening of Caron House, Batoche NHS, July 18, 1992 – Diane Payment.

The two-phase plan called for a period restoration and furnishing of the church and rectory, the construction of a Visitor Reception Centre with a new storyline and exhibits, and the stabilization and interpretation of cultural resources such as the Caron house, historic trails, and Métis and military rifle pits. The second phase called for a period reconstruction of the east village site, in particular, the Letendre home. Central to all these initiatives was the relocation of highway 225 further east to protect site resources and facilitate visitor access. This proposal raised some local opposition, especially from elders who were concerned about change and the creation of a Parks Canada compound or "fortress" in their midst.[63] The issues of visitor safety and noise eventually won over.

One proposal that was dear to Métis hearts was the reconstruction of the village to interpret Métis life. The old village site was symbolic of Métis economic success and enterprise in the late nineteenth and early twentieth century and a testimony of their persistence after 1885. It was the original location of stores owned by George Fisher, Baptiste Boyer, and the community's founding father, Xavier Letendre *dit* Batoche, and the men and women who accompanied them. Xavier and Marguerite Letendre (née Parenteau) had built an impressive two-storey home with wrap-around verandah, described as "the finest west of Winnipeg," in 1884. In its later years, it was used as a North West Mounted Police barracks before being dismantled in 1921. The other village buildings had met a similar fate, and by the 1930s, only foundations remained and the old village had been virtually abandoned. The village reconstruction was never carried out, due to prohibitive costs, reductions in Parks Canada's budget, and debate over the merits or the lack of integrity of period reconstruction. The reconstruction of the Fortress of Louisbourg, on Cape Breton Island in Nova Scotia in the late 1960s, had been an ambitious and very expensive investment, both in initial construction and operational costs, and Parks Canada was understandably reluctant to initiate another similar project without partnerships. However, visitor access and exhibits were provided in the east village. Unfortunately, the isolation of that site and the lack of a dynamic or self-guiding visitor program resulted in a low profile and less emphasis on the interpretation of the Métis community theme at Batoche. It was perhaps ironic that, apart from in the Visitor Reception area, the Métis story was primarily "attached" to the church and rectory and the military encampment on the Caron farmstead. The Caron house, which was rehabilitated on the exterior but not in the interior was only marginally interpreted to the public.[64] The church and rectory told the story of relations between the clergy and the Métis at Batoche, but the Caron house, the village site, and the few remaining Métis structures in the National Historic Site were more appropriate venues to present the activities and lifestyle of the Métis community.

 A new modern-style corrugated metal Visitor Reception Centre with a vaulted glass hall opened to visitors in 1986. "The Glass House" was controversial as some people had hoped for a more traditional structure. There was not much local consultation on the architecture and fabric of the new centre and the decision was made to erect a building that was distinct from the historical buildings on the site. Whatever its merits, it was an elaborate and impressive complex with a large theatre and exhibit area, which reflected Parks Canada's substantial investment in key national historic sites in the 1980s. Other National Historic Sites in Saskatchewan, such as the Motherwell Homestead and Fort Battleford, did not receive the same level of investment. Batoche became the showcase of Western Canada. The exhibit area featured two large lifelike dioramas depicting the buffalo hunt and 1885 Métis and North West Field Force rifle pits and defence networks. One of the highlights of the VRC was a stirring audio-visual presentation with an evocative musical score by composer Pierre Guérin. The "show's" objective was to celebrate the Métis community at Batoche, emphasize its continuity, and acknowledge its views of the armed conflict of 1885. Some of the literary licence (dramatization) and voices chosen to tell the government's side of the story of 1885 provoked some criticism for its lack of balance or bias in favour of the Métis. It was argued that John A. Macdonald was represented as Riel's nemesis, who despised the Métis, while Middleton sounded like a foolish "Colonel Blimp" or a pompous British officer, whereas:

> Moïse [Ouellette], the principal narrator carries the story … gave through his voice and lines, a sympathetic portrayal of the Métis case.… Sir John A. Macdonald, who would presumably have wished to articulate a case for Canada … comes across as an overbearing, arrogant politician from outside of the region and culture.[65]

Keeping in mind that the storyline was developed in 1985, at a time when relations between the government and the Métis were entering a new era of comparative good will, the audio-visual show promoted much local pride and reconciliation. The public reaction to the show was very positive. This is supported by commentaries from visitors to the site, by the Métis, and by many descendants of regiments who fought at Batoche, in particular those from Western Canada. Parks Canada is currently considering shelving the production or replacing it with a "more balanced" one. In my view, this would be a grave mistake. It is a historical drama which reflects the perspectives and issues of the 1980s. It could be supplemented by more comprehensive videos to address issues such as differing views, historical complexities, and recent interpretations, which were beyond the scope of the 1985 production.

For writer and poet Gregory Scofield (and many others), the audio-visual presentation was a stirring personal journey of discovery and renewal:

> We toured the historical site … there was a theatre which had a special show narrated by Gabriel Dumont's character [sic] and told of the struggles leading up to the resistance. It was so unlike anything I had learned at school … a dignified history.… The half-breeds, under the guidance of Louis Riel, had petitioned the Macdonald government, wanting assurance of the right to keep the lands on which they'd lived for years,

> but their requests were repeatedly ignored.... Louis Riel surrendered three days after the resistance, in the hope that he could legitimize the Métis cause.... By the end of the show, tears were streaming down my face. It was such a mixture of emotion. A surprising new feeling had awoken within me. I looked around the theatre and saw my people.... As we left Batoche I felt my heart sink into the very landscape, my spirit joining those of my ancestors in the empty ravines and coulees. I had searched so long for a place of belonging, and now I had found it.[66]

Some Métis argue that there remains a persistent gulf and irreconcilable differences between the two worldviews, Aboriginal and European, and that the (dominant) Eurocanadian perspective will always prevail in a government-operated site. Others say that it is the government side of the story that is privileged and that much of the interpretation of 1885 is focused on the restored military encampment and the strategies of the North West Field Force. There is also the view that the "government glass house" is like a fortress or a "foreign" place, which is not inclusive of the contemporary Métis community. These views persisted in the 1980s and 1990s.

"Let's Straighten Things Out and Get Back to Basics"

A new management plan in 2000 ushered in a policy of consolidation, restraint, and emphasis based on the Parks Canada policy of "commemorative integrity."[67] The management plan was developed with the participation of the Métis Nation of Saskatchewan (MNS), which signed an agreement for the shared management of the site in 1998. This initiative was in part the result of increased pressure by the Métis Nation since the late 1980s for increased control and eventual takeover of the site. The shared management policy was intended to appease the Métis and give them "a voice" in the operation of Batoche NHS, more specifically through increased employment opportunities, heritage presentation activities, and partnership opportunities. During this period, there were two site superintendents of Métis heritage, Anne Morin and Josie (Heron) Weninger, though they were there only briefly. However, most of the maintenance people were Métis locals, and a long-term employee, Raymond Fidler, eventually became manager. When new interpretive staff were hired, a priority was given to hiring people of Métis heritage. The seasonal interpretive staff is now mainly of French Canadian and Métis cultural origin. The official use of French and recognition of Michif, although supported by the Métis, was not vigorously maintained or promoted by Parks Canada in the last decades. Perhaps this was due to diminishing financial resources or a perception that this service was not essential in rural Saskatchewan. In contrast, bilingual staffing and programs are a priority at Riel House National Historic Site (located in St. Vital, a suburb of Winnipeg), operated by La Société historique de Saint-Boniface.

Financial resources decreased at Batoche in the 1990s and early 2000s, and unforeseen operational costs for the conservation of threatened or impaired cultural resources were encountered. The church needed a new foundation and the VRC required repairs and renovations to accommodate new visitor activities and staff. The focus on "protection and presentation" of cultural resources outlined in Parks Canada Cultural Management policy resulted in increased emphasis on the inventory and protection of tangible remains such as archaeological resources, trails, and the parkland ecosystem and less emphasis on the presentation of non-tangible resources such as the cultural landscape or values of the people and the land.

"Home at Last": Batoche in the Twenty-first Century

The new millennium ushered in new initiatives and partnerships between Parks Canada, the Métis Nation of Saskatchewan and the Métis local, more specifically the formation of the "Friends of Batoche," a non-profit group which manages the food services and gift shop.

The site has been reaching out to the community and elders such as Ed Bruce, Rose Fleury, Senator John Boucher, and Maria Campbell. Métis youth such as writer Gregory Scofield, who now can "hold high my head, proud of the blood thundering through my veins,"[68] are re-asserting their identity and connections with Batoche. Brenda Boyer Percell, who grew up on her grandparents farm in St. Laurent in the 1960s, always had fond memories of those ten years of her youth but had lost touch with her culture over the years. Today, she proudly asserts her heritage and is passing it on to her children. She established a local Métis association in Revelstoke, B.C., and often returns to Batoche and surrounding area to reconnect with her past and visit her extended family. She has traced

6.18. *Rose (Gariépy) Fleury, Mark Calette and Edward Bruce at Batoche NHS, 2005 – Parks Canada.*

her ancestry to the Boyer, Tourond, Ladéroute, and Letendre families of Batoche and James McMillan, one of the founders of Fort Langley, B.C., an empowering discovery.[69] David Venne, a great-grandson of Batoche founders, Xavier Letendre and Salomon Venne, is a professional photographer who is documenting and promoting the cultural landscape of the site. Project manager Mark Calette, a descendant of 1885 Resistance leaders Charles Trottier and Gabriel Dumont, is establishing new partnerships to attract private and corporate investments for special events and new visitor services such as the interpretation of the Caron home, the revitalization of the east village, access to the west side, the repatriation of artefacts, and the updating of exhibits.

This Métis pride and empowerment are a great change from the 1970s when most people at Batoche identified as either French Canadian or Scottish. There is increased openness and good will between Parks Canada and the Métis community. Although Métis politics is sometimes divisive and certainly controversial, there has been more interaction with Métis locals at the provincial and national organizations, particularly with respect to the annual July "Back to Batoche" celebrations. Batoche National Historic Site of Canada (NHSC) has participated more actively in the Métis celebrations by holding special events such as masses in the historic church and wagon tours of the site. The Gabriel Dumont Institute's collections and ongoing publications have also benefited the site's interpretive program. The issue of "many voices" and differing views of history may never be resolved to the satisfaction of both Parks Canada and the Métis, but a diverse collection of resource materials ensures a rich and lively interpretive program.

The cultural and natural landscape of Batoche has also evolved and changed considerably in the last decades.

6.19. *Brenda (Boyer) Percell: "Proud to be Métis," ca. 1995 – Brenda Percell.*

Whereas there were still many log structures along the riverlots between Gabriel's bridge and the St. Laurent ferry in the 1980s, most of these have now been torn down. Only a few remain as a testimony to the many homes occupied by extended families such as the Carons, Pilons, Parenteaus, and St. Germains. The post office and store operated by the Chénier family was closed and more recently the 1980s church. A number of lots have been purchased by the One Arrow Cree Nation further to land entitlement agreements. In the past, there have been some conflicts and rivalries over land between the Métis and the Cree.[70] The Métis feel very strongly about their homeland and historic rights at Batoche, whereas the One Arrow Cree Nation, which was economically disadvantaged and suffered extensively under the old reserve system, is interested in developing its new property. Some of the changes in

6.20. *Wagon rides, Back to Batoche Days, July, 2005 – Diane Payment.*

the Métis landscape are the inevitable result of the march of time. There is also evidence of renewal, especially south of Batoche. The Fiddler (Fidler) families have expanded their holdings, and some of the grandchildren of original Batoche families are "coming home."

"Ms. Batoche's" journey has been a long one with many joys, challenges, and deceptions. I will always remember the strong, tenacious, and special people I met at Batoche. They were sometimes understandably wary but always warm and generous. I learned a lot about tolerance and respect. I made many friends especially among elders, who were a source of inspiration. Batoche NHS has become "a Métis place" where its rich culture and heritage are celebrated. The land is protected for present and future generations of Métis and other Canadians. It is a rich legacy, which I was privileged to be part of. As the old people humbly used to say: *mârci bein – excousez la!*

Appendices

Appendix 1 (Related to Chapter 1)

1.1. MÉTIS WINTERING AT ST. LAURENT DE GRANDIN MISSION, 31 DECEMBER 1871

HEADS OF FAMILIES	Men	Women	Children	Total	Horses
(André, Father Alexis)*	1			1	2
(Bourgine, Father)*	1			1	
Batoche [Letendre], André	1	1	6	8	1
Batoche [Letendre], Louison Jr.	1	1	3	5	10
Batoche [Letendre], Louison Sr.	1	1		2	12
Batoche [Letendre], Xavier	1	1	3	5	16
Boyer, Baptiste	1	1	4	6	12
Cadieux [Cayen], Alexandre	1	1	6	8	8
Colin, Maxime	1			1	
Dumont, Édouard (A)	1	1	2	4	12
Dumont, Édouard (B)	1			1	
Dumont, Élie	1	1	2	4	10
Dumont, Gabriel	1	1	1	3	10
Dumont, Isidore dit Escapoo	1	1	2	4	20
Dumont, Isidore Jr.	1	1	7	9	18
Dumont, Jean dit Chakasta	1	1		2	18
Dumont, Jean Jr.	1	1	7	9	18
Dumont, Louis	1			1	1
Dumont, Vital	1	1	3	5	8
Falcon, Athanase	1	1	1	3	2
Ferguson, Antoine	1	1	4	6	8
Fisher, Alexandre	1	1	2	4	5
Fleury, Antoine	1	1	2	4	8
Gariépy, Philippe	1	1	4	6	20
Gariépy, Pierre	1	1	9	11	10
Gladu, Antoine	1	1	2	4	5
Hamelin, Alexandre	1	1	4	6	18
Hamelin, Elzéar	1	1	1	3	3
Hamelin, Joseph	1	1	5	7	18
Hamelin, Josué	1	1	5	7	8
Houle, François	1	1	6	8	6
Laframboise, Augustin	1	1	4	6	12
Laverdure, Pierre	1	1	3	5	8
Lafond, Baptiste	1	1	5	7	4

1.1 (cont'd)

HEADS OF FAMILIES	Men	Women	Children	Total	Horses
Landry, Louis	1	1	4	6	6
Masson, François	1			1	
Moreau, [?] widow		1		1	1
Moreau, Jonas	1	1	3	5	5
Ouellette, Marguerite*		1		1	
Ouellette, Moïse	1	1	5	7	18
Parenteau, Alexandre	1	1	3	5	6
Parenteau, Baptiste	1	1	7	9	30
Parenteau, Élie	1	1	3	5	6
Parenteau, Gabriel	1	1	2	4	6
Parenteau, Isidore	1	1		2	6
Parenteau, José	1	1	6	8	12
Parenteau, Joseph Jr.	1	1		2	6
Parenteau, Joseph Sr.	1	1	4	6	12
Parenteau, Louis	1	1	6	8	10
Parenteau, Raphaël	1	1		2	4
Patenaude, Joseph	1			1	2
Plante, Antoine	1			1	5
Plante, Xavier	1	1		2	3
Poitras, Ignace	1	1	7	9	12
Primeau, Baptiste	1	1	1	3	8
Racette, Augustin	1	1	4	6	6
Racette, Charles Jr.	1	1	6	8	12
Racette, Charles Sr.	1			1	
Racette, Joseph	1	1	5	7	12
St. Denis, Célestin	1	1		2	3
Sansregret, Pierre	1	1	5	7	8
Short, James	1	1	6	8	12
Smith, [?] widow		1	6	7	6
Thomas, Charles	1	1	1	3	10
Vandale, Baptiste	1	1	6	8	12
Vandale, Baptiste (B)	1	1	1	3	2
Villeneuve, Théophile	1	1	5	7	6
Welsh, John	1			1	4
TOTALS	63	58	198	321	567

* Except for Fathers André and Bourgine, and Marguerite Ouellette who farmed and worked as a domestic servant, all the others were identified as hunters.

(A), (B) = Two people with the same name.
Source: GA, Richard Hardisty Papers, File 32.

1.2. FAMILIES OF ST. ANTOINE DE PADOUE PARISH, BATOCHE, 1924

François Arcand
Mathew Bilyk
Chrysostome Boyer
Raphaël Boyer
Robert Boyer
Tobie Boyer
Joseph Branconnier
Alfred Caron
Arthur Caron
Eugène Caron
Jean Caron
Patrice Caron
Théophile Caron
Alfred Carrière
Cléophas Champagne
Daniel Charette
Daniel Dumas
Isidore Dumas
Élie Dumont
Cuthbert (Corbet) Fayant
Antoine Ferguson
Antoine Ferguson (Sr.)
Georges Ferguson
Joseph Ferguson
Bruno Fidler
Norbert Fidler
Ambroise Gervais
Clémence Gervais (née Boyer)
Edmond Gervais
Joseph Gervais
Moïse Gervais
Napoléon Gervais
Pierre Gervais
Joseph Ladéroute
Alfred Lafontaine
Joseph Lafontaine
Albert Laplante

Toussaint Laplante
Charles Laviolette
Eugène Letendre
Louis Letendre
Moïse Marcotte
Baptiste Ouellette
Marie Ouellette
   (née Boyer, widow of Moïse Jr.)
Alexandre Parenteau
François Parenteau
Jérôme Parenteau
Joachim Parenteau
Laurent Parenteau
Louis Parenteau
Modeste Parenteau
William Parenteau
Albert Pilon
Alexandre Pilon
Barthélémi Pilon
Henri Pilon
Joseph Pilon Jr.
Joseph Pilon Sr.
Louis Pilon
William Pilon
William John Pilon
Michel Poitras
Félix Potty
Jérôme Racette
Jean-Baptiste Ranger
Raoul St. Denis
Frédéric St. Germain
Raoül St. Germain
François Slater
Francis Tourond
Napoléon Venne
Robert Venne
Widow of Jean-Baptiste Parenteau

Source: Prince Albert Diocese, Batoche File.

1.3. MÉTIS SONGS

I. C'est au champ de bataille (La lettre de sang).
Composition attributed to Louis Riel. Collected in the Lebret, Saskatchewan area. Sung by Gaspard Jeannotte around 1957. Courtesy of G. Burtonshaw, Calgary.

1. C'est au champ de bataille,
   J'ai fait crier mes douleurs,
   Où tant qu'un doute se passe,
   Ça fait frémir les coeurs.
   Or je r'çois-t-une lettre
   De ma chère maman
   J'avais ni plum' ni encre
   Pour pouvoir lui écrire.

2. Or je pris mon canif,
   Je le trempai dans mon sang
   Pour écrir' une lettre
   À ma chère maman.
   Quand ell' r'creva cett' lettre
   Tout écrit' de sang
   Ses yeux baignant de larmes,
   Son coeur s'allant mourant.

3. S'y jette à genoux par terre
   En appelant ses enfants:
   Priez pour votr' p'tit frère
   Qui est au régiment.
   Mourir, c'est pour mourir,
   Chacun meurt à son tour;
   J'aim' mieux mourir en brave,
   Faut tous mourir un jour.

II. *Chanson de Louis Riel.*
Composed in Dakota in honour of his sister Henriette (St. Louis, Saskatchewan version).

Ma soeur tu n'etais que fillette
Au premier beau jour du printemps
Quand j'ai parti, chère Henriette,
Tu n'avais pas encore quinze ans.
De tous mes travaux politiques
Et mes luttes au Canada
Viens me conter les peines publiques
Du peuple que mon coeur fonda.

Banni, je viens auprès des lignes
Contempler mon pays natal
Revoir mes amis bons et dignes
Et mes parents de Saint-Vital.
Ils sont venus me voir par groupes
Chez mon ami Norman Gingras
Ils sont venus boire à ma coupe
Pendant les fêtes et les jours gras.

Ma soeur, tu viens faire ta visite
Au commencement du mois d'août.
En te voyant, mon coeur palpite
Ma soeur, ah je t'aime beaucoup.
Reçois de moi la bienvenue
Mon coeur t'embrasse en soupirant
Lorsque mes yeux t'ont reconnue
C'était ceux d'un frère content.

J'aime ta taille mince et svelte,
Ton marcher modeste et posé
Cet esprit métis, ta silhouette
Joyeuse, franche et sans souci.
Tu prends soin de ta chevelure
Selon les règles du bon sens
Et les attraits de ta figure
Sont beaux sans être extravagants.

Les traits de ta figure brune
Apparaissent à mes yeux contents
Comme la clarté de la lune
Lorsque les nuits sont au beau temps.
Et le point où le jour se couche
Ne sera jamais plus vermeil
Que le sourire de ta bouche.
Ton regard me porte conseil.

Ah! Que mon âme est réjouie
D'entendre résonner ta voix
Elle est plus douce à mon ennui
Que la musique des grands bois.
Retourne chez toi, Henriette,
Dans notre cher Manitoba
Va dire aux personnes inquiètes
Que je languis dans les États.

III. *Courtisan malheureux ou Riche marchand malheureux.*
Sung by Antoine Ferguson (1884–1976), St. Laurent, Saskatchewan (collected by Henri Létourneau, St. Boniface, 1972).

D'un tour plaisant, un riche marchand,
Courtisant une dame, ce pauvre courtisan,
Lui en a bien coûté 50 mille francs
Sans compter toute la belle équipage[1]
Qu'il avait laissée à ce matelot pour gage,
Il s'attendait pas, d'avoir ce beau butin,
Ce beau, ce matelot marin.

Ça faisait bien deux ans qu'il était en voyage.
Et arrivant à son port
Tout aussitôt débarquant de son vaisseau
Pensant d'aller se coucher avec sa femme
Et son coeur brûlait de mille flammes
Il s'en va tout droit chez lui
"Femme, ouvrez la porte à ton cher mari."
La femme tout en tremblant dit au favori:
"Comment allons-nous faire? Retirez-vous d'ici
Car, par ma foi, voilà mon mari.

Bien promptement mettez votre capote
Car aussitôt je vais lui ouvrir la porte
Et quand vous serez esquivé
Je me défendrai comme je pourrai."
En ouvrant la porte il voit un ombrage
Qui fait comme au sauvage
"Femme qu'est-ce qu'il y a ici
C'est-ti le diable ou bien c'est un esprit?"
"Mon cher mari j'en ai point de lumière
Car aussi bien rien de quoi en faire
Couchons bien promptement
Dedans notre lit on sera bien chaudement."

---

1   un bel équipage

Ce matelot marin encore bien plus fin
Mais il savait de quoi en faire
"Et qu'on m'apporte mon batte-feu
Avec lequel je fais du feu quand je veux
Bien promptement et allume la chandelle
Car aussi noir nous aurons de la crelle[2]
Et tous deux jeunes rigodons
Je me croirais foutu de me coucher à tâtons."
Allumant le feu il vit à ses yeux
Une belle équipage, il vit un beau trésor
Une montre d'or, un sac de louis d'or,
Au pied du lit une paire de bottes,
Un bel habit garni de la sorte,
Un beau chapeau pluché
Une paire de culottes toutes enpercelées[3]

Ce matelot marin dit en souriant
Regardant sa femme:
"ma femme quoique tu es jolie
Car par ma foi, il a bien payé ton prix
Il est donc vrai je porte des cornettes
Et mes frères des sonnettes
Et cela mène autant de bruit
Comme tous ces carosses qui roulent dans Paris."

Ce pauvre courtisan vient tout en tremblant
Mais cogne à la porte
En disant qu'il était un marchand
"Qui est celui qui frappe à ma porte
Mais c'est-ti toi que le diable t'emporte
Je garde tout ce qu'il y a
Ça me servira pour faire laver mes draps.

---

[2] unknown word
[3] pearl-studded

Appendix 2 (Related to Chapter 3)

CLAIMS FOR LOSSES SUFFERED IN 1885, BATOCHE AND VICINITY

A: "Loyal" citizens who did not take up arms against the government
B: "Rebels" or persons "who have contributed to their own losses"
C: Persons absent from their homes or travelling during the insurrection

CLAIMANT(S)	Claim granted ($)	Category	($)
Jean-Baptiste Arcand	934.15	B	0.00
Susette Arcand	388.00	B	0.00
Caroline Beauchemin	1,525.00	B	0.00
Abraham Bélanger	325.00	A	10.00
Charles-Eugène Boucher	885.50	A	373.00
Jean-Baptiste Boucher*			
Jean-Baptiste Boyer	9,330.34	A	6,461.13
William Boyer	1,596.75	A	386.10
Ernestine Breland	1,291.55	B	0.00
Félicité Breland (Boyer), wife of Gilbert	186.75	B	0.00
Moïse Bremner	322.00	A	205.00
Marguerite Caron (Dumas), wife of Jean	4,681.50	B	0.00
Virginie Caron (parenteau), wife of Jean Jr.	1,936.00	B	0.00
Cécile Carrière (Beauchemin), wife of Charles	996.00	B	0.00
Patrice Carrière	1,583.00	B	0.00
Philippe C. Chamberland	410.00	A	183.00
Ambroise Champagne	860.00	B	0.00
Cléophas Champagne	435.00	B	0.00
Emmanuel Champagne	13,310.00	B	0.00
Charlotte Delorme (Gervais), wife of Norbert	888.65	B	0.00
Jean-Baptiste Delorme	600.00	B	0.00
William Delorme	253.00	B	0.00
Télesphore Demers	6,805.00	C	0.00
Louise Desjarlais	38.90	B	0.00
Marguerite Desjarlais, wife of Paul	1,216.25	B	0.00
Ambroise Dubois	300.00	B	0.00
Angélique Dubois (Caron), wife of Ambroise	205.50	B	0.00
Rosalie Dubois	40.00	B	0.00
(Mrs.) Gabriel Dufour	380.00	B	0.00
Véronique Dumas (Ouellette), wife of Michel	556.00	B	0.00
Judith Dumont (Parenteau), widow of Isidore	415.00	B	0.00
Justine Dumont (Short), widow of Ambroise	952.50	A	533.10
Isabelle Fayant (McGillis), wife of Cuthbert	769.00	B	0.00
Josephte Fidler (Laplante), wife of François	1,260.75	B	0.00
Véronique Fidler (Gervais), wife of Baptiste	100.00	B	0.00
William Fidler	1,095.00	B	0.00
Alexandre P. Fisher	378.00	B	0.00
George Fisher Sr.	14,283.00	A	10,442.92

CLAIMANT(S)	Claim granted ($)	Category	($)
Patrice Fleury	788.00	B	0.00
Patrice Fleury Jr.	218.50	B	0.00
Azarie Gareau (lt)	492.00	A	50.00
Ludger Gareau (lt)	7,189.21	A	2,598.80
Rosalie Gariépy (Parenteau), wife of Philippe	1,103.70	B	0.00
Françoise Gervais (Lafournaise), wife of Patrice	350.00	B	0.00
Françoise Gervais (Ledoux), wife of Basile	1,212.00	A	583.00
Jean-Baptiste Gervais	596.00	B	0.00
Roger Goulet	1,957.00	A	1,261.00
Catherine Henry (Beauchemin), wife of Pierre	1,058.70	B	0.00
Kerr Brothers	16,343.50	A	3,402.50
François Ladouceur	294.00	B	0.00
Ferdinand Ladret	261.85	A	100.00
Calixte Lafontaine	727.00	B	0.00
Louise Lafontaine (Gervais), wife of Calixte	902.00	B	0.00
Alexandre Lamirande	140.00	B	0.00
Antoine Laplante	343.50	A	228.00
Élise Laplante (Gervais), wife of Toussaint	385.00	B	0.00
Jean-Baptiste Laplante	525.00	B	0.00
Hélène Ledoux (Poitras), wife of Pierre	995.00	B	0.00
Maxime Lépine	1,829.00	B	0.00
Angélique Letendre (Dumas), wife of Louis	682.45	B	0.00
Catherine Letendre (Godon), widow of André	1,443.00	B	0.00
Xavier Letendre dit Batoche	32,972.44	A	19,295.59
Augustin Lévêque	500.50	C	0.00
Clémentine Lévêque	1,073.00	A	270.00
Alexandre McDougall	949.00	B	0.00
Isabelle McGillis (Poitras), wife of Modeste	228.20	B	0.00
Abraham Montour	508.00	C	0.00
Caroline Montour (Dumont), widow of Baptiste	115.00	B	0.00
George Ness	1,805.00	A	831.00
Adolphus Nolin	443.00	A	279.00
André Nolin	189.00	B	0.00
Charles Nolin	9,915.00	A	1,275.00
Jean-Baptiste Normand	10.50	B	0.00
Élisabeth Ouellette (Dumont), wife of Moïse	828.00	B	0.00
Thérèse Ouellette (Houle), widow of Joseph	270.00	B	0.00
Alexandre Parenteau	340.00	B	0.00
Daniel Parenteau	299.66	B	0.00
Gabriel Parenteau	171.00	B	0.00
Hélène Parenteau (Normand), wife of Pierre Jr.	263.00	B	0.00
Jean-Baptiste Parenteau	1,600.00	B	0.00
Joseph Parenteau Jr.	141.50	B	0.00
Léon Parenteau	285.00	B	0.00
Marie-Anne Parenteau (Caron), wife of Pierre	537.00	B	0.00
Patrice Parenteau	224.50	B	0.00
Pierre Parenteau (Pierriche)	2,392.00	B	0.00
Véronique Parenteau (St. Germain), wife of Moïse	242.00	B	0.00
Angélique Pilon, wife of Joseph	1,939.75	B	0.00
Barthélémi Plion	1,657.70	B	0.00
Joseph Pilon Jr.	504.50	B	0.00
Joseph Pilon Sr.	1,776.00	B	0.00
Hélène Poitras (McGillis), wife of Ignace	1,817.25	B	0.00
Caroline Racette (Nolin), wife of Jérôme	410.00	B	0.00
Hélène Racette (Boyer), widow of Charles	140.00	A	115.00
Octave Régnier	773.00	B	0.00

CLAIMANT(S)	Claim granted ($)	Category	($)
Antoine Richard*			
Louis Riguidel	95.00	A	57.00
Jean-Baptiste Rocheleau Jr.	722.00	B	0.00
Marie Rocheleau (Carrière), wife of Baptiste Sr.	2,416.00	B	0.00
Modeste Rocheleau	1,285.00	B	0.00
Catherine Ross (Delorme), widow of Donald	2,477.00	B	0.00
Élise Ross (Dufour), widow of Baptiste	300.00	A	154.00
Frédéric St. Germain	45.00	B	0.00
Louis Schmidt	224.50	A	84.50
Richard Tees	500.00	A	65.00
Hélène Thomas (Letendre), wife of Charles	492.40	B	0.00
Catherine Tourond (Gervais), wife of Pierre	1,171.85	B	0.00
Josephte Tourond (Gervais), widow of Calixte	1,167.85	B	0.00
Josephte Tourond (Paul), widow of Joseph	8,451.00	A	2,804.67
Norbert Turcotte	470.82	B	0.00
Alphonsine Vandal (Henry), wife of Antoine	714.00	B	0.00
Élise Vandal (Champagne), wife of Joseph	528.00	B	0.00
Élisa Vandal (Poitras), wife of Pierre	93.00	B	0.00
Élisa Vandal (Poitras), wife of Pierre	405.00	C	0.00
Isabelle Vandal (Branconnier), wife of Roger	983.00	B	0.00
Isabelle Vandal (Branconnier), wife of Roger	592.50	C	0.00
Jean-Baptiste Vandal	2,341.00	B	0.00
Joseph Vandal Jr. (deceased)	319.00	B	137.50
Virginie Vandal (Boyer), wife of William	739.00	B	0.00
David Venne	6,032.00	A	2,186.90
Napoléon Venne	1,464.00	A	823.00
Salomon Venne	41,899.21	A	10,978.21
Alexandre Vermette	65.00	B	0.00
Marguerite Vermette, widow of Joseph	1,942.00	B	0.00
Marie-Rose Vermette	247.75	B	0.00
Mathilde Villeneuve	447.00	B	0.00
Rosalie Villeneuve (Champagne), wife of Isidore	384.50	B	0.00
Walters and Baker	28,750.00	A	13,236.35

Source: LAC, RG15, vol. 513, 914–916, 931–932.
* Joint claim with Alexandre McDougall (see under that name)

Appendix 3 (Related to Chapters 4 and 5)

NOTES ON QUANTITATIVE ANALYSIS OF HOMESTEAD DECLARATIONS

There were two series of land applications made by the Métis. The 1884 declarations were part of a survey of residents of the South Saskatchewan River district conducted by the Dominion Lands Agent, Mr. G. Duck, accompanied by a local priest, Father A. André, in May and September, 1884. They were described by the government as a preliminary step in the process of actual homestead entry and application for patent or title, in short a sort of pre-entry or information-gathering investigation. The Métis, on the other hand, hoped that this application was a process that would confirm their landholdings or customary usage and that they would receive "free patents." They believed that as an Aboriginal people of the North-West they should not have to conform to the homestead regulations established for Eurocanadian settlers or newcomers. The government, however, did not recognize this principle and status. The Métis would have to abide by the same regulations as the newcomers, that is, make official entry and pay a $10 entry fee, fulfil established residency and cultivation requirements, and then apply for patent. Their Aboriginal claims would be dealt with later and separately.

The local Métis population became frustrated and angry over the refusals and delays, which were one of the main causes of the armed resistance in March 1885. The Métis who made declarations in 1884 were reportedly advised whether or not they could obtain entry for their lands, but no titles were issued subsequent to these applications. In any case, this was not what they had asked for. Many of the 1884 applicants, however, subsequently made official homestead entry and obtained patent for lands requested in 1884 (code 1).

The post-1884 records deal with actual or official homestead entries and applications for patent. Homestead entry was required of all settlers in the North-West, Métis and non-Métis. There is evidence, however, that a number of Métis resided on lands for years without making official entry.

Some subsequently did, while others simply left their land and relocated elsewhere. This pattern is reflected in both 1884 and post-1884 records.

Number of Cases for Each Record Type

Code	Record Type	Cases	Percent
1	1884 – Obtains patent	38	15.0
2	1884 – Does not obtain patent	23	9.1
3	Post-1884 – New. Does not obtain patent	6	2.4
4	Post-1884 – New. Obtains patent	128	50.6
5	Post-1884 – Previous. Obtains patent	40	15.8
6	Post-1884 – Multiple-lot entries	18	7.1
Total		253	100.0

Ethnic Background by Record Type

	Codes						
Background	1	2	3	4	5	6	Total
Métis	37	23	5	98	38	16	217
Non-Métis	1	0	1	30	2	2	36
Total	38	23	6	128	40	18	253

Place of Origin of Métis Homestead Applicants

	Entry in 1884	Entry post-1884	Total No.	Percent
Manitoba	52	59	111	70.3
NWT	7	36	43	27.2
USA	0	4	4	2.5
Total No.	59	99	158	100.0

Missing Cases: 5.
Records of all Métis homestead applicants from 1884, and new applicants making entry after 1884, were used in this table (codes 1, 2, 3, 4).

A quantitative analysis of 253 homestead declarations (217 Métis and 36 non-Métis) provides the basis for the tables and discussion on Métis land entries. There are two series of homestead applications: 1884 special declarations, and post-1884 to ca. 1925 applications for the following communities along the South Saskatchewan River:

St. Laurent, "St. Laurent Settlement"	T44-1-3, lots 1-25
Batoche, "St. Laurent Settlement"	T43-1-3, lots 25-71
Vandal and Fish Creek	T42-1-3
St. Louis (post-1884 only)	T45-1-3, T45-27-2, T45-28-2

Selection was based primarily on riverlot claims on the east bank (south shore) of the South Saskatchewan River, although a few sectional claims in Batoche were also included. A series of frequency charts and cross-tabulations were generated for the two declaration types, using the Statistical Package for the Social Sciences (SPSS). The object of the inquiry was to help illustrate Métis actions and persistence regarding land claims. This was evaluated on the basis of variables such as: absenteeism, history of the land claim (according to unofficial and official documents), years of continuous residence, number of years between residence and entry, number of years between entry and patent, and year of patent. Cultivation and livestock data were also tabulated to illustrate agricultural activities (see chap. 4: Economy). Some of the post-1884 records, more specifically records in Code 5, tabulate previous or 1884 applicants, while the eighteen records in Code 6 show those who made more than one entry– in most cases, for a second homestead. During the analysis, care was taken not to duplicate record data, particularly in the case of codes 5 and 6. Analysis was done from one set of records, and, in the case of codes 4 and 6, for example, personal data were not duplicated.

The two sets of forms, 1884 and post-1884, did not all request the same information. There was more uniformity in the 1884 declaration, although replies were more evasive. Because of the time-span for the post-1884 records (ca. 1884–1925 or later), the application form also varied. In the tables, "missing cases" refer to situations where the information was not reported or not applicable.

Appendix 4 (Related to Chapter 5)

4.1. BENEFICIARIES OF LAND SCRIP, BATOCHE AND VICINITY, 1885–87

I. Beneficiaries according to the 1885–87 orders-in-council: Métis residing in the North-West Territories and born before 15 July 1870.

Name	Scrip ($)	Date
Duck Lake		
Marie Arcand (widow of James Swain)	160	1885
PRINCE ALBERT		
Cléophas Champagne	240	30 September 1886
Élise Champagne (Lafournaise)	240	30 September 1886
Judith Champagne (Langer)	160	30 September 1886
Baptiste Ouellette	240	30 September 1886
Baptiste Parenteau Jr.	240	30 September 1886
Abraham Ouellette	240	1 October 1886
Bernard Ouellette	240	1 October 1886
Joseph Ouellette	240	1 October 1886
Julien Ouellette	240	1 October 1886
Caroline Bélanger	240	6 October 1886
Pierre Ledoux	240	6 October 1886
Alexandre Letendre	240	6 October 1886
André Letendre	240	6 October 1886
Véronique Parenteau (St. Germain)	240	6 October 1886
Virginie Ladret	240	9 October 1886
ST. LAURENT		
John Fayant (as heir)	208	12 October 1886
Azarie Champagne	240	13 October 1886
Louise Desjarlais	160	13 October 1886
Rose Fagnant	208	13 October 1886
William Fayant (as heir)	208	13 October 1886
Marguerite Flamand	240	13 October 1886
Catherine Ledoux (Dubois)	240	13 October 1886
Hélène Malaterre	160	13 October 1886
Marie McGillis	240	1886
Cyprien Ouellette	240	13 October 1886
Joseph Ouellette	160	13 October 1886

Name	Scrip ($)	Date
Elzéar Parisien	240	13 October 1886
Marie-Louise Patenaude	240	13 October 1886
Madeline Paul	160	13 October 1886
Corbet Trottier	240	13 October 1886
Thérèse Vallée	240	13 October 1886
Corbet Fagnant Jr.	208	14 October 1886
Rosalie Laframboise	240	14 October 1886
Louise Ledoux	160	14 October 1886
Norbert Sauvé jr.	240	14 October 1886
Albert Trottier	240	14 October 1886
Marguerite Bottineau (widow of Alex McGillis)	160	15 October 1886
Euphrosine Cayen	160	15 October 1886
Julie Ducharme	160	15 October 1886
Charles Fayant (as heir)	208	15 October 1886
Hélène McGillis (Poitras)	160	15 October 1886
Isidore McKay	160	15 October 1886
Baptiste Ouellette	160	15 October 1886
Charlotte Bourassa	160	16 October 1886
David Lafond	240	16 October 1886
Pierre Lafontaine (alias Fagnant)	240	16 October 1886
Daniel Laframboise	240	16 October 1886
Édouard Laframboise	240	16 October 1886
Marie-Anne McKay	240	16 October 1886
Abraham Montour Jr.	240	16 October 1886
Abraham Montour Sr.	160	16 October 1886
Clémence Montour	240	16 October 1886
Justine Montour	240	16 October 1886
Marie Montour	240	16 October 1886
Marie Pagé	160	16 October 1886
Francis Primeau	240	18 October 1886
Jean-Baptiste Robillard	240	18 October 1886
BATOCHE		
Judith Dumont (widow of Pascal Montour)	240	11 July 1885
Thérèse Arcand (heir of Baptiste Lafond)	50	18 July 1885
Marie Hallet (widow of Louis Letendre Sr.)	160	18 July 1885
Édouard Lafond	11	18 July 1885
Josephte Patenaude	240	18 July 1885
Hélène Letendre (daughter of Xavier)	240	20 July 1885
Marie McGillis	240	20 July 1885
Rose Parenteau	240	20 July 1885
Virgine Racette (heir of Charles)	15	20 July 1885
Josephte Sauvé	240	20 July 1885
Pascal Montour Jr.	240	19 October 1886
André Nolin	240	12 October 1887

II. Beneficiaries by right of inheritance, 1886 Commission

Heirs of	Petitioner (s)	Scrip ($)
BATOCHE		
Élise Ouellette	Marguerite Ouellette and 4 other children	240
Alexandre Poitras	Ignace Poitras	240
Joseph Thomas	Charles Thomas	60
ST. LAURENT		
Joseph Azure	Élisa Champagne	240
Jean-Baptiste Cayen	Isidore Cayen	160
Louis Desnoyers	Arcand children	160
Catherine Desjarlais	Louise Desjarlais	160
Baptiste Fleury	Antoine Fleury	240
Jean-Baptiste Fleury	Patrice Fleury	240
Calixte Gariépy	Louise Lafournaise	240
Josephte Hamelin	Isidore Lafontaine	160
Basile Ledoux	Louise Desjarlais, wife and children	240
Eusèbe Ledoux	Catherine Roussin, wife and 6 children	160
Alexandre McGillis	3 sisters	160
Paul McGillis	5 brothers and sisters	240
Madeleine Montour	Marie-Louise and Hilaire Patenaude	160
Angèle Ouellette	Baptiste Ouellette	240
Cécile Ouellette	Joseph Ouellette	240
Charles Ouellette	Joseph Ouellette	240
St. Pierre Ouellette	Baptiste Ouellette	240
Michel Patenaude	Josephte Parenteau	160
Charles Racette	Hélène Boyer, wife and 4 children	160
Paulet Roussin	Caroline Roussin	160
Norbert Sauvé Sr.	Norbert Jr.	160
André Trottier	Joseph Trottier	240

Source: LAC, RG15, D11, 8(b)(e).

4.2. BENEFICIARIES OF LAND SCRIP, BATOCHE AND VICINITY, 1900

I. Beneficiaries according to the 1899–1900 orders-in-council: 240 acres to Métis born between 15 July 1870 and 31 December 1885

BATOCHE

Jean-Baptiste Beaugrand dit Champagne
Tobie Boyer
Moïse Carrière
Marie Virginie Cayen
Georgine d'Amour
Joséphine Deschamps
Madeleine Deschamps
Bethsey Dumont (née Boyer)
Joseph Dumont (son of Isidore)
Henriette Dumas
Alfred Fayant
Daniel Fayant
Joseph Fayant
Josué Gariépy
John Letendre (son of Xavier)
Mary Jane Letendre
Jean-Baptiste Ouellette
Moïse Ouellette
Modeste Parenteau
Vital Ross
Mathilde Thomas (née Parenteau)
Victor Thomas
Florestine Venne (née Letendre)

DUCK LAKE

Baptiste Arcand Jr.
Marguerite Bourassa
Baptiste Boyer Jr.
Marguerite Boyer (wife of Paul)
Angélique Cardinal
Justine Cardinal
Florestine Colin, widow of Maxime Poitras
Maxime Collin
Marie Deschamps (wife of Baptiste)
Jean Dumont
Joseph Dumont (son of Élie)
Édouard Fisher
Roger Gariépy
Georges Lafleur
François Larocque
Norbert Laviolette
Marguerite Lussier (wife of Thomas)
Patrice Primeau
Mélanie Ross (wife of Joseph)
William Sansregret
Adolphe Smith
Joseph Vandal(e)
William Vandal Jr.

Prince Albert

Joseph Branconnier
Joseph Delorme
Rosalie Dumont
Joseph Ferguson
Victor Gariépy
Élisa Gervais
Louis Gervais
Rosalie Lafond
Marie-Rose Lafontaine
Gabriel Laplante
Hyacinthe Laplante
Marie Laplante
Agathe Lefort (wife of Norbert Henry)
Agnès Marion
George Alex Marion
Alexandre Parenteau
Joachim Parenteau
Élisa Ross (wife of Vital)
François Slater
Baptiste Vandal
Frédéric Vandal

St. Louis

Pantaléon Schmidt

II. Parents inheriting land of deceased children

Batoche

William Boyer
Moïse Carrière
Isidore Dumas
Édouard Dumont
Corbet Fidler
Daniel Gariépy
Lazare Hamelin
Louis Letendre
Baptiste Parenteau
Ignace Poitras
Charles Thomas
William Thorn(e)
Pierre Vandal
Salomon Venne

Battleford

George Ness

Duck Lake

Charles Carrière
Élie Dumont
Ambroise Fisher
Joseph Parenteau
William Vandal Sr.

Lethbridge

Patrice Fleury
Abraham Montour

Pincher Creek

Ludger Gareau(lt)
Madeleine Delorme
Charles Smith
Élisa Delorme

Prince Albert

Charles Adams
Baptiste Deschamps
Antoine Ferguson
Pierre Henry
Louis Marion
Jonas Moreau
Moïse Ouellette
Baptiste Parenteau
Raphaël Parenteau
Jérôme Racette

III. Land scrip issued to Métis formerly from Batoche and vicinity

BATTLEFORD

Baptiste Boyer (son of Baptiste)
Joseph Nault (son of Élie)
Malvina Nault (daughter of Élie)
Éléonore Nolin (wife of Augustin)
Jean Plante (son of Basile)

LETHBRIDGE

Amanda Caron (née Parenteau), wife of Théophile
Job Falcon (son of Athanase)
Léon Nault (son of Napoléon)
Virginie Nault (daughter of Napoléon)
William, Alexandre and Florestine St. Germain (children of Frédéric)

MAPLE CREEK

Alfred Breland

PINCHER CREEK

Alexis Gervais (son of Cuthbert)
Joseph Gervais (son of Cuthbert)

WINNIPEG

Délima Boucher (daughter of Baptiste)
Élie Carrière (son of Napoléon)
Napoléon Carrière (son of Napoléon)
Norbert Lépine (son of Athanase)
Mathilde Nault (née Carrière), wife of André

Source: LAC, RG15, D11,8(c)(e).

FOREWORD

1 "'La vie en rose'? Métis Women at Batoche, 1870 to 1920," Christine Miller and P. Churchryk, eds., *Women of the First Nations: Power, Wisdom and Strength* (Winnipeg: University of Manitoba Press, 1996), 19–37.

2 For instance, Lyle Dick, another Parks Canada historian, has deconstructed the CBC/Radio Canada's highly acclaimed documentary series, "Canada: A People's History." Dick outlines how the series' producers "othered" First Nations and Métis as obstacles to Canada's development. Lyle Dick, "'A New History for the New Millennium': Canada: A People's History," *Canadian Historical Review*, 85.1 (2004): 85–109.

3 Many of the Gabriel Dumont Institute's students and staff with roots from Batoche have Old World French or Walloon names which suggest that the Batoche-area Métis intermarried, as Diane asserts, with these European Francophones, but failed to do so, at the same extent, with their *"Canayen"* cousins.

INTRODUCTION

1 Jennifer S.H. Brown, "People of Myth, People of History: A Look at Recent Writings on the Métis," *Acadiensis* 17, no. 1 (1987): 150–63.

2 Most important among these was the debate between D.N. Sprague and Thomas Flanagan in the 1980s and 1990s. See, e.g., D.N. Sprague, *Canada and the Métis 1869–1885* (Waterloo: Wilfrid Laurier University Press, 1988), and "Dispossession vs. Accommodation in Plaintiff vs. Defendant Accounts of Métis Dispersal from Manitoba, 1870–1881." *Prairie Forum* 1, 16, no. 2 (1991): 137–55; Thomas Flanagan, *Riel and the Rebellion: 1885 Reconsidered* (Saskatoon: Western Prairie Producer Books, 1983 and 1999), *Métis Lands in Manitoba* (Calgary: University of Calgary Press, 1991), and *Louis David Riel: Prophet of the New World* (Toronto: University of Toronto Press, 1979; 1996).

3 See 1990 edition of *"The Free People–Otipemisiwak": Batoche Saskatchewan, 1870–1930*, by this author. Nicole St-Onge, "Race, Class and Marginality: A Metis Settlement in the Manitoba Interlake, 1850–1914" (PhD thesis, University of Manitoba, 1990), revised and published under the title *St. Laurent, Manitoba* (Regina: Canadian Plains Research Center, 2004) and "Variations in Red River: The Traders and Freemen Métis of Saint-Laurent, Manitoba" *Canadian Ethnic Studies* 2, no. 2 (1991): 2–21; Guy Lavallée, "The Métis People of St. Laurent, Manitoba: An Introductory Ethnography" (MA thesis, University of British Columbia,1988), revised and published by the author in 2003 under the title *The Métis of St. Laurent, Manitoba: Their Life and Stories,1920–1988*; Gregory S. Camp, "The Turtle Mountain Plains-Chippewas and Métis" (PhD thesis, University of New Mexico, 1987), and Ruth Swan, "The Crucible: Pembina and the Origins of the Red River Valley Métis"

(PhD thesis, University of Manitoba, 2003).

4 See, e.g., biographies of Xavier Letendre and Charles Nolin by this author in *Dictionary of Canadian Biography* (vol. XIII, 1994: 595–96; 770–72); Raymond Huel, "Louis Schmidt: The Patriarch of St. Louis." *Saskatchewan History* 40, no. 1 (1987): 1–21; and Gerhard Ens, "Métis Ethnicity, Personal Identity and the Development of Capitalism in the Western Interior: The Case of Johnny Grant," in *From Rupert's Land to Canada: Essays in Honour of John E. Foster*, ed. Theodore Binnema et al., 161–77 (Edmonton: University of Alberta Press, 2001).

5 Antoine S. Lussier, "Msgr. Provencher and the Native People of Red River, 1818–1853," *Prairie Forum* 10, no. 1 (1985): 1–15; Emma LaRocque, "Conversations on Métis Identity," *Prairie Fire* 7, no. 1 (1986): 19–24, Ron Bourgeault, "The Struggle for Class and Nation: The Origin of the Métis in Canada and the National Question," in Ron Bourgeault et al., *1492–1992: Five Centuries of Imperialism and Resistance, Socialist Studies*, vol. 8, 153–88 (Winnipeg: Society for Socialist Studies and Fernwood Publishing, 1992).

6 Howard Adams, *Tortured People: The Politics of Colonization* (Penticton: Theytus Books, 1995, 1999) and "Challenging Eurocentric History," in *Expressions in Canadian Native Studies*, ed. Ron F. Laliberte et al., 41–53 (Saskatoon: University of Saskatchewan Extension Press, 2000).

7 J. R. Miller, "From Riel to the Métis," *Canadian Historical Review* 69 (1988): 1–20. As the title suggests, Miller lamented the fact that Eurocanadian writers focussed almost exclusively on Riel and events of 1870 and 1885, ignoring other aspects of Métis history. The late 1980s and 1990s witnessed the coming of age of Métis history.

8 See, e.g., Robert Rumilly, *Histoire de la Province de Québec*, vol. 5, *Louis Riel* (Montréal: Fides, 1973).

9 Denis Combet, ed., *Les mémoires – The Memoirs de/of Gabriel Dumont*, trans. Lise Gaboury-Diallo (St.-Boniface: Éditions du Blé). I am currently editing the accounts collected by Reverend Gabriel Cloutier at Batoche in 1886.

10 Ron Bourgeault, "Louis Riel: Hero of His People?", in *Expressions in Canadian Native Studies*, ed. Ron F. Laliberte et al., 225 (Saskatoon: University of Saskatchewan Extension Press, 2000).

11 Adams, *Tortured People*, 108.

12 Thomas Flanagan, *Louis Riel: Prophet of the New World* (Toronto: University of Toronto Press, 1996). Flanagan has integrated research materials which have come to light since the 1979 first edition, but he maintains his view that Riel was dysfunctional and failed the Métis.

13 Maggie Siggins, *Riel: A Life of Revolution* (Toronto: Harper Collins, 1994), Addendum 3, 453–59.

14 Yvon Dumont, "Metis Nationalism: Then and Now," in *The Forks and the Battle of Seven Oaks in Manitoba History*, ed. Robert Coutts and Richard Stuart, 83 (Winnipeg: Manitoba Historical Society, 1994).

15 Gerhard Ens, "Kinship, Ethnicity Class and the Red River Métis: The Parishes of St. François-Xavier and St. Andrews" (PhD thesis, University of Alberta, 1989), revised and published under the title, *Homeland to Hinterland: The Changing Worlds of the Red River Métis in the Nineteenth Century* (Toronto: University of Toronto Press, 1996); "Metis Ethnicity, Personal Identity and the Development of Capitalism in the Western Interior: The Case of Johnny Grant," in *From Rupert's Land to Canada*, ed. Theodore Binnema et al., 161–77 (Edmonton: University of Alberta Press, 2001).

16 Howard Adams, *Prison of Grass: Canada from the Native Point of View* (Saskatoon: Fifth House, 1989). He argued that, as a result of political and economic subjugation, Métis society became rigid or inflexible or was "ossified" at the pre-industrial stage.

17 Bourgeault, "The Struggle for Class and Nation," 157.

18 "The Dissolution of a Métis Community: Pointe à Grouette, 1860–1885," *Studies in Political Economy* 18 (Autumn 1985):

149–71; *Saint-Laurent, Manitoba: Evolving Metis Identities, 1850–1914* (Regina: Canadian Plains Research Center, 2004).

19 *The People Who Own Themselves: Aboriginal Ethnogenesis in a Canadian Family, 1660–1900* (Calgary: University of Calgary Press, 2004).

20 Paul Chartrand, "A Questionable Approach to Métis Land Claims," *National* 19, no. 2 (Summer 1992): 13, citing Thomas Flanagan, *Métis Lands in Manitoba* (Calgary: University of Calgary Press, 1991), 232.

21 Canada, *Royal Commission on Aboriginal Peoples Report*, "Métis Perspectives," chap. 5, 245–49.

22 See, e.g., the claim of Morin et al. v. Canada and Saskatchewan (Q.B. file 619-1994). The case involves Métis communities in the Treaty 10 Scrip area of north-western Saskatchewan. Between 1999 and 2003, the MatriX Project, led by Frank Tough of the University of Alberta on behalf of the Métis Nation of Saskatchewan, has established a scrip coupon database in an attempt to trace the claims of 1,163 individuals associated with the area. They are in the process of tracing these claims in the massive Department of the Interior and other government records in order to validate them before the courts. See Linda Goyette, "The X files," *Canadian Geographic* (March/April 2003): 70–80.

23 Ibid., 79–80, and Brad Milne, "The Historiography of Métis Land Dispersal, 1870–1890," *Manitoba History* 30 (1995): 39–40.

24 These ethical and professional issues were raised by Arthur J. Ray in "Native History on Trial: Confessions of an Expert Witness," *Canadian Historical Review* 84 (June 2003): 254–73. He states that expert witnesses, regardless of who they represent, are viewed suspiciously by both academics and the public. The adversarial nature of the judicial process and the fluid nature of theoretical discourses in the academy greatly challenge the historical expert whose primary responsibility is to the court rather than to his or her client.

25 The Manitoba Métis Federation case, Dumont et al v. AG Canada [1992] and [2002] argued that the Métis were unjustly deprived of land that they had rights to under the Manitoba Act, 1870. In 2002 the MMF sought leave to amend their statement of claim and the federal and provincial governments asked for an adjournment. Both requests were accepted but the judge noted that the case was not ready for trial due to inadequately documented evidence. The case was finally argued in the Court of Queen's Bench in 2006. In his decision [2007] M.J. No. 448, Judge A.D. MacInnes of the Court of Queen's Bench dismissed the action for declaratory relief. The Manitoba Métis Federation will appeal the decision. It could take years before a final judgment is delivered and meaningful settlements regarding outstanding claims are achieved.

26 The Métis Nation of Saskatchewan case, Morin v. Canada and Saskatchewan (Q.B. file 619-1994) seeks a declaration that the Métis have an Aboriginal title to land and that these rights were not extinguished through scrip. The Métis National council has compiled a genealogical and land claim database to support this and other claims (www.metisnation.ca/database).

27 R. v. Powley, Supreme Court of Canada, no. 28533, [2003].

28 R. v. Blais, Supreme Court of Canada, no. 28645, [2003].

29 Statement of Commemorative Integrity for Batoche National Historic Site, March, 1997.

30 *Royal Commission on Aboriginal Peoples Report*, 1996, chap. 5, "Métis."

31 Bourgeault, "The Struggle for Class and Nation," 168.

32 Adams, *Tortured People*, 106–8.

33 Laura Caso Barrera, "The Canadian Metis and the Mexican Mayas: A Cross Cultural Study of Native Land Struggles" (MA thesis, University of Calgary, 1992), 98.

34 Blair Stonechild and Bill Waiser, *Loyal till Death: Indian and the North-West Rebellion* (Calgary: Fifth House, 1997).

35 Margaret L. Clarke, Review Article, *Prairie Forum* 23, no. 2 (Fall 1998): 268–73.

36 Diane P. Payment, *The Willow Cree of One-Arrow First Nation and the Métis of Batoche, 1870–1920: An Ambivalent Relationship* (Parks Canada, Western and Northern Service Centre, Cultural Resource Services, 1997), 11–15.

37 Darren R. Préfontaine, Review Article on *Loyal till Death*, *Prairie Forum* 23, no. 2 (Fall 1998): 275–78.

38 Archives of Manitoba, Fonds de la Socété historique métisse, MG 10, F1, "Mémoires dictés par Gabriel Dumont," [c. 1903]; Constance Sissons, [Memoirs of] *John Kerr* (Toronto: Oxford University Press, 1946), 161.

39 Alan McCullough, "Parks Canada and the 1885 Rebellion/Uprising/Resistance," *Prairie Forum* 27, no. 2 (Fall 2002): 161. On the other hand, the Métis argue that emphasis is on the military side with less information on the Métis perspectives or accounts of the resistance. This is reiterated by Margaret L. Clarke in "Skinning the Narrative: The Story of Battle of Fish Creek," *Prairie Forum* 27, no. 2 (Fall 2002): 255–62.

40 Canadian Heritage, Parks Canada, Guiding Principles and Operational Policies, *Cultural Resource Management Policy*, 1994, 106.

41 Term coined by Jennifer S.H. Brown in article entitled "Women as Centre and Symbol in the Emergence of Métis Communities," *Canadian Journal of Native Studies* 3, no. 1 (1983): 39–46.

42 Maria Campbell, *Halfbreed* (New York: Saturday Review Press, 1973).

43 Christine Welsh, "Voices of Our Grandmothers: Reclaiming Métis Heritage," *Canadian Literature* 131 (1991): 15–24; *Keepers of the Fire* (Montréal: National Film Board, 1994); with Christine and Signe Johansson (producers) and Norma Bailey (director), *Women in the Shadows* (National Film Board and Direction Films, 1993).

44 Noëlie Palud-Pelletier's highly successful historical novel, *Louis: Fils des Prairies* was first written and published in French by Les Éditions des Plaines in 1983. It was subsequently translated into English and published by Pemmican Publications in 1990 and 2005. Thelma Poirier's novel is another Pemmican publication (1993).

45 Sylvia Van Kirk *'Many Tender Ties': Women in Fur Trade Society* (Winnipeg: Watson & Dwyer, 1980); Jennifer S.H. Brown, *Strangers in Blood: Fur Trade Company Families in Indian Country* (Vancouver: University of British Columbia Press, 1980).

46 Nathalie Kermoal, « Les rôles et les souffrances des femmes métisses lors de la résistance de 1870 et la rébellion de 1885, » *Prairie Forum* 19, no. 2 (1994): 153–68; Sherry Farrell-Racette, "Beads, Silk and Quills: The Clothing and Decorative Arts of the Metis," in *Metis Legacy: A Metis Historiography and Annotated* Bibliography, ed. Lawrence J. Barkwell, Leah Dorion, and Darren R. Préfontaine, 181–88 (Winnipeg: Pemmican, 2001); Diane P. Payment, "'La vie en rose'?: Métis Women at Batoche, 1870–1920," in *Women of the First Nations: Power, Wisdom and Strength*, ed. Christine Miller and Patricia Chuchryk, 19–37 (Winnipeg: University of Manitoba Press, 1996); Nicole St-Onge, "Memories of Métis Women of Saint-Eustache, Manitoba – 1910–1980," *Oral History Forum d'histoire orale* 19 (1999–2000): 89–111.

47 Diane M. Boyd, "The Rise and Development of Female Catholic Education in the 19th Century Red River Region: The Case of Catherine Mulaire" (MA thesis, University of Manitoba, 1999).

48 Madeline Bird and Agnes Sutherland, *Living Kindness: The Dream of My Life: the Memoirs of Metis Elder Madeline Bird* (Yellowknife: Outcrop, 1991).

49 Heather Devine, *The People Who Own Themselves* (Calgary: University of Calgary Press, 2004); Margaret L. Clarke, "Reconstituting Fur Trade Community in the Assiniboine Basin, 1793–1812" (MA thesis, University of Calgary, 1997) and as editor of Métis genealogy newsletter, *Canada Tree*.

50 Dolores T. Poelzer, and Irene A. Poelzer, *In Our Own Words: Northern Saskatchewan*

Women Speak Out (Saskatoon: One Sky, 1986.) See also Mary Crnkovich, *Gossip: A Spoken History of Women in the North* (Canadian Arctic Resources, Committee Publishing Program, 1990).

51 See article by Erin Millions, "Breaking the Mold: A Historiographical Review of Saskatchewan Women's History, 1880–1930," *Saskatchewan History* 54, no. 2 (Fall 2002): 31–49.

52 Lawrence J. Barkwell, Leah M. Dorion, and Audreen Hourie, eds., *Metis Legacy: Michif Culture, Heritage, and Folkways* (Saskatoon: Gabriel Dumont Institute and Pemmican, 2006).

53 Video produced by the Gabriel Dumont Institute (GDI), 2001. Arcand, whose ancestors were from St. Laurent, near Batoche is one of Canada's most accomplished fiddlers.

54 Video produced by the Gabriel Dumont Institute in 2002. Lafferty is a famous fiddler originally from Fort Providence, Northwest Territories.

55 Lynn Whidden (producer) and Ray St. Germain (author and narrator), *A Metis Suite* (Brandon: All Media Musics, 1995).

56 Maria Campbell, *Stories of the Road Allowance People* (Penticton: Theytus Books, 1995).

57 Marcien Ferland, *Au temps de la prairie: L'histoire des Métis de l'Ouest canadien racontée par Auguste Vermette, neveu de Louis Riel* (Saint-Boniface: Éditions du Blé, 2000).

58 Leah Dorion and Todd Paquin (producer), *The Story of the Crescent Lake Métis: Our Life on the Road Allowance* (Gabriel Dumont Institute, 2002).

59 Cheryl Troupe, *Expressing Our Heritage: Métis Artistic Designs* (Saskatoon: Gabriel Dumont Institute, 2001–02), includes a series of gallery prints, manual, and teacher's guide. She also co-produced a video on the artwork at Cumberland House with Leah Dorion entitled: *Our Shared Inheritance: A Tradition of Métis Beadwork* (Gabriel Dumont Institute, 2002).

60 See "The Continuing Problematic of Métis inclusion in Museum Representation," *Proceedings of the Annual Meeting of the American Society for Ethnohistory* (Mashantucket, CT: unpublished reports,1999), 20–23, and "Beads, Silk and Quills: The Clothing and Decorative Arts of the Metis," in Barkwell et al., *Metis Legacy: Michif Culture, Heritage, and Folkways*, 181–88.

61 See, e.g., *En route pour la mer glaciale* (Paris: Letouzey et ane, 1887) and *Traditions indiennes du Canada Nord-Ouest* (Paris: Maisonneuve frères, 1886).

62 Martha McCarthy, *From the Great River to the Ends of the Earth: Oblate Missions to the Dene, 1847–1921* (Edmonton: University of Alberta Press, 1995); Raymond J.A. Huel, *Proclaiming the Gospel to the Indians and the Métis* (Edmonton: University of Alberta Press, 1996).

63 Raymond Huel, "The Oblates, the Métis, and 1885: The Breakdown of Traditional Relationships," *Canadian Historical Association, Historical Studies* 56 (1989): 9–29.

64 Guy Lavallée, *Prayers of a Métis Priest: Conversations with God on the Political Experiences of the Canadian Métis 1992–94* (Winnipeg: Kromar Printing, 1997).

65 Peter Bakker, *A Language of Our Own: The Genesis of Michif, the Mixed Cree-French Language of the Canadian Métis* (New York: Oxford University Press, 1997).

66 Robert Papen, « ‹ Mitchifs, mitchisse, métis … du pareil au même? › : Langue(s) et identité(s) des Métis de l'Ouest canadien », Colloque international *Résistances et Convergences*, Regina, Saskatchewan, le 22 octobre 2005; « La situation linguistique des Mitchifs: un dédale sans issue, » Gabriel Dumont Conference, St. Boniface, Manitoba, September 2006.

67 Patline Laverdure and Ida Rose Allard, *The Michif Dictionary: Turtle Mountain Chippewa Cree* (Winnipeg: Pemmican, 1983).

68 See essays in Robert Coutts and Richard Stuart, eds., *The Forks and the Battle of Seven Oaks in Manitoba History* (Winnipeg: Manitoba Historical Society, 1994). An example of community history is Brenda Macdougall, "Wahkohtowin and Métis Identity and Family: Ramifications for Kinship Studies," American Society for

Ethnohistory Conference Paper, Québec City, 2002, a study of Ile à la Crosse.

69 *Royal Commission on Aboriginal Peoples Report*, chap. 5, "Métis Perspectives," 199–386, and chap. 6, "The North," 428–60, 1996.

70 Olive P. Dickason, *The Myth of the Savage and the Beginnings of French Colonialism in the Americas* (Edmonton: University of Alberta Press, 1984); *Canada's First Nations: A History of Founding Peoples from Earliest Times* (Toronto: Oxford University Press, 1997; 2001).

71 Métis Heritage Association of the Northwest Territories and Parks Canada, *Picking Up the Threads: Métis History in the Mackenzie Basin* (Yellowknife: Outcrop, 1998).

72 Joanne Overvold [Burger], *Our Metis Heritage: A Portrayal* (Yellowknife: Metis Association of the Northwest Territories, 1976).

73 Barkwell et al., *Metis Legacy: A Metis Historiography and Annotated Bibliography*.

74 Leah Dorion and Darren R. Préfontaine, "Deconstructing Métis Historiography: Giving Voice to the Métis People," in Barkwell et al. *Metis Legacy: A Metis Historiography and Annotated Bibliography*, 13–36.

75 Theodore Binnema, Gerhard Ens, and R.C. MacLeod, eds., *From Rupert's Land to Canada* (Edmonton: University of Alberta Press, 2001).

76 See "Wintering, the Outsider Adult Male and the Ethnogenesis of the Western Plains Métis," in *From Rupert's Land to Canada*, ed. Binnema et al., 179–92.

77 "Plains Métis," in *Plains Volume*, ed. Raymond J. DeMaillie, *Handbook of North American Indians*, no. 13, Part 1, 661–76 (Washington: Smithsonian Institution, 2001). See comprehensive bibliography in Part 2.

78 Key sites and databases are: Gabriel Dumont Institute, Virtual Museum. Archivia Net, Library and Archives Canada. Métis Archival Scrip Project, Department of Native Studies, University of Alberta. Voyageur and Métis Scrip Database, University of Ottawa and Métis National Council. Saskatchewan Archives Board, Homestead Files. La Société historique de Saint-Boniface, Métis Resource Centre, and PRD (Programmme de recherche en démographie historique, University of Montréal) provide genealogical research services.

79 See, e.g., Sylvie Van Brabant, *Sur les traces de Riel* (Montréal: Productions du Rapide-Blanc, 2003), which traces Métis history through the life of elder Rose Fleury of Duck Lake, Saskatchewan, and Marcel Collet, producer, *Francophonie Amérique: Le monde qui parlait aux arbres* (St-Boniface: Les Productions Rivard, 2003), which traces the history of the Métis community of St. Laurent, Manitoba.

80 Play by Laurier Gareau of Bellevue, Saskatchewan, a descendant of witnesses to the events of 1885.

81 Great Plains Productions (Millbrook: Fourth Line Theatre, 1999).

82 Leah Dorion, Todd Paquin, and Darren R. Préfontaine, producers, *The Métis People: Our Story* (Edmonton: Arnold Publishing and the Gabriel Dumont Institute, 2000).

83 Produced by Normand Guilbeault in 1999.

84 Richard Preston, ed., *Cree Narrative* (Montreal and Kingston: McGill-Queen's University Press, 2002), Introduction, xvi.

85 Frederic W. Gleach, "Controlled Speculation: Interpreting the Saga of Pocahantas and Captain John Smith," in *Reading Beyond Words: Contexts for Native History*, ed. Elizabeth Vibert and Jennifer S.H. Brown, 21–42 (Peterborough: Broadview Press, 1998).

86 Diane P. Payment, *Plains Métis*, 661–62.

87 Tim Borlase, *The Labrador Settlers, Métis and Kabhunângajuit* (Goose Bay: Labrador East Integrated School Board, 1994); Martin F. Dunn, "All My Relations – The Other Métis," Background paper prepared for the Métis Circle Special Consultation of the Royal Commission on Aboriginal Peoples (Ottawa: March 1994).

88 Dickason, *Myth of the Savage*, 147.

89 Louise Dechêne, *Habitants et marchands de Montréal au 17e siècle* (Paris-Montréal: Plon, 1974), 17.

90 Dickason, *Canada's First Nations*, 169.

91 For an analysis of Eurocanadian perceptions of Aboriginal peoples, see Cornelius Jaenen, *Friend and Foe* (Toronto: McClelland & Stewart, 1976), and Donald B. Smith, "Le Sauvage" d'après les historiens canadiens français des XIXe et XXe siècles. Cahiers du Québec. (Montréal: Hurtubise HNH, 1979).

92 Pierre Simoni, "Science anthropologique et racisme à l'époque de l'expansion coloniale: le cas du Grand dictionnaire universel du XIXe siècle de Pierre Larousse," *Historical Papers/Communications historiques* (1980), 167–84. This incisive article describes the development and pervasiveness of racist thought in the nineteenth century.

93 Christine Bolt, *Victorian Attitudes to Race* (Toronto: University of Toronto Press, 1971), 23.

94 William F. Butler, *The Wild North Land* (Edmonton: Hurtig, 1968); Earl of Southesk, *Saskatchewan and the Rocky Mountains* (Tokyo: C.D. Tuttle & Co., 1967); Marquis of Lorne (Duke of Argyll), *Manitoba and the North-West Territory* (London: Caustin, 1881) and *Memories of Canada and Scotland* (Montreal: Dawson, 1884).

95 Richard White, *The Middle Ground: Indians, Empires and Republics in the Great Lakes Region, 1650–1815* (Cambridge: Cambridge University Press, 1991).

96 Jacqueline Peterson, "Many Roads to Red River: Métis Genesis in the Great Lakes Region, 1680–1815," in *The New Peoples: Being and Becoming Métis in North America*, ed. J. Peterson and Jennifer S.H. Brown, 40–45 (Winnipeg: University of Manitoba Press, 1985).

97 Peterson, "Many Roads to Red River", 63.

98 Alexander Ross, *History of the Red River Settlement: Its Rise, Progress and Present State* (Edmonton: Hurtig, 1972), 107 [originally published in 1856].

99 Cornelius Jaenen, "Miscegenation in Eighteenth Century New-France" in *New Dimensions in Ethnohistory*, ed. Barry Gough and Laird Christie, 92, 106. Canadian Ethnology Service, Canadian Museum of Civilization (Mercury Series, no. 120, 1991). The first identified Prairie Métis, Fleurimond, born around 1735, was sent to school in Montreal and later returned to live in the Dakota region. See A.G. Morice, *La Race Métisse* (Winnipeg: The Author, 1938), 13.

100 Antoine Champagne, *Les LaVérendrye et le Poste de l'Ouest* (Québec: Presses de l'université Laval, 1968), 143–46.

101 The Programme de Recherche en Démographie historique (PRDH) of the Université de Montréal has produced an inventory of Quebec parish records up to the early nineteenth century. Based on these records and an inventory of voyageurs' contracts for that period, Alfred Fortier of La Société historique de Saint-Boniface (SHSB) was able to identify the nineteen compagnons de LaVérendrye who died at "Massacre Island" near Fort St. Charles in 1736. See « Les victimes de l'Île au Massacre: les oubliés de l'histoire, » *Bulletin de SHSB* (hiver 2001–02): 3–6.

102 Diane P. Payment, « Les héritiers et les héritières de Louis Riel : Un aperçu des relations entre les Métis et les Canadiens français dans l'ouest canadien » in *Le dialogue avec les cultures minoritaires*, dir. Éric Waddell, 56–57 (Sainte-Foy: Presses de l'université Laval, 1999), citing missionary and fur trade records.

103 There is much ongoing debate on this subject. See, e.g., Frits Pannekoek, *A Snug Little Flock: The Social Origins of the Riel Resistance, 1869–1870* (Winnipeg: Watson & Dwyer, 1991); Irene Spry, "The Métis and Mixed Bloods in Rupert's Land Before 1870," in *The New Peoples*, ed. Peterson and Brown, 95–118; and Robert Coutts, *The Road to the Rapids: Nineteenth-Century Church and Society at St. Andrew's Parish, Red River* (Calgary: University of Calgary Press, 2000).

104 Term used by Louis Goulet, a Métis who traded in the Battleford district, in reference to his partner, William Gladu. See Guillaume Charette, *L'Espace de Louis Goulet* (Winnipeg: Éditions Bois-Brûlés, 1976), 141.

105 Deschambault referred bitterly to the discriminatory policies of the Hudson's Bay Company towards French Canadians in his correspondence. SBHS, SBAA, letter to H. Northcote, June, 1870. Bélanger was the only French Canadian to attain the rank of Chief Factor. See L.A. Prud'homme, « Horace Bélanger, facteur en chef de la Compagnie de la Baie d'Hudson », *Revue Canadienne* 27 (1891): 464–68.

106 For a revisionist account of the conflict, see L. Dick, "The Seven Oaks Incident and the Construction of a Historical Tradition, 1816–1970," *Journal of the Canadian Historical Association* 2 (1991): 91–113.

107 For an account of the trial, see W.L. Morton, Introduction, in *Eden Colvile: London Correspondence Inward, 1849–1852*, ed. E.E. Rich and A.M. Johnson, lxxix–lxxxix (London: Hudson Bay Record Society, 1956).

108 Lionel Dorge, "The Métis and Canadien Councillors of Assiniboia," *The Beaver* 305 (Summer 1974): 12–19; 305 (Autumn 1974): 39–45; 305 (Winter 1974): 51–58. Riel and other militant Métis and priests were not appointed to the company-controlled Council of Assiniboia.

109 This is documented in the Riel Papers and Papers of La Société historique métisse (PAM, MG3, D2 and MG10, F1).

110 Nicole J.M. St-Onge, "The Dissolution of a Métis Community: Pointe à Grouette, 1860–1885," *Studies in Political Economy* 18 (Autumn 1985): 149–71.

111 *Report of the Royal Commission on Aboriginal Peoples*, "Métis Perspectives," chap. 5, 224–25.

112 Jennifer L. Bellman and Chris C. Hanks, "Northern Métis and the Fur Trade," in *Picking Up the Threads: Métis History in the Mackenzie Basin*, Métis Heritage Association of the Northwest Territories and Parks Canada, 37–38 (Yellowknife: Outcrop, 1998).

113 Diane P. Payment, "Métis People in Motion: From Red River to the Mackenzie Basin" ibid., 69–86.

114 Diane P. Payment, "Jean-Baptiste Letendre dit Batoche," in *Dictionnaire biographique du Canada*, ed. Jean Hamelin, vol. 6, "1821–35," 437–38 (Québec: Presses de l'université Laval,1987). See chap. 1: Society and Culture for a definition of "*nom dit*" and the alias "*dit* Batoche."

115 Marie's father, Henry Hallet (ca. 1722–1844), was in charge of the NWC post at La Montée in 1818–21. Hallet and Letendre retired to Red River around 1821, and in 1825 the customary marriage of their children, Louis Letendre and Marie Hallet was blessed in St. Boniface cathedral. Although largely based in St. Boniface, the Letendre family continued to trade in the Saskatchewan district between 1821 and 1870.

116 Gail Paul Armstrong, "The Métis, The Development and the Decline of Métis Influence in an Early Saskatchewan Community," in *Wood Mountain Uplands: From Big Muddy to the Frenchman River, Wood Mountain, Saskatchewan*, ed. Thelma Poirier, 20–33 (Wood Mountain: Wood Mountain Historical Society, 2000); Clovis Rondeau and Adrien Chabot, *Histoire de Willow Bunch, Saskatchewan, 1870–1970* (Gravelbourg: Diocese of Gravelbourg, 1970; 2nd ed.).

117 For an account of the Prairie Ronde Métis community, see Rita Schilling, *Gabriel's Children* (Saskatoon Métis Local No. 11, 1983). About sixty families were at Petite-Ville between 1868 and 1873.

CHAPTER 1: SOCIETY AND CULTURE

1 SBHS, SBAA, Taché Papers, T28008-11, Father Moulin to Bishop Taché, 14 July 1883.

2 GA, Richard Hardisty Papers, file 31, letter 143, "Condensed Report of a Meeting of Métis Winterers at Saint Laurent ...," 31 December 1871.

3 PAA, OMI, Little chronicle of St. Laurent, Introduction (translation).

4 GA, Richard Hardisty Papers, Census of Métis at St. Laurent near Fort Carlton District in 1871. The St. Laurent Colony or "St. Laurent Settlement Reserve" extended to about sixteen kilometres north of

the crossing operated by Xavier Letendre starting in 1873 and to twenty-four kilometres south of the 1870–71 winter camp (St. Laurent de Grandin), i.e., roughly as far as Gabriel Dumont's Crossing.

5   LAC, RG15, vol. 238, file 10492.

6   See Métis population wintering at St. Laurent in 1871, Appendix 1.1.

7   DA, Father A. André, "Mémorial en réponse au questionnaire du R. P. Visiteur, octobre 1883."

8   PAA, OMI, Bishop V.J. Grandin, List of missions of the Catholic diocese of St. Albert, 1883.

9   Canada, Parliament, *Census of the Three Provisional Districts of the North-West Territories 1884–1885* (Ottawa: Maclean, Roger & Co., 1886).

10 Canada, *Censuses* of 1881, 1891, 1901, and 1911 (Ottawa: Queen's Printer). The 1881 census does not list the Métis, while the 1891 census lists only the total for the Prince Albert District. The 1901 census reports 71 families and 372 persons in Batoche, 889 in Duck Lake, and 227 in St. Louis. No figures are reported for St. Laurent. The 1911 census counted the Métis together with the French Canadians or allowed them to identify themselves as Indians, which few Métis in the area chose to do.

11 *Le Canada ecclésiastique* (Montréal: Beauchemin, 1887–1935); PADA, Parish register, St. Antoine de Padoue Parish, Batoche, 1881–1925; PADA, Spiritual and financial reports, St. Antoine de Padoue Parish, Batoche, 1924–1942.

12 Figures derived from two sources: SABS, Department of the Interior (Canada), Homestead Files, no. 81184 (1884) (hereafter "Homestead Files") and the 1870 Manitoba census: AM, MG2, B3.

13 An expression used by Mrs. Christine (Dumas) Pilon and supported by her journal and family photographs.

14 This analysis is based on a series of documents, in particular, the claims for losses following the 1885 resistance, the Fisher-Deschambault Papers (SBHS, SBAA), the Hillyard Mitchell Papers (SABS), the Homestead Files (SABS), the correspondence of Maxime Lépine (SBAA), Louis Schmidt (SBAA and PAM), C.-E. Boucher (SABS), Alex Fisher (LAC), and other Métis who left eyewitness accounts, as well as on the correspondence of missionaries.

15 SABS, Homestead Files, no. 81184. See also PAA, OMI, Little chronicle of St. Laurent, 1874–1879 [Father André].

16 DA, Xavier Letendre's account of the origins and commercial activities of Batoche, transcribed by Father Valentin Végréville, 1882.

17 The rural society in question is the French Canadian one, whose traditions were present at Batoche. On the subject of French Canadian society at the end of the nineteenth century, see Léon Gérin's study, "L'Habitant de Saint-Justin," *Mémoires de la Société Royale du Canada*, series 2, 4, no. 1 (1898): 139–216; Lionel Groulx, "La famille canadienne-française, ses traditions, son rôle," in *Notre maître le passé*, 115–51 (Montréal: Granger, 1936, 3rd ed.); and the more recent work by Susan M. Trofimenkoff, *The Dream of a Nation: A Social and Intellectual History of Québec* (Toronto: Macmillan, 1982).

18 These conclusions were drawn from a study of the Homestead Files (SABS), the correspondence of missionaries in the district (SBHS [SBAA], PAA [OMI], DA, EAA), and accounts or testimonies by the Métis themselves.

19 Take, for example, the (Xavier) Letendre and (Salomon) Venne families, some of whose members completed secondary school and other professional training. John Letendre obtained a teaching certificate, his sister Josette completed her Grade 12, and David Venne became a notary. Other members of these families (e.g., William and Napoléon Venne and Eugène Boucher) were less educated, but did well in business. Still others had few professional or commercial opportunities and worked as labourers or "hired men."

20 This political alignment was particularly evident in the 1886, 1887, 1888, and 1891 elections. See chap. 3: Political Activism.

21 PADA, Correspondence of Father Pierre E. Myre, Letter to Bishop Prud'homme, 30 November 1927.

22 Charles Nolin's speech on the Métis' National Feast Day, 24 July 1887. See account in *Le Manitoba* (St.-Boniface), 18 August 1887. Louis Riel also raised this theme in his writings.

23 Tamara K. Hareven, "Family Time and Historical Time," in *The Family*, ed. A.S. Rossi, J. Kagan, and T.K. Hareven, 69 (New York: W.W. Norton, 1978).

24 Interview with Mrs. Justine (Caron) St. Germain, Batoche, 1981. She had to do chores such as taking care of the cattle.

25 PADA, List of parishioners in Batoche, 1924, Appendix 1.2.

26 Hareven, "Family Time and Historical Time," 62.

27 PADA, Analysis of parish register of St. Antoine de Padoue, Batoche, 1885–1905.

28 For example, Théophile and Patrice Caron, Joseph Branconnier and Louis Letendre, to cite only a few.

29 AM, St. François-Xavier, Manitoba, parish register, 1834–82. The Delorme, McGillis, Gervais, Fisher, and Boyer families were well-to-do merchant families who intermarried.

30 According to the genealogical records of Métis families in Batoche and vicinity compiled by the author.

31 This union caused a lot of commotion in the family, whose members were aware of the risks of marriage between first cousins. The couple eloped and were married in St. Boniface, Manitoba.

32 There is the example of Xavier Letendre's and Antoine Richard's wills and the estates of Jean Caron Sr. and Salomon Venne.

33 Interview with Mrs. Justine (Caron) St. Germain, Batoche, 1981.

34 Xavier Letendre and his brother-in-law Charles Thomas (husband of Hélène Letendre) fought over lot 48. Letendre finally went to court, which decided in his favour.

35 PAA, OMI, Journal of Brother Célestin Guillet, Batoche, 1895.

36 According to the Homestead Files and correspondence on the subject of lands, SABS. After a quantitative analysis of these sources, the average size varied between 750 and 1310 sq. ft. According to a sample of 130 houses between 1885 and 1933, 46 (35.4%) were 750 to 980 sq. ft. (28.5%) 1,000 to 1,310 sq. ft. About 25 per cent were less than 750 sq. ft. and 11 per cent more than 1,350 sq. ft.

37 Interview with Mrs. Justine (Caron) St. Germain, Batoche, 1981.

38 Ibid. She cited a few cases. Others appear in the court records.

39 LAC, RG15, vol. 914, Testimony before the Commission on Rebellion Losses.

40 Interview with Mrs. Justine (Caron) St. Germain, Batoche, 1981.

41 SABS, Homestead Files, no. 81184.

42 LAC, RG15, vols. 513, 535, 914–18, 923, 928, Testimony before the Commission on Rebellion Losses. Unfortunately, only a few detailed inventories have survived, such as the claims of Ludger Gareau, Xavier Letendre, Salomon Venne, Baptiste Boyer, George Fisher, and Jean Caron Sr.

43 AM, MG9, A31, Memoirs of Louis Schmidt, 4–5 (translation).

44 Charette, *L'Espace de Louis Goulet*, 66–68.

45 Ibid., 66.

46 Ibid.

47 Ibid., 68.

48 Interview with Mr. Élie Dumont, Duck Lake, 1982 and 1983.

49 Interview with Mrs. Justine (Caron) St. Germain, Batoche, 1981.

50 PAA, OMI, Little chronicle of St. Laurent.

51 Interview with Mrs. Alexandrine (Fleury) Nicolas, Duck Lake, 1982.

52 AM, MG9, A31, Memoirs of Louis Schmidt, 1 (translation).

53 SBHS, SBAA, Taché Papers, Father Moulin to Bishop Taché, Ile à la Crosse, 18 March 1867.

54 Interview with Mrs. Alexandrine (Fleury) Nicolas, Duck Lake, 1981 and 1982.

55 Interviews with Mrs. Marie (Caron) Parenteau, Batoche, 1976 and Mrs. Alexandrine (Fleury) Nicolas, Duck Lake, 1981 and 1982.

56 Interview with Mrs. Alexandrine (Fleury) Nicolas, Duck Lake, 1981 and 1982.

57 Interview with Mrs. Adélaïde (Pilon) Ranger, Batoche, 1976 and 1977.

58 Interviews with Mrs. Justine (Caron) St-Germain, Batoche, 1981 and Mr. Omer Courchesne, Duck Lake, 1981. Mr. Courchesne, a former teacher in Batoche and St. Laurent, said that this dish was still very popular in the 1930s.

59 Interview with Mrs. Justine (Caron) St. Germain, Batoche, 1981.

60 Ibid.

61 Interview with Mrs. Alexandrine (Fleury) Nicolas, Duck Lake, 1981 and 1982.

62 Raymond Montpetit, *Le temps des fêtes au Québec* (Montreal: Éditions de l'Homme, 1978), 119 (translation).

63 Interview with Mr. Omer Courchesne, Duck Lake, 1981.

64 GA, Recollections of Eva Pozer Powell. She was the daughter of W.J. Pozer of Duck Lake. Her father had business and social connections with Louis Marion, Xavier Letendre, Patrice Parenteau, and Charles-Eugène Boucher.

65 AM, MG9, A6, Guillaume Charette, « Memoires de Louis Goulet » (translation).

66 Interview with Sister Irène Schmidt, Prince Albert, 1976. Sister Irène was the daughter of Charles-Pantaléon and the granddaughter of Louis Schmidt.

67 GA, Faithful Companions of Jesus Collection, Annals, St. Anne's Convent, Prince Albert, 1887.

68 Interview with Mr. Omer Courchesne, Duck Lake, 1981. He was referring to Mr. Baptiste Ouellette and Léon Ferguson of St. Laurent de Grandin.

69 Interview with Mrs. Alexandrine (Fleury) Nicolas, Duck Lake, 1981 and 1982.

70 SABS, Hillyard Mitchell Papers, A349, B.8-10, Accounts, including those of Xavier Letendre, Patrice Parenteau, George Fisher, Jean Caron, William Boyer, David Venne, and Pierre Parenteau.

71 Ibid.

72 Interview with Mrs. Marie-Louise (Ethier) Langlois (first married to Ernest Caron), Bellevue, 1981.

73 Hector Berthelot, *Le bon vieux temps* (Montréal: Beauchemin, 1916), 87–88.

74 Interview with Mrs. Justine (Caron) St. Germain, Batoche, 1981.

75 AM, MG9, A31, Memoirs of Louis Schmidt, Addenda, 2 (translation).

76 Interview with Mrs. Béatrice (Lépine) Boucher, St. Louis, 1977.

77 Interviews with Mrs. Justine (Caron) St. Germain, Batoche, 1981 and with Mrs. Alexandrine (Fleury) Nicolas, Duck Lake, 1981 and 1982.

78 Interview with Mrs. Adélaïde (Pilon) Ranger, Batoche, 1976 and 1977.

79 Interview with Mrs. Béatrice (Lépine) Boucher, St. Louis, 1977.

80 *Times and North-West Review* (Prince Albert), 3 January 1890.

81 For some examples, see Appendix 1.3.

82 Ottawa, Canadian Museum of Civilization, Canadian Ethnology Department, Richard Johnston Collection, recordings done in St. Louis and Lebret, Saskatchewan, in 1957 and songs recorded in Batoche and Duck Lake by Mr. Henri Létourneau for the St. Boniface Museum in 1972 and 1973.

83 These elements are evident in the collection of recordings in the Canadian Museum of Civilization and in the songs sung for the author by "old-timers" in Batoche and vicinity.

84 *Times* (Prince Albert), 22 January 1892.

85 SABS, At. "G," 117, Father André to A.E. Forget, 17 January 1884.

86 Interview with Mrs. Béatrice (Lépine) Boucher, St. Louis, 1977. Mrs. Boucher was the widow of Frédéric Boucher, singer and story-teller.

87 Interview with Sister Irène Schmidt, Prince Albert, 1976.
88 Interview with Mrs. Justine (Caron) St. Germain, Batoche, 1981.
89 Interview with Mrs. Adélaïde (Pilon) Ranger, Batoche, 1976.
90 Interview with Sister Irène Schmidt, Prince Albert, 1976.
91 *Missions des Oblats de Marie-Immaculée*, Father Fourmond to the Superior-General, 27 December 1878, 193 (translation).
92 Prayer recited by Sister Irène Schmidt, Prince Albert, 1976.
93 For a detailed account of the feast day and its origins, see chap. 3: Political Activism.
94 *Times and Saskatchewan Review* (Prince Albert), 26 July 1889.
95 Interview with Mr. Joseph Jobin, Wakaw, 1976.
96 Interview with Mrs. Lumina Gaudet, Batoche, 1976.
97 Interview with Mr. Joseph Jobin, Wakaw, 1976.
98 Interviews with Sister Irène Schmidt, Prince Albert, 1976, and Mrs. Adélaïde (Pilon) Ranger, Batoche, 1976.
99 *Le Patriote de l'Ouest* (Duck Lake), 16 October 1910.
100 « Pèlerinage à Notre-Dame de Saint-Laurent, Vicariat de la Saskatchewan, 16 juillet 1906 », *Les Cloches de St-Boniface*, 1906, 250–52.
101 Ibid. This hymn was recalled and sung by Mrs. Nicolas in 1982.
102 « Pèlerinage à Notre-Dame de Saint-Laurent », 251.
103 Ibid.
104 Interview with Mrs. Béatrice (Lépine) Boucher, St. Louis, 1977.
105 Interview with Mrs. Justine (Caron) St. Germain, Batoche, 1981.
106 Ibid.
107 LAC, RG15, vol. 914, file 892789, H. Mitchell's declaration, "Rebellion Losses Claims, 1885"; SABS, Hillyard Mitchell Papers, A 349, I 40, Statement and Account of Losses incurred by H. Mitchell in 1885.
108 Interview with Mr. Élie Dumont, Duck Lake, 1983.
109 Interview with Mrs. Justine (Caron) St. Germain, Batoche, 1981 (translation).
110 Interview with Mrs. Alexandrine (Fleury) Nicolas, Duck Lake, 1982.
111 *Missions des Oblats de Marie-Immaculée*, Father Fourmond to the Superior-General, 27 December 1878, 188 (translation).
112 Ibid.
113 There have been a number of studies on the origins and varieties of Michif and an ongoing debate on which is the real Michif or new language. See in particular: Robert Papen, "Un parler français méconnu de l'Ouest Canadien: Le Métis. « Quand même qu'on parle français, ça veut pas dire qu'on est des Canayens! »," in *La Langue, la culture et la société des francophones de l'Ouest*, ed. Pierre-Yves Mocquais, André Lalonde, and Bernard Wilhelm, 121–36 (Regina: Institut de Recherche du Centre d'Études Bilingues, 1984); John C. Crawford, ed., *The Michif Dictionary: Turtle Mountain Chippewa Cree* (Winnipeg: Pemmican, 1983), and Bakker, *A Language of Our Own*.
114 Interview with Sister Irène Schmidt, Prince Albert, 1976 (translation).
115 Interview with Mr. Omer Courchesne, Duck Lake, 1981.
116 See chap. 2: The Métis and the Roman Catholic Church, section on schools and education.
117 Interview with Mrs. Alexandrine (Fleury) Nicolas, Batoche, 1982 (translation). Alexandrine was the daughter of Patrice Fleury Jr. and Justine Montour. Her maternal grandparents were Abraham Montour and Marie Pagé.
118 Robert-Lionel Séguin, *La civilisation traditionnelle de "l'habitant" aux 17ᵉ et 18ᵉ siècles* (Montreal: Fides, 1967), 575 (translation).
119 Ibid.
120 Marius Barbeau, "Blason, géographie et généalogie populaires du Québec," *Journal*

of *American Folklore* 33, No 130 (1920): 346 (translation).

121 These nicknames were mentioned in documents or reported in interviews between the author and elders in Batoche, Duck Lake, St. Louis, and vicinity.

122 Interview with Mr. Joseph Jobin, Wakaw, 1976 (translation).

123 See, e.g., George Manuel and Michael Posluns, *The Fourth World: An Indian Reality* (Don Mills: Collier-Macmillan, 1974), 53.

124 *Times* (Prince Albert), 21 March 1888.

125 *Le Patriote de l'Ouest* (Prince Albert), 1 July 1915.

126 LAC, RG18, C1, vol. 2836, Sergeant Martin to Commanding Officer in Prince Albert, Batoche, 23 May 1891.

127 Ibid., Sergeant Albert J. Mountain to Commanding Officer in Prince Albert, 12 May 1889.

128 Ibid., vol. 2841, Inspector Huot to Commanding Officer in Prince Albert, 9 July 1890.

129 Ibid., vol. 2836, Corporal Lasker to Commanding Officer in Prince Albert, 5 July 1892.

130 Ibid., vol. 2841, Inspector C.F.A. Huot to Commanding Officer in Prince Albert, 9 July 1890. Ironically Huot was a hard drinker and died of liver disease in Duck Lake in 1893.

131 *Times and Saskatchewan Review* (Prince Albert), 26 July 1889.

132 PAA, OMI, Journal of Brother Célestin Guillet, Batoche, 11 October 1895.

133 Interview with with Mrs. Justine (Caron) St. Germain, Batoche, 1981 (translation).

134 Account from the Louis Venne family, who lived nearby and were related to him by marriage.

135 PADA, Correspondence of Father Pierre E. Myre, Letter to Bishop Prud'homme, 30 November 1927, and comments by an informant who chose to remain anonymous.

136 Ibid., 26 March 1872.

137 Interviews with Mrs. Armandine (Gareau) Gaudet, Batoche, 1976, and Bellevue, 1977 (translation).

138 PAA, OMI, Journal of Brother Célestin Guillet, Fish Creek, 22 February 1903.

139 Interview with Mrs. Lumina Gaudet, Batoche, 1976 (translation).

140 May Elizabeth McInnes, *Essentials of Communicable Disease* (St. Louis: C.V. Mioshy, 1975), 121–24. Blacks and "poor Whites" were also victims in the United States.

141 Ibid., 128, and *The Canadian Magazine* (Toronto) 1, no. 8 (October 1893): 628–33.

142 LAC, RG18, C1, vol. 2837, L. Hopper to Commanding Officer at Prince Albert, 15 February 1898.

143 SABS, Department of Agriculture, Lands Branch files, AGII, lot 26, T45-27-2.

144 LAC, RG15, vol. 914, Claims for losses suffered in 1885.

145 Ibid., RG18, C1, vol. 2841, file C, part 2.

146 Ibid., vol. 2845, file R, part 1.

147 Ibid., B5, vol. 2480, file B, part 2.

148 Ibid., vol. 2481, file C, part 1.

149 Ibid., vol. 2485, file "R." The individual will not be identified because of family still living in Batoche.

150 These Plains Cree, also identified as Willow Cree, were descendants of George Sutherland (Okayasiw), a Scotsman who married Cree women.

151 He reportedly told them to kill their cattle and forced the young men on the reserve to come to Batoche. This action and his participation in the armed conflict earned him a prison sentence, but Dumas escaped with Dumont to the United States. After being given amnesty in 1887, he returned to Canada, but the government refused to consider him for another position.

152 The population of the One Arrow Cree Nation (Reserve) was about 200 in 1885. For an account of the relationship between the Cree and the Métis in 1885 and after, see: Diane P. Payment, *The Willow Cree of One-Arrow First Nation and the Métis of Batoche, 1870–1920: An Ambivalent*

Relationship (Parks Canada, Western and Northern Service Centre, 1999).

153 *Dictionary of Canadian Biography* (Toronto: University of Toronto Press, 1966), vol. 11: 1881–1890, "Kàmiyistowesit," 458.

154 LAC, RG18, B5, vol. 2480, Assistant Commissioner to Commanding Officer, June 1897.

155 Martin Robin, *The Bad and the Lonely* (Toronto: S. Lorimer, 1976), 66–93.

156 PAA, OMI, Little chronicle of St. Laurent, 1888 [Father Fourmond].

157 Diane P. Payment, *The Willow Cree of One-Arrow First Nation and the Métis of Batoche,*, 29–34.

158 GNMA, Letters to the Mother-General, vol. 1, Sister Emery to Mother Deschamps, 3 September 1872 (translation).

159 DA, Letters of priests to the Sisters of Visitation of Le Mans, Father Fourmond to Mother Gertrude, 18 April 1888.

160 AM, MG3, D2, Louis Riel Papers, Address of L.R. St. Louis de Gladiou to Louis Riel.

161 GA, Edgar Dewdney Papers, E. Dewdney to John A. Macdonald, [March] 1885.

162 DA, Microfilm 710 of the SBAA, "Notes d'un Père de Prince-Albert" [Father Végréville], 17–19 August 1884.

163 Ibid.

164 SABS, Hillyard Mitchell Papers, A349, I7, Angus Thompson to H. Mitchell, 10 January 1892.

165 This was the conclusion reached in conversations with European French, French Canadians, and Métis.

166 The relations between Bellevue and Batoche were particularly strained from the 1920s to the 1970s. The Métis asserted that this tension was harmful to their maintenance of the French language.

167 Interview with Mr. Fred Anderson, Rosthern, 1976.

168 Interview with Sister Irène Schmidt, Prince Albert, 1976. She was the daughter of Indian Agent Charles-Pantaléon Schmidt and Rose-Délima Boucher, both Métis. She claimed not to have suffered personally from this attitude because her parents were fairly well off and her father was a government official. The family lived in St. Louis, Duck Lake, and Calgary.

169 PAA, OMI, Codex historicus of St. Laurent de Grandin, 1890–92, 5 October 1890.

170 Ibid., 10 October 1890 (translation).

171 SBHS, SBAA, Taché Papers, Bishop Pascal to Bishop Taché, 18 October 1891.

172 Canada, Parliament, *Sessional Papers*, vol. 11, no. 25 (Ottawa: Queen's Printer,1906), 86, "Rapport de l'abbé H.L. Vachon, 11 juillet 1905."

173 See eyewitness account by Gaston Giscard, *Dans la Prairie canadienne – On the Canadian Prairie* (Regina: Canadian Plains Research Center, 1982), on colonization in the Jackfish Lake area and *Le Patriote de l'Ouest* (Prince Albert), 16 April 1914.

174 SABS, Hillyard Mitchell Papers, A349, 120, A.M. Burgess to H. Mitchell, 22 February 1894, citing a letter he had received from Dr. Stewart; *Le Patriote de l'Ouest* (Prince Albert), 16 April 1914.

175 PAA, OMI, Journal of Brother Célestin Guillet, Fish Creek, 1900 and 1901.

176 Ibid., 7 December 1911.

177 Ibid., 16 June 1914 (translation).

178 Marcel Giraud, *Le Métis Canadien* (Paris: Institut d'Ethnologie, 1945), 1211–1286. Giraud personally visited many Métis communities, including Batoche, in 1935–36.

CHAPTER 2: THE MÉTIS AND THE ROMAN CATHOLIC CHURCH

1 Louis Riel to the people at Batoche in March 1885, cited in letter from Father André to Bishop Taché, 20 March 1885 (SBHS, SBAA). It translates as follows: Providence which foresaw this miraculous movement had prepared this church to serve us as a fortress and St. Antoine [Batoche] would become famous in history as the seat of the emancipation of the North-West.

2   Huel, *Proclaiming the Gospel*; Robert Choquette, *The Oblate Assault on Canada's Northwest* (Ottawa: University of Ottawa Press, 1995) and McCarthy, *From the Great River to the Ends of the Earth*.

3   It was a religious order founded in France in 1816 and established in Québec in 1842. In 1845, it sent two missionaries to St. Boniface: Fathers Aubert and Taché. In less that 10 years, the Oblates set up a chain of missions in the Saskatchewan, Athabasca and Mackenzie districts of the North West Territories.

4   SBHS, SBAA, Provencher Papers, Father J.B. Thibault to the Bishop of Québec, 18 June 1843, pp. 1805–1808 (copy and translation).

5   In 1863, the Lac Ste. Anne mission was moved to St. Albert, a more favourable location for the institution.

6   One example was the conflict over money between Fathers Caër and Rémas and Father Lacombe in St. Albert in the early 1860s and between Father André and priests in St. Laurent in the 1870s. The Grey Nuns and other female religious orders who worked with the Oblates also complained of mistreatment and lack of financial resources.

7   Testimony of Mr. Isidore Ledoux (1874–1976), Prince Albert, 1976 and Élie Dumont (1886–1985, Duck Lake) in 1982. Both men believed in spells cast by good and bad spirits and in foretelling.

8   SBHS, SBAA, Taché Papers, Father Lacombe to Bishop Taché, St. Paul des Cris Mission, 1866 and Carlton, 3 July 1867 (translation).

9   Ibid., Carlton, 7 August 1862 (translation).

10 Ibid., Father Moulin to Bishop Taché, Gros Ventres forks, [South Saskatchewan River], 8 November 1870. Father Moulin was probably at the Petite Ville wintering site or north in the vicinity of the future St. Laurent de Grandin mission.

11 Stobart was located northeast of the present village of Duck Lake at the site of the Stobart, Eden & Sons store, established in 1875.

12 Unfortunately, difficulties with the local authorities (Hudson's Bay Company and North West Mounted Police) soon put an end to this initiative. See chap. 3: Political Activism.

13 PAA, OMI, Little chronicle of St. Laurent, 1875 (translation).

14 DA, Father Fourmond to the Sisters of Visitation of Le Mans (hereafter Le Mans), 7 January 1876 (translation).

15 Ibid., 17 August 1880.

16 Born at La Gouesnière, Brittany, in 1830, he arrived in St. Boniface in 1858. During the following years, he served as missionary at Ile à la Crosse and Lac Caribou (Reindeer Lake), founded the Lac Vert (Green Lake) mission, and was finally sent to Batoche in 1882. He stayed there until his retirement in 1914. He was nicknamed Father Caribou by the Métis because of all the years he spent as a missionary among the Chipewyan at Lac Caribou and also reportedly because of his character. He died in St. Albert in 1920.

17 PAA, OMI, Little chronicle of St. Laurent, 1875 [Father André] (translation).

18 Ibid., 1876.

19 Ibid., 1877.

20 As models of "adaptation," they cited elders Isidore Dumont Sr. and Louis Letendre, committed farmers Jean Caron and Michel Dumas, government officials Louis Schmidt and Charles Nolin, and the merchants Xavier Letendre, Jean-Baptiste Boyer, and Salomon Venne.

21 See chaps. 4: Political Activism, and 5: Economy for a discussion of these themes.

22 PAA, OMI, Little chronicle of St. Laurent, 1874 [Father André].

23 Ibid., 1875.

24 Ibid.; Jean Caron, one of the early Métis in the district, settled on a farm in St. Laurent in 1879 and then moved to lot 52, the land adjoining the mission at Batoche, in 1881. He wanted lot 51 for his eldest son but agreed to take lot 53 instead.

25 PAA, OMI, Father André to Jean Caron, 21 July 1882 (translation).

26 PAA, OMI, Father Végréville to Father André, 26 May 1882.

27 DA, Father Végréville to Superior General, Rome, 16 May 1886; 3 November 1893. He also complained that his letters to Bishop Grandin were intercepted and that he and Father Touze were generally ill-treated by Father André.

28 PAA, OMI, Father Végréville to Father André, 6 May 1882.

29 As superior, Father André was in charge of financial affairs, but it is obvious that in this instance he acted against the directives of Bishop Grandin, who had supported the appointment of a parish council in Batoche to manage the construction funds.

30 PAA, OMI, Father Végréville to Father André, St. Antoine de Padoue, 26 May 1882 (translation).

31 DA, Father Moulin to Superior General, Rome, 31 March 1883.

32 PADA, Reverend P.E. Myre to Bishop J.H. Prud'homme, 30 November 1927.

33 PAA, OMI, Journal of Brother Célestin Guillet, Batoche 1895–96; 1900. He wrote that it was difficult to work for the father who did not want him to cook anything with butter or sugar and restricted his diet. He could not play the harmonium or sing, and he had trouble getting the father to wash and change his clothing and infested bed linens.

34 DA, Father Moulin to Superior General, Rome, 30 November 1892 (translation).

35 Brother Guillet reported that Father Moulin had saved his money and was hoping to visit his family in France but that the church council opposed his departure. He finally went in 1899. PAA, OMI, Journal of Brother Célestin Guillet, 23 April 1895.

36 DA, Father Moulin to Superior General, Rome, 8 February 1896 (translation).

37 SBAA, Taché Papers, Father Fourmond to Bishop Taché, 30 July 1883.

38 PAA, OMI, Little chronicle of St. Laurent, 1877 [Father André] (translation).

39 One of the most famous and dedicated of these lay missionaries was Mlle Onésime Dorval (1845–1932), who worked diligently in those three Oblate missions and was the first professional bilingual teacher in the district of Saskatchewan. When she was at Batoche, she donated all her salary to the Oblates. She also "adopted" two orphaned children, Marie Giroux and Georgine d'Amours [later Mrs. Lenglet]. See biography: Diane P. Payment, "Onésime Dorval: « la bonne demoiselle »," *Saskatchewan History* 55, no. 1 (Spring 2003): 31–35.

40 *Missions des Oblats de Marie-Immaculée*, 1885, Father Fourmond's account, 26 December 1885, 197 (translation). It seems that the Métis were initially not supportive of female teachers or may have resented that one of their own was not hired as teacher.

41 *The Consolidated Ordinances of the North West Territories of Canada, Being a Consolidation of the Revised Ordinances of the Territories, 1888, with the Subsequent Public General Ordinances* (Regina: Queen's Printer, 1899), chap. 75, nos. 3, 36–38, 110, 709, pp. 684–757.

42 Brother C. Guillet reported that in 1895 John Letendre, the son of Xavier Letendre *dit* Batoche, was trying to get the teaching position at Batoche. PAA, OMI, Journal of Brother Célestin Guillet, 9 March 1895. Pierre Tourond and Josephte Gervais (first married to Calixte Tourond who died in 1885 and then Boniface Lefort) taught at la couli des Tourond (Fish Creek) in the 1890s.

43 SBHS, SBAA, Taché Papers, Father Moulin to Bishop Taché, 31 December 1897.

44 See Jules Le Chevallier, « Aux prises avec la tourmente: les missionnaires de la colonie de Saint Laurent de Grandin durant l'insurrection métisse de 1885 », *Revue de l'université d'Ottawa*, 1940, and, in particular, *Batoche: Les missionnaires du Nord-Ouest pendant les troubles de 1885* (Montréal: Presse dominicaine, 1941), chap. 5, 47–48.

45 Giraud, *Le Métis Canadien*, 1203 (translation).

46 Huel, *Proclaiming the Gospel*, 210–11.

47 Between 1881 and 1884, at least seven petitions were sent to the federal and territorial governments with the support of the priests in the district. When the Métis became more militant in the winter of 1884–85, the clergy became critical and defensive. For more details on these petitions, see chap. 3: Political Activism.

48 SBHS, SBAA, Taché Papers, Louis Schmidt, « Mouvement des Métis à Saint Laurent, Saskatchewan, Territoires du Nord Ouest en 1884 », p. 29793 (translation).

49 Ibid.

50 PAA, OMI, Little chronicle of St. Laurent, 1885 [Father Fourmond] (translation).

51 LAC, MG26, A, vol. 105, Bishop Grandin to Prime Minister J.A. Macdonald, 13 June 1884.

52 SBHS, SBAA, Louis Schmidt, « Mouvement des Métis à Saint Laurent », p. 29798 (translation).

53 SBHS, SBAA, Taché Papers, « Notes d'un Père de Prince Albert », [Father André], 12 December 1884 (translation).

54 SBHS, SBAA, Taché Papers, Father Végréville to Bishop Taché, 6 December 1884 (translation).

55 Ibid.

56 PAA, OMI, Little chronicle of St. Laurent, 1885 [Father Fourmond] (translation).

57 DA, Father Fourmond to Mother Gertrude, Le Mans (France), 15 June 1885 (translation).

58 Ibid.

59 Charles Nolin (1836–1907), former MLA and minister of agriculture in Manitoba, had moved to St. Laurent de Grandin in 1882. An initial supporter of Riel and the resistance, he suddenly changed position after the miraculous recovery of his wife Rosalie Lépine in late 1884. He fled to Prince Albert during the battle of Duck Lake and later agreed to act as a witness for the Crown. This latter act aroused much resentment in the Métis community and earned him the label of *vire-capot* (turncoat). According to Louis Schmidt (SBAA, Taché Papers, « Mouvement des Métis à Saint Laurent », p. 29796), Nolin was a big talker who loved intrigue and action as long as it did not compromise him.

60 The informers included Fathers André and Végréville, and they were joined by Louis Schmidt, Amédée Forget, and Captain Sévère Gagnon of the Mounted Police.

61 Riel stayed with friends, first at Moïse Ouellette's, then at Charles Nolin's, and finally in the old St. Laurent school house. According to Philippe Garnot: "There was no furniture, only a borrowed stove, their beds and they slept on the floor. During the day Riel often came to see Father Fourmond to eat, talk and pray. His family was poorly dressed. In the fall [1884], Baptiste Boyer gave him some clothes and made a feast for him. About a month before the conflict, people collected money which they presented to him in a nicely embroidered purse." SBHS, SBAA, Journal of Father Gabriel Cloutier, 1886, p. 5264 (translation).

62 For a fascinating and comprehensive biography of William Henry Jackson, known as Honoré Joseph Jaxon after his baptism and "conversion" to the Métis cause, see Donald B. Smith, *Honoré Jaxon: Prairie Visionary* (Regina: Coteau Books, 2007).

63 Ibid., Taché Papers, Father André to the Bishop [Grandin], 2 March 1885 (translation).

64 Ibid., Father Végréville to Superior General, 11 May 1885; PAA, OMI, Little chronicle of St. Laurent, 1885 [Father Fourmond].

65 Not everyone embraced Riel's beliefs and some were more or less pressured into armed resistance. Out of about 300 men who took up arms, perhaps a third were firmly committed. See the testimonies of the Métis in SBHS, SBAA, Journal of Father Gabriel Cloutier, 1886.

66 Ibid., pp. 5260–5261 (translation).

67 Jules Le Chevallier, *Batoche: Les missionnaires du Nord-Ouest pendant les troubles de 1885* (Montréal: Presse dominicaine, 1941), 185–91. A.G. Morice, *Histoire de l'Église catholique dans l'Ouest canadien,*

1659–1905 (Winnipeg: The Author, 1912), 2:369.

68 SBHS, SBAA, José Arcand's testimony in Journal of Father Gabriel Cloutier, 1886, 520; Auguste-Henri de Trémaudan, *Histoire de la nation métisse* (Montréal: Editions Albert Lévesque, 1935), 297.

69 GA, Faithful Companions of Jesus Collection, Journal of the St. Laurent House, 17, 18, and 19 April 1885 (translation). Riel's sister Sara, who had died in 1883, was a Grey Nun, which may explain Riel's particular regard for the Sisters.

70 For a detailed account of the four days of the battle, see Walter Hildebrandt, *The Battle of Batoche: British Small Warfare and the Entrenched Métis* (Ottawa: Parks Canada, 1985).

71 DA, Father Moulin to Superior General, Rome, 7 July 1885 (translation). Captain James Peters, who took photographs of the North West campaign, took a picture of General Middleton and his aides meeting the priests in front of the rectory. Library and Archives of Canada, C-3462.

72 Father Moulin's desperate words: "the government will take everything you do into account" and Bishop Grandin's response: "no doubt, the dear father [Moulin] saw farther than the tip of his nose," were reported in *Missions des Oblats de Marie-Immaculée*, 1886, Report of Bishop Grandin to Superior-General, 17 October 1885 (translations).

73 GA, Faithful Companions of Jesus Collection, Journal of the St. Laurent House, 9 May 1885.

74 DA, Father Végréville to the Superior General, 11 May 1885.

75 SBHS, SBAA, Taché Papers, T31424-27, Father Moulin to Bishop Taché, Prince Albert, 27 May 1885.

76 Father Le Chevallier (*Batoche*, 198) cites Father Végréville's journal in support of this charge. In a letter to his Superior-General (see preceding note), Father Végréville mentions only a stray bullet.

77 DA, Father Végréville to the Superior-General, 11 May 1885 (translation).

78 Testimony of Élie Dumont, nephew of Isidore Dumont, who died at the battle of Duck Lake and Alfred Boyer of St. Louis whose grandfather, Isidore Boyer, died at Batoche.

79 PAA, OMI, 22-733, Mémoire de Philippe Garnot, February, 1886. (typescript).

80 SBHS, SBAA, Taché Papers, Father André to Bishop Taché, 4 June 1885. Father André, a man of many moods and a fiery temper, acted without reservation whenever he espoused a cause. Bishop Taché reprimanded him for his outspoken statements in the press, reminding him that they could have grave repercussions for the clergy. In a letter to the Department of the Interior, published in *Le Manitoba* (St.-Boniface) on 18 July 1885, Father Moulin also explained the difficulties and despair that had driven the Métis to take up arms and implored the government to recognize its errors and come to their aid.

81 PAA, OMI, Little chronicle of St. Laurent, 1885 [Father Fourmond] (translation).

82 PAA, OMI, Father André to Father Lacombe, 31 August 1885 (translation).

83 DA, Father Moulin to Superior General, Rome, 4 January 1887 (translation).

84 PAA, OMI, L. Clarke to Bishop Grandin, Prince Albert, 24 September 1886.

85 Ibid., Reply, 1 October 1886 (translation).

86 DA, Father Moulin to Superior General, Rome, 4 December 1889 (translation). When the mission at St. Laurent de Grandin closed in 1894, the parishioners went to Batoche. The parish of St. Antoine de Padoue (Batoche) also extended to Fish Creek and Bellevue until the early 1900s. A chapel for new Polish immigrants was built in Fish Creek in 1901 and a new church at Bellevue in 1902.

87 DA, Father Moulin to Superior General, Rome, 17 November 1888 (translation). For information on the development of the parish, see Diane Payment, *A Structural and Material Culture History of St. Antoine de Padoue Mission at Batoche* (Parks Canada, Microfiche Report, no. 92, 1981–82).

88 PAA, OMI, Journal of Brother Célestin Guillet, 1895–96, 1900.
89 PADA, Father L. de G. Belleau to Bishop Prud'homme, 8 December 1925, in a letter protesting his dismissal. He was accused of irresponsibility and financial mismanagement.
90 Ibid., Albert Caron to Bishop Prud'homme, 21 May 1926.
91 Ibid., Tobie Boyer, president, Patrice Caron and Ambroise Gervais, councillors, Petition to Bishop Prud'homme, 19 August 1926 (translation).
92 Ibid., Father P.E. Myre to Bishop Prud'homme, 30 November 1927.
93 Ibid., Petition of the Batoche parishioners to Bishop Prud'homme, 5 November 1927, presented by William Parenteau and Patrice Caron.
94 Ibid. (translation).
95 Ibid. (translation).
96 Ibid. (translation)
97 Ibid., 7 November 1928; ibid., [around 1931]. Father Myre justified his position by stating that he was going to replace the Bank of Montreal, Sun Life, and other speculators as landholder at Batoche.
98 *Le Patriote de l'Ouest* (Prince Albert), 7 August 1929.
99 PADA, Batoche Parish, Spiritual and financial reports, 1927–32.
100 Interview with Mr. Henri Pilon, Batoche, 1976 (translation).
101 PADA, Reverend H. Robert to Father Olivier [1932] (translation).
102 Interviews with Marie Parenteau (née Caron) and Adélaïde Ranger (née Pilon), Batoche 1976.
103 Lavallée, *Prayers of a Métis Priest*.

CHAPTER 3: POLITICAL ACTIVISM

1 The laws of the buffalo hunt in the Red River Settlement were recorded by individuals such as Father Georges A. Belcourt, Reverend Louis Laflèche, who accompanied the Métis on numerous expeditions, as well as Alexander Ross, a local popular historian. The rights and freedoms of the group took precedence over the individual during the hunts. There was also an administrative or governing hierarchy composed of the chief or president of the hunt, guides, and ten captains, each with ten soldiers or *dizaines* under their command who protected the caravan from theft and attack and enforced the obedience of the laws of the hunting expedition. See Alexander Ross, *The Red River Settlement* (Edmonton: Hurtig, 1972, reprint of an 1856 edition), 249–50.

2 On June 25, 1815 in Red River, Métis leaders Cuthbert Grant, Bostonnais Pangman, Willliam Shaw, and Bonhomme Montour were involved in a dispute with the Selkirk Settlers and their sponsors, the HBC, whom they accused of infringing on their territorial and trading rights. See Marcel Giraud, *The Métis in the Canadian West* (Edmonton: University of Alberta Press, 1986; translation of 1945 edition), 1:435–37. Even though many Métis were more closely allied with the NWC, it is important to note that they took advantage of the fur trade rivalry and allied themselves with the NWC during the Pemmican Wars of 1814–16 because it was to their economic and social advantage.

3 See petition cited in Barry Cooper, *Alexander Kennedy Isbister: A Respectable Critique of the Honourable Company* (Ottawa: Carleton University Press, 1988), 129.

4 SBAA, Taché Papers, Father Lacombe to Bishop Taché, St. Paul des Cris, 12 September 1870. He also refers to an earlier memorandum by the Métis in St. Albert to codify their laws of the prairie. Yet the Métis of the North West made their political interests known very early on. During the negotiations for the creation of the Province of Manitoba in 1870, they had expressed their disappointment at their exclusion.

5 Glenbow Archives, Richard Hardisty Papers, GA 1A, vol. 2, file 34, "Condensed Report of a Meeting at St. Laurent on Dec. 31, 1871" [translation] signed by pen name "Blaireau." HBC officer Lawrence Clarke chaired the meeting with Father André.

The first meeting was probably held at the Dumont wintering camp at Petite Ville on the South Saskatchewan River.

6   LAC, RG18, vol. 6, no. 333-75, "Copy of Laws and Regulations established at the Colony of St. Laurent on the Saskatchewan," 1872-75, signed by Father André [English translation]. The original petition in French appears to have been lost or destroyed.

7   Ibid., and PAA, OMI, Little chronicle of St. Laurent, 1872-75.

8   George F.G. Stanley, *The Birth of Western Canada* (Toronto: University of Toronto Press, 1966), 180. Stanley refers to the St. Laurent council as a provisional government, but I would argue that it was a formally constituted local self-government. It did not challenge Canadian authority over the territory, and it was based on the natural right of Aboriginal peoples to govern themselves and initiate any form of civil authority.

9   PAA, OMI, Little chronicle of St. Laurent, 1872-75 [Father André].

10 PAA, OMI, Little chronicle of St. Laurent, 1875 [Father André] (translation).

11 George F.G. Stanley, "The Half-Breed Rising of 1875," *Canadian Historical Review* 17, no. 1 (December 1936): 399-412. For a Métis perspective of the conflict, see Lawrence J. Barkwell, "Early Law and Social Control among the Metis," in *The Struggle for Recognition: Canadian Justice and the Metis Nation*, ed. Samuel W. Corrigan and Lawrence J. Barkwell, 33-34 (Winnipeg: Pemmican, 1991).

12 PAA, OMI, Little chonicle of St. Laurent, 1875.

13 L.H. Thomas, in *The Struggle for Responsible Government in the North West Territories, 1870-1897* (Toronto: University of Toronto Press, 1978), chap. 3, discusses in depth the nature and weaknesses of this administration, particularly its lack of legislative and fiscal power.

14 Pascal Breland (originally Berland *dit* Boishué), a Cypress Hills merchant residing in Manitoba, was a member of the first council in 1872-75. He had some political experience as a member of the Council of Assiniboia in Red River from 1857 to 1869 and subsequently as a member of the first Legislative assembly of Manitoba from 1870 to 1874. He was married to Maria, daughter of Cuthbert Grant who was pro-Hudson's Bay Company. Breland kept his seat until 1888, the date of the first general election and the creation of the legislative assembly. No St. Laurent Settlement Métis was appointed to the council.

15 The Dumont, Ouellette, Lépine, Gariépy, Carrière, Delorme, and Nault families in the Batoche area were the most closely associated with Riel.

16 Joseph Royal, Quebec journalist and politician, settled in Manitoba in 1870, where he founded the newspaper *Le Métis*. He was a member of the Manitoba legislature from 1871 to 1879 and subsequently the federal member for Provencher until 1888. He served as lieutenant-governor of the North West Territories from 1888 to 1893. Pierre Delorme and James McKay (Macaille) were Métis of considerable wealth and prestige in Manitoba, but they did not sit on the council after it was reconstituted in 1878. They were conservative and did not represent the interests of the Saskatchewan traders and freighters.

17 There were some longer-term plans for legislative and fiscal reform with a view to creating an assembly. See Thomas, *The Struggle for Responsible Government*, 75-79.

18 SABS, *Journal of the Legislative Council of the North West Territories* (1878).

19 Thomas, *The Struggle for Responsible Government*, 92; Canada, Parliament, House of Commons, *Debates* (1878), vol. 5, Hon. D. Mills vs Hon. H.L. Langevin, Questions about the administration of the North West Territories, 8 May 1878, pp. 2542-2544.

20 SABS, *Journal of the Legislative Council of the North West Territories* (1878-79), Appendix A; PAA, OMI, Little chronicle of St. Laurent, 1880 [Father André].

21 *Saskatchewan Herald* (Battleford), 23 February 1880.

22 PAA, OMI, Little chronicle of St. Laurent, 1881 [Father André]; PAM, MG9, A31, Memoirs of Louis Schmidt, 1912, 97.

23 PAA, OMI, Little chronicle of St. Laurent, 1879 [Father André] (translation). Father André and the missionaries always portrayed themselves as indispensable and positive mediators with the government.

24 The Métis interpreters were Peter Erasmus, James McKay, and Pierre Léveillé.

25 The proximity of the Métis communities necessitated interaction between the two. There was intermarriage and trade between the Cree and Métis, but the government negotiators discouraged the Métis from participating in the treaty. For a discussion of this issue, see Diane P. Payment, *The Willow Cree of One-Arrow First Nation and the Métis of Batoche 1870–1920* (Parks Canada, Western and Northern Service Centre, Cultural Resource Services, 1997), 7–10.

26 PAA, OMI, Little chronicle of St. Laurent, 1876 [Father André] (translation).

27 They included Isidore and Jean Dumont, Xavier Letendre, and François Gingras. A. Morris, *Treaties of Canada with the Indians* (Toronto: Coles, 1971; reprint), appendix, 357.

28 Batoche and vicinity constituted a distinct constituency from 1888 to 1908.

29 See in particular the Prince Albert *Times* from September 1884 to March 1885 and the Battleford *Herald* for 12 July 1884.

30 The 1881 census was too early and too general to establish even an approximate number. In a memoir written in 1883, Father André established the specific population of Batoche at 500. See DA, Alexis André, "Mémorial en réponse au questionnaire du R.P. Visiteur, automne 1883."

31 Owen E. Hughes was married to an "English Metis," Mary Inkster.

32 Journalist by profession and a Liberal in politics, David Laird was Minister of the Interior in the Mackenzie government from 1873 to 1876. In 1876, he was appointed lieutenant-governor of the North West Territories, a position he occupied until 1881. He was succeeded by Edgar Dewdney (1881–88), when John A. Macdonald appointed him Minister of the Interior and Superintendent of Indian Affairs. Laird was generally more favourable to the political demands of the Métis. In view of the growing Métis population, the Lorne district would have been entitled to another representative in 1883, but Governor Dewdney did not grant this request.

33 Louis Schmidt *dit* Laferté emigrated from St. François-Xavier to present-day St. Louis in 1880. He was a protégé of Bishop Taché, who sent him to Quebec to pursue his studies, along with Louis Riel and Daniel McDougall in 1858. He returned to Red River and was secretary in Louis Riel's provisional government in 1869–70. He was elected to the Manitoba legislature as member for St. Boniface West from 1870 to 1874 and for St. François-Xavier in 1878–79. In 1882 he was appointed justice of the peace for the district, and in 1884 he received an appointment at the Land Titles Office in Prince Albert. A government agent and staunch Roman Catholic, he opposed the armed resistance of 1885.

34 SBHS, SBAA, Taché Papers, Letter of Louis Schmidt to A.M. Burgess, 6 May 1885; ibid., Louis Schmidt, « Mouvement des Métis à Saint Laurent ».

35 PAA, OMI, Little chronicle of St. Laurent, 1883 [Father André].

36 SBHS, SBAA, Father André to Sir John A. Macdonald, winter 1882–83 (copy in Taché Papers).

37 Philippe Garnot (1859–1916) was a French Canadian who came out West to Manitoba in 1870 with his father Odilon, a member of the Wolseley Expedition. In 1882 they moved to the South Saskatchewan River district, on land next door to Gabriel Dumont. Philippe was college-educated, a teacher and sometime law student. By 1884 he operated a small hotel or stopping place at Batoche, which sold liquor and where patrons played pool. Adventurous and outspoken, he was described as a dissolute character by the strict local clergy. Garnot had met Riel in Montana in 1883 and was a staunch admirer and supporter, although

he would later deny this. He served briefly as Riel's secretary in the council of 1885 and was arrested and imprisoned by the Canadian army at the end of the armed conflict. He then wrote a memoir of the Métis Resistance for Bishop Taché, returned to Batoche, and married Florestine Arcand, widow of Joannet Parenteau, a victim of 1885. They settled at Moon Hills near Carlton, where he worked as postmaster and teacher and was active in politics.

38 SBHS, SBAA, Taché Papers, T31062-67, Louis Schmidt to Bishop Taché, 8 April 1885. The clergy was opposed to Philippe Garnot's candidacy because of his resistance to civil and religious authority.

39 J.A. Gemmill, ed., *The Canadian Parliamentary Companion* (Ottawa: J. Durie, 1885), 368: Macdowall received 279 votes and Dr. Porter 120.

40 SBHS, SBAA, Journal of Father Gabriel Cloutier, Charles Nolin's and Maxime Lépine's depositions, p. 5177. Among those present were: Xavier Letendre, Gabriel Dumont, Michel Dumas, Baptiste Boyer, Moïse Ouellette, and Jean-Baptiste Boucher, and the English Metis: Charles Adams, Thomas Scott, and Henry Monkman.

41 Ibid., pp. 5174–5176, and Charles Nolin's testimony, LAC, RG13, B2, C-1231. Two assemblies were held at Baptiste Boyer's and Abraham Montour's. A subsequent meeting with the English Metis took place in the spruce grove opposite Maxime Lépine's house, mid-way between St. Laurent and St. Louis.

42 SBHS, SBAA, Journal of Father Gabriel Cloutier, p. 5176. According to Nolin's account, the emissaries were authorized to explain the grievances to him and to invite him to come and lead them "as he had done in Manitoba."

43 The meeting in Prince Albert was a success, despite Lawrence Clarke's and D.H. Macdowall's opposition and Father André's concerns.

44 LAC, MG26, A, John A. Macdonald Papers, vol. 105, June 1884, « Mémorial présenté par l'entremise de Mgr Grandin ».

45 SBHS, SBAA, Taché Papers, Father André to Bishop Taché, 6 January 1883 (translation).

46 Ibid., Louis Schmidt, « Mouvement des Métis à Saint Laurent ». The visit took place on 19 August. Judge Rouleau was not sympathetic to Métis claims. See GA, Edgar Dewdney Papers, vol. 6, Charles B. Rouleau to E. Dewdney, 5 September 1884. At the end of the armed conflict in 1885, he sentenced eleven Cree and Assiniboine to death by hanging at Fort Battleford.

47 SBHS, SBAA, Taché Papers, Louis Schmidt, « Mouvement des Métis à Saint Laurent ».

48 SBHS, SBAA, Taché Papers, Louis Schmidt, « Mouvement des Métis à Saint Laurent » (translation); LAC, MG27, IC4, Edgar Dewdney Papers, vol. 4, D.H. Macdowall to E. Dewdney, 24 December 1884; ibid., MG26, A, vol. 107, Father André to E. Dewdney, 21 January 1885.

49 DA, microfilm 710 of SBAA, "Notes d'un Père de Prince Albert" [Father Végréville], 17 August 1884 (translation).

50 Ibid., 15 September 1884 (translation).

51 DA, Father Fourmond to Mother Gertrude, Sisters of Visitation, Le Mans (France), 17 September 1884.

52 *Le Manitoba*, 18 October 1884.

53 DA, Father Fourmond to Mother Gertrude, 15 June 1885; SBAA, Journal of Father Gabriel Cloutier, 1886, Father Fourmond's testimony. In his memoir, Philippe Garnot states that Colonel Williams sent him to fetch the flag (PAA, OMI, Memoir de Philippe Garnot, 1886). Father Fourmond gives the most precise description of the flag adopted by the Saskatchewan Métis in 1885. There are other versions, including the one proposed by Peter Charlebois in *The Life of Louis Riel* (Toronto: New Canada Publications, 1975), 196. A later flag of the Union Nationale Métisse St. Joseph du Manitoba, known at the "François Marion flag" incorporated the British Union Jack. It dates from around 1910, the year the Union Nationale was reorganized. François Marion of St. Vital was

a member of the executive. Mrs. Marion reportedly made the flag, and it was then presented to the Batoche chapter (SBHS, Union Nationale Métisse St. Joseph du Manitoba, Minutes, 1887–1930).

54 DA, Father Fourmond to Mother Gertrude, 27 September 1884.

55 GA, Faithful Companions of Jesus Collection, Journal of the St. Laurent House, 24 April 1885.

56 LAC, MG27, I, F3, vol. 2, no. 49 (translation).

57 DA, Father Fourmond to Mother Gertrude, 22 September 1884. The author of the national hymn is unknown but possibly Riel.

58 LAC, RG15, vol. 335, file 83808.

59 SBHS, SBAA, Taché Papers, Father Végréville to Bishop Taché, 26 February 1885. Father Fourmond reported that it was manifest that, while the ministers were well disposed towards the Métis, they did not want to deal with Riel, on the pretext that he was a naturalized American, but in reality because "they hated and feared him" (translation). PAA, OMI, Little chronicle of St. Laurent, 1885 [Father Fourmond].

60 AM, MG9, A31, Memoirs of Louis Schmidt, 1912, 101–2; SBHS, SBAA, Journal of Father Gabriel Cloutier, 1886, p. 5174, testimonies of Charles Nolin's and Maxime Lépine.

61 PAA, OMI, Little chronicle of St. Laurent, 1885 [Father Fourmond] (translation).

62 For a detailed account of the Battle of Batoche, see Hildebrandt, *The Battle of Batoche*.

63 See the account of the trial in Desmond Morton, ed., *The Queen vs Louis Riel* (Toronto: University of Toronto Press, 1974). The most notorious example was Charles Nolin's testimony.

64 This term was used in a fairly wide sense to designate either a liberal or a radical, while a Conservative was called a *bleu* (blue).

65 GA, Edgar Dewdney Papers, vol. 5, J. Anderson to E. Dewdney, 25 November 1885.

66 Ibid., Report of a Mr. Badger to Thomas White, cited in a letter from Sir H. Langevin to E. Dewdney, 28 October 1885.

67 Ibid., A. McKay to E. Dewdney, 8 January 1886.

68 Ibid.

69 Ibid., M. Nichol to E. Dewdney, 13 May 1886.

70 Ibid., vol. 3, E. Dewdney to John A. Macdonald, 2 and 13 March 1886. Bishops Taché and Grandin intervened in their favour.

71 PAA, OMI, Journal of Brother Célestin Guillet, 8 May 1887.

72 O.D. Skelton, *Life and Letters of Sir W. Laurier* (Toronto: McClelland & Stewart, 1981, reprint) [Carleton Library Series, no. 21], vol. 1: "1841–1896," 85.

73 The French Canadian battalion was not sent to fight against the Métis, as authorities feared they might refuse to fight or join them. The French Canadian soldiers were very surprised to learn that the Métis were their compatriots and spoke their language.

74 Arthur Silver, "French Québec and the Métis Question, 1869–1885," Carl Berger and Ramsay Cook, eds., *The West and the Nation: Essays in Honour of W.L. Morton* (Toronto: McClelland & Stewart, 1976), 102–6. See the reports in *Le Manitoba* (St.-Boniface), a conservative Catholic weekly, during the summer of 1885.

75 See the Métis testimonies gathered by Reverend Cloutier in Batoche in 1886 (SBHS, SBAA, Journal of Reverend Gabriel Cloutier), particularly that of Philippe Gariépy, p. 5171, Charles Nolin and Maxime Lépine, pp. 5174–5175, as well as Father Fourmond's account, p. 5096.

76 Testimonies gathered in Batoche during interviews in 1978, 1979, and 1981.

77 AM, MG3, C14, Capt. George H. Young, Notes regarding Royal Commission on Rebellion Losses, 1886.

78 Queen's University Archives, George H. Young Papers, book C, Notes accompanying declarations of losses suffered in 1885.

The commission also had at its disposal documents seized in Batoche as well as testimony from the Regina trials.

79 See Morton, *The Queen vs Louis Riel*. See also testimony of several witnesses in a confidential report by Superintendent Perry, 29 August 1887: SABS, Department of the Attorney-General, Series "G" (hereafter cited as At "G"), file 4344.

80 PAA, OMI, Mémoire de Philippe Garnot, 1886.

81 Ibid.

82 SAB (Regina), C-Y 861, "Champagne vs Queen," Testimony of G.H. Young in Exchequer Court, Winnipeg, 14 September 1892, 15, 26.

83 LAC, RG15, vol. 632, file 237041, Philippe Gariépy to Sir John A. Macdonald, 22 November 1889.

84 There were no official parties in the Territories in 1886, but the Métis favoured Laird (a liberal) rather than Macdowall, the (conservative) government candidate.

85 SBHS, SBAA, Taché Papers, Father Fourmond to Bishops Taché and Grandin, 20 October 1886 (translation).

86 PAA, OMI, Little chronicle of St. Laurent, 1885 [Father Fourmond].

87 J.A. Gemmill, ed., *The Canadian Parliamentary Companion*, 381. Hughes received 141 votes and Porter 133.

88 PAA, OMI, Little chronicle of St. Laurent, 1886 [Father Fourmond].

89 Ibid., 1887 (translation). Interestingly, [Joseph] Campeau is my paternal ancestor, while Préfontaine is an ancestor of Darren Préfontaine of the Gabriel Dumont Institute.

90 LAC, RG15, vol. 510, file 144363.

91 Octave Régnier (1852–1899) was originally from Québec and came to St. François-Xavier, Manitoba, and then to St. Louis in 1882. He became a teacher and served briefly as Riel's secretary in 1885. Jean Caron Sr. (1833–1905), was born in St. Norbert, Manitoba, first settled in St. Laurent and then at Batoche. He took up arms with his elder sons in 1885. He supported the conservatives in 1887, but changed sides in 1888.

92 For example, they rejected the offer of seed grain that had liens attached to it.

93 LAC, RG15, vol. 510, file 144363, Confidential Memorandum of T. White, Minister of the Interior, to Privy Council, 23 May 1887.

94 SABS, At "G," file 3744, "Pétition des habitants de Saint Antoine de Padoue au lieutenant-gouverneur Dewdney, 13 mai 1887."

95 At the end of the armed conflict, Gabriel Dumont took refuge in Montana. He then went to New York State and Montreal, where he met with politicians and gave lectures with the aim of sensitizing the Franco-Americans and French Canadians to the condition of his Métis compatriots. Fearing that he had been excluded from the October 1886 amnesty, he hesitated to return to Canada. He visited the Riel family in St. Vital, Manitoba, in 1888, went to Batoche in the spring of 1889, where he made official entry for his land, but travelled back and forth in Western Canada and was a guest speaker in France before his return to Batoche a few years before his death in 1906. For an account of the life of Gabriel Dumont, see G. Woodcock, *Gabriel Dumont* (Edmonton: Hurtig, 1975).

96 This correspondence with Maxime Lépine, Alex Fisher, and Philippe Garnot in 1887–88 was carried on mainly with a view to drafting a petition to Wilfrid Laurier and the Liberals (see LAC, MG26, G, vol. 2). Dumont wrote mainly through his Franco-American friend E. Riboulet, with whom he was staying. Dumont's letters (or copies of them) were passed on to the North West Mounted Police by Maxime Lépine with the promise that they would not be published. These letters had been handed over to Col. Herchmer, who sent them to his superior F. White. The latter passed them on to Dewdney. The French originals of Dumont's letters have been lost and only English translations have survived.

97 There were few other options in 1888. Dumont tried repeatedly to revive the possibility of armed resistance during his visits to Métis camps and settlements in Dakota and Manitoba. He also tried in vain to

obtain the support and intervention of the American authorities. See GA, Edgar Dewdney Papers, 6:1563.

98 Ibid., 1605.

99 SBHS, SBAA, Taché Papers, Jean Caron to Father G. Cloutier, 18 March 1887.

100 LAC, MG26, G, vol. 737, pp. 208184–208187, Alex Fisher to W. Laurier, 17 December 1887.

101 Ibid., 2:669–70. Alex Fisher to W. Laurier, 7 March 1888 (translation).

102 Ibid., 671, Alex Fisher to G. Dumont, 7 March 1888 (translation).

103 Charles Nolin's second wife was Rosalie Lépine, cousin of Maxime. One of Maxime's sons, Patrice, married Lucie Nolin, Charles's daughter, in 1892. Howard Adams (great-grandson of Lépine) did not divulge the association between Nolin and Lépine and identified only Nolin and Garnot as "traitors." See Adams, *Prison of Grass*, (Saskatoon: Fifth House, 1999) 69–75.

104 Philippe Gariépy had supported the Liberals in 1887. According to Alex Fisher, he had been bought by the Conservatives, who had offered him a contract for installing telegraph poles. See LAC, MG26, G, vol. 2, A. Fisher to W. Laurier, 7 March 1888, 670.

105 Emmanuel Champagne (1820–1904), born in St. Norbert (Manitoba), was married to Marie Letendre, an aunt of Xavier Letendre. He relocated to Batoche in 1878 and was a prosperous trader with a large herd of cattle and horses in 1885.

106 The petition was received by the House of Commons on 19 April 1888, but was not printed. See Canada, Parliament, *Journal of the House of Commons* (1888), (Ottawa: A. Sénécal), 22:199. The Laurier fonds does not contain the original or final text. A translation in the Pearce Collection (UAA, MG9/2) is almost identical in content if not form with the petition dated 17 December 1887. See LAC, MG26, G, vol. 737, pp. 208184–208185.

107 LAC, MG26, G, vol. 2, A. Fisher to W. Laurier, 20 March 1888.

108 Ibid., 737:671–72 (translation).

109 LAC, MG26, G, vol. 2, 14 March 1888, 676–96.

110 UAA, MG9/2, William Pearce Papers, John R. Hall to William Pearce, Ottawa, 5 May 1888. He objected in particular to the granting of lands and scrips to Métis born between 1870 and 1885.

111 *The Consolidated Ordinances of the North-West Territories, 1898* (Regina: Queen's Printer, 1899), 12–13. St. Louis was incorporated into the Kinistino constituency.

112 LAC, RG15, vol. 589, file 198086. Reply to the petition of Xavier Letendre and signatories, Ottawa, 5 March 1889.

113 For a discussion of this question, see chap. 4: Economy, section on Agriculture.

114 It was only in the 1898 election that the candidates for the territorial assembly affiliated themselves to a political party or grouping.

115 DA, Father Fourmond to Superior General, Rome, 15 January 1889.

116 He was not a member of the Ouellette family of St. Laurent, but a French Canadian who had recently arrived in Prince Albert.

117 The official result was 82 votes against 65: see J.A. Gemmill, ed., *The Canadian Parliamentary Companion*, 397.

118 PAA, Little chronicle of St. Laurent, 1888 [Fourmond].

119 SABS, *Journals of Legislative Assembly of North West Territories* (Regina: R.B. Gordon, 1888) (hereafter cited as *NWT Legislative Assembly*), 1:90, "Report of Standing Committee on Privilege and Elections."

120 Ibid., 91.

121 DA, Rome, Father Fourmond, 15 January 1889. Fourmond was more concerned with French language and Catholic rights than with Métis rights.

122 SABS, *NWT Legislative Assembly*, 1:75.

123 LAC, MG25, A, 335:151350A–151361, D.H. Macdowall to John A. Macdonald, 12 April 1890; PAA, OMI, Little chronicle of St. Laurent, 1890 [Father Fourmond]. He was accompanied by O.E. Hughes, a former member of the Territorial assembly,

James McKay, a Prince Albert lawyer and Métis, and R.S. McKenzie, an Indian agent in the Duck Lake district.

124 PAA, OMI, Little chronicle of St. Laurent, 1890 [Father Fourmond].

125 Son of Jean-Baptiste Boucher and Caroline Lespérance, he was born in St. François-Xavier, Manitoba, in 1864. In 1882, he emigrated with his family to St. Louis, Saskatchewan. In 1884–85, he was a clerk in Xavier Letendre's store in Batoche and in 1886 he married his eldest daughter, Hélène Letendre. Unlike his father and some of his brothers, he did not support the armed resistance. From 1891 to 1898, he sat in the Territorial assembly as a member for the Batoche constituency. Afterwards, he spent a few years ranching in Montana and then returned to his farm in St. Louis. He was a well-known singer, and some of his compositions are part of the local folklore. He died in 1926.

126 LAC, MG26, A, 335:151360, D.H. Macdowall to John A. Macdonald, 12 April 1890.

127 J.A. Gemmill, ed., *The Canadian Parliamentary Companion*,194.

128 Election campaigns were very lively, especially during these years, because the successful candidate had patronage to dispense. Voters were regularly bribed with liquor and fights often broke out.

129 SABS, *NWT Legislative Assembly*, vol. 5, Session of 2 August to 1 September 1892, 9. Boucher was declared elected in August 1892. The journals of the assembly provide no details of inquiry. On the other hand, the Prince Albert *Times* of 11 November 1891 reports that the voting took place in doubtful circumstances, that the polling station was open before eight o'clock, that several votes were rejected, and that the register was removed from the polling station. Several legal proceedings followed, including one against Francis Tourond for perjury. See the *Times*, 16 December 1891.

130 The record shows only four members opposed to the motion. Among them were the two francophone representatives: Boucher (Batoche) and Prince (St. Albert). French was banished from the assembly and could be taught only in primary school. This motion by F.W.G. Haultain, member of the territorial assembly from 1888 to 1905 and opponent of the Catholic francophone minority, could be cited as one of the political repercussions of 1885 and the abolition of French in Manitoba in 1890. See Thomas, *The Struggle for Responsible Government*, 208 and 214. However, it is important to emphasize that the 1891 bill to make English the only official language was never proclaimed. Since Saskatchewan was created out of the Territories in 1905, it may therefore be maintained that French is still legally an official language of the legislative assembly and the courts.

131 SABS, *NWT Legislative Assembly*, vol. 7, 1893, 97.

132 Ibid., 1894, 93.

133 David Venne's brother Bruno was married to Florestine Letendre, sister of Hélène Boucher (née Letendre).

134 Thomas, *The Struggle for Responsible Government*, 243.

135 H. Mitchell, former member for Batoche (1888–91) and member for Mitchell (which included Duck Lake) from 1891 to 1898, was a member of the executive council under Haultain. He supported Haultain on the abolition of French.

136 PAA, OMI, Journal of Brother Célestin Guillet, Batoche, 1 November 1900.

137 See D.J. Hall, "T.O. Davis and Federal Politics in Saskatchewan," *Saskatchewan History* 30, no. 2 (Spring 1977): 56–62. In 1904, he was appointed to the Senate. James McKay, the Conservative candidate had some support among members of the Métis bourgeoisie, including Xavier Letendre and Charles Nolin.

138 J.A. Gemmill, ed., *The Canadian Parliamentary Companion*, 202.

139 Laurier campaigned personally in the West in 1893–94. He visited Prince Albert (electoral district of Saskatchewan) with the aim of consolidating the position of the Liberals, who came to power in 1896. Israël Tarte, minister of Public Works, visited Batoche and other

francophone centres where he presented the Liberals' bill to restore the teaching of French.

140 Son of George Fisher, fur merchant of Fort Qu'Appelle, and Émilie Boyer, he was born in St. François-Xavier in 1865. His elder brother, George Jr., was a candidate in Batoche in 1888. Charles studied at St. Boniface College and at St. John's College in Winnipeg. He was a member of the legislative assembly from 1898 to 1905. He was appointed Indian agent at Mistawasis and subsequently worked for the Department of Indian Affairs in Ottawa. He died in Duck Lake in 1907.

141 Grant had come west from Ontario. He operated a store in Fish Creek in the late 1890s and rented Letendre's store in Batoche in the early 1900s, which he operated with his brother, Donald.

142 Turgeon was an Acadian from New Brunswick. The difficulties of getting a Catholic French Canadian elected in the predominantly Protestant anglophone constituency of Prince Albert City prompted Grant to take this step. See Grant's letter to Premier Scott, 13 October 1907, cited in P. Morissette, « La carrière politique de W.F.A. Turgeon » (MA thesis, University of Regina, 1975), 61. This thesis provides an incisive analysis of Turgeon's career, a man regarded by his compatriots and co-religionists as their official representative in the Scott and Martin governments from 1907 to 1921.

CHAPTER 4: ECONOMY

1 SAB (Regina), Surveyors' Correspondence, I. 320, file 1234, E. Hubbell to E. Deville, 30 June 1906.

2 Manuel and Posluns, *The Fourth World*, 19 and 53. This was also confirmed by Médéric McDougall in an interview in 1982.

3 Interviews with Sister Irène Schmidt, Prince Albert, September 1978, and Mr. Martin Dumont, Duck Lake, 1983.

4 E.Z. Massicotte, "Congés de traite conservés aux Archives de la province de Québec, 1739–1752," *Rapport de l'archiviste de la province de Québec*, 1922–23, 192–265;

ibid., "Répertoire des Engagements pour l'ouest conservés dans les Archives judiciaires de Montréal (1670–1804)," 1930–31, 353–453; and 1931–32, 243–365.

5 SABS, A.S. Morton, "Historical Geography of Saskatchewan to 1870," vol. 4, unpublished manuscript. According to Morton's investigations around 1925, the South Branch House of the Hudson's Bay Company was located on the northeast quarter of section 35 and lot 13, township 44-1-3, and the North West Company House on the southeast quarter of section 11, township 45-1-3.

6 W.K. Lamb, ed., *Sixteen Years in the Indian Country: The Journal of Daniel Harmon, 1800–1816* (Toronto: Macmillan, 1957 reprint), 96–97. Several employees were killed. The survivors fled to Fort St. Louis and Fort à la Corne.

7 According to Morton, "Historical Geography of Saskatchewan to 1870," Carlton House and South Branch House II were located on the eastern half of section 9, township 44-1-3.

8 G.C. Davidson, *History of the North West Company* (New York: Russell, 1967 reprint), 239.

9 Diane P. Payment, "Jean-Baptiste Letendre dit Batoche," in *Dictionary of Canadian Biography* (DCB), vol. 6: "1821–1835," ed. F.G. Halpenny and Jean Hamelin, 1987, 437–38.

10 Elliot Coues, ed., *New Light on the Early History of the Greater North West: The Manuscript Journals of Alexander Henry and David Thompson, 1799–1814* (Minneapolis: Ross & Haines; 1965 reprint), 2:484n.48; Morton, "Historical Geography of Saskatchewan to 1870," 10:484c.

11 AM, Hudson's Bay Company Archives, E. 243, 1825–26, "Summary of a journey from York Factory to the Saskatchewan and continued at Carlton, 1825–26," 7, 24 August 1825.

12 Ibid., 26 August 1825, 7.

13 Jules Le Chevallier, « Saint-Laurent et Saint-André de la Prairie-Ronde », *Le Patriote de l'Ouest* (Prince Albert), 14 July 1937. According to the account, some

caravans at the Forks of the Gros Ventres stayed there all year round.

14 SBHS, SBAA, Fisher-Deschambault Papers, J.G. Harriott to H. Fisher, 22 November 1853. He advised him that several merchants were dealing with Mr. Kittson.

15 Ibid., McGillivray to H. Fisher, 17 November 1853. All these people subsequently settled around Batoche.

16 See, in particular: Father Belcourt to Father Cazeau, 25 November 1843, Account published as an appendix to *Rapports des missionnaires du diocèse de Québec* (Quebec, 1845–53), 35–49, and SBHS, SBAA, Provencher Papers, Father Laflèche to the Bishop of Quebec, June 1845.

17 A. Ross, *The Red River Settlement* (Edmonton: Hurtig, 1972, reprint of an 1856 edition), 243–74.

18 SBHS, SBAA, Provencher Papers, Father Laflèche, 1 June 1845 (translation).

19 Ibid. (translation).

20 Ibid. (translation).

21 SBHS, SBAA, Taché Papers, Father Belcourt, 15 April 1857 (translation).

22 Ibid., Father Lestanc to Bishop Taché, 22 May 1871 (translation).

23 Butler, *The Wild North Land*, 47.

24 LAC, MG26, A, vol. 104, « Pétition des Métis de la rivière Qu'Appelle, 1874 », pp. 41996–41999. They made it clear that they wanted to be consulted about the particulars of this legislation.

25 Ibid., « Pétition des Métis de Cypress Hills, septembre 1878 ».

26 SABS, Department of Agriculture (Saskatchewan), Lands Branch files, AG II, southwest quarter of section 20 (river-front lots 21 and 22), township 42-1-3, Dumont's declaration.

27 PAA, OMI, Little chronicle of St. Laurent, 1880 [Father Fourmond].

28 SABS, Department of the Interior (Canada), Homestead Files, no. 81184. Under pressure to declare that they were farmers, some probably hesitated or refused to say that they still went hunting.

29 SABS, Hillyard Mitchell Papers, F. Stobart to H. Mitchell, 29 May 1889.

30 Ibid., 10 June 1891.

31 SABS, Department of the Interior (Canada), Homestead Files, no. 81184.

32 Ludger Gareau (1855–1954) arrived in the North West from Quebec in 1878. He was a noted carpenter and builder in Batoche. Xavier Letendre hired him between 1878 and 1884 to build his house and store. Gareau also built the rectory and church in Batoche. During the 1885 Resistance he was away on his honeymoon with his wife, Madeleine Delorme (1867–1958), daughter of Urbain Delorme Jr. and Marie Desmarais. Their home was burned down by the Canadian army. In 1886, the family left Batoche and settled in Pincher Creek, Alberta, where they had a ranch. Philippe Garnot, another French Canadian, had a contract to freight 500 bags of flour from Prince Albert to Green Lake in 1883. AM, MG9, A6, Guillaume Charette, « Mémoires de Louis Goulet », 108.

33 GA, Richard Hardisty Papers, file 34, L. Clarke to D. Smith, 15 January 1872.

34 Norbert Delorme, son of Urbain Delorme, a rich merchant from St. François-Xavier (Manitoba), was in the North West on his father's business in the 1870s. He opened a small store on his land, lot 56, at Batoche. He moved to Pincher Creek, AB in the 1890s.

35 SBHS, SBAA, Taché Papers, Lists of freighters employed by the archdiocese (around the 1870s); ibid., Maxime Lépine to Bishop Taché, 8 March 1892.

36 AM, MG9, A6, Guillaume Charette, « Mémoires de Louis Goulet », 105–6 (translation).

37 Frédéric St. Germain and his wife, Mélanie Parenteau, came to Saskatchewan from St. Vital, Manitoba, in 1882. He settled near Gabriel's Crossing. He died in Batoche at the age of 101 on 21 August 1953.

38 Prince Albert Historical Society, "Reminiscences of Patrice Fleury," [around 1940].

39 SABS, Department of the Interior (Canada), Homestead Files, nos. 21884,

4 875–650, and 3 112 059. Abraham Bélanger Sr. and Jr. were on lots 48 and 49 of township 42-1-W3.

40 DA, Rome, Father Moulin to Father Sardou, 5 February 1885. Moulin said that the price was 15 to 20 francs per 100 pounds. In 1885, the franc was worth about 20 American cents.

41 PAA, OMI, Little chronicle of St. Laurent, 1886 [Father Fourmond] (translation).

42 AM, Hudson's Bay Company Archives, B. 276/6/1, p. 128, H. Adams to G.S. Davison, 31 July 1891.

43 Ibid., 15 July 1891, 126.

44 Ibid., B. 332/2/2, Prince Albert Office, 26 July 1891.

45 Ibid., B. 276/6/1, 128, 31 July 1891.

46 DA, Correspondence of Father Végréville, Xavier Letendre's account of the founding of Batoche, [around 1882] (translation); Diane P. Payment, "Monsieur Batoche," *Saskatchewan History* 32, no. 3 (Autumn 1979): 81–103, and "François-Xavier Letendre dit Batoche," *Dictionary of Canadian Biography*, vol. 13, 1987: 646–48.

47 LAC, RG15, vol. 914, file 892789, claim no. 15. Ludger Gareau testified that the house was decorated with fine wood panelling and moulding brought from Winnipeg.

48 Ibid.

49 Moïse Parenteau was the brother of Letendre's wife Marguerite. Charles (Châlins) Thomas was married to Hélène Letendre, and Édouard Dumont (brother of Gabriel) was married to Sophie Letendre, both of them sisters of Xavier. William Letendre was the son of Louis, Xavier's elder brother.

50 For more on Boucher, see the chap. 3: Political Activism. Philippe Chamberland (1861–1954), a French Canadian settled in Bellevue, worked as a cook for the Provisional government at Batoche in 1885.

51 LAC, RG15, vol. 914, file 892789, Xavier Letendre's testimony.

52 DA, Correspondence of Father Végréville, Xavier Letendre's account of the founding of Batoche, [around 1882] (translation).

53 The first steam threshing machines arrived in Prince Albert around 1880. But the Prince Albert *Times* did not start advertising the agricultural implements of A. Harris & Sons until 1888. Xavier Letendre may have brought his thresher directly from Winnipeg by rail and wagon via Troy or by steamboat around 1883–84.

54 In 1885, he had two sons at St. Boniface College, and, in 1890, he had two daughters in the boarding school at St. Anne's Convent, a bilingual institution run by the Faithful Companions of Jesus in Prince Albert.

55 DA, Correspondence of Father Végréville, Xavier Letendre's account of the founding of Batoche, [around 1882]. Boyer and Letendre were cousins.

56 LAC, RG15, vol. 914, file 892789, Jean-Baptiste Boyer's claim.

57 Ibid., vol. 531, file 153221.

58 Ibid., vol. 535, file 155386, George Fisher Jr.'s claim. Another son, Michel, was a merchant at Nut Lake.

59 Those who had billiard tables in the community were: Baptiste Boyer, Xavier Letendre, George Fisher, Joseph Vandal, and Gabriel Dumont.

60 LAC, RG15, vol. 535, file 155386, George Fisher Jr.'s claim.

61 Born ca. 1820 and died in 1904 at Batoche, he was the son of a French Canadian, Emmanuel Beaugrand *dit* Champagne, and a Métis woman, Madeleine Ladéroute, from St. Norbert (Manitoba). In 1849, his father had one of the largest farms in St. Boniface. See AM, Red River Settlement Census, 1849, no. 448; ibid., Hudson's Bay Company Archives, B. 235/a/15, "Extracts from William Black's Red River Journal," 17 October 1853.

62 LAC, RG15, vol. 914, file 892789, Ludger Gareau's testimony; ibid., claims register, vol. 931, no. 129, Emmanuel Champagne's claim; SBAA, Taché Papers, E. Champagne to Bishop Taché, 6 March 1886.

63 Born in St. Norbert, Manitoba, Salomon Venne (ca. 1829–1922) was the son of Pierre-Jean Venne and Marie Charette. He married Josephte St. Arnaud. His family was one of the most enterprising and prosperous in the district.

64 LAC, RG15, vol. 916, file 892789 and claims register, vol. 931, no. 99.

65 SABS, Hillyard Mitchell Papers, accounts, Patrice Parenteau, 1895–96; *Henderson's Directory of the North West Territories*, 1895–1905. He may have managed Grant's store (formerly Letendre's) at Batoche.

66 LAC, RG15, vol. 914, file 892789, H. Walters' declaration and Ludger Gareau's testimony; Baker family history by Dr. Fred Baker, 2005–06.

67 The two brothers had come west from Ottawa, Ontario, and had operated businesses in Winnipeg in Saskatoon.

68 LAC, RC15, vol. 513, file 145780, G. and J. Kerr to the Minister of the Interior, 15 November 1887.

69 After their flight from Batoche, they took a strong position against the Métis. Afterwards, they had trouble gathering testimony to support their claims and maintained that they did not receive a fair indemnity.

70 Guillemette was from Manitoba and, according to Bishop Taché's correspondence, was the Métis who had given the *coup de grâce* to Thomas Scott, who was executed by the Métis Provisional Government in March, 1870. He had gone into hiding in North Dakota and Minnesota and came to Batoche in 1892 and then Fish Creek. He left the district in 1905 and died in St. Boniface (Manitoba) in 1909.

71 On Macdonald's National Policy and its impact in the West, see V.C. Fowke, *The National Policy and the Wheat Economy* (Toronto: University of Toronto Press, 1957), and Kevin H. Burley, ed., *The Development of Canada's Staples, 1867–1938: A Documentary Collection* (Toronto: McClelland & Stewart, 1970). The latter statement is corroborated by an examination of the files of the Department of the Interior from 1886 and 1900 and especially by the correspondence about Métis lands and their petitions.

72 LAC, RG15, vol. 632, file 237041, Philippe Gariépy to John A. Macdonald, 22 November 1889. The claims of Xavier Letendre, Ludger Gareau, Salomon Venne, George Fisher, and Jean Caron for losses suffered in 1885 give evidence of this prosperity.

73 LAC, MG26, A, vol. 106, G.A. Kerr to John A. Macdonald, April 21, 1885; ibid., C.A. Boulton to his father, 23 May 1885.

74 SBHS, SBAA, Taché Papers, E. Champagne to Bishop Taché, 6 March 1886 (translation). His wife was Marie Letendre, Xavier Letendre's aunt.

75 LAC, RG15, vol. 914, file 892789, no. 15, Xavier Letendre's testimony.

76 SAB (Regina), R.K. Allan, Diary kept during the North West Rebellion, 1885.

77 It was reportedly taken by Colonel Winslow and the Midlanders and loaded on a steamboat with the troops. It is probably the bell that was on exhibit in Millbrook, Ontario, for over a hundred years as a symbol of the long-standing animosity of Irish Protestants towards French Catholics, and rivalry between eastern and western Canada. This author first uncovered the bell in the town in 1978 and reported its whereabouts to Parks Canada and the Manitoba Métis Federation. It was repatriated by the Métis in a well-planned coup in 1991 but was subsequently hidden and embroiled in local Métis politics. It is the wish of the Métis people and the citizens of Millbrook, that it will one day return to Batoche. It is also possible that the bell in Millbrook was from Onion Lake or Frog Lake, rather than Batoche as the three were taken by the troops. The bells were similar or identical and bore Bishop Grandin's coat of arms.

78 LAC, RG15, vol. 928, George Fisher Sr., Rebellion Losses Claim, John Macdonald to G. Fisher, 23 May 1885.

79 Jean-Baptiste Boucher Jr. (1861–1943) was a deputy lands officer from 1888 to 1895. At about the same time, Jean-François Hubert Huysmans de Neftal, a minor

French nobleman, worked in the lands office at Duck Lake. He married Corinne de la Gorgendière and died at the age of 30 in 1904.

80 Georgine d'Amours (1884–1975) was the daughter of Théophile d'Amours and Marguerite Bourassa. Georgine's mother died when she was very young, and she was adopted by Mlle Dorval and lived with her in Battleford and Batoche. In 1900, she married the twice-widowed Frenchman Auguste Lenglet, who was more than twice her age. They had two daughters, Liliane and Edna. The family lived in Duck Lake, where Mr. Lenglet, and afterwards, Georgine, managed the post-office. For additional information, see Diane P. Payment, "Onésime Dorval: « la bonne demoiselle »," *Saskatchewan History* 55, no. 1 (Spring 2003): 31–35.

81 A native of Quebec, Odilon St. Denis (1861–1934) served at the Batoche and Duck Lake posts during the 1890s. He was married to Marie Boucher (formerly Lavallée) of St. Louis, where he owned a farm and where he later retired. Inspector Joseph-Victor Bégin (1856–1932) was in Battleford and Prince Albert between 1886 and 1910 and then moved to Maple Creek (Alberta). He accompanied Xavier Letendre to Ottawa to present his petition in 1888.

82 C.F.A. Huot was posted at Batoche in 1887–88 and then at Duck Lake. He was a friend of the Boucher family, and Joseph Boucher wrote a song about Huot's drinking sprees entitled: "Capitaine Huot et sa bouteille."

83 See chap. 1: Society and Culture, section on relations with First Nations.

84 LAC, RG18, C1, vol. 2836, Inspector Bégin to the Commanding Officer in Prince Albert, 18 May 1887; ibid., A.J. Mountain to the Commanding Officer, 16 September 1888; ibid., A. Huot to the Commanding Officer, 31 May 1890.

85 LAC, RC18, C1, vol. 2837, Sergeant Bird to the Commanding Officer, 4 June 1894.

86 *Prince Albert Times and Saskatchewan Review*, 6 December 1889 and 14 February 1890.

87 Ibid., 29 November 1889 and 21 March 1890.

88 GA, Barnett LeRoy, "The Buffalo Bone Trade," unpublished manuscript, n.d.

89 Ibid., D. 621, Dixon Brothers, Maple Creek, 1882–1906. The North-Western Fertilizer Company of Chicago paid $19 a ton in 1888.

90 Mitchell (1853–1923) was born in England and came west with the Wolseley Expedition during the Red River Resistance in 1870. He came to Duck Lake in 1876, first as an employee of Stobart & Co. of Winnipeg and then as an independent trader. He became one of the region's most prosperous merchants, ranchers, and politicians. Although influential and respected by the immigrants, he was disliked by some Métis for his anti-Riel stance during the 1885 Resistance. He died in Victoria, B.C. He had two daughters with his wife, who later left him, and according to local lore, he was the biological father of Jules Fisher, son of Rose Chalifoux (wife of Ambroise Fisher, his long-time employee).

91 SABS, Hillyard Mitchell Papers, contract dated 5 November 1885.

92 Ibid., contract dated 12 February 1898.

93 GA, Richard Hardisty Papers, file 31, "Condensed Report of a meeting of Métis winterers of St. Laurent," 31 December 1871.

94 Ibid., file 34, L. Clarke to D.A. Smith, 15 January 1872.

95 DA, Correspondence of Father Végréville, Xavier Letendre's account of the founding of Batoche, [around 1882] (translation).

96 This breakdown of their farming activities is derived from SABS, Department of the Interior (Canada), Homestead Files, no. 81184.

97 PAA, OMI, Little chronicle of St. Laurent, 1879 [Father André] (translation).

98 Ibid., 1876 (translation).

99 LAC, MG26, A, vol. 104, Petition of the Métis of rivière Qu'Appelle, 11 September 1874; ibid., Resolution of the Métis of Cypress Hills, 1878; ibid., Petition of the Métis of St. Laurent de Grandin, February 1878.

100 PAA, OMI, Little chronicle of St. Laurent, 1884 [Father Fourmond].

101 SABS, Department of the Interior (Canada), Homestead Files, no. 81184.

102 LAC, RG15, vol. 923, claim no. 493; ibid., MG26, A, vol. 106, J. and G.A. Kerr to John A. Macdonald, 21 April 1885.

103 LAC, RG15, vol. 914, file 892789, no. 15, Ludger Gareau's testimony; ibid., vol. 931, no. 129, Emmanuel Champagne's testimony; ibid., vol. 916, file 892789, no. 99, Salomon Venne's testimony; vol. 928, no. 708, A. MacDonald on George Fisher's claim.

104 *Le Manitoba* (St.-Boniface), « Échos du Nord Ouest », 31 July 1884.

105 PAA, OMI, Little chronicle of St. Laurent, 1884 [Father Fourmond] (translation).

106 GA, Faithful Companions of Jesus Collection, Annals, St. Laurent Convent, 1884.

107 *McPhillips' Alphabetical and Business Directory of Saskatchewan, North West Territories* (Qu'Appelle: "The Progress" Book Job Office, 1888), 22. It should be noted that these figures are based on the seed grain advanced by the government.

108 LAC, RG15, vol. 105, file 144363, Petition of St. Laurent de Grandin, 24 February 1886, J. Caron, O. Régnier et al.; ibid., MG26, G, vol. 737, pp. 298286–298287, Petition of Alex Fisher, P. Garnot et al., April 1888; ibid., RG15, vol. 589, file 190886, Petition of Letendre, Nolin et al., December 1888.

109 Ibid., RG15, vol. 105, file 144363, Petition of St. Laurent de Grandin, 24 February 1886; ibid., Communication of Minister of the Interior T. White to the Privy Council, 23 May 1887.

110 SABS, Department of Agriculture (Saskatchewan), Lands Branch files, AG II, lots 19 and 63, T43-1-3.

111 LAC, RG18, C1, vol. 32, no. 221–289, Superintendent A. Bowen Perry to the Commissioner, 25 March 1889.

112 *Prince Albert Times and Northwest Review*, 20 February 1890.

113 LAC, RG18, C1, vol. 2837, Sergeant Bird to the Commanding Officer, Prince Albert, 13 November 1893; ibid., 7 May 1894.

114 See chap. 5: Land Claims on the South Saskatchewan River.

115 SABS, Department of Agriculture (Saskatchewan), Lands Branch files, AG II, lots 1 to 12 and 17 to 19, T43-1-3.

116 Ibid., lot 3, T43-1-3; François Parenteau on lot 4 had fewer animals but cultivated 55 acres between 1913 and 1919.

117 These figures are derived specifically from lots 53 to 69.

118 A quantitative analysis of land claims in the area, and more specifically, of lots 1 to 13, T45-1-3, lots 11 to 40, T45-27-2 and lots 3 to 12, T45-28-2, south bank.

119 SABS, Department of the Interior (Canada), Homestead Files, no. 442-62.

120 Née Josephte Paul (1831–1928), she and her husband, Joseph Tourond, emigrated from St. François-Xavier with their family in 1882. They gave the name *la couli des Tourond* to their place of residence near the site of present-day Fish Creek. Her husband died in 1883, and she took over the management of the farm with her sons. She lost two sons at the battle of Batoche and one to tuberculosis in 1885. She lost four other children before 1900. She later moved to a second homestead at Batoche, next door to her daughter Élise and her husband Raphaël Boyer.

121 SABS, Department of the Interior (Canada), Homestead Files, no. 881793 (lot 56); no. 2328642 (lot 58); ibid., Department of Agriculture (Saskatchewan), Lands Branch files, AG II, lots 59, 68, and 69, T43-1-3.

122 Ibid., Department of the Interior (Canada), Homestead Files, no. 4049585. The ranch was situated on the southwest quarter of section 16, T41-28-2.

123 SABS, Department of Agriculture (Saskatchewan), Lands Branch files, AGII, file 3744, Petition of the inhabitants of Batoche to Lieutenant-Governor Dewdney, 13 May 1887.

124 The industrial schools were special schools for First Nations, administered by the federal government and run by religious communities (such as the Oblates) in the Canadian West, starting in the 1880s. The aim of these schools was to suppress the culture and lifestyle of Aboriginal peoples. They were taught mainly trades and farming methods with a view to turning them into a class of labourers. Some Métis attended the schools. There was an industrial school for First Nations in Duck Lake and Lebret, Saskatchewan, and one of the Métis at St. Paul des Métis, in northern Alberta. For more on the subject, see: John S. Milloy, *A National Crime: The Canadian Government and the Residential School System, 1879 to 1986* (Winnipeg: University of Manitoba Press, 1999), and Huel, *Proclaiming the Gospel*.

125 See communications from Minister of the Interior White to the Privy Council: NA, RG15, vol. 105, file 144363, 23 May 1887 and vol. 589, file 198086, 5 March 1889. According to White, even Bishop Taché was against the industrial schools, saying that the Métis needed practice rather than theory.

126 Interview with Sister Irène Schmidt, Prince Albert, 1976 (translation).

127 Interview with Mr. Fred Anderson, Duck Lake, 1976.

128 DA, Rome, Father Moulin to Father Soullier, 17 June 1893 (translation).

129 PADA, Parish registers of Lac Maskeg (Aldina), (St. Vital) Battleford, Leask, and Jackfish Lake.

130 Information from descendants of the Nault family of Jackfish Lake and the Carrière family of Crystal Springs, whom the author met at Batoche in the 1990s.

CHAPTER 5: LAND CLAIMS AND THE SOUTH SASKATCHEWAN RIVER

1 René Fumoleau, *As Long As This Land Shall Last* (Calgary: University of Calgary Press, 2004), xxiii.

2 Treaties and land acquisitions by Europeans began in present-day Central Canada as early as 1764. That year, the British at Forth Niagara purchased some land from the Saulteaux (Ojibwe). The reserve system had been established much earlier in the late seventeenth century. Wendat (Huron) villages or reserves were set up between 1680 and 1750, and in 1786 a Mikmaq reserve was established in St. Margaret's Bay (Nova Scotia). For more information, see Olive P. Dickason, *Canada's Founding Peoples from Earliest Times* (Toronto: McClelland & Stewart, 1992).

3 It is important to underline that First Nations were ready to share *their* lands with the newcomers but not to give them up as they were forced to do. Moreover, they didn't consider the treaties as permanent and immutable agreements but as something to be negotiated in the future. See John L. Tobias, "The Origins of the Treaty Rights Movement in Saskatchewan," in *Native Society in Transition*, ed. F.L. Barron and J.B. Waldram, 241 (Regina: Canadian Plains Research Center, 1986); Dickason, *Canada's Founding Peoples from Earliest Times*, 273–77.

4 Alexander Morris, *The Treaties of Canada with the Indians* (Toronto: Belfords, Clarke & Co., 1880) [Coles Canadiana Collection, 1971], 50 and 69.

5 SBHS, SBAA, Provencher Papers, « Soumission des habitants de la Rivière Rouge pour un missionnaire, 1817 », copy. The petitioners stated that they had been in the region for over twenty years. See also Arrowsmith's map of the Red River Colony in 1816 and early plans of the Red River Colony by W. Kempt (1822–24) and G. Taylor (1836) AM, HBCA, E.6/10, E.6/11, E.6/13, E.6/14.

6 Lot 754 of the Hudson's Bay Company Survey (hereafter no. 81 and no. 82 of the Dominion Lands Survey) was reserved for the use of the inhabitants of small lots (*emplacements*) 684 to 753 until around 1881. SBAA, Report on the Community of St. Boniface, n.d. [ca. 1881].

7 AM, MG2, C12, M169, Hudson's Bay Company Land Register "B" and Correlation Book 1908; HBCA, E.6/3 to E.6/14, Land Register Books Nos. 1 and 2, E.6/13,

Holders of Land at Red River Settlement with Plans of the same, 1836.

8   Ibid.

9   SBHS, SBAA, Provencher Papers, G.A. Belcourt to C.F. Cazeau, 4 August 1842, copy (translation).

10 D.N. Sprague, "The Manitoba Land Question, 1870–1882," *Journal of Canadian Studies* 15, no. 3 (1980): 74–84.

11 Manitoba Métis Federation, *Riverlots and Scrip, Elements of Métis Aboriginal Rights* (Winnipeg: Manitoba Métis Federation Press, 1978), 1–47.

12 Sprague, "The Manitoba Land Question, 1870–1882," 74–84; "Government Lawlessness in the Administration of Manitoba Land Claims, 1870–1887," *Manitoba Law Journal* 10, no. 4 (1980): 415–41; For an in-depth discussion of Métis land claims pursuant to sections 31 and 32 of the Manitoba Act, see Paul L.A.H. Chartrand, *Manitoba's Métis Settlement Scheme of 1870* (Saskatoon: Native Law Centre, 1991). Thomas Flanagan disputes these views and argued that the government met its obligations to the Métis in *Métis Lands in Manitoba* (Calgary: University of Calgary Press, 1991).

13 Sprague, "The Manitoba Land Question, 1870–1882," 83.

14 Gerhard Ens, "Métis Lands in Manitoba," *Manitoba History* 5 (Spring 1983): 2–11.

15 Sprague, "The Manitoba Land Question, 1870–1882," 83n.47.

16 SABS, Saskatchewan Land Surveys Branch (hereafter SLSB), M. Aldous, Notebook 747.

17 SABS, Department of the Interior (Canada), Homestead Files, no. 81184.

18 LAC, MG26, A, 105: 42343, A.N. Burgess to D.L. Macpherson, 18 April 1885; SABS, J.L. Reid, "Plan of Township 43-1-W3, 1879."

19 SABR, Surveyors' Correspondence files, IV, 4 "Halfbreed Grievances in the Prince Albert District, 1884–1886," V. Végréville to E. Deville, 19 January 1884. The same is repeated in a petition through the intermediary of Bishop V.J. Grandin, 13 June 1884, LAC, MG26, A, 105:42261–70: « Mémorial de Messieurs Charles Nolin, Maxime Lépine et al. ».

20 LAC, MG26, A, 105:42343, A.M. Burgess to D.L. Macpherson, 18 April 1885.

21 SABS, SLSB, M. Aldous, Notebook 747.

22 Ibid.

23 SABS, Department of the Interior (Canada), Homestead Files, no. 81184.

24 LAC, MG26, A, 105:42334, "Memorandum regarding North West Half-Breeds." This was stated repeatedly by Commissioner William Pearce, although George Duck, the local agent at the time, contradicted this statement, saying the majority had settled previous to the survey. See UAA, W. Pearce Papers, MG 9, Letterbooks, Land Claims, G. Duck to Surveyor General E. Deville, 14 March 1882.

25 SABS, SLSB, J.L. Reid, Notebook 882.

26 LAC, MG26, A, 105:42098–110, "Copy of a memorial from Lawrence Clarke, Member of the North West Council to Lieutenant Governor in Council, 7 June 1881:" and "Copy of a Petition from Father André of Duck Lake to Lieutenant Governor in Council:" UAA, W. Pearce Papers, MG 9, Land Claims, 1:28, W. Pearce to Minister of the Interior, 19 January, 1884.

27 SBHS, SBAA, L. Schmidt to A.M. Burgess, 26 May 1885, copy.

28 SABR, Surveyors' Correspondence files, IV, 4, V. Végréville to E. Deville, 19 January 1884 (translation). G. Duck wrote to the Surveyor-General requesting a resurvey. UAA, W. Pearce Papers, MG 9, Letterbook, Land Claims, vol. 2, G. Duck to E. Deville, 11 March 1882.

29 Ibid., V. Végréville to E. Deville, 19 January 1884 (translation).

30 The government proposed the following plan to adapt a section of 640 acres divided into four quarters of 160 acres each to the riverlot system. Each quarter section was divided into eight 20-acre parcels – 32 per section.

31 UAA, W. Pearce Papers, MG 9, Letterbooks, Land Claims, vol. I, A.M. Burgess to G. Duck, 21 September 1882.

32 In "Métis Land Claims at St. Laurent: Old Arguments and New Evidence," *Prairie Forum* 12, no. 2 (Fall 1987): 245–55, Thomas Flanagan argued that the Métis had no reason for mistrust and that the government was responding to their demands. He cited Mr. Duck's schedule of 1884 declarations, which showed that claimants could enter lands on odd-numbered sections and reserves. I would argue, however, that not all of Mr. Duck's recommendations were approved by his superiors in Ottawa, as subsequent events and the government's official report revealed.

33 The Métis had petitioned for the appointment of one of their own to the position of assistant lands agent, but the appointment went to Valmore Gauvreau, an anglophile. He subsequently moved to Battleford and married Minnie Laurie, the daughter of P.G. Laurie, publisher of the *Battleford Herald*.

34 SABR, Surveyors' Correspondence files, IV, 4, W. Pearce to A.M. Burgess, 18 January 1886.

35 Schmidt was appointed sub-agent at the Prince Albert Land Office in May, 1884, but he did not get out into the field or accompany Mr. Duck. Schmidt was fluent in French, English, Cree and Ojibway (Saulteaux) and was also aware of the cultural and political concerns of the Métis.

36 LAC, RG15, vol. 335, file 83808. Petition dated 16 December, 1884, addressed to the federal government to which the latter responded evasively in February, 1885, one month before the formation of the provisional government and the resort to arms.

37 SABS; William Pearce, *Detailed Report upon all Claims to Land and Right to Participate in the North-West Half-Breed Grant by Settlers along the South [Saskatchewan] and Vicinity* (14 December 1885) (Ottawa: Maclean, Roger & Co., 1886), 1–17; GA, George B. Coutts Papers, Typescript, 1923, W. Pearce to Chairman of Alberta Military Institute, no. 13, 16 October 1923.

38 SABS, Pearce, *Detailed Report* (1886), 1–17. Pearce's figures and cases do not correspond with the evidence in the Homestead and Land Survey Branch files.

39 UAA, Pearce Papers, MG 9, series 5, vol. 1, file 6; Ibid., Claims regarding T45-28-2, vol. 5, 1886).

40 PAA, OMI, Mémoire de Philippe Garnot (translation).

41 GA, Richard Hardisty Papers, file 30A, A.G. Archibald to J.C. Christie, 11 January 1872.

42 GA, Edgar Dewdney Papers, vol. 3, Sec. 4, E. Dewdney to J.A. Macdonald, 4 February 1885, copy.

43 Ibid. The Métis were also informed of this decision by a telegram sent to Charles Nolin, rather than to Louis Riel, whom the government refused to deal with.

44 SAB, Regina, Surveyors' Correspondence files, I-273, E. Deville to C.F. Leclerc, 26 December 1888.

45 Ibid.

46 SABS, SLSB, C.F. Leclerc, Notebook 4928, 1889 (translation).

47 SAB, Regina, Surveyors' Correspondence files, I-417, E. Deville to Deputy Minister of the Interior, 17 August 1896.

48 Ibid., E-418, E. Deville to A.M. Burgess, 8 May 1889.

49 Ibid., I-320, G. McMillan to E. Deville, 26 September 1908 and 16 February 1909.

50 SABS, Department of Agriculture (Saskatchewan), Lands Branch files, riverlots 11–14, "St. Laurent Settlement"; ibid., Department of the Interior (Canada), Homestead Files, no. 2578579.

51 Chester Martin, *"Dominion Lands" Policy* (Toronto: McClelland & Stewart, 1973) [Carleton Library Series, no. 69], 157–74; James M. Richtik, "The Policy Framework for Settling the Canadian West, 1870–1880," *Agricultural History* 49, no. 4 (October 1975): 613–28.

52 SABS, Department of the Interior (Canada), Homestead Files, nos. 4049585, 3333836, 2850508, 781078, 2492466, and ibid., Department of Agriculture (Saskatchewan), Lands Branch file, riverlot 16, "St. Laurent Settlement."

53 Ibid., Homestead and Lands Branch files with particular reference to lots 28, 34, 39, and 41 ("St. Laurent Settlement").

54 Ibid., Homestead Files, no. 645177.

55 Ibid., Homestead and Lands Branch files regarding lot 48, T42-1-3, Vandal (Abraham Bélanger Jr.); lot 12, T44-1-3, St. Laurent (François Arcand); lot 8, T45-28-2, St. Louis (Célestine Régnier); lot 52, T43-1-3, Batoche (Jean Caron Sr.); and lot 2, T42-1-3, Vandal (Frédéric St. Germain).

56 Ibid., Department of the Interior (Canada), Homestead Files, nos. 81184, 564192, and 692951; ibid., Department of Agriculture (Saskatchewan), Lands Branch files, riverlots 27, 39, and 41 ("St. Laurent Settlement Survey"). A 1930 order-in-council cancelled grain mortgages, enabling many Métis to obtain their patents. It was too late, however, for others who had already moved.

57 Ibid., Department of the Interior (Canada) Homestead Files, no. 81184, and Department of Agriculture (Saskatchewan), Lands Branch regarding sections 7 and 8, T43-1-3.

58 Ibid., Department of Agriculture (Saskatchewan), Lands Branch files, NW quarter-section 18, N half-section 8, T43-1-3; ibid., Department of Natural Resources (Saskatchewan), Provincial Lands Branch, Correspondence about the St. Laurent Settlement, Commissioner J.W. Martin to Registrar of Land Titles in Prince Albert, 4 April 1930.

59 Ibid., Department of Agriculture (Saskatchewan), Lands Branch file, riverlot 48, T42-1-3.

60 Ibid., Department of the Interior (Canada), Homestead Files, no. 281532.

61 Canada, House of Commons, *Debates*, 1885, 3208–09, cited in John L. Taylor, "An Historical Introduction to Métis Claims in Canada," *Canadian Journal of Native Studies* 3, no. 1 (1983): 157. M.P. Joseph Royal, who was being quoted, was a former editor of *Le Métis* [St.-Boniface] (1871–81) and former Manitoba member of the Legislature, who had also dealt in scrip. He knew the situation of the Métis.

62 The resolution was adopted by the executive council of the North West Territories on 2 August 1879. See also, Canada, Parliament, *Consolidated Statutes of Canada*, 1879, Victoria, ch. 31, sec. 125; sub-sec. (e).

63 Robert Painchaud, *Un rêve français dans le peuplement de la Prairie* (St. Boniface: Éditions des Plaines, 1987), 13–18.

64 AM, MG3, D1, letter 414, Bishop Taché to Louis Riel, 4 October 1884; GA, Richard Hardisty Papers, file 30A, Plan of bishops Taché and Grandin.

65 LAC, RG15, vol. 239, file 13984, "Petition of Half-breeds of St. Laurent of the North West Territories, 1 February 1878," under the direction of Gabriel Dumont and Alex Fisher.

66 J.S. Dennis also proposed a reserve for the Métis. The plan was essentially for a grant of 160 acres of non-negotiable scrip to be located on vacant Dominion Lands for which title would be withheld for a ten-year period. See Canada, Parliament, *Sessional Papers*, vol. 7, no. 12 (Ottawa: Maclean, Roger & Co., 1884), 93–96.

67 Ken Hatt, "The North West Scrip Commissions as Federal Policy – Some Initial Findings," *Canadian Journal of Native Studies* 3, no. 1 (1983): 117–29. The author quotes an article by D.B. Smiley, "Canada and the Quest for a National Policy," *Canadian Journal of Political Science* 8 (1974): 40–62.

68 LAC, RG2, 28 January 1885, P.C./135.

69 LAC, RG2, 30 March 1885, P.C./688. The three commissioners appointed were: W.P.R. Street, Chairman, Roger Goulet, a Métis and surveyor from St. Boniface, and Amédée E. Forget, clerk of the North West Council and future lieutenant-governor of Saskatchewan.

70 LAC, RG15, vol. 88, order-in-council 688/85, 105–6 and Canada, Parliament, *Consolidated Statutes of Canada*, vol. 1, 1884–85.

71 Ibid.

72 LAC, RG15, vol. 632, file 236942, D.H. Macdowall to A.M. Burgess, 19 July 1980. Macdowall reported that 260 Métis took land scrip at Fort Qu'Appelle. According to a report by Street in the 1886 Canada, Parliament, *Sessional Papers*, vol. 12, no. 45, p. 2, the Street Commission approved 1142 claims of which 236 were taken in land.

73 LAC, RG2, 18 April 1885, P.C./821; ibid., 13 April 1886, P.C./657.

74 A second commission headed by Roger Goulet assisted by N.O. Côté was appointed on 1 March 1886. It dealt with 1,414 claims of which 1,164 were allowed. See Canada, Parliament, *Sessional Papers*, 1887, vol. 6, no. 7, pp. 76–77.

75 LAC, RG15, DII 8(e). Forms E. and J., for Batoche only.

76 PAA, OMI, Little chronicle of St. Laurent, 1886; DA, V. Fourmond to Mother Gertrude (Sisters of Visitation, Le Mans), 20 October 1886 (translation).

77 LAC, RG15, vol. 632, file 236942, D.H. Macdowall to A.M. Burgess, 25 August 1890.

78 Ibid.

79 LAC, RG15, vol. 510, file 144363, Petition of 24 February 1886 by Jean Caron, et al.

80 SBHS, SBAA, Father Fourmond to Bishop Taché, 20 October 1886. Petition of John Ross et al.

81 Ibid. (translation).

82 Ibid.

83 LAC, MG26, vol. 6, 737, pp. 208184–87 (translation).

84 LAC, RG15, vol. 589, file 198086 (translation).

85 LAC, RG18, vol. 32, no. 22-89, A.B. Perry to Commissioner in Regina, 25 March 1889.

86 PAA, OMI, Little chronicle of St. Laurent, 1890. See also LAC, RG15, vol. 492, file 138650, « Pétition d'Emmanuel Champagne, le député C.-E. Boucher et cent soixante-trois signataires en faveur des scrips, 1895 » (translation).

87 LAC, RG15, vol. 100, order-in-council, 29 April 1899 and 6 May 1899, 171–73 and Canada, Parliament, *Canada Gazette*, 1899, order-in-council 918/1899.

88 Ibid.

89 LAC, RG15, vol. 492, file 138650, « Pétition des Métis de Batoche et de Duck Lake (Lac au Canard), 24 janvier 1900, présentée par le député Charles Fisher ». See order-in-council of 2 March 1900: RG2, P.C./438.

90 LAC, RG15, DII, 8(e).

91 LAC, RG15, DII, 8(e), vol. 1539, Names, Date of Patent, Assignee.

92 LAC, MG26, G, vol. 118, C. Fisher to W. Laurier, 14 July 1899. The Métis of Saskatchewan and the Northwest Territories are still in the process of vindicating their claims and obtaining their land rights more than a hundred years later.

CHAPTER 6: "HARD TIMES AND COMING OF AGE": BATOCHE SINCE THE 1930s

1 Hartmut Lutz, Murray Hamilton, and Donna Heimbecker, eds., *Howard Adams: Otapaway!* (Saskatoon: Gabriel Dumont Institute, 2005).

2 Diane P. Payment, « ‹ On n'est pas métchifs nous autres ›: un aperçu des relations entre les femmes francophones au Manitoba durant les années 1810–1920 », *Bulletin de la Société historique de Saint-Boniface* 3 (1992): 13–18.

3 Interview transcript, Duck Lake, 14 March 1984, 10. Saskatoon Native Women's Association and Batoche Centenary Corporation (SNWA &BCC), Gabriel Dumont Institute (GDI) Collection. Mr. Courchesne, exhibited the views and attitudes of many of his contemporaries. A respected Duck Lake elder in 2005, he appeared to have moderated his views and spoke fondly of his former Métis students.

4 Interview transcript, Duck Lake, 27 March 1984, 6-7-11. SNWA &BCC, GDI Collection.

5   Interview transcript, Duck Lake, 5 April 1984, 5. SNWA & BCC, GDI Collection.

6   Interview transcript, Debden, 4 August 1982, 7. GDI Collection.

7   Interview transcript, St. Louis, 4 August 1982, 3. GDI Collection.

8   Interview transcript, Maxime Parenteau, Duck Lake, 13 March 1984, 3–4. SNWA & BCC, GDI Collection.

9   Interview transcript, St. Louis, 12 July 1973, 17. Saskatchewan Archives Board (SAB), GDI Collection.

10 Interview transcript, Debden, 22 July 1982, 8. GDI Collection.

11 Interview transcript, Duck Lake, 17 April 1984, 1–3. SNWA & BCCC, GDI Collection.

12 Interview transcript, Debden, 4 March 1984, 9. SNWA & BCC, GDI Collection.

13 Interview transcript, Duck Lake, 11 July 1973, 8. SAB, GDI Collection.

14 Interview transcript, Duck Lake, 14 March 1984, 3. SNWA & BCC, GDI Collection.

15 Interview transcript, Duck Lake, 27 March 1984. SNWA & GDI Collection; Film featuring Rose Fleury in which this author participated: *Sur les traces de Riel*, with Normand Guilbeault and Rose Fleury, produced by Sylvie Van Brabant (Montréal: Les Productions du Rapide-Blanc, 2003).

16 Born at Batoche in 1926, she was the daughter of Arthur Caron and Octavie Parenteau and was raised by her grandmother Octavie Parenteau (née Pilon). "Growing Up in an Orphanage," in *Métis Women: Telling Our Stories* (Ottawa: Métis National Council, 1997), 13–17.

17 Informal discussions between this author and Métis women at Batoche, 1990s.

18 Interview with Marie-Louise Langlois (née Ethier) formerly Caron, Batoche, 1981.

19 Brenda Percell (née Boyer) family history and biographies, 2003–05.

20 Interview transcript, 12 July 1973, 10–11. SAB, GDI Collection.

21 Interview with Euclide Boyer of St. Laurent (Sk), in *Remembrances: Métis Veterans* (Regina: Gabriel Dumont Institute, 1997), 17.

22 Interview transcript, 5 April 1984, 9–10. SNWA & BCC, GDI Collection.

23 Interview with Archie Nicolas of Duck Lake, in *Remembrances*, 95.

24 Interview transcript, 5 April 1984, 9. SNWA & BCC, GDI Collection.

25 Interview with Archie Nicolas, in *Remembrances*, 98.

26 Interview in *Remembrances*, 43–45.

27 Interview transcript, 14 July 1973, 10–12. SAB, GDI Collection.

28 See Diane P. Payment, "'La vie en rose'?: Métis Women at Batoche, 1870–1910," in *Women of the First Nations*, ed. Christine Miller and Patricia Chuchryk, 19–37 (Winnipeg: University of Manitoba Press, 1996); Kermoal, « Les rôles et les souffrances », 153–68.

29 Story told to the author by Mme Boucher's descendants, Réal Boucher and Senator John Boucher.

30 Interview with Médéric McDougall, 12 July 1973, 11–12, transcript, SAB, GDI Collection.

31 For biographies of these leaders, see *Métis History through Biography* (Winnipeg: Pemmican, forthcoming<UPDATE?>).

32 Schilling, *Gabriel's Children*, 143–46.

33 Edward D. Noonan and Percy G. Hodges, "The Saskatchewan Métis" Saskatoon: Gabriel Dumont Institute, Métis Historical Collection, 1943), 135–36.

34 Interview transcript, 12 July 1973, 15–16. SAB, GDI Collection.

35 Interview transcript, 18 August 1976, 8. SAB, GDI Collection.

36 Ibid., 21; Interview transcript, Joseph Vandale, Debden, 4 March 1984, 3. SNWA & BCC, GDI Collection.

37 Ibid., 25.

38 F. Laurie Barron, "The CCF and the Development of Métis Colonies in Southern Saskatchewan during the Premiership of T.C. Douglas, 1944–1961," Métis Nation website reprint, 2004, 252 <www.mnc.ca>. The Duck Lake colony, established in 1948, was in operation only for a few years. It provided land leases to Métis farmers who had to agree to work the land collectively or as a co-operative. It was the same approach that was used in other colonies established in Saskatchewan in the 1940s, such as Green Lake in the north and Lebret and Willow-Bunch in the south. They all failed to address the all-important issue of traditional Métis self-reliance, and they were assimilationist and in many cases exploited Métis labour. T.C. Douglas was himself sensitive towards the disadvantaged, but like most of his contemporaries, he believed that there was a "racial flaw" in the Métis character, which was responsible for their poverty and misfortune.

39 Mentioned in informal conversations with this author between 1981 and 1984.

40 Interview transcript, Batoche, 5 April 1984, 13–14. SNWA & BCC, GDI Collection.

41 The history of the family has been written by a descendant, Réal Boucher, in a book entitled: *Marin Boucher 1588–1671 to Jean Baptiste Boucher 1838–1911 and his Descendants* (The Author: 2001). The family was originally from Berthier (Quebec). The Bouchers of St. Louis (Saskatchewan) are descendants of North West Company voyageur Jean-Marie Boucher and Catherine Mincy [Maskégone], a Cree Métis who lived in St. Boniface and St. François-Xavier (Manitoba).

42 William Albert Boucher (1889–1976), son of Jean-Baptiste Boucher Jr. (1861–1943) and Marie-Louise (Maria) Bremner (1863–1959), was the second Métis in Canadian history (preceded in this honour by Richard Hardisty in Alberta) to be appointed to the Senate. His father, Jean-Baptiste, and his uncle Charles-Eugène were both nineteenth-century "Liberal-Conservatives" and staunch defenders of Catholic and francophone rights in Saskatchewan. "Boss" was a Liberal, a strong supporter of Prime Minister Louis St. Laurent, and an advocate of the creation of a National Historic Site at Batoche, who called for the government's acquisition of the historic rectory in 1953. We had a symbolic meeting in 1976 on my first trip at Batoche when his remains arrived from Ottawa. I was told that the Métis senator and supporter of the historic site was on his last trip and I was on my first to fulfil his mission.

43 In translation: "Shut up, Boss; I asked God to give me a priest and not a politician." Account in Solange Lavigne, *Kaleidoscope Many Cultures – One Faith: The Roman Catholic Diocese of Prince Albert 1891–1991* (Muenster: Abbey Press, 1990), 389.

44 Réal Boucher, *Marin Boucher 1588–1671 to Jean Baptiste Boucher 1838–1911 and his Descendants*, 186. Msgr. Boucher had suffered from tuberculosis in his youth and his health was affected, which may have also been a factor. A pious, humble, and sociable man, he did not seek the appointment, but his proud family was offended by the oversight.

45 Ibid., Léo Blais was Bishop of Prince Albert between 1952 and 1959. He reportedly resigned due to financial issues and personality conflicts.

46 Dr. Howard Adams (1926–2001) was born and raised in St. Louis, Saskatchewan. He was the great-grandson of 1885 provisional government councillor Maxime Lépine. He left St. Louis as a young man and was a constable in the RCMP for two years and then became a probation officer in British Columbia. He graduated from the University of British Columbia and became a teacher and then went to the University of California at Berkeley. where he graduated with a PhD in Educational History in 1965. He returned to Saskatchewan as a "Red Power advocate." Adams taught at the University of Saskatchewan and was president of the Saskatchewan Métis Association from 1968 to 1970. He subsequently taught Native American Studies at the University of California from 1975 until his retirement in 1988. Adams was a persistent advocate of Aboriginal rights and a provocative writer. His uncle Médéric

McDougall, who supported his ideals but not always his style, stated that: "Howard really got things going and brought us to life again. In some ways he was a little bit like Louis Riel – at times a fanatic when he would set his mind on something. I didn't always approve but since I was a strong socialist I went along with him in lots of ways." Interview, September 14, 1979.

47 Interview transcript, 12 July 1982, 12. GDI Collection.

48 Interviews with the author in 1976 and 1977.

49 "Owning Ourselves: A History of the Gabriel Dumont Institute in Documents: 1980–1996," GDI Collection.

50 Interviews with this author between 1976 and 1981.

51 He was MP for Prince Albert from 1940 to 1979 and Prime Minister of Canada from 1957 to 1963.

52 Interview transcript, Saskatoon (family originally from Duck Lake), 19 February 1984, 9. SNWA & BCC, GDI Collection.

53 These thoughts were echoed in interviews with Médéric McDougall and Walter Fidler in the 1980s during public consultations on development plans for Batoche National Historic Site.

54 The rectory and plot of land were purchased from the Corporation Épiscopale de Prince Albert for $5,000, and Albert Caron was paid $300 for the military trenches on his farm.

55 Interview with Edward Bruce, Batoche, May 9, 1990. Parks Canada.

56 Parks Canada (Prairie and Northern Region), Batoche Realty Files C8616-107B3, Site Map, ca. 1972. By 1976, Parks Canada had acquired 980 hectares (2,700 acres) at Batoche, most of the land (680 hectares) as a buffer zone on the west side of the South Saskatchewan River.

57 Cited in Alan McCullough, "Parks Canada and the 1885 Rebellion/Uprising/Resistance," *Prairie Forum* 27, no. 2 (Fall 2002): 185. According to McCullough this meant only the Métis point of view.

58 Ibid., 186.

59 Interview with Edward Bruce, Batoche, May 9, 1990. Parks Canada.

60 See McCullough, "Parks Canada and the 1885 Rebellion/Uprising/Resistance,", 187–88.

61 Diane P. Payment, *Batoche* (Saint-Boniface: Éditions du Blé, 1983) and *"The Free People/Les Gens Libres – Otipemisiwak": Batoche 1870–1930* (Ottawa: Environment Canada-Parks, 1990).

62 Walter Hildebrandt, *The Battle of Batoche: British Small Warfare and the Entrenched Métis* (Ottawa: Parks Canada, 1985).

63 Comments made by Médéric McDougall, Martin Dumont, and Murray Hamilton during Management Plan consultations in 1982.

64 The exterior of the Caron house was conserved to reflect its history over time, from ca. 1895 to ca. 1970, when it was occupied by the Caron family. The interior of the house has been repaired and redecorated along the same principles. The visitor program at the house has been enhanced, and the refurbished main floor opened to the public in 2007.

65 McCullough, "Parks Canada and the 1885 Rebellion/Uprising/Resistance," 189.

66 Gregory Scofield, *Thunder through My Veins: Memories of a Métis Childhood* (Toronto: Harper Collins, 1999), 166.

67 Parks Canada, Cultural Resource Management Policy (Ottawa: Department of Canadian Heritage, 1994). A Commemorative Integrity Statement based on this policy was developed for each National Historic Site of Canada.

68 Scofield, *Thunder through My Veins*, 167.

69 Personal family history and genealogy communicated to the author since 2002.

70 Diane P. Payment, *The Willow Cree of One-Arrow First Nation and the Métis of Batoche, 1870 to 1920: An Ambivalent Relationship* (Parks Canada: Western Canada Service Centre, 1999).

Selected Bibliography

ORAL HISTORY INTERVIEWS

Parks Canada (by the author)

Anderson, Fred (1890–1976), Duck Lake, 1976
Boucher, Béatrice née Lépine (1893–1979), St. Louis, 1977.
Boyer, Alfred (1987–1982), St. Louis, 1981.
Bruce, Edward (born 1933), Batoche National Historic Site, 1990.
Campbell, Marguerite née Branconnier (1903–78), Rosthern, 1976.
Courchesne, Omer, Duck Lake, 1982.
Dumont, Élie (1886–1985), Duck Lake, 1982, 1983.
Fayant, François (1899–1982) and Malvina née Parenteau, St. Louis, 1981.
Ferguson, Walter (ca. 1910–1982), St. Laurent [de Grandin], 1981.
Fisher, Arthur, Regina, 1981.
Gaudet, Lumina née Gaudet (1886–1983), Batoche, 1976.
Jobin, Joseph (1884–1979), Wakaw, 1976.
Langlois, Marie-Louise née Éthier, formerly Caron (1910–2007), Batoche, 1981.
Ledoux, Isidore (1874–1976), Prince Albert, 1976.
Letendre, Jean-Baptiste (ca. 1896–1980), Shellbrook, 1976.
Moffatt, Thérèse née Lenglet (born 1891), Batoche, 1976.
Nicolas, Alexandrine née Fleury (1887–1986), Duck Lake, 1981, 1982.
Nogier, Justine née Branconnier, formerly Caron (1897–1993), Batoche, 1976.
Parenteau, Émile, Batoche National Historic Site, 1990.
Parenteau, Marie née Caron (1888–1978), Batoche, 1976, 1977.
Perillat, Marguerite (1909–89), Duck Lake, 1981–1986.
Pilon, Henri (1888–1980) and Amanda née Caron (1898–1992), Batoche, 1976 and 1981.
Ranger, Adélaïde née Pilon (1891–1981), Batoche 1976, 1977, 1978.
St. Germain, Justine née Caron (1903–83), Batoche, 1978, 1981.
Schmidt, Sister Irène (1901–78), Prince Albert, 1976.
Venne, Louis (1898–1991), Wakaw, 1980, 1981.

Gabriel Dumont Institute

Saskatoon, Saskatoon Native Women's Association and Batoche Centenary Corporation 1982, 1984.

Adams, Graham, St. Louis, 1982.
Adams, Howard, Saskatoon, 1984.
Arcand, Alice née St. Denis, (Duck Lake) Debden, 1982.
Arcand, Damase, (Duck Lake) Debden, 1982.
Dumont, Aimé, Duck Lake, 1984.
Dumont, Élie, Duck Lake, 1984.
Dumont, Martin, Duck Lake, 1982.
Dumont, Victoria née Laframboise, Duck Lake, 1984.
Fidler, Walter, Batoche, 1984
Fidler, Marie née Parenteau, Batoche, 1984.
Fleury, Rose née Gariépy, Duck Lake, two interviews, 1984.
Laframboise, Marge (Duck Lake) Saskatoon, 1984.
McDougall, Médéric, St. Louis, two interviews, 1984
Parenteau, Délima née St. Germain, Batoche, 1984.
Vandale, Joseph (Vandal/Fish Creek), Debden, 1984.

Saskatchewan Archives Board, "Towards a New Past Series"

Boyer, Alfred, St. Louis
Carrière, Pierre, (Batoche) Cumberland House, 1976.
Nicolas, Alexandrine née Fleury, 1973.

UNPUBLISHED MANUSCRIPT SOURCES

Archives of Manitoba [AM]

Hudson's Bay Company Archives:
    B. 276/631 Correspondence, Duck Lake;
    B. 332/2/2 Correspondence, Prince Albert office.
MG3, C13, George A. Flinn journal.
MG3, C14, Capt. George H. Young, notes on Royal Commission for Rebellion Losses, 1886.
MG3, D1 and D2, Louis Riel Papers.
MG9, A6, Guillaume Charette, Memoires de Louis Goulet.
MG9, A31, Mémoires de Louis Schmidt.
MG10, F1, Société historique métisse, Mémoires de Gabriel Dumont [1902].
MG14, B26, Joseph Dubuc, correspondence and memoirs.

Canada. Canadian Museum of Civilization. Canadian Ethnology Department

Richard Johnston Collection, recordings and transcripts of Métis songs, St. Louis and Lebret, Sk. 1957.

Deschâtelets Archives [DA], Oblates of Mary Immaculate (Ottawa)

Alexis André, « Mémorial en réponse au questionnaire du R.P. Visiteur, octobre 1883. »
Letters of priests to the Sisters of Visitation (Le Mans, France), copies.
Fathers André, Fourmond, Moulin, Végréville to the Superior-General in Rome, 1878–1900, copies.

Edmonton Archdiocesan Archives [EAA]

Letters of Bishop V.J. Grandin to Father J. Moulin.
Register of letters by Father H. Leduc.

Glenbow Archives [GA]

Edgar Dewdney
Recollections of Eva Pozer Powell.
Faithful Companions of Jesus (Fidèles Compagnes de Jésus)
    Annals;
    Journal of the Prince Albert House;
    Journal of the St. Laurent House;
    Annual reports.
George B. Coutts Papers.
Diary of George H. Young.
Marie-Rose Delorme Smith, accounts and reminiscences.
Richard Hardisty Papers.

Fisher, Arthur (Art)

Personal family history, genealogy and photographs 1977–88.

Library and Achives Canada [LAC]

MG26, A, John A. Macdonald
MG26, G, Wilfrid Laurier
MG27, IC4, Edgar Dewdney
RG13, Department of Justice
RG15, Department of the Interior
RG18, North West and Royal Canadian Mounted Police

Percell, Brenda née Boyer

Personal family history, genealogy and photographs, 2002–05.

Prince Albert Diocesan Archives [PADA]

Actes de visites, Batoche.
Reverend Pierre-Elzéar Myre correspondence.
Parish registers:
    Notre Dame de Pontmain (Maskeg Lake), Aldina-Leask; St. Antoine de Padoue, Batoche;
    St. Laurent de Grandin; St. Louis de Langevin;
    St. Vital (Battleford);
    St. Sacrement (Duck Lake).

Provincial Archives of Alberta [PAA], Oblates of Mary Immaculate [OMI], 71.220 and 84.400

Administration vicariale of Prince Albert.
Codex Historicus of St. Laurent de Grandin.
Correspondence of Bishop Albert Pascal.
B-VII-27, Correspondence of Father Julien Moulin.
B-VII-38, Correspondence of Father Valentin Végréville.
D-112-12, 13, 16. Journal of Brother Célestin Guillet, Batoche, 1895–96 and 1900–01.
D-IV-126, Journal of Brother Valentin Végréville.
D-IV-125, Little chronicle [Petite Chronique] of St. Laurent, 1874–91.
D-IV-119, Mémoir de Philippe Garnot, 1886.
D-IV-123, Riel Rebellion Files.
St. Antoine de Padoue (Batoche) records.
St. Laurent de Grandin parish records.

Ranger, Omer

Personal family history and photographs

Saskatchewan Archives Board (Saskatoon) [SABS]

Canada, Department of the Interior:
:   Homestead Files 81184;
    Townships 42-13, 43-1-3, 4-3,45-1-3, 45-27-2 files.
    St. Laurent Settlement file;
    Journals and Correspondence of Surveyors.
"Evidence of George H. Young in Champagne vs. Queen," Winnipeg, Exchequer Court, 14 September 1892.
Hillyard Mitchell Papers, A349, accounts and correspondence.
Journals of the Legislative Council of the North West Territories, 1877–1887.
:   Morton, A.S., "Historical Geography of the Canadian West to 1870," Vols. 4 and 10.
North West Territories Government (1870–1905):
:   Orders-in-council; Petitions;
    Sessional Papers 1887–1900 (microfilms).
Saskatchewan, Department of Justice, Land Titles Offices,
Prince Albert, land files relating to Batoche Survey Maps, Townships 42, 43, 44, 45, 1-3, 27-2, 28-2.
Saskatchewan, Department of Agriculture, Lands Branch files, AG II.
Saskatchewan, Department of the Attorney-General, Series "G", Correspondence.
Saskatchewan, Department of Natural Resources,
:   Journals and Correspondence of Surveyors.
    Provincial Lands Branch files
Saskatchewan, Department of Tourism and Renewable Resources, Land Surveys Branch, Field Notebooks.

St. Boniface Historical Society [SBHS] (Société historique de Saint-Boniface)

St. Boniface Archdiocesan Archives [SBAA] (also Corporation archiépiscopale catholique romaine de Saint-Boniface)
Bishop Langevin Papers:
:   Letters from Father Julien Moulin
Bishop Provencher Papers;
:   Copies of letters to Bishop of Québec, 1843–53.
Bishop Taché Papers:
:   Letters from Emmanuel Champagne, Maxime Lépine and Louis Schmidt
    Letters from Fathers André, Fourmond, Lacombe, Lestanc, Moulin and Végréville
    Louis Schmidt, « Mouvement des Métis à Saint Laurent, Saskatchewan, Territoires du Nord Ouest en 1884. »
    Louis Schmidt to A.M. Burgess, deputy-minister of the Interior, 26 May 1885 about petitions sent by the Métis between 1881 and 1885 (copy).
    Journal of Reverend Gabriel Cloutier, 1886.

Fisher-Deschambault Papers
    Correspondence and genealogies.
Pierre Picton Papers:
    Genealogies of Métis families.
Union Nationale Métisse de Saint-Joseph du Manitoba Papers.
    Minutes 1887–1930

University of Alberta Archives [UAA]

MG92, William Pearce Papers.

University of Saskatchewan Archives

A.S. Morton Collection.

PUBLISHED SOURCES

Adam, Graeme Mercer. *The Canadian Northwest: Its History and Troubles from the Early Days of the Fur Trade to the Era of the Railway and the Settlers; with Incidents of Travel in the Regions and the Narrative of the Three Insurrections.* Toronto: Rose Publishing, 1885.

Adams, Howard. *Prison of Grass: Canada From the Native Point of View.* Saskatoon: Fifth House, 2nd ed., 1989.

———. *A Tortured People: The Politics of Colonization.* Penticton: Theytus Books, 1995.

Armstrong, Gail Paul. "The Métis, The Development and the Decline of Métis Influence in an Early Saskatchewan Community." In *Wood Mountain Uplands: From Big Muddy to the Frenchman River, Wood Mountain, Saskatchewan*, ed. Thelma Poirier. Wood Mountain: Wood Mountain Historical Society, 2000.

Bakker, Peter. *A Language of Our Own: The Genesis of Michif, the Mixed Cree-French Language of the Canadian Métis.* New York: Oxford University Press, 1997.

Ballentyne, Robert M. *Hudson Bay; or Everyday Life in the Wilds of North America During Six Years Residence in the Territories of the Honourable Hudson's Bay Company*, 2nd ed. Edmonton: Hurtig, 1972.

Barbeau, Marius. "Blason, géographie et généalogie populaires du Québec," *Journal of American Folklore* 33, no. 130 (1920): 346–66.

Barkwell, Lawrence, Leah Dorion, and Audreen Hourie, eds. *Metis Legacy: Michif Culture, Heritage, and Folkways.* Saskatoon: Gabriel Dumont Institute and Pemmican Publications, 2006.

Barkwell, Lawrence J., Leah Dorion, and Darren R. Préfontaine, eds. *Metis Legacy.* Winnipeg: Pemmican Publications, 2001.

Barrera, Laura Caso. The Canadian Métis and the Mexican Mayas: A Cross Cultural Study of Native Land Struggles. M.A. thesis, University of Calgary, 1992.

Barron, F. Laurie. "The CCF and the Development of Métis Colonies in Saskatchewan during the Premiership of T.C. Douglas 1944–61." Métis National Council website, 2004.

Battiste, Marie, and James Youngblood Henderson. *Protecting Indigenous Knowledge and Heritage: A Global Challenge.* Saskatoon: Purich Publishing, 2000.

Begg, Alexander. *History of the North West.* Toronto: Rose Publishing, 1894–1895, 3 vols.

Bellman Jennifer L., and Chris C. Hanks. "Northern Métis and the Fur Trade." In *Picking Up the Threads: Métis History in the Mackenzie*, Basin, Métis Heritage Association of the Northwest Territories and Parks Canada, 37–38. Yellowknife: Outcrop, 1998.

Berthelot, Hector. *Le bon vieux temps.* Montréal: Beauchemin, 1916.

Binnema, Theodore, Gerhard Ens, and R.C. MacLeod, eds. *From Rupert's Land to Canada.* Edmonton: University of Alberta Press, 2001.

Bird, Madeline, and Agnes Sutherland, *Living Kindness: The Dream of My Life: the Memoirs of Metis Elder Madeline Bird.* Yellowknife: Outcrop, 1991.

Black, Norman F. *History of Saskatchewan and Old North West.* Regina: North West Historical Society 1913, 2 vols.

Bolt, Christine. *Victorian Attitudes to Race.* Toronto: University of Toronto Press, 1971.

Borlase, Tim. *The Labrador Settlers, Métis and Kabhunângajuit.* Goose Bay: Labrador East Integrated School Board, 1994.

Boucher, Réal. *Marin Boucher 1588–1671 to Jean-Baptiste Boucher 1838–1911 and his Descendants.* N.p.: The Author: 2001.

Bourgeault, Ron. "Louis Riel: Hero of His People?" In *Expressions in Canadian Native Studies*, ed. Ron F. Laliberte et al., 222–26. Saskatoon: University of Saskatchewan Extension Press, 2000.

———. "The Struggle for Class and Nation: The Origin of the Métis in Canada and the National Question." In *1492–1991: Five Centuries of Imperialism and Resistance*, ed. Ron Bourgeault et al., 153–88. *Socialist Studies*, vol. 8. Winnipeg: Society for Socialist Studies, Fernwood Publishing, 1992.

Bourgeault, Ron, et al., eds., "1492–1991: Five Centuries of Imperialism and Resistance," *Socialist Studies*, vol. 9. Winnipeg: Fernwood Publishing, 1992.

Boyd, Diane M. The Rise and Development of Female Catholic Education in the 19th Century Red River Region: The Case of Catherine [Lacerte] Mulaire. MA thesis, University of Manitoba, 1999.

Brabant, Sylvie. *Sur les traces de Riel*. Montréal: Productions du Rapide-Blanc, 2003.

Brown, Jennifer S.H. "People of Myth, People of History: A Look at Recent Writings on the Métis," *Acadiensis* 17, no. 1 (1987): 150–63.

———. *Strangers in Blood: Fur Trade Company Families in Indian Country*. Vancouver: University of British Columbia Press, 1980.

———. "Women as Centre and Symbol in the Emergence of Métis Communities," *Canadian Journal of Native Studies* 3, no. 1 (1983): 39–46.

Bumsted, J.M. *Louis Riel v. Canada: The Making of a Rebel*. Winnipeg: Great Plains Publications, 2001.

Burley, Kevin H., ed., *The Development of Canada's Staples, 1867–1938: A Documentary Collection*. Toronto: McClelland & Stewart, 1970.

Butler, William F. *The Wild North Land*. Edmonton: Hurtig, 1968; reprint of 1872 edition.

Camp, Gregory S. The Turtle Mountain Plains-Chippewas and Métis. PhD thesis, University of New Mexico, 1987.

Campbell, Maria. *Halfbreed*. New York: Saturday Review Press, 1973.

———. *Stories of the Road Allowance People*. Penticton: Theytus Books, 1995; 2nd ed.

Canada. Parliament. *Annual Report of the Department of the Interior*, 1884–1916.

———. *Annual Report of the North West and Royal North West Mounted Police Commissioner*, 1886–1910.

———. "Census of population and agriculture of the North West provinces, Manitoba, Saskatchewan, Alberta." *Sessional Paper No. 17A*. Ottawa: King's Printer, 1907.

———. *Census of the Three Provisional Districts of the North West Territories 1884–85*. Ottawa: Maclean, 1886.

———. *Consolidated Statutes of Canada*, 1873, 1874, 1880, 1885.

———. *Debates*, House of Commons, 1878–1900.

———. *Journals*, House of Commons, 1884–1888.

———. *Report of the Halfbreed Commissioners*, 1899, 1900.

———. *Sessional Papers*, 1884–1887, 1900–1902.

Carrière, Gaston. *Dictionnaire biographique des Oblats de Marie-Immaculée au Canada*. Ottawa: Éditions de l'université d'Ottawa, 1976–1979, 3 vols.

Chabot, Richard. *Le curé de campagne et la contestation locale au Québec de 1791 aux troubles de 1837–1838*. Montréal: Hurtubise HMH, 1975.

Champagne, Antoine. *Les La Vérendrye et le poste de l'Ouest*. Québec: Presses de l'université Laval, 1968.

Charette, Guillaume. *L'Espace de Louis Goulet*. Winnipeg: Éditions Bois-Brûlés, 1976.

Charlebois, Peter. *The Life of Louis Riel*. Toronto: New Canada Publications, 1975.

Chartrand, Paul L.A.H. *Manitoba's Métis Settlement Scheme of 1870*. Saskatoon: Native Law Centre, 1991.

———. "A Questionable Approach to Métis Land Claims," *National* 19, no. 2 (Summer 1992): 19.

Choquette, Robert. *The Oblate Assault on Canada's Northwest*. Ottawa: University of Ottawa Press, 1995.

Clarke, Margaret L. Reconstituting Fur Trade Community in the Assiniboine Basin, 1793–1812. MA thesis, University of Calgary, 1997.

———. Review of Blair Stonechild and Bill Waiser, Loyal till death: Indians and the North-West Rebellion. Calgary, Fifth House, 1997. *Prairie Forum* 23, no. 2 (Fall 1998): 267–73.

———. "Skinning the Narrative: The Story of the Battle of Fish Creek," *Prairie Forum* 27, no. 2 (Fall 2002): 255–62.

Collet, Marcel, producer, *Francophonie Amérique: Le monde qui parlait aux arbres*. St-Boniface : Les Productions Rivard, 2003.
Combet, Denis, ed., *Les mémoires – The Memoirs de/of Gabriel Dumont*. Trans. Lise Gaboury-Diallo. St. Boniface: Éditions du Blé.
Cooper, Barry. *Alexander Kennedy Isbister: A Respectable Critique of the Honourable Company*. Ottawa: Carleton University Press, 1988.
Corrigan, Samuel W., and Lawrence J. Barkwell, eds., *The Struggle for Recognition: Canadian Justice and the Métis Nation*. Winnipeg: Pemmican Publications, 1991.
Coues, Elliot, ed. *New Light on the Early History of the Greater Northwest; The Manuscript Journals of Alexander Henry and David Thompson, 1799–1814*. Minneapolis: Ross & Haines, 1965, vol. 2: "The Saskatchewan and Columbia Rivers" reprint.
Coutts, Robert. *The Road to the Rapids: Nineteenth-Century Church and Society at St. Andrew's Parish, Red River*. Calgary: University of Calgary Press, 2000.
Coutts Robert, and Richard Stuart, eds., *The Forks and the Battle of Seven Oaks in Manitoba History*. Winnipeg: Manitoba Historical Society, 1994.
Crawford, John C., ed., *The Michif Dictionary: Turtle Mountain Chippewa Cree*. Winnipeg: Pemmican, 1983.
Crnkovich, Mary. *Gossip: A Spoken History of Women in the North*. Canadian Arctic Resources, Committee Publishing Program, 1990.
Davidson, G.C. *History of the North West Company*. New York: Russell, 1967, reprint.
Dechêne, Louise. *Habitants et marchands de Montréal au 17e siècle*. Paris-Montréal: Plon, 1974.
Devine, Heather. *The People Who Own Themselves*. Calgary: University of Calgary Press, 2004.
Dick, Lyle. "The Seven Oaks Incident and the Construction of a Historical Tradition, 1816–1970," *Journal of the Canadian Historical Association* 2 (1991): 91–113.
Dickason, Olive P. *Canada's First Nations: A History of Founding Peoples from the Earliest Times*. Toronto: McClelland & Stewart, 2001, 3rd ed.
———. *Canada's Founding Peoples from Earliest Times*. Toronto: McClelland & Stewart, 1992.
———. *The Myth of the Savage and the Beginnings of French Colonialism in the Americas*. Edmonton: University of Alberta Press, 1984.
Dorge, Lionel. "The Métis and Canadien Councillors of Assiniboia," *The Beaver* 305 (Summer 1974): 12–19; 305 (Autumn 1974): 39–45; 305 (Winter 1974): 51–58.
Dorion, Leah, Todd Paquin, and Darren R. Préfontaine (producers). *The Métis People: Our Story*. Edmonton: Arnold Publishing and the Gabriel Dumont Institute, 2000.
———. *The Story of the Crescent Lake Métis: Our Life on the Road Allowance*. Gabriel Dumont Institute, 2002.
Dumont, Yvon. "Metis Nationalism: Then and Now," In *The Forks and the Battle of Seven Oaks in Manitoba History*, ed. Robert Coutts and Richard Stuart. Winnipeg: Manitoba Historical Society, 1994.
Dunn, Martin F. "All My Relations – The Other Métis." Background paper prepared for the Métis Circle Special Consultation of the Royal Commission on Aboriginal Peoples, Ottawa: March 1994.
Dusenberry, Verne. *The Métis of Montana*. New York: Hasting House, 1965.
Ellis, George E. *The Red Man and the White Man in North America*. Boston: Little, Brown and Co., 1882.
Ens, Gerhard. *Homeland to Hinterland: The Changing Worlds of the Red River Métis in the Nineteenth Century*. Toronto: University of Toronto Press, 1996.
———. "Métis Ethnicity, Personal Identity and the Development of Capitalism in the Western Interior: The Case of Johnny Grant." In *From Rupert's Land to Canada: Essays in Honour of John E. Foster*, ed. Theodore Binnema et al., 161–77. Edmonton: University of Alberta Press, 2001.
———. "Métis Lands in Manitoba," *Manitoba History* 5 (Spring 1983): 2–11.
Ferland, Marcien. *Au temps de la Prairie: l'histoire des Métis de l'ouest canadien racontée par Auguste Vermette, neveu de Louis Riel*. Saint-Boniface: Éditions du Blé, 2000.

Flanagan, Thomas. *First Nations? Second Thoughts*. Montreal and Kingston: McGill-Queen's University Press, 2000.
———. *Louis "David" Riel: Prophet of the New World*. Toronto: University of Toronto Press, 1979; 2nd ed., 1996.
———. *Métis Lands in Manitoba*. Calgary: University of Calgary Press, 1991.
———. *Riel and the 1885 Rebellion Reconsidered*. Saskatoon: Western Prairie Producer Books, 1983; 2nd printing in 1999.
Foster, John E. "Wintering, the Outsider Adult Male and the Ethnogenesis of the Western Plains Métis," *Prairie Forum* 19, no. 1 (Spring 1994): 1–13. Reprinted In *From Rupert's Land to Canada*, ed. Theodore Binnema, Gerhard J. Ens, and R.C. Macleod. 179–92. Edmonton: University of Alberta Press, 2001.
Fowke, V.C. *The National Policy and the Wheat Economy*. Toronto: University of Toronto Press, 1957.
Frémont, Donatien. *Les secrétaires de Riel, Louis Schmidt, Henry Jackson et Philippe Garnot*. Montréal: Éditions Chanteclerc, 1953.
Friesen, Gerald. *River Road: Essays on Manitoba and Prairie History*. Winnipeg: University of Manitoba Press, 1996.
Fumoleau, René. *As Long As This Land Shall Last: A History of Treaty 8 and Treaty 11, 1870–1939*, 2nd. ed. Calgary: University of Calgary Press, 2004.
Gabriel Dumont Institute. *Remembrances: Métis Veterans*. Regina, 1997.
Gareau(lt) [family]. *Histoire de Ludger Gareault et de sa famille*. Bellevue, Saskatchewan: n.p., n.d.
Gérin, Léon. "L'Habitant de Saint-Justin," *Mémoires de la Société Royale du Canada*, series 2, 4, no. 1 (1898): 139–216.
Giraud, Marcel. *Le Métis canadien: Son rôle dans l'histoire des provinces de l'Ouest*. Paris: Institut d'Ethnologie, 1945.
———. *The Métis in the Canadian West*. Edmonton: University of Alberta Press, 1986.
Giscard, Gaston. *Dans la Prairie canadienne – On the Canadian Prairie*. Regina: Canadian Plains Research Center, 1982.
Gleach, Frederic W. "Controlled Speculation: Interpreting the Saga of Pocahantas and Captain John Smith." In *Reading Beyond Words: Contexts for Native History*, ed. Elizabeth Vibert and Jennifer S.H. Brown, 21–42. Peterborough: Broadview Press, 1998.
Goyette, Linda. "The X files," *Canadian Geographic* (March/April 2003): 70–80.
Groulx, Lionel. "La famille canadienne-française, ses traditions, son rôle." In Lionel Groulx, *Notre maitre le passé*, 115–51. Montréal: Granger, 1936, 3rd ed.
Hall, D.J. "T.O. Davis and Federal Politics in Saskatchewan," *Saskatchewan History* 30, no. 2 (Spring 1977): 56–62.
Hareven, Tamara K. "Family Time and Historical Time." In *The Family*, ed. A.S. Rossi, J. Kagan, and T.K. Hareven. New York: W.W. Norton, 1978.
Harvard, V. *The French Half-breeds in the Northwest: Report of the Smithsonian Institution*. Washington: Government Printing Office, 1880.
Hatt, Ken. "The North West Scrip Commission as Federal Policy – Some Initial Findings," *Canadian Journal of Native Studies* 3, no. 1 (1983): 117–29.
Hawkes, John. *Saskatchewan and its People*. Chicago and Regina: S.J. Clark, 1924, 2 vols.
Henderson's Directory of the North-West Territories [title varies], 1895–1905. The Henderson Directory Company, Winnipeg.
The Herald (Battleford). 1878–88.
Hildebrandt, Walter. *The Battle of Batoche: British Small Warfare and the Entrenched Métis*. Ottawa: Environment Canada-Parks, 1985.
Howard, Joseph Kinsey. *Strange Empire*. Toronto: Swan Publishing, 1965.
Huel, Raymond. "Louis Schmidt: The Patriarch of St. Louis." *Saskatchewan History* 40, no. 1 (1987): 1–21.
———. "The Oblates, the Métis, and 1885: The Breakdown of Traditional Relationships," *Canadian Historical Association, Historical Studies* 56 (1989): 9–29.

———. *Proclaiming the Gospel to the Indians and the Métis*. Edmonton: University of Alberta Press, 1996.
Jaenen, Cornelius. *Friend and Foe*. Toronto: McClelland & Stewart, 1976.
———. "Miscegenation in Eighteenth Century New-France." In *New Dimensions in Ethnohistory*, ed. Barry Gough and Laird Christie. Canadian Ethnology Service, Canadian Museum of Civilization. Mercury Series, no. 120, 1991.
Jérôme, Martin. *Coup d'oeil rétrospectif sur ce qu'a été la nation métisse dans les affaires politiques lors de l'entrée de la province dans la confédération et ce qu'elle est de nos jours*. Winnipeg: Manitoba Free Press, 1892.
Kermoal, Nathalie. « Les rôles et les souffrances des femmes métisses lors de la Résistance de 1870 et de la Rébellion de 1885 », *Prairie Forum* 19, no. 2 (Fall 1994): 153–68.
Lagassé, Jean. *The People of Indian Ancestry in Manitoba*. Winnipeg: Manitoba Department of Agriculture and Immigration, 1957.
Laliberte, Ron F., et al., eds. *Expressions in Canadian Native Society*. Saskatoon: University Extension Press, 2000.
LaRocque, Emma. "Conversations on Métis Identity," *Prairie Fire* 7, no. 1 (1986): 19–24
Lavallée, Guy.*The Métis of St. Laurent, Manitoba: Their Life and Stories,1920–1988*. Winnipeg: The Author, 2003.
———. *Prayers of a Métis Priest: Conversations with God on the Political Experiences of the Canadian Métis 1992–94*. Winnipeg: Kromar Printing, 1997.
Laverdure, Patline, and Ida Rose Allard, *The Michif Dictionary: Turtle Mountain Chippewa Cree*. Winnipeg: Pemmican, 1983.
Lavigne, Solange. *Kaleidoscope: Many Cultures–One Faith, The Roman Catholic Dioceses of Prince Albert, 1891–1990*. Muenster: St. Peter's Press, 1990.
Le Chevallier, Jules. *Batoche; les missionnaires du Nord-Ouest pendant les troubles de 1885*. Montréal: Presse dominicaine, 1941.
———. « Aux prises avec la tourmente; les missionnaires de la colonie de Saint Laurent de Grandin durant l'insurrection métisse de 1885 ». Ottawa: Revue de l'université d'Ottawa, 1940.
———. « Saint-Laurent, et Saint-André de la Prairie-Ronde », Le Patriote de l'Ouest (Prince Albert), 14 July 1937.
Le Patriote de l'Ouest (Duck Lake and Prince Albert, Saskatchewan), 1910–15; 14 July 1937.
Lischke, Ute, and David T. McNab, eds. *Métis Identities and Family Histories*. Waterloo: Wilfrid Laurier University Press, 2007.
Lorne, Marquis of (Duke of Argyll). *Manitoba and the North-West Territory*. London: Caustin, 1881.
———. *Memories of Canada and Scotland*. Montreal: Dawson, 1884.
Lussier, Antoine S., and D. Bruce Sealy, eds. *The Other Natives, the–les Métis, 1700–1885*. Winnipeg: Manitoba Métis Federation Press and Éditions Bois-Brûlés, 1978, 3 vols.
Lutz, Hartmut, Murray Hamilton, and Donna Heimbecker, eds., *Howard Adams: Otapaway!* Saskatoon: Gabriel Dumont Institute, 2005.
Le Manitoba (Saint-Boniface). "Échos du Nord-Ouest," 1883–1900.
Manuel, George, and Michael Posluns. *The Fourth World: An Indian Reality*. Don Mills: Collier-Macmillan, 1974.
Martel, Gilles. *Le messianisme de Louis Riel (1844–1885)*. Waterloo: Wilfrid Laurier University Press, 1984.
Martin, Chester. *"Dominion Lands" Policy*. Toronto: McClelland & Stewart, 1973; Carleton Library Series, No. 69.
Massicotte, E.Z. « Congés de traite conservés aux Archives de la province de Québec, 1739–1752, » Rapport de l'archiviste de la province de Québec, 1922–23.
———. *Nos Canadiens d'autrefois*. Montréal: Granger, 1923.
McCarthy, Martha. *From the Great River to the Ends of the Earth: Oblate Missions to the Dene, 1847–1921*. Edmonton: University of Alberta Press, 1995.

McCullough, Alan. "Parks Canada and the 1885 Rebellion /Uprising/ Resistance," *Prairie Forum* 27, no. 2 (Fall 2002): 185.

McInnes, May Elizabeth. *Essentials of Communicable Disease.* St. Louis: C.V. Mioshy, 1975.

McPhillips' Alphabetical and Business Directory of Saskatchewan, North West Territories. Qu'Appelle: "The Progress" Book and Job Office, 1888.

Métis Association of Northwest Territories and Parks Canada. *Picking Up the Threads: Métis History in the Mackenzie Basin.* Yellowknife: Outcrop, 1998.

Miller, J. R. "From Riel to the Métis," *Canadian Historical Review* 69 (1988): 1–20.

Millions, Erin. "Breaking the Mold: A Historiographical Review of Saskatchewan Women's History, 1880–1930," *Saskatchewan History* 54, no. 2 (Fall 2002): 31–49.

Milloy, John S. *A National Crime: The Canadian Government and the Residential School System, 1879 to 1986.* Winnipeg: University of Manitoba Press, 1999.

Milne, Brad. "The Historiography of Métis Land Dispersal, 1870–1890," *Manitoba History* 30 (1995): 39–40.

Missions des Oblats de Marie-Immaculée. 1871–1915.

Montpetit, Raymond. *Le temps des fêtes au Québec.* Montreal: Éditions de l'Homme, 1978.

Morice, Adrien-Gabriel. *Dictionnaire historique des Canadiens et des Métis français de l'Ouest.* Saint-Boniface: The Author, 1908.

———. *La race métisse: Étude critique en marge d'un livre récent.* Winnipeg: The Author, 1938.

Morris, Alexander. *The Treaties of Canada with the Indians of Manitoba and the North-West Territories.* Toronto: Coles Publishing, 1971; reprint of 1880 edition.

Morton, Arthur S. *A History of the Canadian West to 1870–71.* Toronto: University of Toronto Press, 1973; 2nd ed.

Morton, W.L. Introduction. In *Eden Colvile: London Correspondence Inward, 1849–1852*, ed. E.E. Rich and A.M. Johnson, lxxix–lxxxix. London: Hudson Bay Record Society, 1956.

Mulvaney, C.P. *The History of the North-West Rebellion of 1885.* Toronto: A.H. Hovey, 1886.

Noonan, Edward D., and Percy G. Hodges. "The Saskatchewan Metis." Saskatoon: Gabriel Dumont Institute, Métis Historical Collection, 1943, 139p.

North West Territories Legislature. *The Consolidated Ordinances of the North West Territories, 1898.* Regina: Queen's Printer, 1899.

———. *Journals of the Legislative Assembly of the North West Territories.* Regina: R.B. Gordon, 1888–1902; vols. 1–9.

Ouimet, A., and B.A.T. de Montigny. *Riel, la vérité sur la question métisse.* Beauceville: Presses de l'Éclaireur, 1979; originally published in 1889.

Overvold [Burger], Joanne, *Our Metis Heritage: A Portrayal.* Yellowknife: Metis Association of the Northwest Territories, 1976.

Painchaud, Robert. *Un rêve français dans le peuplement de la Prairie.* Saint-Boniface: Éditions des Plaines, 1987.

Palud-Pelletier, Noëlie. *Louis: Fils des Prairies.* Éditions des Plaines, 1983 (English trans: Pemmican, 1990; 2005).

Pannekoek, Frits. "Métis Studies: The Development of a Field and New Directions." In *From Rupert's Land to Canada*, ed. Theodore Binnema, Gerhard J. Ens, and R.C. Macleod, 111–28. Edmonton: University of Alberta Press, 2001.

———. *A Snug Little Flock: The Social Origins of the Riel Resistance, 1869–1870.* Winnipeg: Watson & Dwyer, 1991.

Papen, Robert. "Un parler français méconnu de l'Ouest Canadien: Le Métis. « Quand même qu'on parle français, ça veut pas dire qu'on est des Canayens! »." In *La Langue, la culture et la société des francophones de l'Ouest*, ed. Pierre-Yves Mocquais, André Lalonde, and Bernard Wilhelm, 121–36. Regina: Institut de Recherche du Centre d'Études Bilingues, 1984.

Payment, Diane P. "Batoche," In *The Oxford Companion to Canadian History*, ed. Gerald Hallowell, 155. Toronto: Oxford University Press, 2002.

———. *Batoche: 1870–1910.* Saint-Boniface: Éditions du Blé, 1983.

———. "Batoche after 1885: A Society in Transition." In *1885 and After: Native Society in Transition*, ed. Laurie Barron and James B. Waldram, 173–87. Regina: Canadian Plains Research Center, 1986.
———. "Charles Nolin." In *Dictionary of Canadian Biography*, dir. Ramsay Cook and Jean Hamelin, vol. 13: "1901–1910," 770–72. Toronto: University of Toronto Press, 1994.
———. The Ferry Crossing and Related Trails, ca. 1870–1921 and Caron Sr. House Study. Parks Canada. Microfiche Report No. 409, 1986-87.
———. *"The Free People – Otipemisiwak": Batoche, Saskatchewan 1870–1930*. Ottawa: Environment Canada-Parks, 1990.
———. « *Les gens libres – Otipemisiwak* » *: Batoche, Saskatchewan 1870–1930*. Environnement Canada–Service des Parcs, 1990. English trans. published as: *The Free People – Otipemisiwak: Batoche, Saskatchewan, 1870–1930*.
———. « Les héritiers et les héritières de Louis Riel: Un aperçu des relations entre les Métis et les Canadiens français dans l'ouest canadien », *Le dialogue avec les cultures minoritaires*, dir. Eric Waddell, 53–76. Québec: Presses de l'université Laval, 1999.
———. "Jean-Baptiste Letendre dit Batoche." In *Dictionary of Canadian Biography*, ed. F.G. Halpenny and Jean Hamelin, vol. 6: "1821–1835." Toronto: University of Toronto Press, 1987. www.biographi.ca.
———. "Jean-Baptiste Letendre dit Batoche." In *Dictionnaire biographique du Canada*, dir. Jean Hamelin, vol. 6: "1821–35," 437–38. Québec: Presses de l'université Laval, 1987.
———. "Maxime Lépine." In *Dictionary of Canadian Biography*, ed. F.G. Halpenny and Jean Hamelin, vol. 12: "1891–1900," 602–3. Toronto: University of Toronto Press, 1990.
———. "The Métis," *Plains Volume, Handbook of North American Indians*, Raymond J. De Maillie, ed., 1, No. 13, Part 1. Washington: Smithsonian Institution, 2001, 661–76.
———. "The Métis Nation of the Northwest Territories: The Historic Athabasca-Mackenzie," *Metis Legacy*, ed. Lawrence J. Barkwell, Leah Dorion, and Darren R. Préfontaine, 157–68. Winnipeg: Pemmican Publications, 2000.
———. "Métis People in Motion: From Red River to the Mackenzie Basin." In *Picking up the Threads: Métis People in Motion in the Mackenzie Basin*, 69–109. Yellowknife: Outcrop, 1994.
———. "Monsieur Batoche," *Saskatchewan History* 22, no. 3 (Autumn 1979): 81–103.
———. « ‹ On n'est pas métchifs nous autres ›: un aperçu des relations entre les femmes francophones au Manitoba durant les années 1810–1920 », *Bulletin de la Société historique de Saint-Boniface* 3 (1992): 13–18.
———. "Onésime Dorval: « la bonne demoiselle »," *Saskatchewan History* 55, no. 1 (Spring 2003): 31–35.
———. A Structural and Material Culture History of St. Antoine de Padoue [Mission and Parish], Batoche. Parks Canada, Microfiche Report No. 92, 1981–82.
———. "'La vie en rose?': Métis Women at Batoche 1870–1920." In *Women of the First Nations*, ed. Christine Miller and Patricia Chuchryk, 19–37. Winnipeg: University of Manitoba Press, 1996.
———. The Willow Cree of One-Arrow First Nation and the Métis of Batoche, 1870–1920: An Ambivalent Relationship. Parks Canada, Western and Northern Service Centre, Cultural Resource Services, 1997.
———. "Xavier Letendre." In *Dictionary of Canadian Biography*, dir. Ramsay Cook and Jean Hamelin, vol. 13: "1901–1910," 595–96. Toronto: University of Toronto Press, 1994.
Pearce, William. "Causes of the Riel Rebellion: A Personal View," *Alberta Historical Review* 16, no. 4 (Autumn 1968): 19–26; presented to Alberta Land Surveyors' Association in 1926.
———. *Detailed Report upon all Claims to Land and the Right to Participate in the North-West Halfbreed Grant by Settlers along the South [Saskatchewan] and Vicinity*. Ottawa: Maclean, Roger & Co., 1886.
Pelletier, Émile. *Le vécu des Métis*. Winnipeg: Éditions Bois-Brûlés, 1980.
Peterson, Jacqueline. "Many Roads to Red River: Métis Genesis in the Great Lakes Region, 1680–1815." In *The New Peoples: Being and Becoming Métis in North America*, ed. J. Peterson and Jennifer S.H. Brown, 40–45. Winnipeg: University of Manitoba Press, 1985.

Peterson, Jacqueline, and Jennifer S.H. Brown, eds. *The New Peoples: Being and Becoming Métis in North America*. Winnipeg: University of Manitoba Press, 1985.

Petitot, Émile. *En route pour la mer glaciale*. Paris: Letouzey et ane, 1887.

Poelzer, Dolores T., and Irene A. Poelzer. *In Our Own Words: Northern Saskatchewan Women Speak Out*. Saskatoon: One Sky, 1986.

Poirier, Thelma. *The Bead Pot*, Winnipeg: Pemmican, 1993.

Préfontaine, Darren R. Review of *Loyal till Death*, *Prairie Forum* 23, no. 2 (Fall 1998): 275–78.

Preston, Richard, ed., Introduction. In *Cree Narrative*. Montreal and Kingston: McGill-Queen's University Press, 2002.

Prud'homme, L.A. « Horace Bélanger, facteur en chef de la Compagnie de la Baie d'Hudson », *Revue Canadienne* 27 (1891): 464–68.

Ray, Arthur J. "Native History on Trial: Confessions of an Expert Witness," *Canadian Historical Review* 84 (June 2003): 254–73.

Richtik, James M. "The Policy Framework for Settling the Canadian West, 1870–1880," *Agricultural History* 49, no. 4 (October 1975): 613–28.

Rivard, Ron, and Catherine Littlejohn. *The History of the Metis of Willow-Bunch*. Saskatoon: The Authors, 2003.

Robin, Martin. *The Bad and the Lonely*. Toronto: S. Lorimer, 1976.

Robinson, H.M. *The Great Fur Land or Sketches of Life in the Hudson's Bay Territory*. Winnipeg: Coles Canadiana, 1972.

Rodwell, Lloyd, W. "Land Claims in the Prince Albert Settlement," *Saskatchewan History* 19, no. 1 (Winter 1969): 1–33.

Rondeau, Clovis, and Adrien Chabot, *Histoire de Willow Bunch, Saskatchewan, 1870–1970*. Gravelbourg: Diocese of Gravelbourg, 1970, 2nd ed.

Royal Commission on Aboriginal Peoples Report. "Métis Perspectives," 5: 199–384. Ottawa, 1996.

Rumilly, Robert. *Histoire de la province de Québec*. Montréal: Fides, 1973, 2nd ed., Vol. 5: *Louis Riel*.

Saskatchewan Archives Board. *Directory of the Council and Legislative Assembly of the North West Territories, 1876–1905*. Saskatoon, 1970.

Scofield, Gregory. *Thunder through My Veins: Memories of a Métis Childhood*. Toronto: Harper Collins, 1999.

Schilling, Rita. *Gabriel's Children*. Saskatoon Métis Local No. 11, 1983.

Séguin, Robert-Lionel. *La civilisation traditionnelle de "l'habitant" aux 17e et 18e siècles*. Montreal: Fides, 1967.

Siggins, Maggie. *Riel: A Life of Revolution*. Toronto: Harper Collins, 1994.

Silver, Arthur. "French Québec and the Métis Question, 1869–1885," In *The West and the Nation: Essays in Honour of W.L. Morton*. ed. Carl Berger and Ramsay Cook, 102–6. Toronto: McClelland & Stewart, 1976.

Simoni, Pierre. "Science anthropologique et racisme à l'époque de l'expansion coloniale: le cas du Grand dictionnaire universel du XIXe siècle de Pierre Larousse," *Historical Papers/ Communications historiques* (1980): 167–84.

Sissons, Constance. [Memoirs of] *John Kerr*. Toronto: Oxford University Press, 1946.

Skelton, O.D. *Life and Letters of Sir W. Laurier*. Toronto: McClelland & Stewart, 1981 (reprint) [Carleton Library Series, no. 21], vol. 1: "1841–1896."

Smith, Donald B. *Honoré Jaxon: Prairie Visionary*. Regina: Coteau Books, 2007.

———. "Honoré Joseph Jaxon: A Man Who Lived For Others," *Saskatchewan History* 34, no. 3 (Autumn 1981): 81–102.

———. Le "Sauvage" d'après les historiens canadiens français des XIXe et XXe siècles. Cahiers du Québec. Montréal: Hurtubise HMH, 1979.

Southesk, Earl of. *Saskatchewan and the Rocky Mountains*. Tokyo: C.E. Tuttle, 1969; reprint of 1875 edition.

Sprague, Donald N. *Canada and the Métis, 1869–1885*. Waterloo: Wilfrid Laurier University Press, 1988.

———. "Government Lawlessness in the Administration of Manitoba Land Claims, 1870–1887," *Manitoba Law Journal* 10, no. 4 (1980): 415–41.
———. "The Manitoba Land Question, 1870–1882," *Journal of Canadian Studies* 15, no. 3 (1980): 74–84.
Sprague, Donald N., and R.P. Frye, eds. *The Genealogy of the First Métis Nation: The Development and Dispersal of the Red River Settlement 1820–1900*. Winnipeg: Pemmican, 1983.
Spry, Irene. "The Métis and Mixed Bloods in Rupert's Land Before 1870." In *The New Peoples*, ed. J. Peterson and Jennifer S.H. Brown, 95–118. Winnipeg: University of Manitoba Press, 1985.
Stanley, George F.G. *The Birth of Western Canada*. Toronto: University of Toronto Press, 1966; 2nd ed.
———. "The Half-Breed Rising of 1875," *Canadian Historical Review* 17, no. 1 (December 1936): 399–412.
———. *Louis Riel*. Toronto: University of Toronto Press, 1963.
Stonechild, Blair, and Bill Waiser, *Loyal till Death: Indian and the North-West Rebellion*. Calgary: Fifth House, 1997.
St-Onge, Nicole. "The Dissolution of a Métis Community: Pointe à Grouette, 1860–1885," *Studies in Political Economy* 18 (Autumn 1985): 149–71.
———. "Memories of Métis Women of Saint-Eustache, Manitoba – 1910–1980," *Oral History Forum d'histoire orale* 19 (1999–2000): 89–111.
———. *St. Laurent, Manitoba: Evolving Metis Identities, 1850–1914*. Regina: Canadian Plains Research Center, 2004.
———. "Variations in Red River: The Traders and Freemen Métis of Saint-Laurent, Manitoba" *Canadian Ethnic Studies* 2, no. 2 (1991): 2–21.
Swan, Ruth. The Crucible: Pembina and the Origins of the Red River Valley Métis. PhD thesis, University of Manitoba, 2003.
Thomas, L.G., ed. *The Prairie West to 1905: A Canadian Sourcebook*. Toronto: Oxford University Press, 1975.
Thomas, L.H. *The Struggle for Responsible Government in the North-West Territories, 1870–97*. Toronto: University of Toronto Press, 1978; 2nd ed.
Times (Prince Albert). Variously titled: *Times and Northwest Review* or *Times and Saskatchewan Review*, 1885–95.
Tobias, John L. "The Origins of the Treaty Rights Movement in Saskatchewan." In *Native Society in Transition*, ed. F.L. Barron and J.B. Waldram. 241–52. Regina: Canadian Plains Research Center, 1986.
Tough, Frank. *'As Their Natural Resources Fail': Native Peoples and the Economic History of Northern Manitoba, 1870–1930*. Vancouver: UBC Press, 1996.
Trémaudan, Auguste-Henri de. *Histoire de la nation métisse*. Montréal: Éditions Albert Lévesque, 1935; reprinted by Éditions du Blé in 1979.
Trofimenkoff, Susan M. *The Dream of a Nation: A Social and Intellectual History of Québec*. Toronto: Macmillan, 1982.
Troupe, Cheryl. *Expressing Our Heritage: Métis Artistic Designs*. Saskatoon: Gabriel Dumont Institute, 2001–02.
Van Kirk, Sylvia. *'Many Tender Ties': Women in Fur Trade Society*. Winnipeg: Watson & Dwyer, 1980.
Weekes, Mary. *[Norbert Welsh] The Last Buffalo Hunter*. Saskatoon: Fifth House, 1994; reprint.
Welsh, Christine. "Voices of Our Grandmothers: Reclaiming Métis Heritage," *Canadian Literature* 131 (1991): 15–24.
Whidden, Lynn (producer) and Ray St. Germain (author and narrator), A Metis Suite. Brandon: All Media Musics, 1995.
White, Richard. *The Middle Ground: Indians, Empires and Republics in the Great Lakes Region, 1650–1815*. Cambridge: Cambridge University Press, 1991.
Woodcock, George. *Gabriel Dumont*. Edmonton: Hurtig, 1975.

Index

A

Aboriginal beliefs and practices, 93, 95
  Church's new tolerance for, 122
Aboriginal land rights, 204. *See also* Métis Aboriginal rights; Métis land rights
  French colonial period, 204
  reaffirmed in Proclamation of 1763, 204
Aboriginal peoples, 22–23, 81
  Aboriginal women, 11, 23, 78, 95
  communal land tenure, 203
  Métis as, 21
Aboriginal rights, 128, 206. *See also* Métis Aboriginal rights
Aboriginal self-determination, 19
Acadians, 21, 41
Adair, Marjorie (Caron), 261
Adams, Graham, 257
Adams, Howard, 2–5, 9, 249, 272, 277
  advocate of union between Métis and Non-Status Indians, 280
  Red Power advocate, 280
Adamson, A.J., 247
agricultural activities. *See* farming
Aicawpow, Isidore. *See* Dumont *dit* Aicawpow, Isidore
Alberta, 124, 192, 257
  demand for young cowboys, 200
  Métis land base, 274
alcohol, 64, 67, 120, 267, 281
  accepted in French Canadian society, 77
  drunkenness and fighting, 78, 81
  homebrewers and bootleggers, 77–78
  increased consumption after 1885, 79
  land speculators and, 78
  licenses, 77, 89
  missionaries' opposition, 98
  and prejudices about Aboriginal peoples, 77–78
  prohibition, 77–78, 80
  stills, 64, 78
Aldous, Mr. (surveyor), 209–10
Allard, Father O., 120
Almighty-Voice, Gabriel, 86–87, 181
Amyotte, Joe, 267, 277
Anderson, James, 140
André, Father Alexis, 34, 96–97, 101, *115*, 116, 125–26, 128, 131, 133, 187, 212
  inflexibility, 98, 100
  intermediary with Canadian government, 37, 96
  meeting with Riel, 110
  North West Mounted Police and, 111
Arcand, Alice (St. Denis), 258
Arcand, Bella (Vandale), 257
Arcand, Florestine (Garnot), 201
Arcand, François, 235
Arcand, Jean-Baptiste, *46*, *65*
Arcand, Nancy (McKay), *46*, *65*
assimilation, 2, 52, 281
Assiniboine, 9–10, 23, 164–65
L' Association Canadienne-Française [de la Saskatchewan], 92
Association of Métis and Non-Status Indians of Saskatchewan (AMNSIS), 281
Athabaska *(le Rabasca)*, 26

B

Back to Batoche Days, xiv, 281–82, 297
Baie St. Paul, 166

Baker, Fred, 177
Bakker, Peter, 14
Ballendine, Peter, 125
bannock, 58, 188
Barbeau, Marius, 75
Barrera, Laura Caso, 9
Batoche, 1, 18, 42, 69, 71, 91, 97, 127, 161, 226
- at center of network of trails, 169
- church (*See* St. Antoine de Padoue)
- cliques, 41–42
- customs and traditions, 52–77
- 1885 Resistance, 84, 112, 139–40
- encroachment of One Arrow reserve, 212
- entrepreneurial spirit, xii
- evolving "cultural community," 18–19, 297
- farm community, 185–86, 191 (*See also* farming)
- Father Myre's colonization campaign, 120
- first families of hunters and winterers, 33
- founding of, 27
- freighting, 169, 171–72
- fur trade, 165
- identification as French Canadian or Scottish (1970s), 296
- immigration from Manitoba and North West Territories, 35
- known for its dancers, 67
- land lots reverted to Municipality of St. Louis, 236
- language, 15, 73–75
- legacy of fear of outsiders and "government agents," 289
- local in new Métis association, 279
- located in parkland belt, 251
- love of good times, 67
- marriage to outsiders (*See* marriage)
- memories of Riel, 4
- "Métis capital of Canada," xvii, 19
- Métis culture maintained, 281
- no career opportunities for young women (1940s and 50s), 263
- North West Mounted Police (NWMP) post at, 154, 180
- occupations, 41, 168
- parish council, 41, 118
- part of Territorial constituency of Lorne, 129, 236
- permanent settlement, 35
- petitions, 131, 149, 153–54, 189, 211, 238
- political activism in 1880s, 267, 275–76
- political power (1888-1908), 159, 161
- population, 36
- population movements within farming community, 190–91
- "the promised land," 201
- prosperity, 179
- railway and, 181, 183
- regrouping of families, 235
- rejection of Métis reserve plan (*See* Métis reserves)
- riverlots, 207, 236
- scrip claims, 190–91, 240, 242, 244
- social organization (1890s), 41
- social relations, 54
- teachers, 106
- transitional period (1880s), 37

Batoche (Catholic Public school), 104
Batoche (Payment), 290
Batoche, Jean-Baptiste. *See* Letendre dit Batoche, Jean-Baptiste
Batoche, Louis [*dit* Batoche], 166
Batoche, Xavier. *See* Letendre *dit* Batoche, Xavier
« Batoche Avenue, » 175
Batoche merchants, 173–77, 183
Batoche Museum, 122, 283–84
Batoche National Historical Site, xiii, xiv, 282–84, 297
- "a Métis place," 299
- audiovisual presentation, 292–93
- buffalo hunt display, 292
- Métis and North West Field Force rifle pits, 291–92
- Métis employees, 287–89, 294–95
- Métis Nation's pressure to take over, 294
- "Métis point of view," 286–87
- misrepresentations, 250
- new management plan (2000), 294
- North West Rebellion theme, 287
- official use of French, 295
- recognition of Michif, 295
- resistance-rebellion debate, 8, 10
- village reconstruction proposal, 291–92
- Visitor Reception Centre (VCR), 286, 291–92

Batoche parish. *See also* St. Antoine de Padoue
- administered by Oblates from Duck Lake after 1936, 120
- Reverend Myre, 119–20
- during 1940s and 1950s, 122
- Tertiaries of St, Francis, 103

Batoche parish register
- dispensations for marriage between cousins, 52

"Batoche Post," 165
Batoche Sports Day, 257
Batoche stores, 173, 175–77, 192, 258, 291
   clothing and fabrics, 57
Batoche's Crossing, 207, 210
"les batochiens," xiii, 251
The Battle of Batoche (Hildebrandt), 290
Battle of Tourond's Coulee/Fish Creek National Historic Site, xiii
Battleford, 91, 103, 169, 171, 191, 200–201, 276
Battleford council. *See also* Territorial government
   adopted St. Laurent Council's regulations, 127
Battleford *Herald*, 129
The Bead Pot (Poirier), 12
Beardy, Chief. *See* Kàmiyistowesit (Beardy), Chief
Beaulieu, François, 16, 27
Bélanger, Abraham Jr., 235–36
Bélanger, Abraham Sr., 166, 171–72, 191, 201
Bélanger, Horace, 24
Bélanger, Marie-Anne (Charette), 201
Bélanger, Norbert, 172
Bélanger brothers, 186
Belcourt, Father, 94, 166–67, 205
Belgian immigrants, 87, 161, 191
Belleau, Father, 118
Bellevue, 41, 90, 118–19, 161, 199, 251, 258
   prejudice against « les batochiens, » 251
Billings, Montana, 141
Birch Hills, 201
Bird, Madeline (Mercredi), 12
The Birth of Western Canada (Stanley), 3
birth rates, 36
bison, 58–59
   demand for coats, 167
   demise of, 164
   extinction, 167–68
bison bones, 183
bison hunt, 25
   controls, 168–69
   hierarchical paramilitary structure, 166
   risks, 167
   timing of social activities and births, 36
   winter hunts, 167
Blackfoot (Siksika), 141–42, 164
blacksmith shop, 175
blacksmiths, 181
Blais, Ernie, 8
blazons. *See* nicknames; *sobriquets*
Bois-Brûlés, 23
la boisson. *See* alcohol

Bonne Madone, 90, 201
"borrowed" spouses, 54#
Bossé, Father Léo, 120
Boucher, Albina. *See* St. Denis, Albina "La Pie" (Boucher)
Boucher, Alfred (Monsignor), *278*, 279
   considered in line to become bishop, 252, 280
Boucher, Baptiste Sr., 41, 48, 51, *51*,141, 159, 180, 183,191, 228, 279
Boucher, Caroline (Lespérance), 48, 51,*51*
Boucher, Charles-Eugène, *51*, 67–68, 86, *156*, 173, *178*, 200, 237
   advisory committee on agriculture, 159
   French language and, 158
   MLA for Batoche, 279
   opposition to Métis reserve plan, 157, 243
   prize herds from Montana, 192
   support for scrip, 158
   supported just compensation for losses, 158
Boucher, Élise, *51*
Boucher, Emma, *51*
   Grey Nun, 48, 252, 279
Boucher, Frédéric, *51*, 67
Boucher, Jean-Baptiste Sr. *See* Boucher, Baptiste Sr.
Boucher, Jean-Marie, *51*
Boucher, John B., 280, 295
Boucher, Joseph, *51*
Boucher, Marguerite. *See* Lépine, Marguerite (Boucher)
Boucher, Caroline (Lespérance), *51*
Boucher, Marie-Louise (Bremner), 272
Boucher, Marie-Rose, *51*
Boucher, Réal, 250, 274
Boucher, Rose-Délima, *51*, 80, 279
Boucher, Rose « La Rose » (Ouellette), 76
Boucher, Salomon, *51*, 191
Boucher, Sara (Marion), *51*, 201
Boucher, Véronique (Marion), 201
Boucher, William Albert "Boss," 279, 283
Boucher family, 42, 48
   conflict with Prince Albert Colonization Company, 214
   education (first generation), 75
   political and religious elite, 279
   socio-economic elite, 41
Boucher Settlement, 97, 210–11
Bourgeault, Dr., 181
Bourgeault, Ron, 2–3, 5–6, 9
Bourget, Bishop, 113

Bousquet, Julienne. *See* Boyer, Julienne (Bousquet)
Bouvier, Catherine Beaulieu. *See* Lamoureux, Catherine Beaulieu Bouvier
Bouvier family, 27
Boyd, Diane, 12
Boyer, Alfred, 258, 270
Boyer, Baptiste, 34, 147, 151, 153–54, *174*, 244, 291
Boyer, Baptiste Jr., 201, 244
Boyer, Baptiste, Tobie, 244
Boyer, Berthe (Ladéroute), *46*, 262, 263
Boyer, Brenda. *See* Percell, Brenda (Boyer)
Boyer, Chrysostome, 201
Boyer, Clémence. *See* Gervais, Clémence (Boyer)
Boyer, Edmond, 265, *266*
Boyer, Élise (Tourond), 270
Boyer, Émilie (Breland), 201
Boyer, Estelle, 263
Boyer, Euclide, 275
Boyer, Eveline (Caron), 260, *261*
Boyer, Félicité. *See* Breland, Félicité (Boyer)
Boyer, Hélène. *See* Racette, Hélène (Boyer)
Boyer, Isidore, 270
Boyer, Jean-Baptiste, 68, 112, 169, 176
　dedicated farmer, 186
　land title, 229
　store at Batoche, 175
Boyer, Joe, *261*
Boyer, Julienne (Bousquet), *46*
Boyer, Kokum Clémence. *See* Gervais, Kokum Clémence (Boyer)
Boyer, Magloire, 270
Boyer, Marguerite (Bremner), 270
Boyer, Raphaël, 177, 180, 192, 258
Boyer, Tobie, 244
Boyer, William, *46*, 147, 151, 172, 175, 177
　dedicated farmer, 186
　second "free" homestead entry, 228
Boyer family, 42, 62, 152, 251, 284, 296
Boyer-Fisher families, 47
Brady, Jim, 267, 274–75, 277
Branconnier, Joseph, 177
Breland, Félicité (Boyer), *46*
Breland, Gilbert, *46*, 181, 186, 201
Breland, Pascal, 126–27
Breland family, 25
Bremner, Marie-Louise. *See* Boucher, Marie-Louise (Bremner)
Brown, Jennifer S.H., 1, 12
Bruce, Edward, *288*, 289, 295, *296*
　early Métis presence at Batoche NHS, 287
Bruce, William, 82, 181
Bruneau, François, 25
buffalo. *See* bison
Buffalo Lake, 258
Bungee dialect (Cree-Ojibwe-Gaelic), 24
Burgess, A.M., 131, 215, 243
Butler, Captain, 22
butter-making, 66

C

Calette, Mark, 296, *296*
Campbell, Maria, 13, 295
　Halfbreed, 11
Canada Territories Corporation, 247
Canada's First Nations (Dickason), 16
Canadian French language, xii, xiii
Canadian government. *See also* government patronage
　claims to the lands of the North West, 206
　Department of Indian Affairs, 86, 253
　Department of the Interior, 212, 214–15
　discriminatory attitude towards the "Halfbreed rebels," 177
　fear of uprising of First Nations and Métis, 141
　hiring of Métis to make pemmican, 183
　immigration policy, 90, 157
　land policies (*See* Dominion Lands Act; land claims)
　military expedition to control Manitoba, 26
　spy network, 140
　tariff policy, 140
Canadian Pacific Railway, 169, 181, 183
Canadiens (of New France), 21
"Canayen" French language, xii
Canoe Lake, 176
capitalism, 2, 6
Carlton House, 165
Carlton Trail, 169, 176, 286
Caron, Albert, 119, 285
Caron, Angélique (Dubois), 201
Caron, Eveline. *See* Boyer, Eveline (Caron)
Caron, Jean Jr., 52, 118, 76
Caron, Jean Sr., 41, 48, *49*, 55, 76, 100, 149, 151–52, 189, 192, 229, 235, 285
carpenter, 181
　veteran of 1885, 269

Caron, Jeannette. *See* Gervais, Jeannette (Caron)
Caron, Joe, *256*
Caron, Lisa (Gervais), *49*
Caron, Marguerite (Dumas), 48, *49*, 76, 192, 234, 272
Caron, Marie. *See* Parenteau, Marie (Caron)
Caron, Marie-Anne, 48
Caron, Marjorie (Adair), 261
Caron, Mrs. Ti-Jean (Virginie Parenteau), 52, 64
Caron, Pierre, 118, 189
Caron, Théophile, *49*, 200
Caron, Ti-Jean-Vieux-Jean. *See* Caron, Jean Jr.; Caron, Jean Sr.
"Caron clique," 42
Caron family, 26, 42, 48, 284, 285, 297
Caron house, 291–92, 296
carpenters, 181
Carrière, Charles, 186
Carrière, Damase, 133, *269*
Carrière, Pélagie Parenteau, 201
Carrière, Pierre, 275
Carrière family, 25, 191, 210
Carrot River, 91, 173, 201
Carscadian and Peck, 173
casting of spells, 95, 123
Catholic Church, 77, 92. *See also* clergy; missionaries
    changes in attitude, 122
    criticism of Métis, 97
    help against Anglo-Protestant enemy, 94
    policy of assimilation and federal control, 274
    punitive toward single mothers, 263
    Riel's challenge to, 3
cattle, 86, 164, 187–88, 191, 205, 255
    customs duties, 149, 192
    destroyed and moved in 1885, 197
    herd sizes, 188, 191–92, 198
    inheritance, 54
cattle and horse ranching, 192. *See also* ranching
Cayen, Marie (Dumont), 201
Cayen family, 10
celebrations and visits with parents and friends, 66, 78
cellars, 61–62
« chain migration, » 42
Chakasta, Jean. *See* Dumont *dit* Chakasta, Jean
Chamberland, Philippe, 41, 173, 88
Champagne, Antoine, 23
Champagne, Cléophas, 189

Champagne, Emmanuel, 25, 37, 42, *140*, 152, 172, 179, 192, 210, 234
    cattle herd, 188
    employment of freighters, 169
    home, 55
    land title, 229
    no compensation, 147
    seasonal farmer, 186
    traded with First Nations, 176
Champagne, François, 200
Champagne, Johnny, 284
Champagne, Marie (Letendre), 19, 42, 234, 272
Champagne, Patrice, 284
Champagne family, 26, 41
Charette, Daniel, 67, 172, 191, 201
Charette, Kokum Mary-Jane (formerly Racette, née Ouellette), *254*
Charette, Marie-Anne (Nault), 201
Charette, Moïse, 82
Charette family, 25
Chartrand, Paul, 7, 15
Châtelain, Louis, 165
« les chavages ont passé, » 22
Chénier, Avila, 258
Chénier family, 297
Chicots, 23
children, 12, 75, 281
    cause of death, 81
    clothing, 57–58
    "missing from history," 11
    natural children, 54
    orphans, 45, 260
    single parent children, 253, 261, 263
    source of labour, 45
church bell (Marie Antoinette), 18, 179, 272
Clarke, Lawrence, 34, 117, 125, 127, 129, 131, 169
    campaign against Riel, 133
Clarke, Margaret, 12
"class marriages," 47
clergy. *See also* Catholic Church; missionaries
    attempt to transform Métis into sedentary people, 94, 98
    avoided political issues after 1885, 117
    belief in Christianity's superior spirituality, 94, 97
    collaboration with government against Riel, 133
    favoured Métis reserve, 243
    Métis petitions to Canadian government and, 131

plans for francophone colonization, 89–91, 161, 238
recruited Métis as auxiliaries, 94
refused sacraments to Métis, 112–13, 115
support for 1869-70 Resistance, 94
support for Métis' claims against Hudson's Bay Company, 94
support for Métis self-governing council, 96
supported Conservatives, 148
ultramontane ideology, 94
clothing, 55–58
adoption of Eurocanadian dress, 55, 57–58
children, 57–58
cowboy outfits, 57
craint-rien capes, 56
Co-operative Commonwealth Federation (CCF), 276
avoided land-claims and self-determination, 277
Catholic opposition to, 277, 279
The Collected Writings of Louis Riel (Stanley), 1
colonialism, 2–3, 5, 9
colonization, 2, 6, 89–91, 161, 238
Comité Historique of the Union Nationale Métisse St. Joseph du Manitoba, 3
la commune, 205
conjuring rituals, 95
conscription, 263
Conservatives, 142, 147, 153, 276
clergy support for, 148
Métis resentment after 1885, 148
on scrip rights, 243
Conservatives of Batoche
petition to Sir John A. Macdonald, 153–54
Constitution Act (1867)
Métis status under, 7
Constitution Act (1982)
Métis Aboriginal rights, 7–8
"consumption" (tuberculosis), 36, 80–81
Corporation Épiscopale de la Saskatchewan, 247
corvée (building bee), 100
Council of Assiniboia, 124
"Council of Public Instruction," 104
country fairs, 70
Courchesne, Omer, 253
coureurs de bois, 23
court cases, 7, 82–83
cowboys, 200
Cree, 9, 83–84, 96, 165
intermediaries in fur trade, 164

small pox epidemic (1870), 80
Cree and Ojibwe women, 23
passed on cultural and linguistic training, 42
Cree language, 73, 95, 125, 281
recording and transmission, 282
Cree songs, 68
Creighton, Donald, xi
Crescent Lake (road-allowance community), 13
crimes, 81, 83, 86
Crooked Lake, 201
Crossings (The Bell of Batoche), 18
Crystal Springs, 201
Cumberland House, 17, 169
Cumberland Trail, 169
custom exemptions for live animals, 149, 192
Cypress Hills, 27, 168

D

dairy house, 64
Dakota (Sioux), 10, 23, 84, 141–42, 172
dancing, 66–67
Daniels, Douglas, 4
Dauphinais, Joseph, 166
Davis, T. O., 159
Dease family, 25
death
causes of, 81 (*See also* disease)
death rates, 36, 45
Debden, 276
Dechêne, Louise, 21
Deh Cho region, 16
Delorme, Élise (Ness), 201
Delorme, Madeleine. *See* Gareau, Madeleine (Delorme)
Delorme, Marie Desmarais, 25
Delorme, Norbert, 133, 141, 171, 192, 200
Delorme, Pierre, 25, 126
Delorme, Urbain « Pezzan » Jr., 200
Demers, Télesphore, 188
Dene, 26–27
Department of Indian Affairs, 86, 253
Department of the Interior, 212, 214
Depression years, 2, 255–59, 275
extended absence of fathers and sons, 255, 257, 259
Deschambault, Georges, 24
Deschamps, Baptiste, 81
Desjarlais, Caroline (Moreau), 201

Desjarlais family, 6, 17
Desmarais, Jean, 200
Desmarais, Marie. *See* Delorme, Marie Desmarais
"Devil's Lake," 80
Devine, Heather, 12, 17, 249
  The People Who Own Themselves, 6
Dewdney, Edgar (Lieutenant-Governor), 88, 129, 133, 215
Dickason, Olive, 21–22
  Canada's First Nations, 16
  The Myth of the Savage and the Beginning of French Colonialism in America, 16
Diefenbaker, John, 283–84, *284*
diet, 44, 58–62, 66
  beverages, 64
  Depression years, 255
  purchased food, 58, 64, 259
  typical Métis dishes, 60
Dion, Joe, 274
diphtheria, 80–81
disease, 80
doctors, 180
Dominion Lands Act, 214–15, 226, 242
  corrupt and inefficient bureaucracy, 228
  no special provisions for Métis, 227–28
  reserved lands, 235
Dominion Lands regulations
  for the benefit of Eurocanadian settlers, 237
  confusion over, 237
  incompatible with riverlot system, 210–11
  Métis compliance, 208
Domrémy, 161
Dorion, Leah, 13, 16
Dorion trading family, 17
Dorval, Onésime, 75, *105*, 106, 118
Douglas, T.C., 276–77
dowry (or trousseau), 54
dreams, 71
drought, 187, 189
Dubois, Ambroise, 201
Dubois, Françoise (Rocheleau), 201
Dubois, Maxime, *140*, 201
Dubois, Pélagie (Parenteau), *269*
Dubuc, Father Denis, 122, 283
Dubuc, Joseph, 143
Duck, Mr., 212, 214, 226
Duck Lake, 34, 41, 127, 171, 199, 258, 275
  active Métis local, 279, 281
  fair and farm show, 70
  freighting, 172
  heterogeneous population, 89
  new constituency of, 161
  NWMP post established, 126
  petition to Territorial government, 211
  population, 35, 42
  private convent boarding school, 75
  rejection of Métis reserve plan, 157
Duck Lake battle, 138
Duck Lake merchants, 247
Duck Lake parish, 103, 118
Duck Lake picnic, 257
Dumas, Angélique (Letendre), 48, 192
Dumas, Christine. *See* Pilon, Christine (Dumas)
Dumas, Daniel, 48
Dumas, Geneviève (Ladéroute), 192
Dumas, Isidore, 192
Dumas, Joseph, 200
Dumas, Marguerite. *See* Caron, Marguerite (Dumas)
Dumas, Michel, 9, 84, 140–41, 171, 200, 211
  farming instructor, 133, 180
Dumas family, 88
Dumas-Letendre, Angélique. *See* Dumas, Angélique (Letendre)
Dumont, Aimé, 255, 257, 265, 275
Dumont, Ambroise, 200
Dumont, Caroline « Câline » (Montour), 76
Dumont, David, 265
Dumont, Édouard, 42, 140, 173, 192
Dumont, Élie, 235, 257
Dumont, Elisabeth. *See* Ouellette, Elisabeth (Dumont)
Dumont, Gabriel, 2, 27, 37, 68, 88, 96, 114, 116, 135, 139, *139*, 140–42, 166, 296
  acres under cultivation, 186
  adjutant-general of provisional government, 138
  afraid to return to Canada, 149
  Albert Caron's description, 285
  on bison extinction, 168
  denounced by missionaries, 111
  dramatization (conflict with Moulin), 18
  guerilla warfare tactics, 4
  honoured by GDI, 282
  hunting feud with Mistahimaskwa (Big Bear), 10
  memoirs of 1885 conflict, 3
  president of St. Laurent Council, 124–26
  succeeded Louis Riel as political leader, 151
  support for Batoche church, 100
  veteran of 1885, 269

Dumont, Isidore, 34, 132, 166, 187
Dumont, Isidore Jr., 124, 172, 201
Dumont, Jean, 34, 140
Dumont, Jean Jr., 124
Dumont, Sophie (Letendre), 42
Dumont, Victoria (Laframboise), 258–59
Dumont, Yvon, 4
Dumont *dit* Aicawpow, Isidore, 34, 37
Dumont *dit* Chakasta, Jean, 34, 37
Dumont family, 10, 27, 42
Dumont-Ouellette families, 47

E

economy, 5, 163
   agricultural activities, 185–93
   buffalo hunt, 167–68
   freighting, 169–72
   fur trade, 164–65
   merchant trading, 173–77
   mixed economy, 234
Les écrits complets de Louis Riel. See *The Collected Writings of Louis Riel* (Stanley)
education. *See* schooling
1885 Resistance, xi, 3, 10, 20, 138–43, 215
   Alex Fisher's account of, 153
   anguish and despair after, 83
   arrests and reprisals, 86, 116
   centennial, 1–2, 225, 290–94
   compensation for losses, 147, 152, 155, 158
   deprivation following, 188, 239
   descendants reclaiming a political voice, 275
   Duck Lake battle, 138
   fear of Métis/First Nations uprising following, 141–42
   First Nations' division over, 84
   First Nations' participation, 9
   French Canadian and French neutrality, 89
   French Canadian public opinion, 142
   general amnesty, 142
   Le grand silence, 269
   interviews with veterans, 269
   leaders dispersed, 141
   legacy of fear and resentment, 270, 272, 275
   la loge des femmes, 272
   Métis / clergy tensions, 108–15, 131–32
   Métis differences, 4, 10, 139
   Métis exodus after, 140, 180, 200
   Métis prisoners at Stony Mountain, *141*
   monument to Métis and First Nations victims, 270
   Parks Canada interpretation, xiii (*See also* "North West Rebellion")
   "success stories," 270
   vindicating Métis actions, 250
   war dead, 266
   women's actions, 272
Elbow trail, 169
elders, 11, 71
   aged parents, 44–45 (*See also* grandparents)
   imitation of model farm, 186
   old people, 258
   respect and authority, 123
electoral division, 154
   unfair to Métis, 129
emplacements, 205
endogamy, 47
engagés, 23
English ancestry, 24, 36, 47, 131–32
English language, 104, 125, 158, 260, 281
   language of instruction, 74, 158
"English Metis," 131–32
Ens, Gerhard, *Homeland to Hinterland*, 5
Escapot. *See* Dumont, Isidore
Éthier, Marie-Louise (Caron, Langlois), 106, 261
ethnocentrism, 3
Eurocanadians
   demand for "hard-working Halfbreed girls," 258
   favoritism from government and church, 199
   integrated with Métis, 87
   lack of sympathy for Métis "Indian" heritage, 89
   looked down on slower rhythm of Métis life, 163
Eurocentricism, 2
evil spirit or "Wendigo," 123
Ewing Commission, 274
exogamy, 48
Exovidate, 112
Expressing Our Heritage: Métis Artistic Designs, 13

F

Failhant, Cuthbert (Corbert). *See* Fayant (Failhant), Cuthbert « Corbet »
Falcon, Athanase, 200, 236
Falcon, Jean-Baptiste, 166
Falcon, Pierre, 25
family, 44
    "chain migration," 42, 44
    changes in family relationships, 54, 260
    at core of Métis society, 42
    deserting one's family, 82
    family life cycle, 45
    freedom and privileges to boys, 45, 54
    inheritance, 54, 153–54
    interdependence, 54
    principle of unity, 44
    roles and tasks, 44–45, 52
    tensions, quarrels, 54
    traditional values, 44
    young couples, 44, 54
family and kinship networks, 6, 12, 20–21, 52, 84, 128
    whole families relocated, 42
family antecedents
    social standing and, 37, 41
family history, 12
family sizes, 36
Far Northwest and Saskatchewan, 26–28
farm shows, 70
farming, 25, 37, 41, 163–64, 168, 185–03
    absences, 186, 208, 226, 234
    acres under cultivation, 186–87, 194–96
    "burnt stump" agriculture, 23
    cattle, 19, 54, 86, 149, 164, 187–88, 191–92, 197, 205, 255
    complementary to hunting, trading, freighting, 186, 199, 208, 226
    consolidation, 191–92
    farmers (new class of diligent), 41, 186
    Kàpeyakwàskonam (One Arrow) Cree Nation reserve, 86
    land as pasture and vegetable garden, 208
    markets, 189, 199
    method of cultivation, 199
    Métis *vs.* Eurocanadians, 194–95
    prosperous farmers at Batoche (1940s-1960s), 258
    Red River, 205
    seasonal farmers, 186
    St. Laurent Settlement, 185
    stock farmers, 197
    subsistence, 164
    success, 195
    unprofitable in poor soil, 98
farming instructors, 75, 133, 180
    wives of, 180
Farrell-Racette, Sherry, 12–13
Fayant, Joe, 265
Fayant, Mélanie, 201
Fayant, Napoléon, *256*
Fayant, Patrice, 185
Fayant (Failhant), Cuthbert "Corbet," 34, 173, 210
federal election (1896), 159
Ferguson, Charles, 191
Ferguson, Emma, *53*, 76
Ferguson, Ernest, 266
Ferguson, Ernestine, *53*
Ferguson, Léon, 265–66
Ferguson, Marie-Rose, 234
Ferguson (Fercuson), Antoine, 34, *53*, 67–68
ferry operators, 181
Fête des Michifs (Métis Days)
    reestablished as "Back to Batoche Days," 281
fête nationale, 69
F.G. Baker. *See* Walters & Baker store
Fiddler, Tom, 276
Fiddler (Fidler) families, 299
Fidler, François, 201
Fidler, Jean-Baptiste, 200
Fidler, Raymond, 294
Fidler, Walter, 257, 279
Fidler, William, 183
Fidler family, 42, 191, 284, 299
File Hills, 33
La Fille. *See* Ferguson, Emma
First Nations, 16, 21, 23, 141, 176. *See also* Aboriginal peoples
    First Nations women and Eurocanadian fur traders, 23
    fringe of society, 185
    land rights, 203–4 (*See also* Aboriginal rights)
    loyalty to Queen, 9
    Métis relations with, 10, 83–86, 94, 128–29, 181, 204, 297
    no restrictions on hunting, 168
    participation in resistance / rebellion, 9–10
First Nations Industrial School, 277
First Nations living on reserves
    alcohol prohibition, 77

First World War, 263–65
  work and adventure, 263
Fish Creek. *See also* Tourond Coulee, 27, 35, 84, 91, 177, 192, 200, 227, 272
  abandoned by Métis, 161, 191, 199, 235
  acres under cultivation, 186, 191
Fisher, Alexandre Pierre, 42, 113, 148–49, 151–53, 209, 236
Fisher, Ambroise, 152, 183, 244
Fisher, Art, 250
Fisher, Charles "Le Marquis," 159, *160*
  on abuses of scrip, 248
Fisher, George Jr., 68, 89, 136, 147, 179
  immigration committee, 90
  justice of the peace, 176, 180
  liquor licence, 78, 176
  merchant trading, 183
  postmaster, 176
  store in Batoche, 176
  store in Duck Lake, 176
Fisher, George Jr., 154, *174*, *178*
Fisher, George Sr., *170*, 175, 176
  cattle herd, 188
  employment of freighters, 169
  fur sales, 169
Fisher, Henry, 24
Fisher, Joseph, 176
Fisher family, 48
  education (first generation), 75
  local bourgeoisie, 152
  socio-economic elite, 41
fishing, 25, 276
fishing and hunting rights, 168, 204. *See also* natural resources
Fishing Lakes, 173
Flanagan, Thomas, 6
  anti-Métis agenda, 7
  Louis 'David' Riel, 4
Fleury, Alexandrine. *See* Nicolas, Alexandrine (Fleury)
Fleury, Antoine, 34
Fleury, Norman, 14
Fleury, Pascal-Pasquette (sobriquet/nickname), 76
Fleury, Patrice, 171, 185, 270, *271*
Fleury, Patrice Jr., 200
Fleury, Rose (Gariépy), xiii, 18, 253, 255, 281, 295, *296*
  community activist and respected elder, 260
  returned to school to become social worker, 260

flour mills, 187
flu epidemics, 36, 80
food. *See* diet
forewarnings, 72, 93
Fort à la Corne, 164–65, 173, 176
Fort Assiniboine, 141
Fort Battleford, 292
Fort Carlton (La Montée), 33–34, 84, 95–96, 165, 169, 171
  itinerant missions, 94, 96
  smallpox, 80
Fort des Prairies, 164
Fort Edmonton region, 94
Fort Garry (Winnipeg), 169
Fort la Jonquière, 164
Fort St. Louis (Nipawin), 164
Foster, John, 17
Fourmond, Father Vital, 68, 97, 102–3, 110–13, 135, 137, 154–55, 157
  immigration committee, 90
  sympathetic towards Riel, 109
  on Métis reserve, 243
  model farm, 186–87
  supported Conservatives, 153
  on why Métis chose money scrip, 240
Fournier, Gustave, *178*
The Fourth World (Manuel), 163
Simonin, Father, François-Xavier, Father, *46*
The Free People (Payment), 290
"the free people," (gens libres) 95–96, 164
free traders, 25. *See also* freemen
freeman Métis culture and identity, 17
freemen, 25, 165–66
freighting, 168, 191
  Métis skill, 169
  replaced by mechanization, 173
  risky economic activity, 172
  trails, 169
French, Colonel, 126, 128
French Canadian elite, 252
French Canadian settlers, 22, 41, 87, 120, 161
  from Manitoba, 88
  neutrality during 1885 resistance, 89
  from Quebec, 88, 90
  views of Métis, 89–90, 251
French Canadian songs, 68
French Canadian voyageurs, 24, 27, 33, 84, 95, 164. *See also* Boucher, Jean-Marie; Letendre *dit* Batoche, Jean-Baptiste
French Canadians in Middleton's army, 142

French immigrants (near Batoche), 41, 87–88, 191
  allegiance to Riel, 88
  neutrality during 1885 resistance, 89
French language, 68, 125, 155, 158
  discrimination against, 74
  granted status by Battleford council, 127
  resistance to, 95
  taught in school, 74
  useful in the army, 265
"French" shoes, 57
"Frenchness" cultivated to avoid discrimination, 252
"Friends of Batoche," 295
Frigon, A.M., *85*
Frobisher family, 27
From Rupert's Land to Canada, 17
fruits, 58, 61–62, 188, 259
Fumoleau, René, 203
fur trade, 16–17, 84, 164–65, 169
furniture and possessions, 55

G

Gabriel Dumont Institute (GDI), xiii, 16, 18, 249, 282, 297
Gabriel Dumont's Crossing, 34, 42, 191, 207, 227
games, 68
Gardepuis' (Philippe Gariépy's) Crossing, 207, 210
Gardepuis [sic], Philip[pe], 34, 41, 131, 147, 171, 172, 211
Gareau, Azarie, 41, 88
Gareau[lt], Ludger, 37, 41, *50*, 88, 135, 169, 192
  builder, 181
  ranch in Pincher Creek, 200
Gareau, Madeleine (Delorme), *50*
Gareau, Napoléon, 88
Gariépy, Baptiste, 124
Gariépy, Daniel, 189, 235
Gariépy, « La Moëlle » (Daniel), 171
Gariépy, Philippe, 34, 41, 131, 147, 171, 172, 211
  enticed into Conservative Party, 152
  guide and interpreter, 181
  released from prison, 141
Gariépy, Pierre, 124, *140*
Gariépy, Rose. *See* Fleury, Rose (Gariépy)
Gariépy (Gardipy) families, 10

Garnot, Philippe, 42, 78, 88, 116, 131, 133, *140*, 147–49, 152, 169, 188, 201, 214, 237, 243
  left committee (went to conservatives), 151
  released from prison, 141
  secretary of provisional government, 138
Garnot *vs.* Malfaire trial, 82
Gautier de Rues, Dr., 180
Gauvreau, Valmore, 212
gender equality, 45, 52
gens libres. *See* freemen, 25
Gervais, Clémence (Boyer), *46, 49*
Gervais, Corbet, 186, 192
Gervais, Cuthbert, 200
Gervais, Émile, 266
Gervais, Jean-Baptiste, 189, 235
Gervais, Jeannette (Caron), 260
Gervais, Lisa. *See* Caron, Lisa (Gervais)
Gervais brothers, 172
Gervais family, 284
Gingras, Antoine, 166
Gingras, François, 25, *174*
Gingras, Marguerite (Ouellette), 200
Gingras, Narcisse, 166
Gingras family, 25
Giraud, Marcel, xi, 92, 270, 290
  Le Métis Canadien, 2–3, 108
Goodfellow Brothers, 247
Goulet, Elzéar, 17
Goulet, Keith, 249
Goulet, Louis, 56–57, 73, 171
Goulet, Roger, 92, 171, 240
Goulet family, 25
government contracts supplying First Nations, 177
government patronage, 148, 152, 159, 161, 181, 185, 276
government surveys. *See* land surveying system
Grain Adjustment Board, 235
Le grand silence, 269
Grandin, Bishop Vital-Justin, 100, 104, 110, 112, 117, 131
  accepted request for patron saint, 135
  interceded with Macdonald, 132
  support for Métis reserves, 238
grandmothers, 11, 42, 76
  "the real teachers," 253
grandparents, 44–45, 260, 263
Grant, Cuthbert, 25
Grant, George, 177
Grant, Johnny, 2, 5

Grant, William, 159, 177
Great Depression. *See* Depression years
Great Lakes communities, 23
Great Lakes Métis, 8, 22–23
Green Bay, 23
Green Lake, 171, 173, 176, 201, 258
    militant Métis from, 276
    store, 175
    trading post, 169
"La Grenouillère" (Seven Oaks), 25
Grey Nuns, 48, 252, 279
    convent schools, 75, 95
    of Métis descent, 95
Grézaud, Paul, 177
la grippe, 80
Gros Ventres (Haaninin), 84, 164–65
Gros Ventres Forks
    winter camps, 33
Grosse-Butte, 27, 166, 236
Groulx, Lionel, xiv
Guérin, Pierre, 292
guerre nationale. *See* 1885 Resistance
Guillemette, Pierre, 177
Guillet, Célestin, Brother, 70, 101, 118

H

Halfbreed (Campbell), 11
"Halfbreeds," 24
Hallet, Marie (Letendre), 27
Hamelin, Alexandre, 34, 124
Hamelin, Baptiste, 34, 124
Hamelin, Daniel, 172
Hamelin, Joseph, 37
Hamelin family, 25
Hamilton, Murray, 249
The Handbook of North American Indians, 17
Haultain, F.W.G., 159
health care, 123, 255
    "Indian medicine," 72
    medical doctors, 180–81
    traditional healers and midwives, 72, 181
    Western medicine, 72
Henry, Catherine (Grant), 159
Heron, Josie. *See* Weninger, Josie (Heron)
high school. *See* schooling
Hildebrandt, Walter, 250
    The Battle of Batoche, 290

L'Histoire de la Nation Métisse, 3
Historic Sites and Monuments Board of Canada, 10, 122
    plaque commemorating "Northwest Rebellion," 270, 282–83
hivernements (wintering camps), 27, 124, 164, 166
Hobbs, Rena, 106
Hoeppner, D., 247
holidays, religious and civil, 67–70, 78–79, 122, 135. *See also* Métis feast days
Holy Childhood and Propagation of the Faith allowances, 100
Homeland to Hinterland (Ens), 5
homes or dwellings (1870s-1920s), 54–55
Homestead Act, 239, 247
homestead applications, 187, 226, 228
    cultivation requirements, 228
    delays in applying for patent, 232
    interval between entry and patent, 226, 229
    interval between occupation and entry, 230–31
    leaving land without obtaining title, 189
    time taken to obtain title, 196–97
homestead declarations
    Métis *vs.* non-Métis, 226
homestead residence requirements, 214, 224, 228
    absenteeism or comings and goings, 188, 208–9, 226, 234
horses, 188, 191–92, 198. *See also* ranching
Houle, Julie (Parenteau), 201
Hryciuk, Bernice (St. Germain), 285
Hryciuk, Dmytro, 285
Hryciuks, 286
Hudson's Bay Company (HBC), 23–24, 126–27, 165, 204
    armed protest against, 25
    conflicts with North West Company, 123–24
    created Aboriginal class of wage labourers, 6
    employment of freighters, 169
    landholding system, 205
    Métis claims against, 94
    Métis labourers, 24, 171
    reserved land, 206, 212, 236
    supplier to merchants, 173, 176
    survey of property in Red River Settlement (1836-38), 205
    trading monopoly, 25, 124, 166
Hudson's Bay Company (HBC) census, 34
Huel, Raymond, 14, 108
Hughes, O. E., 129, 148

hunting, freighting, and trading, 37, 84, 123, 163–64, 186. *See also* bison hunt
    basic to Métis economy, 97–98
    missionaries' lack of recognition, 97
hunting rights, 8. *See also* natural resources
    Métis / First Nations disputes, 10
Huot, Inspector (C.F.A.), 78, 181
Huysmans de Neftal, Baron, 41, 180

I

I. & R. Friesen, 247
Ile à la Crosse, 95, 124, 171, 176
    language, 15
    Métis communities established, 26
    store, 175
    trading post, 169
immigration. *See* settlers
In Our Own Words: Northern Saskatchewan Women Speak Out, 12
independent traders, 25. *See also* freemen
Indian Act of 1876, 204
indigenous rights. *See* Aboriginal rights
inheritance, 54, 190–91
insurance agents, 180
intermarriage, 22–23, 47, 84
Irish ancestry, 36
Isbister, Alexander, 124

J

Jackfish Lake, 173, 191, 201
Jackson, William Henry (alias Honoré Joseph Jaxon), 111, 213
John Arcand and his Métis fiddle (video), 13
Josephte (Cree wife of Jean-Baptiste Letendre *dit* Batoche), 27
justices of the peace, 180

K

Kalispell, Montana, 200
Kàmiyistowesit (Beardy), Chief, *115*, 128
Kàmiyistowesit (Beardy) reserve, 75, 83
    government reprisals, 86
    participation in 1885 Resistance, 10

Kàpeyakwàskonam (One Arrow) Cree Nation reserve, 9, 75, 83, 128, 177, 297
    encroachment on Métis land, 19, 212
    mixed farming, 86
    participation in 1885 Resistance, 10
Kermoal, Nathalie, 12
Kerr, George, 177
Kerr, John, 177
Kerr Brothers of Batoche, 188
kinik-kinik, 61, 72
Kinistino, 201
kinship networks. *See* family and kinship networks
Kittson, Norman, 166
Kittson family, 25
Klondike Gold Rush, 183
kokums. *See* grandmothers
Korean War, 265–66

L

labourers, 37, 163
Labrador, 15, 21
Lac la Biche, Alberta, 26
Lac la Ronge, 169
Lac Ste. Anne, 26, 80, 95
Lacombe, Father, 96
Ladéroute, Joseph, 192
Ladéroute family, 251, 296
Ladret, Ferdinand, 37, 88, 180
Laferté, Louis. *See* Schmidt *dit* Laferté, Louis
Laflèche, Father (Louis), 94, 166–67
Lafond, Cyrille, 173
Lafontaine, Calixte, 192
Laframboise, Augustin, 266
Laframboise, Edouard, 172
Laframboise, Marge, 281, 283
Laframboise, Victoria. *See* Dumont, Victoria (Laframboise)
Lagimodière, Elzéar, *268*
Lagimodière, William, *268*
Lagimodière family, 25
Laird, David, 127, 129, 148
Lalonde, Aldina (Venne), 201
Lamoureux, Catherine Beaulieu Bouvier, 16
land base, 274
    loss of, 6–7, 236
    Red River, 25

land claims, 20, 203–36, 274. *See also* Métis land rights; Métis landholding customs; Métis reserves
    direct Métis land grant, principle of, 153, 155, 215, 226
    government surveys (*See* land surveying system (Dominion Lands))
    homestead entries, 187, 189, 207–15, 226, 228, 239, 247
    language issues, 209, 212
    Manitoba Métis land claims case, 7
    Manitoba precedent, 203–7
    Métis persistence, 211
    petitions to Territorial government, 211
    request for riverlot surveys, 211
    resurveys and homestead entries (1885-ca. 1925), 216–36
    through scrip, 237–48
land prices, 247
land scrip, 207, 240
    confused with homestead entries, 242
    location of, 244
    sale of, 247
    socio-economic circumstances and, 244
land speculators, 78
land surveying system (Dominion Lands), 209–14
    ignored riverlot system, 131, 209, 213
    language difficulties, 209, 212
    Métis suspicion, 213, 215, 227
    resurveys and homestead entries (1885-ca. 1925), 216–36
land surveying system (Hudson's Bay Company), 205
land surveys and homestead entries (1878 - 1885), 207–15
landholding and ownership concepts
    Aboriginal *vs* European, 203–4
Landry, Pierre, 34
Landry family, 88
language, 13–15, 17, 52, 68, 73–74
    bilingual teachers, 75, 104
    Cree, 9, 83–84, 96, 165, 282
    distinguishing Métis groups, 24
    English, 74, 104, 125, 158, 260, 281
    French, 68, 74, 95, 125, 127, 267
    land surveying and, 209, 212
    Michif (*See* Michif-Cree; Michif French language)
Laplante, Father J.-O., 118–19
Laplante, Josephte Fidler, 201
Laplante, Toussaint, 172

Larocque, Joseph, 275
LaRoque, Emma, 2
Lasker, Corporal, 78
Laurier, Wilfrid, 148–49, 151–53, 159
Lavallée (hunter), 165
Lavallée, Guy, Father, 14, 122
Laverdure, « Beau-Blé, » 76
Laviolette, Charles, 55, 181
Le Chevallier, Father Jules, 108, 113, 115
Lecoq, Father (Pierre), 97
Ledoux, Jérôme, 185
Ledoux, Magloire, 201
Leduc, Father Louis-H., 211
Lemieux, E., 78
Lenglet, Auguste, 78
Lenglet, Georgine d'Amours, 180
Lépine, Achilles (Archie), *273*, 274
Lépine, Marguerite (Boucher), *85*, 180
Lépine, Marie-Anne. *See* McDougall, Marie-Anne (Lépine)
Lépine, Maxime, 3–4, 37, 41, 48, 116, 131, 138, 148–49, *150*, 171, 211
    crossover to Conservatives, 151–52
    denounced by missionaries, 111
    offered government contract, 133
    passed Dumont's letters to NWMP, 149
    released from prison, 141
Lépine, Maxime Jr., 75, *85*, 180, 183, 191
Lépine, Octavie (Pilon), *57*
Lépine, Rosalie (Nolin), 70, *146*
Lépine, Thomas, 236
Lépine family, 25, 42, 48, 88
Lespérance, Caroline. *See* Boucher, Caroline (Lespérance)
Lespérance family, 27
Letendre and Letendre *dit* Batoche family, 34, 41, *43*, 47, 48
Letendre, André, 42
Letendre, Azarie, *264*
Letendre, Baptiste, 191
Letendre, Emmanuel, 80
Letendre, Eugène, 191
Letendre, Jean-Baptiste *dit* Batoche 27, 165
Letendre, John, 75, 79–80, 180, 244, 247
Letendre, John-Baptiste, *264*
Letendre, Joseph, 191
Letendre, Louis Jr., 63, 189, 191, 244
Letendre, Louis(on), Jr., 42, 48, 192, 211
Letendre, Louis(on) Sr., 37, 25, 27, 37, 76
Letendre, Marguerite (Parenteau), *39*, 42, 291

Letendre, Marie (Champagne), 42, 192, 234, 272
Letendre, Sophie. *See* Dumont, Sophie (Letendre)
Letendre, Virginie (Pilon), 201
Letendre, William, 173, *174*, 201
Letendre, Xavier, 2, 27, 34, 37, 42, 48, 68–69, 132, 147, 158, *174*, 176, *178*, 210, 296
   acres under cultivation, 186
   alcohol consumption, 79
   cattle herd and horses, 188, 192
   children's education, 75
   delivered petition to Macdonald, 153
   employment of freighters, 169, 171, 173
   house, 55, 154, 173, 291
   liquor license, 78
   local bourgeoisie, 152
   losses in 1885, 175
   merchant trading, 173, 175, 183
   prosperity, 168, 173
   ranch in Minichinas Hills, 175, 192
   on scrip rights, 243
   second "free" homestead entry, 228
   support for Batoche church, 100
   support for formal education and training, 175
Letendre-Champagne families, 47. *See also* Letendre family
Letendre *dit* Batoche, André, 210
Letendre *dit* Batoche, François-Xavier, *38*
Letendre *dit* Batoche, Jean-Baptiste, 27, 165
Letendre *dit* Batoche, Louis(on) Sr., 25, 27, 34, 42, 63, 191–92, 211
Letendre *dit* Batoche, Xavier, 110, 151, 291
Letendre *dit* Batoche family, 34
Letendre family, 41, *43*, 48. *See also* Letendre-Champagne families; Letendre *dit* Batoche family
Letendre store, 177
Lethbridge, 200
Lévesque, Clémentine, 82
Lewiston, 200
Liberal government, 283
Liberal Party, 147–48, 159, 263, 276, 279
   support for scrip without restrictions, 243–44
liens against land. *See* seed grain mortgage liens
life expectancy, 45
   "ideal" life cycle, 48
   infant mortality, 36, 48
liquor licenses, 77–78, 176
"Little Canada" (store), 177
"little provisional government of Saskatchewan," 112, 138
"living in the present," 163

Lorne, Marquis of, 22
Lorne district, 129, 131
   created 1881, 127
Louis: Fils des Prairies (Palud-Pelletier), 12
Louis 'David' Riel (Flanagan), 4
Louis Riel Institute, 16
Louisbourg, 286, 292
Loyal till Death, 9
Lussier, Antoine, 2
Lussier, Toussaint, *140*, 173
Lyon Mackenzie Powis, 176

M

Macdonald, John A., 129, 148, 153, 157, 215
Macdowall, D.H., 111, 129, 131, 215, 239–40
   campaign against Riel, 133
   clergy and Métis "bourgeoisie" support, 148
   Métis land rights and, 157
   support for Métis reserve, 157, 243
Mackenzie, Alexander, 27
Mackenzie, R.S., *115*, *178*, 247
Mackenzie River, 26
Macpherson, David, 215
Madigan, Luke, 181
"madness," 81, 83
Mandela, Nelson, 280
mangeux d'gallette (bannock eaters), 265
Manitoba, 23, 26
   Métis hunting rights, 8
   provisional government (*See* Provisional Government of Red River)
Manitoba Act, 26, 124, 237
   recognized principle of Métis land rights, 204, 206
   terms never fulfilled, 7
Manitoba Métis. *See also* Red River
   attempts to register land, 207
   massive relocation, 207
   move to Batoche area, 191
   scrip, 206–7
Manitoba Métis Federation, 5
Manitoba Métis land claims case, 7
Mannix, Florence (Venne), 201
Manuel, George, *The Fourth World*, 163
"many voices," 297
Marcelin, 90, 119, 201, 247
"Marie-Antoinette" (church bell), 18, 179, 272
Marion, Albert, 201

Marion, Andronique (Ross), 180
Marion, Jules, 201
Marion, Louis, 75, 86, 133, 177, 180, 244
Marion, Narcisse, 25, 166
Marion family, 25
marriage, 36, 48
    à la façon du pays, 22–23
    age of, 47, 259–60
    "borrowed" spouses, 36
    "class marriages," 47
    between cousins, 47–48, 52
    customary marriages, 21, 54
    divorce and separation, 54
    endogamy, 47
    intermarriage, 22–23, 47, 84 (*See also* miscegenation)
    ménage à trois, 54
    outsiders, 47–48, 52
    polygamy, 95
    remarriage, 47, 52
    second marriages, 48
    serial monogomy, 95
    "successful marriages," 48
la maudite police, 272
McCarthy, Martha, 14
McCullough, Alan, "Parks Canada and the 1885 Rebellion/Uprising/Resistance," 10
McDougall, Brenda, 249
McDougall, Marie-Anne (Lépine), *276*
McDougall, Médéric, 257, 263, 270, 272, 275, *276*, 277
McGillis, Cuthbert and Daniel, 25
McGillis, Modeste, 201
McGillis family, 96
McIntyre, J., 247
McKay, Alex, 141
McKay, James, 25, 126, 159
McKay, Nancy (Arcand), *46*, *65*
McMillan, James, 296
Meadow Lake, 169, 176, 201, 275
meat (wild meat), 259. *See also* bison
meat preservation, 62
medicine. *See* health care
Medicine Hat, 200
Mennonites, 77, 161, 199, 247, 251
merchant trading, 25, 173–77
merchants, 173–77, 183
    adopted culture of Eurocanadians, 163
    employment of freighters, 169
Mercier, Honoré, 142, 148

Mercredi, Madeline. *See* Bird, Madeline (Mercredi)
Mercredi (originally Macardy) family, 27
methodology, 18–20
methodology of "controlled speculation," 12, 20
Métis
    Aboriginal heritage, 42
    anti-Métis bias, 11, 16, 155
    "coming of age," 18
    coming out in early 1970s, 249, 281
    community rather than individual, 44, 54
    cultural brokers and interpreters, 10, 14, 84, 94, 181
    customs and traditions, 52–57
    diversity and complexity, 1–2, 14, 18, 25
    ethnocentric view of, 3
    European diseases, 80
    European heritage, 24
    forgotten in English-Canadian literature, 2
    of French Canadian descent, 47
    identification as, 19, 21–22, 24, 92, 204, 251, 297 (*See also* Métis identity)
    identified or passed as "whites," 253
    independent and wary people, 189
    integration into Aboriginal mother's culture, 23
    integration into anglophone community, 92
    looking for a good time, 66–67
    limited schooling (*See* schooling)
    loss of land base, 6, 236 (*See also* land claims)
    marginalization, xii, xiii, 5–6, 79, 251
    meaning of term, 21
    métissage, 21–22, 252
    Michel Giraud's view of, 2–3
    mobility, 20, 37, 187
    multilingual tradition, 15 (*See also* language)
    "on the fringe" of Western society, 251
    perceived as inferior to "real Indians," 22
    political resurgence (*See* Métis political consciousness)
    prejudice, 91, 252, 261
    re-affirmation of identity and culture, 251
    reluctance to accept welfare, 189, 255, 258
    Roman Catholic faith, 70, 87 (*See also* Métis cosmology or religious beliefs)
    of Scottish or English ancestry, 47
    slower rhythm of life, 163
    tradition of sharing, 52, 54, 163
    transition from hunting to farming, 164, 187, 190, 226
    value attached to work, 163, 257

Métis / French Canadian relations, xiii, 89–90, 92, 251
Métis Aboriginal rights, 6–8, 128, 151, 214, 237
    not acknowledged by colonial authorities, 204
    petitioning for, 238
    through scrip not through homesteads, 228
Métis art works, 17
Métis Association of Alberta and the North West Territories, 274
Métis Association of Saskatchewan, 275
Métis associations, 274–81
    reorganized provincially in mid-60s, 277
Le Métis Canadien (Giraud), 2, 108
Métis colonies (northern Alberta), 274
Métis colonies rehabilitation scheme, 277
Métis "colony" in Duck Lake, 277
Métis cosmology or religious beliefs, 13
    syncretism of indigenous and Christian beliefs, 14
Métis cultural revival and renewal, 281–84
Métis culture, language, and spirituality, 12–15, 17, 24
Métis diaspora, 17
Métis economy. *See* economy
Métis expressions, 73–74
Métis feast days, 69–70. *See also* holidays, religious and civil
    national feast day, 78–79, 122, 135
Métis films, 17
Métis flag, 13, 135–36
Métis food. *See* diet
Métis history
    challenging traditional white concepts of, 251
    "hidden," 16, 249
    re-assessed by ethnohistorians, 289
    recovery of, 1, 15, 17, 19
    rehabilitation, 250, 267, 282
Métis identity, 15, 52
    fluid and varied, 21
    group, xiv, 21–23
Métis ideological culture *(mentalité)*</i>, 12
Métis in urban centers, 263
    hid ancestry from children, 281
    poverty and alcoholism, 281
Métis land rights, 1, 6–7, 15, 157, 237. *See also* land claims
    under Manitoba Act, 204, 207
Métis landholding customs, 5, 132, 205
    "absenteeism" or seasonal movements, 208, 226, 234
    confused and angered land agents, 230
    flexible approach to ownership and exchanges, 205
    hay and wood lots, 214, 229
    occupied land "unofficially" before making entry, 226
    riverlot system, 205–7, 209–10, 213, 229
Métis law, 123
Métis Legacy, 16–17
Métis Legacy II, 13
Métis literature (oral history and stories), 16–17. *See also* Métis writers
Métis material culture, 13, 17
Métis merchants, 163, 169, 173–77
Métis museum and genealogy center in Duck Lake, 260
Métis music, 13, 17
Métis Nation of Saskatchewan (MNS), 294–95
Métis National Council, 15, 280
Métis national hymn, 137
The Métis People (interactive CD-ROM), 18
Métis perspective, xii, xiii, 2, 9, 15–16
"Métis Perspectives," 15
Métis petition to Laurier and Liberal party, 149, 151–52
Métis petitions to government, 131, 149
    on draught animals and ploughing implements, 189
    for industrial school, 192–93
    on mortgage clause, 189
    on ploughing implements and seed grain, 187
    re land rights, 238
    requesting representative government, 124
    Riel's (1885), 138, 213
    on scrip, 242, 244
    support from clergy, 108, 110
    to territorial government, 149, 211
Métis police officers, 181
Métis political consciousness, 11, 267, 276–80. *See also* political activism
Métis priests, 122
Métis recreational activities, 66–68, 98
Métis relations with First Nations, 83–86, 128–29, 297
    assimilating role, 83–86
    complicity with NWMP, 181
    cultural differences, 10
    hunting disputes, 10
    treaty negotiations, 94, 204
Métis relations with Roman Catholic Church, 93–122, 133
    cultural, social, religious differences, 97–98

1885 resistance and, 108–13
new phase of dialogue and renewal, 122
relations after 1885, 117–22
Métis relations with settlers, 87–92, 199, 235. *See also* Métis / French Canadian relations
Métis reserves, 238, 243
clergy support for, 157, 243
Métis opposition to, 157, 238
Métis rights, 8, 143, 204, 280
Aboriginal (*See* Métis Aboriginal rights)
challenged by HBC and Canadian authorities, 125
discussed away from strangers, 270, 272
land (*See* Métis land rights)
Riel's role, 4
Métis sash, 13, 56–57, 280
Métis scholars, 5
attempts to document heritage, 13
Métis school teachers, 180
Métis settlement periods, 231
Métis Society of Saskatchewan, 277
Métis soldiers. *See* war experiences
Métis spirituality
syncretism, 4, 14, 93
Métis Studies, xii, xiv
A Métis Suite (video), 13
Métis veterans. *See* war veterans
Métis voyageurs, 56, 58, 84, 95
Métis women, 17, 20, 66
absence from literature, 2
agency, xi, 255
bookkeeping and teaching First Nations, 180
bosses in the home, 255
clothing, 56, 58
cultural and economic brokers, 12
death rates, 45, 81
"domestic scientists," 259
education, 75
farming, 192, 259
Grey Nuns, 95
health care and childbirth, 255
homestead declarations, 234
involvement in politics, 12, 281
lacking career opportunities, 263
la loge des femmes (women's camp), 272
matriarchs, 192
"missing from history," 11
nuns and spinsters of a certain age, 42
"old maids," 47
quilts and knitted items, 258

recruited by clergy, 94
resisted Western patriarchal values (child before mother), 255
role in bison economy, 167
role in 1885 Resistance, 272
role in fur trade, 12
single mothers, 263
skillful with needle and thread, 57, 258
smoking, 72
status, 42, 95
"strong like two people," 12
taught Aboriginal languages to missionaries, 94
unmarried mothers, 261
valued for cultural and linguistic training, 42
values of self-reliance and enterprise, 260
war experiences, 266
widows, 44
work outside the home, 253, 258–59
Métis Women's Association, 260
Métis writers, 249
Métis youth
reasserting identity and connections with Batoche, 295, 299
"métisness," 22, 252
métissage, 21–22
Michif-Cree, 15
declared official historic language of Métis Nation, 15
Michif French language, 14–15, 73, 153, 158, 212, 270, 281
discrimination against, 74
forbidden in schools, 253, 260
promotion of, 267
singing in, 68
spoken in the home, 74, 253
Michif languages, xii, 14, 295
dismissed as bad French, 13
need for funding status, 15
recording and transmission, 282
suppression, 92
Michilimakinac, 23
Middleton, General, 114–15, *115*, 138–39, 147, 283, 285
"Middleton's chair," 285
millers, 181
miracles, 70–71, 93
miscegenation, xii, 16, 22–23
missionaries, 14, 96, 98, 166. *See also* Catholic Church; clergy
Métis guides and interpreters, 83

Métis support of, 95
missionaries' culture and ideology
    counter to Métis traditions, 97, 106
Missouri, 17
Mistahimaskwa (Big Bear), 10, *132*
Mitchell, Hillyard, 154, 159, 169
    government patronage, 185
    Métis employees, 183, 185
    opposed French-language rights, 155
Mitchell's in Duck Lake
    clothing and fabrics, 57
    food, 64
"Mixed bloods," 24
mixed farming, xii, 37, 86
    lands suited to, 185
Le Monde qui parlait aux arbes (film), 18
Monet, Irène (Sansregret), 201
money scrip, 207, 237–48
    clergy opposition to, 243
    negotiable at face value, 240
    powers of attorney or assignment, 244
    reasons for choosing, 244
Monkman, Albert, *140*
Montana, 17, 140–41, 172, 200
« La Montée, » 33–34, 80, 84, 94–96, 165, 169, 171
Montour, Abraham, 34, 42, 124, 171, 186, 200
Montour, Caroline. *See* Dumont, Caroline « Câline » (Montour)
Montour, Marie (Pagé), 75
Montour, Nicolas, 165
Montour, Pascal, 34
Montreal, 24, 169, 173
Montreal Lake, 172
Moose Hills Reserve, 84
Moreau, Jonas, 34, *46*, 201
Morice, Father (A-G.), 113
Morin, Anne, 250, 294
Morin, Father, 90
Morris, Alexander, Lieutenant-Governor, 128, 204
Morton, W.L., 8
Motherwell Homestead, 292
Moulin, Father Julien, 42, 83, 96–97, *101*, *105*, 106, 111, 113, 115, 117–18, 181, 200
    dramatization, 18
    mutual affection for Métis, 102
    paternalistic but sensitive, 252
    postmaster, 102, 176, 180
    signed Batoche petition, 131
    struck by bullet, 114
    teacher in Batoche school, 104
Mulaire, Catherine Lacerte, 12
multilingualism, 15, 124
Museum era, 285–86
musical instruments, 67
Muskootao Point, 27
Mylymok, Thérèse, 106
Myre, Father Pierre-Elzéar
    French Canadian nationalist views, 251
    prejudice against Métis, 119–20, 252
    priest-colonizer, 119–20
The Myth of the Savage and the Beginning of French Colonialism in Americas (Dickason), 16
mythology, 17

N

names. *See also* nicknames (*sobriquets*)
    French pronunciation of English or Scottish names, 77
    nom dit custom, 76
national consciousness, 25, 47
National Council of Veterans Association, 267
national feast days, 122, 135
    alcohol use, 78
    drunkenness and fighting, 79
National Métis Senate, 280
National Policy of Western settlement, 238
Nationalists (Quebec), 148
"Native English"
    administrative positions with Hudson's Bay Company, 24
    integration into parent Métis society, 24
Natural Resource Transfer Agreement (1930), 8
natural resources. *See also* fishing and hunting rights
    Métis Aboriginal rights to, 7–8
Nault, André Sr., *268*
Nault, André Jr., 171, 200
Nault, Élie, 141, 200–201
Nault, Napoléon, 141, 171, 200
Nault family, 25, 88
Ness, George, 201, 210
New Democratic Party, 279
New France, 21–23
"New Nation of the Northwest," 9, 25
The New Peoples (Peterson), 1
new social history of the 1980s, 289

New Year's, 68–69
nicknames (*sobriquets*), 75–76
   significance, 76
Nicolas, Alexandrine (Fleury), 68, 250, *250*, 259–60, 266
Nicolas, Archie, 265–67, 281
Nicolas, Robert, 266
Nogier, Armand, 285
Nogier family, 285
   did not identify as Métis, 258
   prosperous farmers at Batoche (1940s-1960s), 258
Nolin, Charles, 2, 10, 25, 37, 41, 67, 70, 131, 138, *146*, 148, 153–55, 157, 237
   arrest, 79
   associated with conservative faction, 152
   denounced by missionaries, 111
   fled during battle, 147
   immigration committee, 90
   offered government contract, 133
   respect for maternal ancestors, 42
   on scrip rights, 243
   at service of government, 151
   witness for prosecution at Riel's trial, 147
Nolin, Dolphus, 171
Nolin, Jean-Baptiste, 23
Nolin, Rosalie (Lépine), 70, *146*
Nolin, Virginie (Boyer), 201
nom dit custom, 76–77
Non-Status Indians, 280–81
Normand family, 27
Norris, Malcolm, 274–75, 277
North American Indigenous Games, 13
North Dakota, 140, 200
North Slave region, 16
North-West, 23
North West Company (NWC), 23, 27, 165
   conflicts with HBC at Red River, 123–24
   promotion of French Canadian employees, 24
North West Field Force, 138, 147
North West Mounted Police (NWMP), 48, 82, 88, 149, 243
   on alcohol, 77
   confrontation with Almighty-Voice, 181
   contracts for supplying goods, 83, 181
   distrust of St. Laurent Council, 125
   employment of freighters, 172
   employment of Métis, 83, 86, 181
   insensitive to Métis way of life, 127, 247
   post at Batoche, 154
   post at Duck Lake, 126
   resentment of, 272
   retreat at Duck Lake, 138
   sub-post in Batoche, 180
   use of Cree labourers, 86
"North West Rebellion," 8, 290
North West Rebellion centennial, 225, 282, 290–94
North West Rebellion plaque (1925)
   Métis resentment, 270, 282
   replaced by bilingual plaque (1949), 283
North-West Scrip Commission, 238
"North West Territorial Act," 103
   revisions (1875, 1877), 126
   seat of government moved from Winnipeg to Battleford, 126
North West Territories, 15, 17, 124
   legal ownership of, 8
Northcote (steamer), 153, 270
notaries, 180

O

Oblates of Mary Immaculate, 93–95, 118. *See also* Catholic Church
occupations, 16, 24, 28, 41, 47, 163, 180–81, 226
   Depression years, 255, 257–58
   social standing and, 41
Official Languages Act, 15
Ojibwe, 204
Ojibwe (Saulteaux) language, 73
Ojibwe women, 23
old people. *See* elders
"old wives tales," legends, and prophecies, 71
Oliver, Frank, 158
Oliver ballot. *See* secret ballot
One Arrow Cree Nation. *See* Kàpeyakwàskonam (One Arrow) Cree Nation reserve
Onion Lake, 201
oral history, xi, xii, 3, 6, 12–14, 16, 19–20, 249, 280
   1815 Resistance, 269
oral traditions, 22, 251
Order of Canada, 280
orphans, 253
   institutional care, 260
   taken in by grandparents or others, 45
Ouellet, Rodolphe, 154
Ouellette, Alexandrine (Boyer), 201

Ouellette, Elisabeth (Dumont), *46*
Ouellette, Joseph, 34, 41, 187
Ouellette, Marguerite, 34, 210, 234
Ouellette, Mary-Jane. *See* Charette, Kokum Mary-Jane (formerly Racette, née Ouellette)
Ouellette, Moïse, *46*, 69–70, 103, 135, 138, 226
    acres under cultivation, 191
    councilor of St. Laurent Council, 124
    veteran of 1885, 269
Ouellette, Moïse Jr., 244
Ouellette, Pierre, 200
Ouellette, Rose. *See* Boucher, Rose « La Rose » (Ouellette)
Ouellette family, 42

P

Pagé, Marie. *See* Montour, Marie (Pagé)
Pagé, Xavier, 200
Pagé family, 96
Palud-Pelletier, Noëlie, *Louis: Fils des Prairies*, 12
Pambrun, Leonard, 281
Pannekoek, Frits, 17
Papen, Robert, 14
Parenteau, Alexandre, *63*
Parenteau, André, 42
Parenteau, Baptisens, 34, *46*
Parenteau, Baptiste, 186
Parenteau, Baptiste-Baptisens, 76
Parenteau, Délima (St. Germain), 253, 259
Parenteau, « Dodet » (Joseph), 171, 185, 200
Parenteau, Élise (Ledoux), 201
Parenteau, Émile, 289
Parenteau, Gabriel, 173
Parenteau, Gustave, 177
Parenteau, Isidore « Wabash, » 200
Parenteau, Jean-Baptiste, 79
Parenteau, Joseph, 82
Parenteau, Joseph « Dodet, » 34, 201, 209
Parenteau, Kokum, 260
Parenteau, Louis, 42
Parenteau, Marguerite. *See* Letendre, Marguerite (Parenteau)
Parenteau, Marie (Caron), *121*, 281
Parenteau, Maxime, 257, 281
Parenteau, Modeste, 244
Parenteau, Moïse, 42, 48, 173
Parenteau, Patrice, 67, 176, *178*, 183
Parenteau, Pélagie. *See* Carrière, Pélagie Parenteau; Dubois, Pélagie (Parenteau)
Parenteau, Pierre, *140*, 235
Parenteau, Pierre-Pierriche, 42, 76
Parenteau, Pierre Sr., 138
Parenteau, Véronique, 234
Parenteau, Virginie (Caron), 52, 64
Parenteau family, 48, 297
parish registers, 35–36
Parisien, Baptiste, 165
Parisien, Elzéar, 186, 236
Parisien, Hyacinthe, 166
Parisien, Laventure, 165
Parks Canada
    commemoration of government military sites, 285
    Cultural Resource Management Policy, 11, 295
    historical status quo, xiii, xiv
    land expropriation, 286
    partnerships with, 295–96
    policy of "commemorative integrity," 294
    took over church as historic site, 122
"Parks Canada and the 1885 Rebellion/Uprising/Resistance" (McCullough), 10
party politics, 148–61
The Pas, 169
Pascal, Bishop Albert, 90
Pascal, Dr., 180
paternal blessings, 68–69
Le Patriote de l'Ouest, 91, 120
patronage appointments. *See* government patronage
Paul, Élise (Trottier), 253
    Métis nationalist, 255
    spiritual woman, 255
Paul, Josephte. *See* Tourond, Josephte, Mme, "La veuve"
Paulhus, Ferdinand, 258
Payment, Diane, 12
    Batoche, 290
    The Free People, 290
pays d'en haut (Great Lakes and the Ohio valley), 22–23
pchi-coup (drink). *See* alcohol
Pearce, William, 153, 212–15
Pembina, North Dakota, 2, 13, 23
Pembina River, 166
pemmican, 25, 58, 165, 168, 183
The People Who Own Themselves (Devine), 6
people's council or *exovidate*, 138

Percell, Brenda (Boyer), 251, 295, *297*
Père Caribou. See Moulin, Father Julien
Perillat, Marguerite, 250
Perry, Superintendent, 243
"perverse effect thesis," 7
Peterson, Jacqueline, 23
    The New Peoples, 1
Petit, Claude, 265–66
Petit, Norris, 266
« le petit provisoire de la Saskatchewan, » 214, 267
Petite-Ville, 27, 33, 80, 166
Petitot, Émile, (Father), 14
Picking Up the Threads, 16
"La Pie." *See* St. Denis, Albina « La Pie » (Boucher)
pied-à-terre, 27, 171, 209
pilgrimage of Our Lady of Lourdes, 70–71
Pilon, Adélaïde (Ranger), *57*, 68, *121*, 281, 285
Pilon, Azarie, 201
Pilon, Barthélémi, 118, 181, 228
Pilon, Christine (Dumas), 37, *57*, 272
Pilon, Jean, 191
Pilon, Joseph Sr., 41, 48, 55
Pilon, Joseph Caton Jr., *63*, *191*
Pilon family, 42, 67, 284, 297
Pincher Creek, 200
Piquet, Brother, 70
Pointe-à-Grouette (Ste. Agathe), 6, 26
Poirier, Thelma, *The Bead Pot*, 12
Poitras, Ignace, 34, *140*
Poitras, Isabelle (McGillis), 201
political activism, 123, 269
    Batoche's tradition of, xii, 275–76
    Métis political consciousness, 11, 267, 276–80
Portage La Loche brigades, 27
Porter, Dr., 131, 148
Posluns, Michael, 163
postmasters, 41, 180
Powley, Steve, 7
Pozer, W.J., *178*
Prairie du Chien, 23
Prairie Ronde, 27, 166
Préfontaine, Darren R., 16, 249
priest-colonizers, 90, 119
Primeau, Baptiste, 165, *264*
Primeau, Marie. *See* Vandal, Marie (Primeau)
Prince Albert, 82–83, 104, 118, 127, 161
    anglophone commercial interests, 129
    land agents, 212
    local Métis association, 275–76

    Sacred Heart Cathedral, 280
    surveys laying out village, 208
Prince Albert Colonization Company, 214, 227
Prince Albert Historical Society, 270, 283
Prince Albert Land office, 211, 214
Prince Albert *Times*, 129
Prince Albert Trail, 176
Princess Patricia Regiment, 266
Proclamation of 1763, 204
Les Productions du Rapide-Blanc of Montreal, 18
Productions Rivard of St. Boniface, 18
prohibition, 77–78, 80
prophecies (predictions), 71
Proulx, Paul, *268*
provisional government (Saskatchewan). *See* « le petit provisoire de la Saskatchewan »
Provisional Government of Red River, 26, 126, 204, 276
Pruden, Charles, 141
Prud'homme, Bishop J.-H., 118, 120
psycho-cultural persistence, 18

Q

« Qu'Apelle, Longlac and Prince Albert » (railway line), 181
Qu'Appelle, 124, 171–72, 176, 207, 209
Qu'Appelle Council, 125
Qu'Appelle River winter camps, 33
Qu'Appelle Valley, 27, 235
Quebec, 60, 88, 148, 169
    appel à la race (nationalist outcry), 142
Quebec nationalist literature, 23
    Riel and Dumont in, 2
Québécois settlers (near Batoche), 41

R

Racette, Charles, 34
Racette, Damase, *178*
Racette, Hélène (Boyer), *46*, 234
Racette, Jérôme, 181
Racette, Mary-Jane. *See* Charette, Kokum Mary-Jane (formerly Racette, née Ouellette)
racism, xiv, 15–16, 22
railway, 169, 183
    source of employment, 181
railway land, 229

ramancheur (bonesetter), 72
ranching, 183, 191–92, 200
Ranger, Adélaïde (Pilon), 57, 68, *121*, 281, 285
RCMP, 274
RCMP Aboriginal Advisory Board, 280
ready-made clothes, 57–58
"Rebellion Losses Commission of 1885," 54
  bias and injustice, 143, 147, 151
  Métis resentment, 143, 147
recorded memories. *See* oral history
Red Power, 280
Red River, 13, 23–26, 84, 94, 166
  buffalo hunt, 166–67
  Canada's authority in, 8
  census, 24
  "class marriages," 47
  connections to Métis of Northwest, 27
  diet (both Aboriginal and French-Canadian traditions), 59
  divergent political views, 25–26
  fishing, trapping, farming, 25
  independent traders, 25
  intermarriage, 23 (*See also* marriage)
  land claims, 203–7 (*See also* scrip)
  linguistic and religious rights, 26
  merchant and freighting entrepreneurs, 25
  Métis dispossession and forced relocation, 26
  missionary correspondence, 24
  Montreal or St. Paul fashions, 56
  national consciousness, 25
  occupations, 25
  political elite, 25
  relocation to South Saskatchewan River, 28, 33
  riverlots, 205
  wintered on farms, 205
Red River cart, 13
Red River Settlement (1836-38)
  Hudson's Bay Company survey, 205
Reed, Hayter, 211
Régnier, Célestine (Lépine), 235
Régnier, Octave, 88, 149, 180, 211, 237
Reid, J.L. (surveyor), 209–10, 216
Resistance of 1869-70, 25–26, 33
  clergy support, 94
  firsthand accounts, 13
resistance-rebellion debate, 8–11, 290. *See also* 1885 Resistance
Richard, Ambroise, 83
Richard, Antoine, 228

Richard family
  conflict with Prince Albert Colonization Company, 214
Richard Lafferty: The Muskeg Fiddler (video), 13
Riel (multimedia package), 18
Riel: A Life of Revolution (Siggins), 4
Riel, Alexandre, *268*
Riel, Joseph, 267, *268*
Riel, Louis, xi, 1, 10, 25–26, 88–89, *107*, 114, 126, *132*, 136, 143, 270, 272, 279
  clergy opposition to, 108–11
  established chapel, 112
  exile, 26
  Father André (Alexis) on, 116–17
  founded first Métis association, 267
  martyr-hero, 4
  moderate and conciliatory agenda, 4
  new petition (1885), 138, 213
  official plotting against, 111, 133
  official recognition as a founder of Manitoba, 5
  prophet and leader, 3, 14
  proposals to "rehabilitate," 5
  recognized as prophet, 122
  respect and devotion of Métis people, 110
  respect for maternal ancestors, 42
  syncretic spiritual and political beliefs, 4
  trial, 116
  vision of a distinct nationality for Métis, 110, 135
Riel, Louis Sr., 25
Riel family, 5, 25, 142
Riel House National Historic Site, 8
  bilingual staffing and programs, 295
Riel's execution, 2
  outcry in Quebec, 142
  political consequences, 142
Riguidel, Louis, 41, 88
Ritchot, Father Noël-Joseph, 94
riverlots, 206–7, 210–11, 213, 229, 236
road-allowance community of Crescent Lake, 13
Robert, Father Henri, 120
Rocheleau, Frédéric, 201
Rocheleau, Jean-Baptiste, 83
root-house. *See* cellars
« La Rose. » *See* Boucher, Rose « La Rose » (Ouellette)
Ross, Alexander, 23, 166
Ross, Andronique. *See* Marion, Andronique (Ross)
Ross, Joe, 275
Ross, John, 82

Ross, Julie (Parenteau), 82
Rosthern, 247, 251
rouges. *See* Liberal Party
Roussel, Father Georges, *121*
Royal, Joseph, 126, 131, 158, 211
Royal Commission on Aboriginal Peoples, 7, 15

S

Sansregret, « Brilliant » (André), 76
Sansregret, Johnny, *140*
Sansregret, Marie-Rose (Sauvé), 201
Sansregret, Norbert, 201
sash *(ceinture fléchée)*, 13, 56–57, 280
Saskatchewan, 23, 27, 124
    "betterment and civilization of Halfbreeds," 253
    French-speaking minority, 155
    Métis self-governing before 1905, 35
    municipalities established after 1909, 35
Saskatchewan Urban Native Teacher's Education Program (Suntep), 282
Saskatchewan Valley Land Company, 247
Saskatoon, 275–76
    assimilation, 281
    bone (bison) depository, 183
    prejudice, 281
Sault Ste. Marie, 7
Sauvé, Mr., 100
Sauvé, William, 201
Sayer, Guillaume, 25
Sayer, Pierre-Guillaume, 124
Schley, Paul, 88, 135
Schmidt, Charles-Pantaléon, 180, 244, 279
Schmidt (*dit* Laferté), Louis, 2, 37, 48, 56–58, 69, 92, 109, 130, 131, 138, 155, 236–37, 244
    disputed claims, 211
    government official, 180
    justice of the peace, 180
    memoirs, 73
    Métis appointee to Land office, 212
    request for resurvey, 211
Schmidt, Rose-Délima (Boucher), *51*, 180, 279
Schmidt family, 48
school ordinances for the North West Territories, 103
school trustees, 41
schooling, 16, 106, 175
    bilingual teachers, 104
    conflict between Métis, Church, and government, 102–4
    convent boarding schools, 75, 252
    difficult for Métis, 251–53, 257
    government funding, 103–4
    influence on social status, 37
    instruction in English, 253
    language, 75, 253
    secondary education, 75, 252
    as source of prestige, 42
    during war service, 267
    way of reaching a "higher" class, 41
Scofield, Gregory, 293, 295
Scottish ancestry, 24, 36, 47
scrip, 149, 157, 159, 190–91, 228, 275. *See also* land scrip
    accounts with merchants, 247
    attempt to extinguish Métis land and resource rights, xii, 206, 237–48
    complex and largely unregulated, 247
    eligibility, 158, 239
    fraud and misrepresentation, 26, 248
    freeing land for Eurocanadian settlement, 247
    irregularities, 242
    Manitoba precedent, 237–48
    petitions, 242
    powers of attorney and assignments, 247
    speculators, 237, 247
    varied over years, 207
scrip for cash. *See* money scrip
seasonal jobs for "wages," 44
seasonal workers, 41
Second World War
    employment and adventure, 263
    steady income, 265
secondary education, 75, 106, 252
secret ballot, 158
seed grain, 189
seed grain mortgage liens, 235
Selby Junction (Hill), 200
self-government, 9, 15, 25, 35. *See also* St. Laurent Council
serial monogamy, 95
settlers, 87–92, 185, 199–201, 209, 237
    Belgian and French, 41, 87–89, 161, 191
    Eurocanadian, 237, 247
    French Canadian, 22, 41, 87–90, 120, 161, 251
    Mennonite (*See* Mennonites)
    relocation of Métis, 235
Short, James, 34

Short, James (Timous), *140*
sick, treatment of. *See* health care
Siggins, Maggie, *Riel: A Life of Revolution*, 4
Sinclair, Bruce, 18
Sinclair, Jim, 280
singing, 67
single parent children, 253
    Métis acceptance of, 263
    raised by grandparents, 261
Siouan Languages, 73
Sisters Faithful Companions of Jesus, 113, 188
    school in St. Laurent, 103–4
Sisters of Charity. *See* Grey Nuns
skilled workers, 41
Slater, François, 244
small pox epidemic (1870), 33, 80
smoking, 61, 72–73
sobriquets (nicknames), 75–76
social classes, 36–37
    bourgeoisie, 148, 152
    choice of spouse and, 47
    French Canadian elite, 252
    local bourgeoisie, 152
social evenings, 67
social standing
    community leaders, 37, 41
    criteria for, 41
    socio-economic elite, 41
La Société historique de Saint-Boniface, 295
Société historique métisse, 3
Soldier Settlement grants, 263
"South Branch Houses," 165
South Saskatchewan River area, 124
    buffalo hunt, 167
    First Nations / Métis contact, 83–84
    government agents or officials, 180
    land claims along, 207
    Métis exodus, 200–201
    regrouping 1886 to 1900, 191
    riverlots, 207, 247
    winter camps, 95
South Saskatchewan River Métis, 28, 33, 35, 37, 47
    censuses, 35
    claims and grievances, 132
    community leaders, 41
    exogamy, 48
    few class distinctions (during 1870s), 37
    of First Nation (Cree and Ojibwe) and French Canadian descent, 36, 47
    marriage within social class and among relatives, 47
    marriages between cousins, 48
    occupations, 27–28, 37
    petitions to Canadian government, 129, 131, 214, 238
    politically conscious group, 28
    population, 35–36
    relocated from Manitoba, 28, 35–37
    relocated from Pembina area, 36
    request for survey of "St. Laurent Settlement," 209
    of Scottish, Irish, or English descent, 36
    social stratification, 36
    from St. Joseph (St. Joe) area in Dakota, 36
    whole families relocated together, 42
specialized skills (carpenters, teachers), 37
spirit helpers, 93
Sprague, D.N., 6
St. Albert, Alberta, 95, 124, 171
St. Albert Council, 125
St. Ann's boarding school, Prince Albert, 75
St. Antoine de Padoue church, 122
    purchased by Parks Canada, 285–86
St. Antoine de Padoue mission, 175
    attempts to raise funds, 100
    founding of, 98
St. Antoine de Padoue parish, 35, 97, 122
    expanded and flourished late 1880s and 1890s, 118
    no resident priests from 1915 to 1924, 118
St. Antoine de Padoue registers, 36
St. Antoine de Padoue two-room school, 252
St. Boniface, 24, 75, 94, 166, 205, 263
St. Boniface College, 75
St. Denis, Albina « La Pie » (Boucher), 255
St. Denis, Alice. *See* Arcand, Alice (St. Denis)
St. Denis, Odilon (Sergeant), 86, 181
St. Denis, R.O., 276
St. Eugène mission, 97
St. François-Xavier (White Horse Plain), 24–25, 27, 36, 88, 166, 206
    "class marriages," 47
    Grey Nuns' convent school, 75
St. Germain, Bernice, 285
St. Germain, Délima. *See* Parenteau, Délima (St. Germain)
St. Germain, Emile, 265
St. Germain, Frédéric, 171, 200, 235, 270
St. Germain, Joseph, 267

St. Germain, Raoül, 67
St. Germain, Ray, 13
St. Germain, Véronique (Parenteau), 48
St. Germain family, 26, 297
St. Jean-Baptiste, Manitoba, 200
St. Jean Baptiste Day, 135
St. Joe (Walhalla), North Dakota, 141
St. Joseph, 270
    adopted as patron saint of Métis nation, 110, 135
    feast of, 122
St. Joseph (itinerant mission), 96
St. Joseph Society, 135
St. Joseph's Day, 69–70
St. Laurent de Grandin mission, 34, 124
    model farm, 186
    pilgrimage of Our Lady of Lourdes, 70
St. Laurent (de Grandin, Saskatchewan) 75, 127, 200, 226, 236, 243
    acres under cultivation, 186, 191
    became permanent settlement, 35
    Council (St. Laurent Council) 125–26, 128, 129
    exodus of Métis, 235
    freighting, 169, 172
    homes, 54
    immigrants from Manitoba and North West Territories, 35
    marriage, 47
    mixed farming, 185
    occupations, 168
    population, 35
    schools, 103–4
    smallpox, 80
St. Laurent, Louis, 279, 283
St. Laurent, Manitoba, 2, 6
    historical documentary of, 18
    language, 14–15
"St. Laurent Settlement"
    founded to promote farming, 185
    immigration from Manitoba, 34
    population, 34
    survey, 209–14
St. Louis, 88, 183, 200, 210, 212, 226, 251, 258, 275
    active Métis local, 279, 281
    became permanent settlement, 35
    cattle, 191
    famous for singers, 67
    freighting, 169

    heterogeneous population, 89
    immigration from Manitoba and North West Territories, 35
    land survey and registration issues, 209–10, 214, 226
    land under cultivation, 191
    marriage, 47
    Métis culture maintained, 281
    population, 35, 48
    private convent boarding school, 75
    regrouping of families, 235
    scrip claims, 244
    social stratification, 41
St. Louis de Gladiou, Louis, 41, 88, *178*
St. Michael's Industrial School, 252
St. Norbert (Manitoba), 24–25, 36, 75, 206
St. Patrick's orphanage in Prince Albert, 260
St. Paul (Minnesota), 166, 169
St. Sacrement mission, 96
St. Vital, Manitoba, 25, 141, 200, 206, 267
    memories of Riel, 4
St-Onge, Nicole, 6, 12
Stanley, G.F.G., xi, 8, 125
    The Birth of Western Canada, 3
    The Collected Writings of Louis Riel, 1
Stewart, Dr., 91
Stobart & Sons, 176
Stobart and Eden Company, 187
story-telling as educational tool, 253
Street Commission (1885), 239
Supreme Court
    Métis Aboriginal rights to natural resources, 7
Sur les Traces de Riel (film), 18
survey system. *See* land surveying system
syncretism, 4, 12, 14

T

Taché, Bishop Alexandre-Antonin, 94, 109, 131, 238, 279
Tait, W., 247
Tatro, Harry, 287
taureau (pemmican), 58, 60
teachers, 37, 86, 103, 106, 180, 237, 252–53
    bilingual teachers, 75, 104
    Métis, 103, 180
Tees, Richard, 175
Territorial elections, 131, 148, 154, 157–59

Territorial government, 132
    Métis representation, 126–27
    recommendation of scrip, 238
    undermined St. Laurent Council, 126
Tertiaries of St. Francis, 103–4, 106
Thibaudeau Frères, 173
Thibault, Father Louis, 94
"Third Church," 14
Thomas, Charles, 42, 173
Thomas, Hélène (Letendre), 42
Thomas, Victor, 244
Tompkins, Peter, 274
Touchette, Dr., 181
Touchwood Hills, 27
Tourond, David, 141
Tourond, Élise. *See* Boyer, Élise (Tourond)
Tourond, Francis, 180
Tourond, Josephte (Paul) la veuve, *144*, 147
    nationalist, 270
    rancher and farmer, 192
Tourond family, 251, 296
Tourond's Coulee (Fish Creek), 28, 35, 84, 171, 192, 227, 272
    Métis victory, 138
    occupations, 168
Tourond, Patrice, *140*
Touze, Father Louis, 113
traditional healers and midwives, 72, 181
traditional knowledge, 6, 19, 37
traditional songs, 67
traditional stories and legends, 13
traditional values, 44, 123
La Trahison/The Betrayal (film), 18
trapping, hunting, and fishing, 25, 169, 276
treaties (1871-1877), 84
Treaty No. 6, 128, 209
    imminent arrival of immigrant settlers, 209
    land rights for Métis who lived with or as "indians," 204
    Métis interpreters and witnesses, 84, 128
Treaty No.3 (North West Angle), 204
Trottier, Charles, 84, 166, 255, 296
Trottier, Élise. *See* Paul, Élise (Trottier)
Troy, 169, 171
tuberculosis, 36, 80–81
Tucker, Walter, 283
Turcotte, Norbert, 180
Turgeon, Alphonse, 159, 161
"turning off" of spouses, 123. *See also* marriage
Turtle Mountain, North Dakota, 2, 15, 141

U

Ukrainians, 199, 251
Union Nationale Métisse St. Joseph du Manitoba, 3, 5, 92, 267, 270
United Nations Human Rights Commission, 267
United States, 90, 200, 257
"unity within a diversity," 11
urban centers, 263
    assimilation, 281
    immigrant interest in, 91
Urton, W.S., *178*

V

Van Kirk, Sylvia, 12
Vandal (Settlement), 191, 226
Vandal, Baptiste, 34, *140*
Vandal, Joseph, 68
Vandal, Marie (Primeau), 192
Vandal, Pierre, *140*
Vandal, Roger, 200
Vandal family, 42
Vandale, Joseph, 255, 259, 276
Vandale, Mike, 276
vegetable gardens, 44, 61–62, 186–88, 205, 208, 255, 259
Végréville, Father Valentin, 97–98, 111, 131, 211
    established mission near Fort Carlton, 95
    fear of Riel's ascendancy, 110
    guest of Xavier Letendre, 100
    held in rectory during battle, 113
    re-assigned to St. Laurent, 101
    on surveyors, 209
Venne, Alexandre, 141, 176, 200–201
Venne, Bruno, 192
Venne, David, 75, 158, 176, 192, ~~296~~
    guide and interpreter, 181
    liquor license, 78
    notary and postmaster, 180
    great-nephew, 296
Venne, Napoléon, 86, 176, *182*, 192, 201
    liquor license, 78
    postmaster, 180
Venne, Salomon, 37, 236, 244, 296
    cattle herd, 188
    children's education, 75
    employment of freighters, 169
    fur trader, 169, 176

home, 55
liquor outlet, 176
post office, 176
ranch near Wakaw, 192
store in Batoche, 176
Venne, William, 176, 201
Venne family, 25, 48, 62
    local bourgeoisie, 152
    socio-economic elite, 41
La Vérendryes, 23
Vermette, Auguste, 13
Versailles, Marie-Anne (Bélanger), 201
Vieux-Jean. *See* Caron, Ti-Jean-Vieux-Jean
Villeneuve, Isidore, 186
"Vingt-Deuse" (French Canadian Regiment), 265
Visitor Reception Centre (VRC), 286, 291–92
    audio-visual presentation, 292
    "The Glass House," 294
    voyageurs, 24, 27, 33, 56, 58, 164. *See also* Boucher, Jean-Marie; Letendre *dit* Batoche, Jean-Baptiste

W

Wahpahissco (White Cap), Chief, 84–86
Wahpeton, 84
Wakaw, 251
Wakaw School Unit, 106, 192
Walker-Côté Commission, 244
Walters & Baker store, 176–77
war experiences, 263–73. *See also* 1885 Resistance
    equal treatment (in active service), 265
war legacies
    alcoholism, 267
    schooling and training during enlistment, 267
    training for political leaders of 1940s and 1950s, 267

war veterans
    discrimination, 253
    1815 Resistance, 269–70
    experience in dealing with bureaucracy, 275
    First World War, 263
    prejudices, 265–66
    still fighting for compensation, 267
weddings, 66–67
Welsh, Christine, 11
"Wendigo," 123
Weninger, Josie (Heron), 294
Whidden, Lynn, *A Métis Suite*, 13
White Cap. *See* Wahpahissco (White Cap), Chief
White Horse Plain. *See* St. François-Xavier
wild fruits, 58, 61, 188, 259
"wild" meat, 59. *See also* bison
Wilkie, David, 140
Wilkie, Jean-Baptiste, 166
Willow Bunch, 201, 207
Wilson, Inspector (surveyor), 216
Winnipeg, 126, 169, 171–73, 176
Winslow, Robert, 18
winter camps, 33, 56–57, 80, 95. *See also* hivernements
women. *See* Métis women
women's artwork, 282
Wood Mountain, 27, 80

Y

Youville de, Sainte Marguerite, 279

www.ingramcontent.com/pod-product-compliance
Lightning Source LLC
Chambersburg PA
CBHW070747230426
43665CB00017B/2280